Business Enterprise in American History

To our families

Business Enterprise in American History

Third Edition

MANSEL G. BLACKFORD
K. AUSTIN KERR

Ohio State University

 **WADSWORTH**
CENGAGE Learning

Australia • Brazil • Japan • Korea • Mexico • Singapore • Spain • United Kingdom • United States

WADSWORTH
CENGAGE Learning™

Business Enterprise in American History, Third Edition
Mansel G. Blackford,
K. Austin Kerr

Sponsoring Editor:
  Sean W. Wakely

Development Editor:
  Susan Yanchus

Senior Project Editor:
  Carol Newman

Editorial Assistant: Celena Sun

Associate Production/Design
  Coordinator: Caroline Ryan

Senior Manufacturing
  Coordinator: Priscilla Bailey

Marketing Manager:
  Rebecca Dudley

For product information and
technology assistance, contact us at **Cengage Learning
Customer & Sales Support, 1-800-354-9706**

For permission to use material from this text or product,
submit all requests online at **www.cengage.com/permissions**
Further permissions questions can be emailed to
permissionrequest@cengage.com

Library of Congress Control Number: 93-78665

ISBN-13: 978-0-395-66849-8

ISBN-10: 0-395-66849-2

Wadsworth
20 Channel Center Street
Boston, MA 02210
USA

Cengage Learning is a leading provider of customized learning solutions with office locations around the globe, including Singapore, the United Kingdom, Australia, Mexico, Brazil, and Japan. Locate your local office at **www.cengage.com/global**

Cengage Learning products are represented in Canada by Nelson Education, Ltd.

To learn more about Wadsworth, visit
www.cengage.com/wadsworth

Purchase any of our products at your local college store or at our preferred online store **www.cengagebrain.com**

Printed in the United States of America
3 4 5 6 7   15 14 13 12 11

FD361

Contents

Preface

The third edition of *Business Enterprise in American History* again focuses on the major themes that underlie the development of American business: the history of the business firm and the history of government-business relations.

This text examines the history of business over three centuries of American history. From colonial times to the present, the book explores the ways in which Americans channeled their entrepreneurial ambitions into the firms that did so much to transform and enrich America. In our view, business history is more than the study of the firm, however. The firm is most broadly understood in the context of the society and the political system in which it operates and which the firm, in turn, influences. And, in the democratic society that exists in the United States the larger political setting in which the firm has evolved provides an added dimension to its story. The history of government and business are inseparable in the United States. Thus, the text probes the political and legal settings in which business has operated.

CHANGES IN THE THIRD EDITION

Those political settings have changed dramatically over time, and at no point more so than over the past few years. The collapse of the Soviet Union and the changes in Eastern Europe are the most evident alterations. But, nearly as important were changes taking place in Asia and other parts of the world. One of the strengths of this edition of *Business Enterprise* is its greatly increased coverage of the post-World-War-II period. Well over half of this volume deals with the twentieth century, much of it on the past fifty years. The chapters dealing with the postwar years have been completely rewritten in light of changing world affairs. Two completely new chapters, 12 and 13, analyze business alterations in America in light of global political and economic changes that have occurred since 1971. New case studies put important trends and characteristics of business in perspective. In the Third Edition, we introduce readers to new cases on *B.F. Goodrich*, the changing dynamics of the automobile industry, the decline of IBM as a corporate giant—and in contrast the success of Microsoft Inc.

We have also updated the entire text in light of the most recent scholarship. In particular, we have broadened our coverage of the contributions that women and minorities have made to the development of America's business system. We have also examined more fully the dynamic roles small firms have played in the evolution of American business. In the text as a whole, we have retained the traditional chronological approach used in the first two editions of this work and the mix of narrative and case-study examples of how early businesses evolved. We continue to explore fully the monumental business changes that took place in the mid- and late nineteenth century, especially the rise of big business and the alterations the development of big business brought to America's business system.

Our book should, therefore, continue to serve two types of students: history students who are particularly interested in learning more about American business and students enrolled in a business school curriculum who want a better understanding of the workings of the American business system. Both groups will benefit from our examination of the development of business in the context of its global economic and political setting.

ACKNOWLEDGMENTS

We have been fortunate to enjoy the support of scholars across the country whose remarks, along with the comments of our students, have guided and encouraged us in the preparation of this revised edition:

Erling Erickson, University of the Pacific
Joe Gowaskie, Rider College
Patrick Reagan, Tennessee Technological University
Diane Lindstrom, University of Wisconsin—Madison
Gregory Segretti, Anne Arundel Community College
Richard Ortquist, Wittenburg University

Our colleagues at Ohio State University provide us with a special place in which to work as scholars and teachers. Special thanks go to E. Gordon Gee, our president, for providing visionary leadership during time of economic distress, and to Joseph A. Alutto for invigorating leadership of our College of Business, and to Michael Hogan, our history department Chair, for his support of high quality teaching and scholarship.

K. Austin Kerr
Mansel G. Blackford

Business
Enterprise
in
American
History

Introduction

Business is the very soul of an American; he pursues it, not as a means of procuring for himself and his family the necessary comforts of life, but as the fountain of all human felicity. . . . It is as if all America were but one gigantic workshop, over the entrance of which there is the blazing inscription, "No admission here except on business."

—FRANCIS J. GRUND
The Americans in Their Moral, Social and Political Relations (1837)

Business, the name commonly given to the organization of the production, distribution, and exchange of valued material goods and services, permeates American civilization, and our book focuses on business as a central topic of American history. The central position of business in the history of America, as the quotation above suggests, has long been recognized by citizens and scholars alike. In examining American business history we will explore some of the institutions, practices, attitudes, and values that have evolved over more than three hundred years.

In our exploration we shall focus on two main topics in American business history: the development of the business firm and the development of government-business relations.

The first major topic of the history of business in the United States is *the development of the firm.* Business firms are institutions and, like other human institutions, have changed over the centuries; thus, this book is in part about alterations in the American business firm—the conditions that cause them and, in turn, their effect on American life. Firms, moreover, are built and run by people—entrepreneurs and managers. Entrepreneurs hold a position of central importance in the history of the firm, for they are the individuals who transform businesses in some important way. Entrepreneurs are innovators. They may observe and seize profitable opportunities, taking risks in doing so, or they may observe some new way of creating or organizing a firm and thereby

1

alter the practice of business. The entrepreneur and the firm are thus inextricably linked, but not all firms, or all persons engaged in business, necessarily create new practices or new institutions. Throughout American history some individuals have operated established enterprises in routine ways, and naturally it would always be correct to refer to such individuals simply as businessmen or businesswomen. In modern times, such individuals are usually called managers or executives.

In the study of the firm, business history is closely related to economic history. Economic historians concern themselves with the larger forces—such as economic expansions and depressions—that shape the formation of material wealth. Those forces are the settings in which business firms arise, mature, and decline. Because business activities are economic activities, distinctions between business history and economic history are easily blurred. But business historians examine institutions, not larger economic forces. They study individual firms and the patterns of their development. Those patterns and the ways in which firms relate to one another constitute the business system. Business historians understand business firms as components, in modern times, of larger industries—the steel or auto industries, for example. Those industries, in turn, are parts of the whole economy.

The larger forces that economic historians study are, of course, important for an understanding of business history. Not only do the activities of business firms help create those forces, but the economic setting influences opportunities available to business entrepreneurs and managers. Business historians are concerned with individuals and firms seizing opportunities created by larger economic forces; so understanding those opportunities, having an awareness of the setting—the economic history—in which Americans have engaged in business, provides a necessary dimension for understanding business history. Our book will briefly describe the economic contexts in which Americans have engaged in business.

The second main topic of business history is *the development of government-business relations*. All business firms operate in environments framed by law and politics, among other things. Business entrepreneurs and business managers have always sought to influence government policy in this country. In addition, people affected by business firms—consumers and workers, for instance—have often tried to influence the legal and political framework in which business activities occur. The importance of government and politics to business as well as the efforts of business owners to influence government policy are inescapable realities of American life.

In its second main topic, *government-business relations*— what is traditionally known as the political economy—the discipline of business history is closely related to political history. Business historians share a concern with political historians in seeking to understand how the political system of the United States has interacted with the business system of the nation throughout its history. Indeed, government policy and the framework of the law have helped shape not only the opportunities available for entrepreneurs but also the evolving economic setting. Politics, broadly conceived, has always affected the strategies of American entrepreneurs and the structure of the American firm. In American society, furthermore, neither business leaders nor political leaders have ever been autonomous groups. Some business executives have been politicians and vice versa. And politicians have often defended or promoted some form of business practice. In brief, the two subjects of politics and business have always been closely intertwined throughout American history.

The student of business history should have two principal objectives: first, to learn about particular aspects of the history of the American firm and the American political economy; and second, to gain insights into the larger framework, the big picture, of the American business system. This book, in approaching the first objective, examines the appearance of new aspects of business at various times in American history. We will note, for instance, the appearance of cost accounting in business and explain the reasons for its development as some entrepreneurs encountered unprecedented problems in the middle of the nineteenth century. Such matters as production management and marketing strategies were, at one time, a result of entrepreneurial innovation. So too were political policies, such as those relating to development of the nation's interior resources and regulation of firm size and competition.

An understanding of these and other aspects of American business history will lead the student to the second objective, comprehending the larger framework of the American business system, which of course is vastly different now from the business system first established in North America by the British in the seventeenth century. When Francis Grund observed in 1837 that America was a "gigantic workshop," Americans had not yet witnessed the rise of "big business." We will tell the story of the growth of the giant firm and of how giant U.S. firms themselves changed as the nation matured. By looking at differences in business firms and government policies historically and by exploring how business and the political economy developed over many generations, the student will gain a better appreciation of how changes in the business world of the nineteenth century laid the foundations for the business world of the late twentieth century.

STAGES AND THEMES OF AMERICAN BUSINESS HISTORY

To help the student understand the main topics of American business history, we will identify and briefly describe significant parts of the larger story. Americans have bought and sold goods and services, used natural resources, developed and exploited technologies, and worked through government to shape their economy and society in ways that have exhibited both continuity and change over nearly four centuries. The overriding theme of American business history is the story of entrepreneurs who seized changing opportunities and, in doing so, fashioned and refashioned the institution of the firm and the conduct of business.

The firm lies at the heart of business history, and the history of the American firm has been one of overlapping stages. During the first stage in colonial times, the most visible firm was the *general merchant and planter*, which both led economic activity and dominated the colonies' social and political affairs. The general merchant and planter, sometimes referred to as "all-purpose" business firms, enjoyed wealth that could not be invested profitably in just one main economic activity, so investments went in a variety of "general" directions. For instance, the general merchant or planter might have concurrently engaged in the production, shipping, wholesaling, and retailing of goods.

In the British colonies in America, the general merchant and planter operated alongside of and in conjunction with small firms that specialized in just one activity. During the second stage, which began shortly after the conclusion of the American Revolution in 1781, those small, specialized firms proliferated in a national economy of expanding economic opportunities. In this second stage of *specialized businesses*, which characterized business history during Grund's time, opportunities enlarged so that even the general merchant and planter could focus sizable capital investments on one particular business activity, and the old colonial "all-purpose" firm disappeared.

The second stage in the history of the business firm lasted until about 1850, when new kinds of business institutions began to appear: these fundamentally differed from the firms of Grund's generation in both size and complexity. Thus, during the third stage in the history of the American firm, some businesses grew large and became known as *big business*. After the midcentury, entrepreneurs saw advantages to investing very large sums of capital to construct complex human organizations termed "bureaucracies." A bureaucracy, quite simply, is an institution with a life of its own, which is independent from the lives of the persons who work for it and which applies expertise to the problems at hand on a continuing basis. A key to bureaucracies is the idea that they are "ongoing" institutions. The business bureaucracies that began to appear on the American scene in the middle of the nineteenth century did indeed last a long time, and some still exist today.

These new big businesses invested very large sums of capital in complex human organizations in order to apply their expertise toward integrating various processes concerned with either producing goods or providing services. Big businesses developed first in the railroad industry during the 1840s and 1850s to coordinate train services and make them more profitable. Big businesses developed in some forms of manufacturing later, after 1870, when the use of experts working in bureaucracies enabled firms to produce and distribute goods more profitably than small independent businesses could.

This third stage, big business, did not mean that small independent businesses disappeared as an institutional form in the way that general merchants and planters had earlier. Small business firms have existed side by side with big business firms in the United States since 1850. But because big business firms came to dominate transportation, communication, and many forms (though certainly not all) of manufacturing during the third stage, Americans emerged with a dual business system, one composed of "center" and "peripheral" firms. Center firms were (and are) big businesses. Since their beginnings in the railroad industry in the mid-nineteenth century and their spread into other lines of economic activity, center firms have tended to accumulate greater and greater sums of wealth and to have concentrated those assets into the hands of fewer and fewer institutions. In other words, big business as a type of enterprise did not replace small business. With fewer assets and less access to capital, small business firms tended to revolve around the periphery of the business world created by big business during the second half of the nineteenth century—so they are commonly referred to as peripheral firms.

Just as big business firms in the third stage brought institutional innovations that did not replace the specialized small firms of the second stage, so too in the fourth stage diversification and decentralization of most big business firms supplemented but did not replace older institutional forms. The fourth stage in the history of the American firm began to unfold in the 1920s and continues today. In this fourth stage of *diversification and decentralization,* big businesses started using their assets to enter more than one field of production, or more than one area of service. That diversification posed enormous administrative problems for the bureaucracies involved. The resolution of those administrative problems brought decentralization of authority within the firm.

A corollary to the stages in the development of the business firm is the series of phases in the evolution of marketing, or distribution. During the first of these phases, in the period before about 1880, firms sold their goods mainly to local, fragmented markets. Nearly all products were unbranded, generic goods. Profit margins on individual items were high and the turnover of stock was slow. During the second phase, beginning in the 1880s and continuing to the present day, a national mass market for some goods developed. Large, successful manufacturing companies emphasized selling a high volume of mass-produced goods, presented to the public by means of national advertising for low prices. Name-brand products replaced generic goods. In the mass market the key to business success lay in making an ever-greater number of sales at low profit margins, with individual items turned over rapidly. Finally, in a third overlapping phase, which began in the 1920s for some goods such as automobiles but after 1945 for many more, segmented markets became important. In many lines of goods and services, the mass market fragmented into segments differentiated by such factors as price and style. Through advertising increasingly aimed at specific groups and often psychological in nature, businesses sought to exploit market segments for their goods.

The shaping and reshaping of the institution of the business firm over the centuries of American history occurred as responses by men and women to evolving opportunities. The availability of some opportunities, notably the abundant natural resources that European settlers found on the North American continent, were beyond human control. After the American Revolution, Americans shaped opportunities for business activity through government in a political process that after 1920 fully included women and, after 1965, blacks. A central theme of American business history thus has been cooperation between private business leaders and public officials to foster entrepreneurial opportunities. The resulting relationship between the governmental and business systems— a relationship referred to as the "political economy"—is the second main subject of this book. Like the business firm itself, government-business relations evolved in stages.

There have been three stages in the history of government-business relations in the United States. (In the colonial period, British subjects lived under a system known as mercantilism, which involved government direction of business activity in order to enlarge the power of the British crown.) After the American Revolution began in 1776, the first stage in government-business relations was *developmental.* Quite simply expressed, Americans used the governments they controlled—local, state, and federal—to develop business opportunities. The first meeting of Congress in 1789 resulted in a tariff law designed both to raise revenue and to protect American manufacturers from competitors abroad, thus providing private individuals with enlarged opportunities to invest their resources in manufacturing firms. That developmental tradition expanded in the nineteenth century, and it continues today.

The second stage of government-business relations, *regulation,* supplemented the developmental tradition established in the earliest days of the Republic. Regulation began in a modern form at the federal level with the establishment of the Interstate Commerce Commission in 1887. The development of regulation was usually a response of business executives, allied with political leaders, to develop a conscious policy of directing business activities in some desired direction. In 1887, regulation of railroads by a federal commission began as the result of various impulses related to the belief that governmental intervention was necessary to ensure the prosperity of carriers and the chances for shippers and passengers to use railroad services at a fair price. Federal regulation spread to other industries after 1900.

The third stage of government-business relations—*the new regulation*—is a more recent phenomenon that began in the 1960s. It did not replace traditional developmental or regulatory policies. The new regulation was innovative in that the spirit guiding it was less involved in providing business opportunities for the producers of goods and services than the traditional forms of regulation have been. The new regulation aimed at protecting consumers, the rights of employees, and especially the chances of all citizens to live and work in a healthful environment. With the success of the maturing business system in producing unprecedented economic wealth, Americans, through the new regulation, expressed concerns that weighed issues of justice, fairness, and health against traditional practices of both government regulators and business executives.

CAPITALISM AND AMERICAN BUSINESS

Capitalism is the social and economic system within which the American business firm has developed, and it is central to the story of American business. *Capitalism* defies precise definition, but in general it can be characterized as the private ownership and control of the means of production. Under capitalism, people invest in factories and stores, and the expectation is that businesses will generate profits and that the owners of the businesses will motivate, discipline, and control their work forces. Individuals have been investing capital in anticipation of profits since ancient times; yet historians usually reserve the term *capitalism* to describe a modern as opposed to medieval or ancient phenomenon. Whatever core meaning is given to capitalism, it must be inclusive enough to embrace a way of thinking as well as certain institutions (such as business firms) and practices that have emerged from that way of thinking.

Americans generally take the capitalistic way of thinking so much for granted that they are only vaguely aware any alternative ways of thinking exist. If it was business that was at "the very soul of an American," as Grund observed in 1837, probably only a few individuals gave more than routine consideration to that aspect of their souls. But in order to understand the development of business in America, more reflection is necessary. Grund quite rightly perceived capitalism as a way of thinking, for he viewed Americans engaging in commercial activities not simply to provide for life's necessities but also to secure personal happiness. He recognized what is often an unspoken assumption of capitalism: that by engaging in business as a rational, profit-seeking activity that people measure in monetary terms, individuals can enjoy fuller, more rewarding lives. In other words, Americans see themselves and others who live in capitalist societies as men and women who participate in the production of goods and services, who value those goods and services, and who profit from them not simply to provide themselves with food and shelter but to benefit the entire society and, indeed, human civilization.

Capitalism is not and never has been a static business system. Like the business firm through which it has worked, capitalism has developed over time. In 1837, Grund assumed that he was observing a nation in which most citizens were either business entrepreneurs or individuals hopeful of becoming business owners. Clearly, his society was a society of capitalism. Today, however, most Americans are neither business entrepreneurs nor individuals hoping or expecting to become business entrepreneurs. The business system has changed radically from Grund's time. In the late twentieth century, most Americans either work for large corporate or government agencies or are employees, not owners, of smaller firms. In another sense, too, capitalism has altered American life: popular values and economic actions have changed together. In the late nineteenth century America possessed a producer-oriented society; in the twentieth century this became a consumer-oriented society. As Americans increasingly came to value consumption, business actions changed. Advertising and matters of style became more and more important aspects of business decision making. Yet, although both American society and American business institutions have changed, the United States is still a capitalistic society. The structure of capitalism in the 1990s differs, of course, from that of capitalism in the 1830s. What remains the same is the assumption that by engaging in business or in providing some service for which there is a monetary reward, Americans are adding not only to their personal benefit but to the benefit of the larger society. The unifying idea between the two periods is the belief that much of that benefit could be measured in monetary terms.

While business in its broadest sense—the making and distribution of goods and services—has existed virtually everywhere on the planet, capitalism has not always prevailed. Indeed, for much of the twentieth century only a minority of the world's peoples lived under capitalistic economic systems. In many societies of this century, public agencies organized the production and distribution of goods and services according to social goals, not according to the individual goals of investors, whether small entrepreneurs or giant corporations. This method of organizing society was called *socialism*. Narrowly speaking, socialism entails the public ownership of the basic means of production and distribution in a society. More broadly speaking, it means that public agencies, claiming to act on behalf of the larger good, direct and control economic activities. Business, in the American sense, does not exist under socialism. Karl Marx, the German historian and philosopher who wrote *Das Kapital* and co-authored the *Communist Manifesto*, was the most important theorist of socialism. The economies of the former Soviet Union and many Eastern European states operated into the 1980s in traditions that stemmed from Marx's theories, and the economy of the People's Republic of China, despite recent changes, still does. State agencies, not the interaction of businesses, determined the quantities and prices of goods produced and distributed.

Sometime around the middle of the twentieth century, the U.S. economy became a "mixed" economy. The term *mixed economy* refers to a special sort of partnership between government and business that matured in the United States in this century. A business system in which private investment decisions do not always guide the economy is generally called a mixed economy. At different times in American history, government has invested funds in projects that were considered too expensive and long term, too developmental, to attract private investors. In the late 1930s, the federal government invested public capital to pursue social goals as part of the effort to end the Great Depression. During both world wars the federal government invested capital to meet war production goals, and following World War II the federal government has continued to provide large capital amounts for defense industries. Never, however, have the public investments that created the mixed economy challenged the basic underpinnings of the American business system: private ownership and control of business enterprises.

Capitalism replaced an older economic system, feudalism. American civilization had its roots in the civilization of Western Europe, and prior to 1500, feudalism was the social and economic system of Europe. In general, feudal society organized human relationships through custom, tradition, and the authority of a few local, militarily powerful figures who protected their neighbors. In feudal Europe, Christian doctrines were also instrumental in organizing human relationships. In a feudal society, human happiness was attained not through business activities or the creation of material abundance but, rather, through the living of life according to established custom, tradition, and church law. Europeans of the feudal period devoted their resources to great cathedrals that served spiritual rather than worldly business functions, unlike modern Americans, whose society has built great office skyscrapers and highly complex factories.

We begin our history of American business with an examination of the feudal origins of business activity in Western Europe. When Europeans first came to North America in the seventeenth and eighteenth centuries, they brought with them European business institutions and practices that had been developed in feudal times. Europeans started coming to North America, however, at a time when feudalism was no longer the prevailing system. Thus, American business had its origins in both the disintegration of feudalism and the rise of capitalism.

Part 1 describes the foundations of American business up to 1790 as part of the growth of capitalism in the western world. This part examines the founding of the North American colonies as business enterprises, traces the development of the colonial American business system, and, by focusing on the political economy, explores changes that occurred in that business system during the years of the American Revolution and its immediate aftermath. Part 2 examines the growth of specialized businesses resulting from new opportunities opening up in the early and mid-nineteenth century and assesses the roles that government played in creating those opportunities. The rise of big business between 1850 and 1920 and the ways in which the development of big business altered government-business relations are the principal topics of Part 3. Part 4 looks at the spread of diversified, decentralized corporations in America between 1920 and 1945 and the changes that this type of business brought to the political economy. Finally, new forms of governmental regulation and promotion of business, together with the still-evolving business firm, are considered in Part 5.

Selected Readings

For those who would like to pursue additional work on their own, at the end of each chapter is a list of books and articles dealing with the topics discussed in that chapter. However, several books deserve particular mention at the outset. Alfred D. Chandler, Jr., *The Visible Hand: The Managerial Revolution in American Business* (Cambridge, Mass.: Harvard University Press, 1977), provides a masterly analysis of the rise of big business in America. Focusing on the firm and its management, this volume shows how the development of big business revolutionized management structures and methods in the United States. Chandler's *Scale and Scope: The Dynamics of Industrial Capitalism* (Cambridge, Mass.: Harvard University Press, 1992) places the development of American big business in international context. Thomas C. Cochran, *Business in American Life: A History* (New York: McGraw-Hill, 1972), examines the evolution of business in the context of social and cultural change in the United States. We urge those who want to know more about the economic history of America to consult Glenn Porter, ed., *Encyclopedia of American Economic History* (New York: Charles Scribner's Sons, 1980), 2 vols. Mansel Blackford, *A History of Small Business in America* (New York: Twayne Publishers, 1991), surveys the development of small firms from the colonial period into the 1990s. And, finally, K. Austin Kerr, Amos Loveday, and Mansel Blackford, *Local Businesses: Exploring Their History* (Nashville: American Association of State and Local History, 1990), guides students in the primary research of business history.

IMPORTANT EVENTS, 1492–1775

1492   Columbus discovers the Bahamian Islands while searching for a trade route to the Orient.

1600   British merchants found the East India Company.

1607   The Virginia Company founds Jamestown.

1611   Colonists in Virginia start raising tobacco.

1624   The Dutch set up a trading post in New York.

1629   The Massachusetts Bay Company is founded.

1630   Some 1,000 Puritans migrate to the Boston area.

1640s   Black slavery becomes an established labor system in some of Britain's North American colonies.

1651–1673   The British Parliament passes the first Navigation Acts.

1681   Pennsylvania is founded, with Philadelphia as its leading city.

1690s   Rice cultivation begins in South Carolina.

1740s   Commercial indigo cultivation begins in South Carolina.

1757   Thomas Willing and Company becomes the first insurance company in colonial America.

1775   Colonial Americans produce 30,000 tons of iron, one-seventh of the world's total.

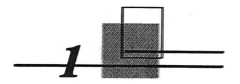

Business in Colonial America

During the Middle Ages, Venetian merchants conducted business on wooden benches in the town square. When a merchant used up his capital, angry creditors broke his bench, putting him out of business. The English word "bankruptcy" (the Italian phrase *banca rotta* means "broken bench") derives from this medieval practice. As this example suggests, the roots of American business lie deep in European soil.

The first American entrepreneurs were, in fact, Europeans whose firms had ties with the British business system, which itself was part of an emerging European capitalism. Until the American Revolution, most people living in the thirteen colonies that became the United States thought of themselves as British. Some of their ancestors had first come to North America from England in 1607, uprooting themselves and risking their lives and fortunes to take advantage of business opportunities. Eventually, business activity flourished in North America as the population grew.

In the colonial American experience, several themes of business development stand out. The British government fostered commerce in America for the benefit of the British Empire under a theory of political economy known as *mercantilism*. Mercantilism embodied the view that the London government should regulate and promote business in order to increase the wealth and power of the British crown. Although overseas trade was the most dynamic arena of commercial opportunity throughout the seventeenth and eighteenth centuries, business opportunities also emerged from colonial Americans' ingenuity in exploiting the bountiful resources of North America. Business opportunities for Americans expanded as the colonial population increased and the colonial economy grew, especially after 1740. In seizing commercial opportunities, Americans followed European customs and business practices that changed very little in the colonial period. Business remained largely a family operation; families and firms amassed wealth and invested in a range of business activities. After 1740, more and more smaller, specialized opportunities for entrepreneurs evolved.

THE GROWTH OF BUSINESS IN EUROPE

The first permanent English settlers in North America, who arrived in 1607, were employees of the Virginia Company, which had been chartered by the crown and opened up to investors as a means of expanding England's imperial power. Such a company, like the policy of mercantilism itself, was a relatively recent development. In the early 1400s, much of Europe was still feudal, and business ventures of the sort represented by the Virginia Company were unknown. During the next two centuries, however, feudalism was essentially shattered, in large part by the business activities and practices of Venetian and other Italian merchants. By the seventeenth century, capitalism was fast emerging as the dominant European economic system.

Feudalism

During the thousand years between the end of the Roman Empire in the fifth century and the discovery of North America in the fifteenth, a social and economic system called feudalism prevailed in Europe. Feudalism differed from place to place, and some of its characteristics changed over the centuries. In general, however, feudalism can be defined by the personal bonds that characterized human relationships. In feudal Europe, central governments were weak, and powerful warrior-lords provided protection to inhabitants of smaller areas. Individuals swore allegiance to these local lords, and this bond became hereditary by custom. The warrior-lords dominated the agricultural lands around their manors, to which serfs, again from a tradition of hereditary allegiance, were bound. As the relationships between lords and their warriors and between lords and their serfs became embedded in custom and tradition, it was those bonds—not formal contracts, wages, or other monetary relationships—that tied society together.

Of course, economic activity did occur within the agrarian world of European feudalism. There were barter relationships in local areas, and some regions produced surplus for trade. Towns emerged where handicraft manufacturing took place and where traders met to exchange goods. Europeans desired commodities, especially spices, from the Orient, and by the tenth and eleventh centuries, traders in northern Italian towns found themselves in a strategic geographical location for conducting business. Feudalism never gained the firm hold in Italy that it had in parts of northern Europe, and this circumstance, combined with the area's trading opportunities, nurtured the entrepreneurial activities and business advances that eventually led to the birth of capitalism. Belgian merchants began converting the surplus wool of northern Europe into cloth that Italian merchants traded in the Orient for spices. Such trade was the principal business opportunity that arose in medieval Europe, but there were others. For instance, Scandinavians exported furs, and German merchants, beer.

While trading opportunities developed throughout Europe's feudal period, personal bonds continued to govern human relationships. The goals of Europeans influenced by the feudal mentality were not monetary or economic success in the modern sense but military security, loyalty to others according to the feudal traditions, and worship of the Christian God. In feudal Europe, most savings went not into capital formation in the modern business sense but into maintenance of a clergy and the construction of cathedrals and other religious edifices, as well as into the castles of the secular nobility.

The Beginnings of Capitalism and New Business Practices

The personal bonds of feudalism were unsuited, however, for the demands of a trading economy operating over long distances through chains of many middlemen. In the satisfaction of these demands, then, were born the business relationships of capitalism that gradually promoted the breakdown of feudalism and the emergence of modern times in Europe. Those modern business relationships first appeared in the towns of northern Italy, and early American entrepreneurs used business practices that had been developed there as early as the twelfth century.

The more important Italian merchants became sedentary. Instead of moving about with their goods from place to place like peddlers, these merchants stayed in one city, where each had an office called a counting house. They relied upon foreign agents, who were usually trusted friends or relatives, to help buy and sell goods in distant lands. Merchants often worked in concert with one another through partnership agreements, which became standardized as time progressed. The business entrepreneurs who appeared to take advantage of the trading opportunities within Europe, and especially between Europe and the Near East, conducted their affairs and measured their success in monetary terms, not according to the bonds of personal loyalty that governed feudal relationships. Italian and other European entrepreneurs sought profits, and they saved their profits to provide capital for investments to secure still more profits. As trade expanded, the web of monetary activities inevitably spread to challenge, subtly but steadily, the traditional personal bonds of feudalism.

New business techniques enabled the Italian merchants to handle the growing volume of their trade. For example, they devised double-entry bookkeeping. Before this innovation, merchants had simply listed their transactions. But in double-entry bookkeeping, they recorded every transaction in two parts—in one place as a debit to one account and in another place as a credit to another account. By periodically balancing their accounts, merchants could readily determine their current financial situation. Merchants also developed the bill of exchange as a financial instrument by which they could handle transactions with one another. Bills of exchange were written agreements between the buyers and sellers of goods. The seller drafted a bill for the goods telling when and how the goods would be paid for and sent the bill to the purchaser. The purchaser, in turn, wrote on the bill that he accepted its terms, thus endorsing it. If endorsed by a reputable merchant, the bill of exchange might pass as currency through the hands of many different people before finally being redeemed and paid off.

By the sixteenth century, the business techniques of the Italian merchants were established elsewhere in Western Europe. Printed manuals taught entrepreneurs double-entry bookkeeping. Selling on credit grew in popularity, and some merchants assumed important roles as bankers. The use of samples in commodity transactions, as in the sale of wheat, was an important merchandising advance.

✱ Mercantilism and the Promotion of Business Enterprise

Along with the emergence of the new business practices and business relationships that fatally weakened feudalism, many other developments contributed to the growth of capitalism in Western Europe. Among the most important was the rise of powerful central governments. By the fifteenth century in England, France, and Spain, the authority of the feudal lord was yielding to that of the crown, and this political development created, among other things, new commercial opportunities. Feudalism rested in part on the power of local lords, but with the advent of stronger, larger political units and eventually modern nations came more opportunities for engaging in regional, national, and even international commerce. For instance, stronger central governments brought a greater measure of security and uniformity (as in such important items as weights, measures, and currencies). And rulers emerged who were interested in furthering business activity and the spread of trade as a way of obtaining funds to support the central governments and their armies and navies.

As capitalism slowly replaced feudalism, mercantilism became the doctrine of political economy that blended old feudal customs with new business attitudes and provided a transition into the modern age of business. Mercantilism was not a set philosophy but, rather, an approach that dominated European economic thought between about 1500 and 1800. According to mercantilist theory, the purpose of having a business system was to enhance the power of the state, not the individual. This emphasis on the community reveals mercantilism's feudal origins. When the British established businesses in North America and settled in the New World, they did not necessarily come as individuals seeking personal gain; instead, they were trying either to establish a new commonwealth in the New World or to work on behalf of the interests of the British crown. Only toward the end of the eighteenth century did the idea spread that the goal of a business system was to enlarge the wealth of individuals and the general population.

Mercantilists sought to have the government intervene vigorously in business affairs in order to increase the power of central rulers over traditional feudal allegiances and to improve the government's ability to wage war and make alliances. Mercantilists espoused several main ideas, all of which involved close government regulation of business opportunities to ensure that the state benefited from commerce. They emphasized that a nation should have a favorable balance of trade; that is, it should export more than it imports. To help bring about this situation, they argued that the government should pass laws to encourage exports and should maintain a strong navy to protect traders. The government should also sponsor agricultural and industrial advances, mercantilists believed, through subsidies called bounties, and should enforce laws to keep skilled artisans and industrial processes at home, out of the hands of rival countries. Finally, mercantilists favored the establishment of colonies, for they viewed them as sources of raw materials not found in the mother country and as markets for their products. A vibrant and growing trade, not simply the possession of treasures of gold and silver, lay at the heart of mercantilists' formulas for national success.

British Mercantilism, British Business, and British Colonies

Because mercantilist philosophy encouraged the establishment of colonies, it was one of the factors behind the great exploratory voyages of the fifteenth and sixteenth centuries that led Europeans to the shores of southern Africa, the Americas, and parts of Asia. Another factor was the growth of Turkish power on the Mediterranean Sea, which reduced commercial opportunities for Europeans along traditional trade routes. Thus the Italian Christopher Columbus, funded by the Spanish crown, began the exploration of the Americas in 1492, searching for an alternative route that traders could follow to Asia. Similarly, Vasco da Gama of Portugal sailed around Africa to India in 1498, and Ferdinand Magellan's expedition returned home to Seville, Spain, in 1522, completing the first trip around the world.

The British crown also encouraged overseas expeditions, and British mercantilism, which eventually led to the settlement of Jamestown, Virginia, in 1607, took a special institutional and business form. By the middle of the sixteenth century, the London government was chartering joint-stock companies to entice private individuals to invest capital in overseas business ventures and thereby help augment British power. Those joint-stock companies were businesses in which individual investors, by sharing ownership, spread their risk; they were legal devices whereby individual investors could readily enter, or leave, a business venture. To encourage trade expansion, the government charter typically granted the joint-stock companies exclusive trading rights in a particular area of the world. The Muscovy Company (1555), the Eastland Company (1579), the Africa Company (1588), the Levant Company (1592), and the East India Company (1600) were all ventures in which British merchants, with the support of their government,

The first English colonists were closely tied to the sea, for ships brought supplies and manufactured goods to them from Europe and carried back their profitable crops and raw materials. This scene depicts the early stages of settlement at Jamestown, the first permanent British settlement. (Virginia State Archives and Library)

sought new trading opportunities by looking for alternatives to traditional medieval trade routes. In the case of the most famous of those firms, the East India Company, the crown granted the firm the right to colonize and govern South Asia in the name of the English king or queen. Meanwhile, the growth of the company's commerce and profits added to the power of the central government.

Chartered in 1606, the Virginia Company was a joint-stock company that, along with several others, the London government expected would further British interests in North America. In a sense, the Virginia Company was part capitalist, part mercantilist, and part feudal. It was a capitalist venture in that the London merchants and landed gentry (wealthy landowners) who invested in the firm's stock anticipated making quick profits. These investors hoped that the firm would discover the fabled Northwest Passage, a water route thought to cross North America, and use it to open a lucrative trade with the Orient. The investors also expected the firm to exploit North America's natural resources, especially its gold and furs. Finally, the investors, observing that the land called Virginia was at the same latitude as the Mediterranean, hoped to grow citrus crops to supply the British market. The English government, in turn, chartered the Virginia Company with mercantilist ambitions. The political leaders favored the "planting" of settlements as a way of blocking French and Spanish ambitions in North

America. The crown expected the colony to strengthen England by supplying products that the nation otherwise had to import from the merchants of rival nations.

The Virginia Company was also, however, partly feudal. The people whom the company sent to Jamestown were expected not to reap individual rewards but, rather, to work on behalf of the common good—for the company and, especially, for the British crown. The instructions issued to the first colonizers, in addition to an admonition to serve and fear God, concluded with the following words: "Lastly and chiefly, the way to prosper and achieve good success is to make yourselves all of one mind for the good of your country and your own."

The Failure of the Virginia Company and the Success of the Virginia Colony

The initial expectations of the investors in Virginia proved unrealistic. The climate of Virginia was unreceptive to the cultivation of citrus fruits. Nor did the adventurers find a Northwest Passage, for no such route exists. Ore sent from Jamestown to England proved to be worthless iron pyrites, not gold and silver. As if the failure of the initial business expectations was not enough of a blow, social problems arose. Disputes over leadership and land rights divided the settlers. Physical and mental disorders, caused by a poor diet and isolation from home, racked them. And conflict with Native Americans gravely injured them, culminating in 1622 in attacks in which the Indians killed nearly one-half of the English residents.

As a result of those problems, the Virginia colony very nearly failed at the start. It experienced a "starving time" that almost wiped it out. In 1607–1608, some 70 of the 108 colonists died. The Virginia Company recruited replacements, but in the winter of 1609–1610, about 440 of the 500 settlers perished. In all, only 1,200 of the 6,000 people who migrated to Virginia in the years 1607 through 1624 remained alive in 1625.

These difficulties led to the reorganization of the Virginia Company, for the original company proved unable to attract new capital investments. At a time when London merchants had put almost £2 million into the East India Company, the Virginia Company could secure only £40,000. In 1609, the Virginia Company began offering its stock free to anyone who would move to Jamestown. Each such stockholder was to receive a hundred acres of land as a dividend after working for the company for seven years. Nine years later, the Virginia Company moved still further in the direction of private rather than corporate landownership by introducing the headright system, giving fifty acres to people paying their own passage to America. At the same time that the company instituted new systems of landownership, it delegated more and more responsibility for running the colony to those in Virginia.

Yet the basic problem of developing a profitable enterprise remained unsolved, as various experiments in growing different crops failed. Tobacco ultimately provided Virginia with a profitable export, despite admonitions from King James I to avoid a custom "so vile and stinking" as smoking. The development of the tobacco trade required time, however, with most of the growth taking place after 1620. London's annual imports of tobacco rose from £161,000 in 1620 to £2 million just eighteen years later.

In the meantime, the Virginia Company was earning no profits, and in 1624 it was disbanded. From that time on, the Virginia Colony existed as a royal colony, with its governor appointed by the English crown (a colonial legislature known as the House of Burgesses, set up in 1619, advised the governor on how best to rule the colony). As the investors in the Virginia Company painfully discovered, developing a plantation economy based on settled agriculture was a much more costly and difficult process than simply opening trade with a distant land.

Thus the founding of Jamestown as a business enterprise was only symbolic of the importance that business was to have in the history of American civilization. The experience of the Virginia Company revealed, moreover, that the New World was inhospitable to old feudal customs. Ancient European traditions of allegiance did not fit the wilderness condition, especially when the leaders resided far away. The colonists' aim was to gain title to the land that they worked as individuals. It was the promise of individual reward that eventually ensured the success of the Virginia Colony.

The Massachusetts Bay Company

If the failure of the Virginia Company and the eventual success of the Virginia Colony were symbolic of the importance of business in the founding of American civilization, the story of British settlement in New England began another theme of American business history—the struggle within the colonies, and eventually throughout American society, to reconcile the sometimes competing interests of individual entrepreneurs and the larger community of which they were a part.

The Massachusetts Bay Company was a joint-stock venture chartered in 1629 to allow a group of English Puritans to establish a new community based on religious values. The Puritans were religious dissenters who sought to purify the Church of England by simplifying its rituals, among other matters. As was not the case with the Virginia Company, the investors themselves traveled to America in 1630 to establish Boston and other towns. The Puritan settlers, led by John Winthrop, envisioned building a new society free from external pressures in which every man respected the worth of every other man—what Winthrop termed "a city upon a hill" that would demonstrate Christian precepts to all people. Winthrop advised his followers to meet one another's needs "in the bond of brotherly affection." In the new land Winthrop believed that "the care of the public must oversway all private respects."

Although Massachusetts Bay was established as a joint-stock company, the first leaders of the colony disdained the commercial practices of merchants who sought profits, if these profits came at the expense of other citizens. So the Puritans' Christian ideals of brotherhood and community soon came into conflict with the ambitions of merchants. The clergymen in control of the colony sought to establish just prices through regulation, for example. They believed, moreover, that men of means should give their wealth to their brothers according to need and regardless of ability to repay.

So the Puritans' Christian ideals soon encountered practical difficulties. The Massachusetts settlers needed to import numerous commodities from Britain and so had to pursue local business opportunities to raise the necessary cash. At first they obtained furs for sale abroad but soon had to find other means of harvesting the region's resources in order to earn a livelihood. The Puritans, in short, required the services of merchants. Moreover, other settlers not imbued with Puritan doctrines came to Massachusetts who were eager to earn profits from those services. Disagreements between merchants and the Puritan clergy led eventually to changes in the government of the colony, whose charter was finally revoked in 1684; Massachusetts was thereafter under royal authority.

The Puritan ideal of "a city upon a hill," however, had lasting repercussions. Throughout the subsequent history of business in America, events would occur and issues would arise that revealed how business entrepreneurs themselves had mixed motives, commercial and communal. Nor were business owners alone in that respect. Throughout American business history there have been and still are occasions when business interests conflict with what Americans define as the public or general interest. Indeed, conflicts between ideas of the public interest and the commercial interests of entrepreneurs, firms, and entire industries have become a significant part of the fabric of government-business relations.

Other Colonies

The Massachusetts Bay Company and the Virginia Company were unique in American colonial history. The British government did not establish most of its North American colonies by chartering joint-stock ventures. Most British settlement in the seventeenth century occurred in *proprietary colonies,* in which the crown granted a large tract of land to a proprietor in exchange for favors. The proprietors, of course, encouraged settlement on their lands, hoping to gain tax revenues—the "quitrent"—for their troubles. Lord Baltimore saw the colony of Maryland as a haven for Catholics from the religious disputes sweeping Britain. And William Penn sought not only British settlers but also Germans and other continental Europeans to emigrate to Pennsylvania.

Although most of the colonies were proprietary, feudalism never took root in North America. The British government encouraged colonization under the doctrines of mercantilism, and, spurred by the necessity of trade with the mother country, capitalism flourished. Moreover, the availability of abundant land undercut attempts to impose feudal controls and encouraged the growth of capitalism. As the settlers overcame the initial trials of their new environment, the colonial American economy began to prosper, and with that prosperity, business opportunities expanded.

BUSINESS IN COLONIAL AMERICA

Once successfully founded, the colonies experienced an uneven growth in population and commercial opportunity. Initially the colonies grew as new settlers migrated to them, but after 1740 more significant growth occurred as opportunities to trade with Great Britain and southern Europe expanded. By the eve of the American Revolution, the colonists had achieved one of the highest standards of living of any people in the world: this population, only one-third that of England, could boast an economic output equal to nearly 40 percent of the mother country's. The colonists had advantages over their compatriots overseas. In America, land was more abundant, water purer, diseases rarer, and energy sources more available. In short, the quality of life became higher in the colonies than in the mother country. By 1776, the thirteen colonies had a population of about 2 million whites, 500,000 blacks, and 100,000 Native Americans.

Colonial Trade and Business Opportunities

Most colonial Americans lived near the seacoast, and the importance of ocean commerce between the colonies and Europe reverberated throughout the colonial economy. Overseas trade stimulated chances for farmers to prosper from their labor and investments as well as opportunities for other colonists to enter overseas trade, thus leading to the creation of many business firms. As farming developed, artisans appeared; these skilled workers made goods and also, as small business owners, sold those goods. American-owned ships sailing the Atlantic linked the Old and New Worlds; in colonial ports, American-owned merchant firms organized cargoes and arranged banking, shipping, and insurance services. By the 1760s and 1770s, some 20 percent of the colonists' income originated directly from their overseas exports, and colonists spent about 25 percent of their income on imports. Table 1.1 lists the exports crucial to the economic advance of the colonies. Foodstuffs and other agricultural goods lead the list.

This substantial overseas trade stimulated regional specialization in colonial agriculture. The colonists learned which crops their areas grew best and produced them for sale in the markets of the British Empire and Europe. The Virginia settlers turned to tobacco as their staple export crop, and a tobacco culture spread throughout Virginia and Maryland in the Chesapeake region. The Carolinas and Georgia grew rice and indigo, a plant used by British textile manufacturers in making blue dye. Farmers in the middle colonies such as Pennsylvania produced more diversified crops, with wheat emerging as an important export. After 1750, the population of Europe increased, but without a corresponding rise in farm production. Colonial American farmers grasped the opportunities to enlarge the production of grain, flax, salted meat, and even beeswax. In the Chesapeake region, its soils exhausted by tobacco, planters shifted to newly profitable wheat. The relatively rocky soil of New England precluded intensive commercial agriculture, but New Englanders exported codfish, whale oil, furs, naval stores, and lumber. Shipbuilding, shipping, and shipping services such as insurance also bolstered the economy of New England.

Although overseas trade was the most powerful engine of colonial business, domestic developments were becoming significant by the eve of the American Revolution in 1775. Marketing networks were reaching out from Philadelphia, Boston, New York, and Charleston to nearby towns and farms; farmers were sending their produce via middlemen to towns and cities for sale in both domestic and overseas markets. In business terms, those networks consisted of hundreds of small specialized firms providing services. For many colonists—a growing proportion as time progressed—"getting and spending" within a commercial economy was the way of life.

From the start, there was a commercial outlook among the people who came to live and work in British North America. Taking advantage of commercial opportunities in the colonies depended in part upon obtaining

Table 1.1   The Value of Major Colonial American Commodity Exports, 1768–1772 (yearly average, in thousands of pounds)

Food grains		
Bread and flour	£410	
Wheat	115	
Indian corn	83	
Rice	312	
Total		£920
Tobacco		766
Fish		154
Wood products		135
Indigo		113
Meat		72
Horses		60
Iron		58
Naval stores		48
Whale oil		46
Flaxseed		42
Potash		35
Rum		22

SOURCE: Gary Walton and James F. Shepherd, *The Economic Rise of Early America* (Cambridge: Cambridge University Press, 1979), pp. 194–195.

people to work in fields and shops. Labor was in short supply relative to Europe. Businesses arose that arranged for a trade in indentured servants. In that trade Europeans came to the colonies under contracts, called indentures, in which they agreed to work for a specified period of time in exchange for their passage and support. From the first, indentured servants were usually commercially minded, viewing their service as a temporary condition. Indentured servants typically looked forward to entering some commercial trade or small farming. Slaves, by contrast, could not aspire to full participation in the world of commerce. Traders from Europe, and to a lesser extent New England, penetrated the slave trade among blacks on the west coast of Africa and resold slaves profitably in the New World. The number of slaves in the thirteen colonies rose from less than 15,000 in 1690 to a half-million by 1776. Slave labor replaced indentured servant labor especially in the less-skilled work of growing rice and tobacco in the southern colonies. By the nineteenth century, however, commercial values had spread into the nation's black population.

The commercial spirit extended to the interior and to the family farm— especially after 1750, with the expansion of foodstuff sales to the growing European population. Before the second half of the eighteenth century, commercial opportunities were limited for many; farmers and artisans in remote regions, isolated from easy access to the Atlantic, were obliged to engage in a simple barter economy to satisfy their needs. In the area around Kent, Connecticut, for instance, before 1750 only one-third of the farms produced any surplus for sale; farmers and artisans bartered, using no middlemen. The value of maintaining the close-knit family farm and links to the local community was important and persisted even as commercial opportunities expanded. Yet the growth of commercial opportunities, especially in the area of providing farm products for European markets, did not substantially change the way of life on the family farm. Instead, farmers successfully expanded the production of surplus foodstuffs, which they then exported through networks of middlemen.

Colonial Businesses as Family Enterprises

Except in isolated areas where subsistence farming was the way of life, business enterprises flourished in colonial America. Like most European businesses, colonial American businesses were family enterprises. American merchants relied heavily upon family members, who served as clerks in their offices, as captains of their ships, and as their representatives in distant cities. At a time when communications were slow and unreliable, merchants had to trust those with whom they worked, and one way to ensure that trust was to conduct business through family networks. Often, artisan businesses and plantations also operated as family ventures. Ties of blood and marriage bound the colonial business world.

In all of these businesses, wives played roles shaped by colonial ideas of the family. In the colonial period, European and American ideas about the family were patriarchal, and when women engaged in commercial activities, they did so within that framework. Husbands were in charge; wives assumed a subordinate position. Women were to guide the house, but not the husband. Within the patriarchal family, however, as long as women's actions aimed at strengthening their families and did not conflict with the wishes of their husbands, wives could and did enter the business world.

In particular, a wife was expected to serve as a business deputy for her husband should circumstances prevent him from filling his position. The wives of fishermen and small merchants, who traveled with their goods, often managed their husbands' businesses in their absence. In 1710, Elizabeth Holmes of Boston met Patience Marston of Salem to settle accounts resulting from a voyage to Newfoundland, though neither woman had been on the ship. They were acting as proxies for their husbands—Captain Robert Holmes, who had commanded the ship, and Benjamin Marston, the shipowner. In a few localities, women as deputy husbands became the norm—as in Nantucket, where men were often away for lengthy periods on whaling or trading voyages, leaving their stores and shops in the hands of their wives. Elsewhere, widows continued family businesses in coachmaking, shipbuilding, rigging, horseshoeing, painting, engraving, and the making of fish pots and fishnets.

There were four main types of businesses in colonial America, in addition to the family farm. In the seaboard towns of the North, entrepreneurs engaged in general mercantile activity. In the Chesapeake region and the southern colonies, there were prominent planters who organized businesses. In the towns, there were skilled artisans who made and sold items. And throughout the colonies, there were itinerant peddlers who bought and sold goods on a small scale.

The Merchant

Colonial Americans usually reserved the word "merchant" for a person conducting an overseas wholesale trade, and in the northern and middle colonies, the largest businesses were those of such merchants. These merchants resembled the Italian merchants of medieval times. The most important colonial merchants were sedentary. They had an office in one city and did not travel from place to place with their goods. The merchant called his office a "counting house," and colonial Americans used the term "house" to describe the merchant's business. Boston, New York, Philadelphia, and lesser cities were the homes of the leading merchants: the Cabots, Lowells, Browns, Jacksons, Hancocks, Beekmans, Willings, Binghams, and Whartons, among others. Colonial merchants operated as single-owner proprietors or as members of partnerships. The partnerships could have been short-lived, limited to the single voyage of a ship, or long-lasting, continuing for a generation or more. Unlike their British counterparts, colonial American merchants did not organize joint-stock companies.

The nerve center of the merchant's business was the counting house, but it was not an elaborate office, even though many different types of business activities originated there. Colonial businesses functioned without a complex hierarchy of managers and officers. Only the largest merchants employed even a bookkeeper and a few clerks. In the counting house the merchant recorded his transactions, with the largest firms using the Italian double-entry method. There he arranged the collection and shipment of various cargoes to different overseas markets. For example, merchants sent salted fish to the West Indies, imported molasses, distilled rum, and sold or exported the spirits. Large merchants supervised the wholesale of goods to smaller merchants, and they operated retail stores.

Some merchants of colonial times were involved in more than trading commodities. They provided a wide variety of services essential to the colonial business system. Many owned or shared ownership in ships. They entered the field of shipbuilding, a lively industry in New England by the eighteenth century. They had interests in wharves and supplied naval stores (lumber, ships' masts, turpentine, and so forth). They engaged in marine insurance services: the first insurance enterprise in America, Thomas Willing and Company of Philadelphia, was formed in 1757. No commercial banks existed in colonial America, but leading merchants performed banking functions by lending money at interest to one another and to smaller business enterprises. Finally, many colonial merchants were deeply involved in real estate projects, both in their cities and on the frontier. Quick profits might have come through speculation, whereas rents tended to provide steadier incomes.

The House of Hancock: A Colonial Merchant

The House of Hancock, the largest colonial business, illustrates the ties between family and business so important in the colonial period. The very use of the word "house" to describe the firm suggests the close connection between family and business life. An eighteenth-century Boston merchant, Thomas Hancock relied heavily upon family and friends in carrying out his far-flung business ventures.

Born in 1703, Hancock was the son of a Puritan minister. Trained as a bookseller and binder, Hancock entered these trades as a small businessman at the age of twenty-one, probably using funds from his father as his initial capital. From the start, Hancock moved in the polite society of Boston and was soon making the personal contacts necessary for business success. In 1730, he married the daughter of Daniel Henchman, a prominent bookseller and merchant, thus solidifying his social and economic position in the city.

Competition in Boston's book trade greatly increased in the 1730s, and Hancock was soon diversifying his business. Over the next few decades, he became one of the leading general merchants in the colonies. He added a growing line of products to the imported books sold in his retail store and eventually got out of the book business altogether. By 1755, clothing made up two-thirds of his sales, but he also sold such items as brass compasses, fire-making steels, hourglasses, swords, and tea. Even more important was Hancock's wholesale trade, the backbone of his business. From his Boston office he resold the goods that he imported from England to country merchants throughout New England. To do so, Hancock had to offer liberal credit terms, up to a full year, to these smaller merchants. In addition, he had to accept the products of the countryside acquired by the country merchants—wheat, corn, whale oil, and less likely items such as harnesses—in payment for their debts to him. In return, Hancock exported these products to England and the rest of the world.

To assist him in making foreign sales, Hancock maintained foreign agents, often friends or family members, in London, Amsterdam, Lisbon, and other cities. Personal ties linked Hancock to his agents; for instance, one agent sent his son to live with the Hancocks for four years. Hancock taught him accounts, and Mrs. Hancock grew so attached to him as a family member that she did not want to part with him when his apprenticeship ended. On another occasion, Hancock's Jamaica agent asked Hancock to take on his son as a boarder: "Let me know what you would Ask with him & remit you sugar or Molasses for that purpose."

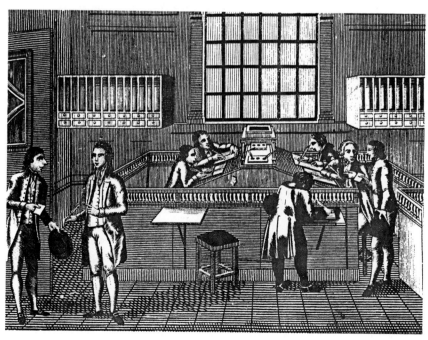

The counting house was the nerve center for the business activities of the colonial merchant. Even the most important merchants, however, employed only a handful of clerks in their counting houses. (The Library Company of Philadelphia)

Hancock took part in other business activities as well. For instance, he dabbled in real estate. In addition to owning one of the major wharves in Boston, he purchased an island off the coast of Nova Scotia with the idea of establishing a fishery there. Hancock was also interested in mining and manufacturing opportunities. He invested in copper and iron mines, but operational difficulties frustrated his search for profits in these ventures. For a twenty-year period, Hancock (joined by several partners) tried intermittently to set up and run a paper-making factory, until he was finally defeated by a lack of good raw materials. Hancock's various activities, especially his trading, made him one of New England's leading merchants. Upon his retirement, his work was carried on by other family members, most notably John Hancock, the signer of the Declaration of Independence.

The Philadelphia Merchants of Late-Colonial Times

Thomas Hancock was a general merchant, a jack-of-all-trades who engaged in a wide range of business activities. Like him, many of the most important merchants of colonial America were general merchants, particularly during the early colonial period. In most of the colonies, markets were too small and too greatly separated by poor transportation to allow merchants to earn large profits from specialized businesses. However, by the close of the colonial period, specialization was becoming increasingly common in some of the larger colonial cities. An increase in the size of markets made specialization possible, and merchants with relatively little capital found in specialization a way to enter and advance in business; to enter a multitude of lines of work simultaneously required too much capital for most. Nowhere in the colonies did mercantile specialization proceed further than in Philadelphia during the years after 1750.

As a rapidly growing city with a prosperous hinterland and an expanding overseas trade, Philadelphia had a large number of merchants: 230 in 1756, 320 in 1774, and 514 in 1785. These were not grocers selling food or shopkeepers running small stores but wholesalers active in overseas trade. About 52 traders, organized into 37 firms, dominated the wholesale trade on the eve of the Revolution. They were the "great oaks" of the Philadelphia merchant community. The hundreds of smaller merchants, the "lesser trees" who labored in their shadows, were much smaller wholesalers. While the large merchants clearly stood out from most Philadelphians by their ownership of luxurious townhouses, country estates, and carriages, the smaller merchants enjoyed lifestyles that were not much different from the better-off artisans, grocers, and shopkeepers.

By the time of the American Revolution, Philadelphia's overseas trading area embraced New England, England, southern Europe, and the Caribbean. Whether importing or exporting, few individual merchants or partnerships enjoyed sufficient capital to trade with all of this vast region, so specialized trading relationships with one or two areas were the norm. Specialization by type of trade also occurred; different groups of merchants came to handle the exportation of foodstuffs (mainly wheat and flour) from Philadelphia and the importation of dry goods (cloth and buttons), hardware, and other manufactured items into Philadelphia. By the 1770s and 1780s, this differentiation by function was pronounced, with only the very largest merchants dealing in more than one type of commodity.

Specialization divided the Philadelphia merchants into two distinct groups. About 250 merchants acted as importers of dry goods from 5 to 10 suppliers in England. The Philadelphia merchants, in turn, sold the imported goods through extensive networks of retailers in small towns around Philadelphia. Some 90 percent of the sales to retailers were made on credit extended for as long as twelve months, and bad debts of retailers often threatened the livelihood of the wholesalers. Most of the other Philadelphia merchants took part in the export trade, conducted mainly on a cash basis. Exporters sent out one or two ships (only the larger firms owned more than two) on regular shuttle runs between Philadelphia and one or two overseas destinations year after year, hoping in this way to establish a secure source of stable profits. In addition to shipping and selling on his own account, a merchant might have acted as a commission agent for other merchants. To fill the holds of their ships, some merchants even promised to leave port on a stipulated day, regardless of whether their ships were full; many also advertised the regularity of their sailings. Thus, the idea of scheduled voyages, fully established by New York packet lines in the early 1800s, was present in embryo form in late colonial Philadelphia.

The Colonial Plantation

The counterpart to the merchant of the middle and northern colonies was the wealthy planter of the Chesapeake and southern colonies who dominated the business systems of the South. Except for Charleston, South Carolina, cities whose businesses served the hinterland never developed in the colonial South. Instead, the population dispersed along navigable waterways, and most business activity centered upon the plantation, often located at a desirable spot near the headwaters of a river. In the Chesapeake region, specialized merchants supplementing the plantation business appeared after 1740 and helped organize both the domestic coastal trade of the region and overseas export trade. By the eve of the American Revolution, some American entrepreneurs even challenged the British merchants who controlled the tobacco trade.

The southern planter produced staple crops for sale within the British Empire. The planter, like other colonials, held no political authority over that economic and political system, which was governed from London. The planter could not control the prices or the markets of staple crops and relied on British supplies of desired manufactured goods and credit. As a result, the largest, wealthiest planters, dependent on imports for luxury goods, followed a strategy of self-sufficiency in everyday items and pursued profits through a variety of entrepreneurial activities.

The heart of the southern plantation was agriculture. Tobacco became the most profitable crop in the tidewater region of the Chesapeake during this period. The cultivation of tobacco was labor-intensive; that is, it required much more in the way of labor than capital to clear the land and grow the tobacco. So in the seventeenth century, especially from the 1680s on, planters began importing large numbers of black African slaves to work their fields. In addition, tobacco cultivation rapidly exhausted the soil, so the planters constantly sought to open new lands in the interior. They sent overseers with slaves to live on and work inland fields. Their base, however, remained the plantation and its wharves reached by ocean-going ships.

The wharf at the tidewater plantation was a center of business activity. From the wharf went the area's exportable produce, and to it arrived manufactured goods from England. There the planter conducted sales from slave ships that called. There too he often maintained a warehouse and a store to service his less-well-off neighbors. The major plantations were impressive indeed: in Virginia, Robert Carter's Nomini Hall had thirty-three outbuildings and looked like a village.

Although the planters grew tobacco, rice, and indigo to earn income from the export trade, they sought self-sufficiency in many other respects. The wealthier planters sometimes owned iron foundries, breweries and

This painting by an unknown artist shows a typical southern plantation. In the southern colonies, planters operating from their plantations often assumed the role of merchant, buying and selling goods for their smaller neighbors. (The Metropolitan Museum of Art. Gift of Edgar Williams and Bernice Chrysler Garbisch, 1963, 63.201.3)

distilleries, and flour mills. They housed artisans who spun thread from wool, wove textiles, sewed clothing, and tanned leather to make shoes and harnesses. Plantation blacksmiths fashioned and repaired tools. Cabinet-makers produced furniture, and coopers made barrels. (By the eighteenth century, the planters had trained slaves to perform these tasks.) The planters sold manufactured goods to neighbors, sometimes bartering for tobacco, which they in turn exported. Nevertheless, planters usually suffered an imbalance of trade because of the luxury goods and manufactured items they imported from Europe.

As time progressed, planters came to depend increasingly upon others for their needs. Southern farming, like colonial trade, became more and more specialized from the mid-1700s on. By the 1760s, for example, tobacco-growing plantations in the upper Chesapeake were surrounded by smaller farms that sold them foodstuffs and were themselves exporting foodstuffs, hemp, flax, and forest products to Great Britain.

George Washington: Planter-Businessman

George Washington's Mount Vernon plantation on the banks of the Potomac River in Virginia in many ways typified the plantation enterprise of the eighteenth century. At the age of twenty-five, Washington owned 3,000 acres of land, which he supervised from his home. The land of Mount Vernon, however, was of poor quality, eroded and exhausted from earlier tobacco cultivation. In his search for income, therefore, Washington sold goods and services to his neighbors and produced profitable export commodities. He was also heavily involved in land speculation in the West, and he sent slaves to till farms near Mount Vernon.

A pioneer in experimenting with agricultural techniques, Washington cultivated a variety of crops under several different conditions and raised animals not common to Virginia, especially sheep and mules. He learned how to grow a high grade of wheat on his tidewater lands and, since wheat was too bulky to ship long distances profitably, entered the flour-milling business. One of his main sources of income came from exporting flour to customers in the West Indies.

From this agricultural base, Washington diversified into a range of business activities. He operated a fishery on the Potomac, supplying the West Indies with dried and salted fish. In 1774, Washington paid taxes on 135 slaves over the age of sixteen, among whom were coopers, smiths, carpenters, spinners, and knitters. His coopers made barrels in which other slaves packed fish, flour, and whiskey. Still other slaves made bricks from local clays and constructed buildings for the plantation. Washington provided services to his neighbors, shipping their produce from his wharf, where he maintained a small store for the retail sale of items he imported. His neighbors paid Washington in kind, usually one-eighth of their wheat for milling or tobacco for shipping. Washington also operated a distillery and, for a time, a ferry service to Maryland.

Like the general merchants operating farther north, Washington broadened his entrepreneurial activities. Both the southern planters and the northern general merchants invested their capital in varied activities, because the opportunities for profit in any one specialized activity were limited. Unlike the northern merchants, Washington used his slave-run plantation as his base. Like Hancock, however, he was successful not only through hard work and entrepreneurial acumen but also because of family connections and inherited wealth.

Artisans and Manufacturers

Although most of the goods manufactured in the Chesapeake region, and farther south, came from the hands of slaves, there were opportunities elsewhere for small-scale craftsmen to satisfy local markets. Small towns from Pennsylvania to the northernmost fringe of settlement had their gristmills, sawmills, tanneries, and smithies. As a growing population broadened markets in the late-colonial period, some of these ventures acquired more than local importance. By 1770, some 140 distilleries clustered in the northern ports, using molasses imported from the Caribbean as their raw material, produced nearly 5 million gallons of rum, about 60 percent of the total consumed in the colonies. In the same year, 26 refineries produced sugar. In the Brandywine valley near Wilmington, Delaware, a complex of water-driven mills took form in late-colonial times: 60 gristmills, 6 sawmills, 4 paper mills, 2 snuff mills, a barley mill, a cotton mill, an iron-slitting mill, and several fulling mills (cloth-making establishments).

In the larger towns and cities, skilled artisans, investing small sums in simple tools, worked as silversmiths and coppersmiths. Printers like Benjamin Franklin published newspapers, pamphlets, and books. Near Franklin, a William Will operated his pewterer's shop, where he sold, at wholesale and retail, mugs, plates, washbasins, and the like that he imported from London or made himself. Such opportunities multiplied many times over in eighteenth-century Philadelphia and other towns as the colonial business system prospered.

The situation of artisans in Charleston was probably typical of that in many colonial cities. This port city had two groups of artisans. The first, consisting of carpenters, bricklayers, carvers, joiners, and tinsmiths, operated as workers but usually did not possess their own shops. The second group—saddlers, cabinetmakers, and shoemakers—operated as small business owners, making goods for sale in their own shops. They usually ran their businesses alone but sometimes took in partners to gain capital and skills. As some of these artisan businesses grew larger, bookkeepers offered in newspaper advertisements to bring their account books up-to-date.

Large-scale manufacturing to supply more than local markets was rare because of the high cost of transportation, but there were initial efforts in a few fields. Between 1763 and 1775, colonial shipbuilders launched 40,000 tons of ships, of which 18,600 tons were sold abroad. Most iron made in

Peddlers criss-crossed the backwoods of colonial America, taking the products of Europe to the countryside. (The Bettman Archive)

the colonies was destined for local use, but some entered intercolonial and international trade. Smelted with charcoal made from America's plentiful hardwood forests, the pig iron was produced at iron "plantations" located in the countryside. (Americans called them "plantations" because of their rural nature; they even grew food crops to feed the ironworkers.) By 1775, the American colonies possessed at least 80 furnaces and 175 forges for making iron, numbers that exceeded those of the corresponding facilities in England. With an annual output of 30,000 tons, these installations in the colonies produced one-seventh of the world's iron, an amount that placed colonial America behind only Russia and Sweden as a manufacturer of iron.

Peddlers

Roaming through the colonies were small-scale merchants known as peddlers. Carrying their trade goods on their backs, on pack horses, or in small wagons, they joined the seaport cities with the inland areas. Bartering their goods for local produce and craft items wherever they went, the peddlers provided commercial links, however primitive, between city and countryside that would not otherwise have existed. Every medium-sized town supported one or two young men who made their living as peddlers, but the number of peddlers more than doubled as economic opportunities broadened at the close of the colonial period. Peddlers sometimes became resident merchants in the interior when they observed trading opportunities at strategic points along rivers.

The Conduct of Business in Colonial America

Several general features characterized the colonial American business system as a whole, whether the entrepreneur was a merchant or planter. As we have seen, commercial people looked outward to the ocean and the British Empire rather than inland to the North American continent. For colonial Americans, most of whom lived along the coast, the larger markets lay overseas because their homeland was still underpopulated. Internal transportation and communication facilities were slow and poorly developed. In 1723, for example, Benjamin Franklin required four days to travel the one hundred miles from New York to Philadelphia. Thus, it was an overseas economy rather than internal commerce that provided merchants and planters more significant opportunities for profit. The southern crops went to market in Europe, and George Washington and his fellow planters did business with English merchants, called *factors,* who sold their goods, lent them money, and filled orders for finer-quality manufactured goods. Without staple crops to export profitably, New England merchants harvested the ocean, built and operated ships, and provided naval stores for the British fleet. Like their southern counterparts, they imported expensive items from Britain and often had to deal with associates abroad.

The overseas nature of many of the business opportunities available to colonial Americans brought considerable risks. Ocean travel was slow; sailing ships took from four to six weeks to cross the Atlantic Ocean (more if the weather was bad). Piracy, shipwreck, and weather-ruined cargoes were risks that all overseas traders had to face, and planters like Washington faced the additional hazard of crop failures. Nor was success guaranteed, even to a ship that survived the perilous ocean crossing. When a ship arrived at a port laden with goods, an oversupply might have depressed prices.

Furthermore, as the American business system was a colonial one, it was supposed to operate mainly for the benefit of the mother country. The British government sought supplies of raw materials and markets for finished products in order to enrich itself, not its colonies. The net cash flow went from the colonies to England and, as a result, American entrepreneurs were sometimes short of money. William Byrd II, a well-known Virginia planter, boasted in 1726 that "half-a-crown [an English coin] will rest undisturbed in my Pocket for many Moons together," in part because his plantation was nearly self-sufficient and in part because the colonial business system operated, of necessity, with little cash. Entrepreneurs, like Washington's neighbors, paid for services in kind (a barter arrangement). Merchants endorsed bills of exchange, just as their Italian counterparts had done centuries earlier, which circulated as a kind of currency.

In American business during the colonial period, business relationships were personal and informal, and the pace of business was necessarily slow. A simple exchange of correspondence could take up to half a year. In towns and cities, merchants transacted business informally among friends in taverns and coffee houses. As the colonial economy grew after 1740, however, business practices began to change somewhat. More of the merchants felt the need to use double-entry bookkeeping. Bookkeeping manuals came into widespread use, and by the mid-1750s, one such guide, *Bookkeeping Methodiz'd* by John Mair, had a section devoted to colonial needs. Merchants' handbooks—guides to standard business practices around the world, arranged alphabetically by city name—helped regularize business methods. Colonial newspapers came to carry more specialized shipping information, local trade statistics, and local commodity prices. In imitation of their European counterparts, late-colonial merchants supported the publication of two types of specialized business newspapers: marine lists and lists of current commodity prices. As specialization took hold in the business system, brokers of various sorts—real estate, insurance, commodity, shipping, and exchange—brought together buyers and sellers. By the close of the colonial period, in some cities brokers met in set places, taverns or "exchange alleys," to make it easier for customers to find them.

Merchant Leadership and the American Work Ethic

The merchants were profit-oriented people who believed in the accumulation of wealth. They took risks and ventured into new fields because they were imbued with the commercial spirit so vital to a capitalist society. As

By the 1730s, Philadelphia had become a bustling port city, whose merchants looked outward to the British Empire for trade possibilities. (Historical Society of Pennsylvania)

the colonial society matured in the eighteenth century, moreover, the merchants became the highest social class, usually closely tied with British colonial officials. Merchants sometimes were elected to colonial legislatures and town councils, and they also advised the royal governors. The merchants and southern planters set themselves apart by living in grand houses, dressing in the latest London finery, and enjoying luxury goods imported from abroad. Not everyone admired their success, or the means by which they achieved it, but their very ability to succeed showed that American society tended to encourage and reward hard work and entrepreneurship.

Ironically enough, the encouragement of hard work and the reaping of its benefits were a Puritan legacy, although perhaps not the one most hoped for by the idealistic settlers whose main goal was to build "a city upon a hill" to serve as a model of Christian precepts. The Puritans followed the theology of John Calvin, a sixteenth-century Swiss cleric who argued that God was so powerful, His wisdom so infinite, that He knew who among humankind had achieved salvation. God, in this view, was omnipotent, and the individual human powerless to determine his or her ultimate fate. Calvinists reasoned that individuals should accomplish good works while on earth as an indication that they were among those whom God had elected to salvation. Hard work, in the eyes of Calvinists, was an important sign of salvation. This view, known as the Protestant ethic, instructed individuals to lead their lives according to the Lord's teachings and to bring forth the fruits of the earth and create wealth.

The Puritans were relatively few in number, but their ideas influenced both colonial society and the course of American history, for they meshed nicely with the needs of a vital, growing country and thus became part of the American culture and the system we know as capitalism. Their ideas were popularized in the writings of Benjamin Franklin, a successful Philadelphia printer who belonged to no church and became both a respected pillar of Philadelphia society and an important political leader. Franklin expressed Puritan values in pithy aphorisms, such as "a penny saved is a penny earned," which became permanent fixtures of the American language. In his *Autobiography,* Franklin admonished Americans to practice "INDUSTRY. Lose no time; be always employ'd in something useful; cut off all unnecessary actions." Such prescriptions promoted the creation of wealth and the growth of the American business system.

THE NAVIGATION ACTS

Despite the vitality of the colonial economy, neither the merchants, the manufacturers, nor the farmers of colonial America were free to pursue business opportunities wherever they found them. Beginning in 1650, the British government, through a series of laws called the Navigation Acts, attempted to regulate business for its own benefit, in accordance with the prevailing mercantilist philosophy. Colonial American entrepreneurs were expected to help make Britain strong while weakening her rivals. (Other European nations had similar regulations, by which they hoped to weaken Britain.) Although the Navigation Acts did little to affect actual business opportunities overall, by the end of the colonial period some colonists saw them as important symbols of British arrogance and power that could be used as instruments of repression.

The Navigation Acts regulated commerce in four major ways. First, most trade between the colonies and the rest of the world had to be carried out in English or colonial ships manned primarily by English or colonial crews. Second, most goods destined for the colonies had to pass through England, even if they had originated in other countries. Third, many items exported from the colonies had to go first to England, even if their final destinations lay elsewhere. These products, known as "enumerated articles," included molasses, indigo, and tobacco. Finally, bounties or subsidies were paid for the production of certain goods, such as indigo and naval stores, and restrictions were placed on some forms of manufacturing in the colonies, such as finished iron products. (See Map 1.1.)

The Navigation Acts helped shape business opportunities for colonial Americans. Clearly, the bounties increased opportunities for producing the selected goods. The requirement that merchants conduct trade using English ships stimulated New England's shipbuilding industry, one of the largest in the world by the mid-1700s. The regulations reduced opportunities in other areas, however. Tobacco exporters in Virginia might have preferred selling tobacco directly to the continental European market, rather than going through British merchants, who charged high commissions for their services.

On the whole, however, the British mercantile regulations affected economic growth very little. For the most part, business opportunities would have occurred as they did without the regulations because the economy of the British Empire was the strongest in the world by the eighteenth century, and colonial American entrepreneurs, as part of that system, enjoyed many advantages. The colonial American entrepreneurs were mostly Englishmen with strong ties of culture and language to the homeland. Southern planters shipped their tobacco to England because of the regulations, but also because they had ties to British merchants who provided credit and desired English books, clothing, furniture, and many other fine manufactured products in return.

The Navigation Acts were intended to benefit British entrepreneurs, not to harm them. Therefore, the rules contained important exemptions that allowed considerable business opportunities for the Americans. Northern merchants sent fish, flour, and rum directly to West Indies markets within the empire and to southern Europe outside of the empire. Trade to these two areas was exempt from the regulation that colonial exports and imports pass through England. Furthermore, in one important measure, the Molasses Act of 1733, British officials allowed violations. In order to help molasses

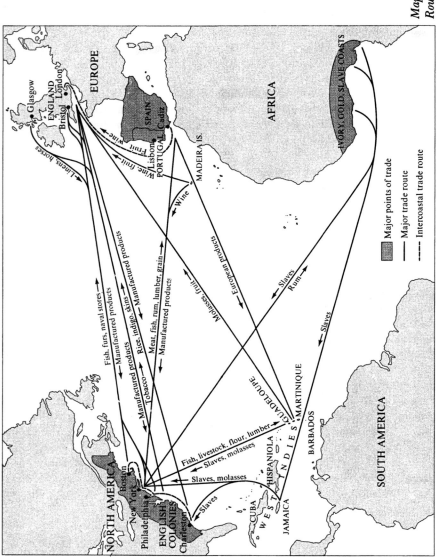

Map 1.1   Atlantic Trade Routes

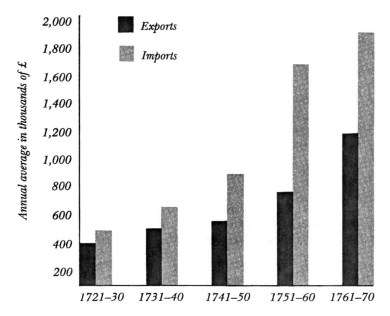

Figure 1.1 Colonial American Commodity Exports to and Imports from England, 1721–1770 [SOURCE: Based on data from James F. Shepherd and Gary M. Walton, *Shipping, Maritime Trade and the Economic Development of Colonial North America* (Cambridge: Cambridge University Press, 1972), p. 42.]

production in the British West Indies, the law placed a prohibitive tariff on the importation of foreign molasses, primarily that made in the French West Indies. This regulation posed a problem to American entrepreneurs, for the supply of British molasses was insufficient to satisfy the American market, and the tariff made French molasses prohibitively expensive. So Yankee traders bribed customs officials in the New England port to allow them to smuggle in French molasses.

Also in accordance with mercantilist philosophy, the thirteen colonies suffered from an imbalance of trade with England: they imported more than they exported. (See Figure 1.1.) But the colonials made up nearly all of the trade deficit through "invisible earnings." The colonies came to supply many of the ships and shipping services for the British Empire, and the earnings from those sources (called "invisible" because they were less apparent than direct returns on trade) helped reduce the annual negative balance of payments with Britain to only a small sum by the close of the colonial period.

Throughout American history, business and politics have been intertwined, as the Navigation Acts demonstrate. The Navigation Acts provided the political framework within which the colonial American economy developed, along with the economy of the rest of the British Empire. The acts were designed to strengthen England, but this consideration did not mean that they hurt the colonies. In reality, the Navigation Acts had relatively little impact on the colonial economies. The economies of the various colonies probably would have developed as they did with or without the Navigation Acts.

Notions of mercantilism went far beyond the Navigation Acts. The British imperial government created a postal service in 1751, with Benjamin Franklin as postmaster, to operate mail routes from Boston to Charleston. The British colonial governments aided the fledgling business system, building wharves and harbors in port towns and constructing roads to facilitate commerce. Governments organized the rapid exploration, surveying, and sale of land, encouraging the transfer of land into private hands. Public loan offices, often called land banks, provided credit to businesses in a credit-hungry economy. Colonial governments minted and printed money, increasing the stock of the circulating exchange medium.

THE CLOSE OF THE COLONIAL PERIOD

If the Jamestown settlers had by some miracle lived to see the American colonies at the close of the colonial period in the 1770s, they would have found them unrecognizable. Prosperous farms and bustling towns and cities stood along the seacoast. What wrought these changes? The clearing of land for farms and the building of businesses by thousands of individuals were responsible. The settlers of 1607 might have recognized the entrepreneurial motives and capitalist mentality of later generations of Americans, but they could not have foreseen how much their business activities would enrich the material well-being of the resulting society.

North America proved to be a hospitable environment for the conduct of business. Geography and abundant natural resources played important roles in the colonial period, as they would after the founding of the new nation. Colonial Americans were the beneficiaries of seas teeming with fish and whales, virgin forests supplying timber for ships and lumber for buildings, land capable of sustaining diversified agriculture, varied mineral resources, and rivers capable of transporting the resulting crops and goods. Colonial Americans were also helped by being part of the largest, most powerful European empire, and of a world economy that was in fact growing and thereby adding to entrepreneurial opportunities. By the eighteenth century, the British political system, on the whole, was conducive to business growth and the further development of capitalism.

By the 1770s, the business system of the American colonies was emerging from its infancy, its core in prosperous farms and plantations, with merchant houses serving as conduits for the sale of their products. Trade mechanisms connecting the colonies to the rest of the world were well developed. America's economic dependence upon Britain was rapidly lessening. Yet the business system of the colonies was far from fully developed, even in the late-colonial period. Though considerably improved over earlier years, internal transportation systems remained primitive, hindering the growth of domestic trade and business specialization. A business infrastructure of insurance companies, banks, and shipping services was just beginning to develop in the years after 1750. Artisans and manufacturers, while significant, would become a more important part of the economy in later years.

As their economy developed, some Americans living in the 1770s came to see the desirability, even the imperative, of breaking with the homeland and establishing a new nation. This break, of course, was primarily a political, not a business, event. During the Revolution and in the founding of an American government, however, would be born new institutions and ideas about political economy that would unleash business activity capable of transforming the North American continent and the world economy.

Selected Readings

For an overview of the economic development of Europe, see Carlo Cipolla, *Before the Industrial Revolution: European Society and Economy, 1000–1700* (New York: W. W. Norton, 1976). Edwin Perkins presents a broad-ranging overview of the colonial economy in *The Economy of Colonial America* (New York: Columbia University Press, 1988), as do Gary Walton and James Shepherd in *The Economic Rise of Early America* (Cambridge: Cambridge University Press, 1972) and John J. McCusker and Russell R. Menard, *The Economy of British America, 1607–1789* (Chapel Hill, N.C.: University of North Carolina Press, 1985). On the origins of industry during the colonial period, see James Mulholland, *A History of Metals in Colonial America* (University, Ala.: University of Alabama Press, 1981). Stuart Bruchey, ed., *The Colonial Merchant: Sources and Readings* (New York: Harcourt, Brace & World, 1966), offers an introduction to that topic. Bernard Bailyn, *The New England Merchants in the Seventeenth Century* (New York: Harper & Row, 1964), and Frederick B. Tolles, *Meeting House and Counting House* (New York: W. W. Norton, 1963), deal with the social and political as well as the business activities of the merchants. Thomas M. Doerflinger, *A Vigorous Spirit of Enterprise: Merchants and Economic Development in Revolutionary Philadelphia* (Chapel Hill, N.C.: University of North Carolina Press, 1986), examines the Philadelphia merchant community.

Standard studies of colonial American businesses include William T. Baxter, *The House of Hancock* (Cambridge, Mass.: Harvard University Press, 1945); Stanley Chyet, *Lopez of Newport* (Detroit: Wayne State University Press, 1970); and J. R. Dolan, *The Yankee Peddlers of Early America* (New York: Bramhall House, 1964). A standard biography is Douglas Southall Freeman, Mary Wells Ashworth, and John Alexander Carroll, *George Washington* (New York: Charles Scribner's Sons, 1948–1957), 7 vols. Finally, Caroline Bird, *Enterprising Women* (New York: W. W. Norton, 1976), and Laurel Thatcher Ulrich, *Good Wives: Images and Reality in the Lives of Women in Northern New England, 1650–1750* (New York: Alfred A. Knopf, 1980), examine colonial businesswomen.

IMPORTANT EVENTS, 1763–1791

1763 The French and Indian War ends with Britain victorious. The Proclamation of 1763 declares the temporary western boundary for colonial resettlement.

1764 The Sugar Act imposes new duties on some imports into the colonies.

1765 The Stamp Act requires tax stamps on most printed materials.

1767 The Townshend Acts impose taxes on British trade goods imported to the colonies.

1773 The Tea Act aims at changing how British tea is sold in the colonies; colonists react against the Act with the Boston Tea Party.

1776 The Declaration of Independence is adopted by the Continental Congress on July 4.
Adam Smith publishes *The Wealth of Nations.*

1781 The Articles of Confederation are ratified by the states. Robert Morris founds the Bank of North America.

1783 The Treaty of Paris ends the American Revolution.

1784 Direct trade between the United States and China begins.

1788 The Constitution is ratified.

1789 The federal government begins operations.

1791 The First Bank of the United States is chartered. Alexander Hamilton presents his report "On Manufactures" to Congress.

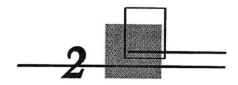

Business in the Revolutionary Era

The formation of the United States of America as a result of the Revolution had significant repercussions in the business as well as the political sphere. Businessmen not only participated in the Revolution as political leaders but also helped fashion a federal political structure capable of enlarging and shaping business opportunities. The American leaders were members of a generation that had begun to reject mercantilism, and they established in its place a new political economy that promoted capitalism. The founding fathers of the United States believed that government should rest on popular consent and that the purpose of the business system was to enlarge material well-being, not enrich the state or its hereditary rulers. In their view, freedom and the success of the new nation depended on a virtuous and independent citizenry who owned property and enjoyed business opportunities. In the 1780s and 1790s, there was dispute about the best methods of fostering opportunity and about what kinds of business to encourage, but there was also much consensus that entrepreneurial opportunity was desirable, even necessary, for the survival of the Republic and the general welfare of its citizens.

The very formation of the United States as one political entity was as significant for the development of entrepreneurial opportunity as the new political economy that leaders eventually instituted. The thirteen colonies, as we have seen, were already among the wealthiest areas of the world by the 1770s. Entrepreneurs successfully exploited both North America's natural resources and the benefits of being part of the British Empire to achieve that wealth. The Revolution, of course, ended benefits of the British imperial system; but in doing so it established other, ultimately more significant, benefits. The United States became the largest free-trade area in the world. Entrepreneurs could operate over a vast territory whose peoples, for the most part, spoke a common language and held a common legal tradition. Political freedom, at least for white males, also meant unprecedented occupational freedom. Common political institutions, abundant natural resources, and occupational freedom resulted in a society with expanding entrepreneurial opportunities.

Some planters and merchants, angered by new British economic policies, were among the most important leaders of the Revolution. However, they could not fully foresee the changes that independence would bring to their businesses. Cut off from the British Empire, they had to develop new trade routes and business institutions. They also had to establish government policies for business development, a task that sorely tried the new American government and led to conflict between its two great leaders, Alexander Hamilton and Thomas Jefferson.

BUSINESS AND THE AMERICAN REVOLUTION

Economic complaints helped cause the American Revolution, and business leaders—colonial merchants like John Hancock, a nephew of Thomas Hancock, and planters like Washington and Jefferson—played major roles in the movement for independence. Objectively viewed, British actions were not oppressive, but many business operators saw them as such. Moreover, the colonists came to look upon English economic regulations as part of a general plot against their liberties.

Increasing Regulation and Taxes

Changes in British mercantile policy prompted the first large-scale complaints. Before 1763, few colonists had complained of the Navigation Acts, but this situation soon changed dramatically. In 1763, England emerged as the winner in a world war fought in Europe, Asia, and the Americas against France. Called the Seven Years' War in Europe and the French and Indian War in the colonies, the conflict was costly. The British found the price of victory great, and England's public debt soared.

The British government responded to those new political and economic conditions by trying to control the costs of defending its larger empire while raising additional revenue to pay for that defense. In order to establish peaceful relations with the Indians, the Proclamation of 1763 forbade white settlement west of the Appalachian Mountains. This decree outraged colonial Americans, especially southern planters speculating in western lands, who saw it as unduly limiting their opportunities. Even worse in the eyes of colonial American merchants was the shift in the goals of the Navigation Acts that occurred after the victory over the French. Parliament passed new postwar measures designed to raise revenue from the colonies, not just to regulate their trade as before. The first of the new laws was the

Map 2.1   European Claims in North America After the French and Indian War (SOURCE: From John P. McKay et al., A History of Western Society, *3rd ed.* Copyright © 1987 by Houghton Mifflin Company.)

Sugar Act of 1764. This measure actually reduced the duty on molasses imported from the French islands in the Caribbean. For the first time, however, the government strictly enforced the tariff and prosecuted smugglers, whose actions had earlier been tolerated. The Sugar Act hurt New England merchants who dealt in molasses and distilled rum. Another tax, the Stamp Act of 1765, required the colonists to affix stamps of various prices to legal documents, newspapers, pamphlets, playing cards, and dice. Two years later, the Townshend Acts placed import duties on tea, glass, paper, and several other items. Finally, the Tea Act of 1773 allowed the British East India Company to establish a monopoly on the importation of tea into the colonies. This measure lowered the cost of tea to consumers by eliminating middlemen, but it outraged the colonial merchants who had earlier handled this trade.

Although the colonists' complaints were business related, they were essentially political in nature. Many Americans complained about these new British policies because they disliked Parliament's passage of laws limiting

The language and images that Americans used to protest the British policies that precipitated the Revolution were often vicious. Here Bostonians gleefully pay the British tax collector with unwanted tea, accompanied by tar and feathers. (Library of Congress)

their freedom without being able to influence those measures. Americans elected no representatives to Parliament and so could try to influence British policy only indirectly, through friends, political agents, and business associates in England. The colonial grievances thus involved more than purely business concerns; "no taxation without representation" was a familiar cry from Americans.

Economic grievances combined with political considerations to convince some leading planters and merchants that they needed a new American government to ensure the representation of their interests, a system they could influence directly. By the 1770s, rebellious Americans perceived Parliament's measures as a plot to destroy freedom and profit in the colonies. By then, the colonists also had a growing confidence in the development of their land. Those who would declare independence and found the new nation were coming to envision an American empire in which a new republican government would protect American commerce, encourage American agriculture, help develop American industry, and promote the settlement of lands in the West—all separate from the British Empire.

Colonial merchants and planters led the resistance to English actions. After the passage of both the Stamp Act and the Townshend Acts, they called upon colonists to boycott English goods. They drew up and enforced agreements that proved remarkably effective in causing substantial declines in the importation of British goods into the colonies. Parliament repealed both the Stamp Act and most of the Townshend duties because of this pressure. The colonial merchants and planters also led the way in petitioning the British government for a redress of colonial grievances. For example, John Hancock participated actively in politics throughout the late-colonial period. The merchants and planters proved adept at securing a fair degree of public support. They succeeded, for instance, in organizing mobs who tarred and feathered officials trying to enforce the unpopular Stamp Act of 1765.

The road to revolution and independence was nonetheless tortuous, and not all merchants trod it easily. The merchants in Philadelphia, for example, were reluctant revolutionaries. Philadelphia merchants feared British infringements upon American rights and were prepared to make financial sacrifices to oppose them. However, their opposition was qualified and inconsistent, and the merchants never offered united, sustained resistance to the British. The British measures after 1763, while disliked, did not lead to any unusual economic hardships. Philadelphia's merchants remained apolitical, accustomed to attending to their commercial affairs. In Pennsylvania other groups—wealthy lawyers, clerics, landed gentlemen, and artisans—were most important in leading the opposition to Great Britain.

Business During the American Revolution

The clash of economic and ideological interests led to the outbreak of war in 1775 and an assertion of American independence a year later. The war disrupted American business, as the British army and navy at various times occupied all of the important towns. Most established merchants, especially the larger ones, suffered from the war. For example, Philadelphia merchants experienced the war's decimation of their opportunities in both coastal and transatlantic trades, as shown in Table 2.1. The Philadelphia merchant community declined from 320 active members in 1774 to only 200 by the close of the war. Only a few merchants were able to take advantage of

Table 2.1 Ships Entering Philadelphia

Origin	1773	1781
Coastwise	293	13
West Indies	286	106
Europe	172	21

SOURCE: From *A Vigorous Spirit of Enterprise: Merchants and Economic Development in Revolutionary Philadelphia*, by Thomas M. Doerflinger. © 1986 The University of North Carolina Press and published for the Institute of Early American History and Culture. Reprinted by permission.

new opportunities during the war years, supplying American troops with food and war material.

Robert Morris was an exception who combined patriotism with private gain. The junior partner of a leading Philadelphia merchant house, Morris was elected to the Continental Congress in 1775 and became a member of committees dealing with trade. At the low point of American military fortunes in 1776 and 1777, Morris was instrumental in maintaining essential American trade in the Atlantic basin but also used his inside knowledge to build up a personal fortune through trade. Always ambitious, Morris resigned from Congress in 1778, left the merchant house with which he had been associated, and participated in nine new business ventures over the next three years. Morris invested in tobacco shipments, military contracting, importation of dry goods, and land speculation, and by the early 1780s, he was the commercial king of Philadelphia.

With the American government in dire financial straits, Morris reentered governmental service. Taking charge of finances for the government, in 1781 Morris formed the Bank of North America in Philadelphia. Morris used deposits of government funds to start the bank, which then provided credit services to the government and merchants. The bank proved to be profitable, paying a 14½ percent return on its capital stock in 1783. Soon other Americans established banks, making American merchants less dependent than before upon British creditors.

Business After the Revolution

The Revolution greatly affected the business opportunities for Americans, and with the advent of peace in 1783, a new business system emerged. American independence meant that American merchants were excluded by the Navigation Acts from trading with much of the British Empire. The British severely restricted trade with the West Indies colonies, for instance, forcing a substantial decline of American exports to that region. During the early 1790s, the British West Indies absorbed only 10 percent of American exports, whereas in late colonial times American traders had sent 27 percent of their exports there. This exclusion hurt many merchants in the short run. However, in the long run it forced traders to develop new business activities, many of which proved to be very profitable. For instance, southern planters and Philadelphia merchants began shipping American tobacco directly to European markets, bypassing the British and Scottish merchants through whom they had earlier been forced to work. By the early 1790s, direct trade with northern Europe took 16 percent of American exports. Trade with Britain declined from 55 to 31 percent of America's exports in the same period.

A dramatic new opportunity was the China trade. In 1784, after the war had ended, New York merchants dispatched the *Empress of China* to Canton with a cargo of ginseng root, which the Chinese believed to be an aphrodisiac and general cure-all, and the merchant adventurers earned a 25 percent return on their investment. (More typically, voyages elsewhere earned a 6 to 10 percent return.) News of this success soon spread, and the scramble to enter the China trade was on. American merchant ships sailed around South America, traded with the Native Americans of the Pacific Northwest for furs, especially sea otter pelts, and then exchanged them in Canton for tea, silk, porcelain, and other fine products. During colonial times the Navigation Acts had prevented direct American trade with China, but soon wealthy Americans were decorating their homes with directly imported Chinese rugs, wearing fine silks, and sipping Chinese tea. In the early nineteenth century, American and British merchants exported opium from Turkey and India to China in exchange for desirable Chinese goods.

The opening of the China trade and the direct export of tobacco were the most spectacular examples of new opportunities, but there were others as well, particularly within the United States. The war cut off access to British manufactured goods, thus encouraging some entrepreneurs to develop domestic manufactures. During the war, American artisans supplied the army with clothing, gunpowder, and guns. Nor did manufacturing opportunities collapse with peace and the return of trade with Britain. By 1790, American mills were supplying paper for an expanding production of newspapers and magazines, and a domestic glass industry had become firmly established. American entrepreneurs felt optimistic that freedom from British mercantilism would mean ample opportunities for the development of internal manufacturing. Tench Coxe, their leading spokesman,

In colonial times merchantmen could be easily converted to wartime privateers. Here the armed schooner Lee *leads the munition ship* Nancy *into Gloucester, Massachusetts. (Henry Beville, courtesy the Mariners Museum, Newport News, Virginia)*

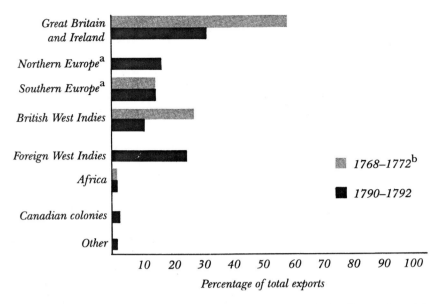

Figure 2.1   Destinations of Exports to Overseas Areas from the Thirteen Colonies (1768–1772) and the United States (1790–1792) [SOURCE: Based on data from Gary M. Walton and James F. Shepherd, *The Economic Rise of Early America* (Cambridge: Cambridge University Press, 1979), p. 190.]
[a]Northern Europe includes Continental European countries north of Cape Finisterre. Southern Europe includes Spain, the Canary Islands, Portugal, Madeira, the Azores, and the Cape Verde Islands.
[b]In 1768–1772, there were no exports to northern Europe, the Foreign West Indies, or the Canadian colonies.

told a Philadelphia audience in 1787 that the "useful arts" and manufactures "must afford the most comfortable reflection to every patriotic mind, to observe their progress in the United States, and particularly in Pennsylvania. . . . The list of articles we now make ourselves, if particularly enumerated, would fatigue the ear, and waste your valuable time." Coxe then named a long list of products anyway. (See Figure 2.1.)

ADAM SMITH AND THE ECONOMICS OF FREEDOM

America's Declaration of Independence, so eloquently worded by Thomas Jefferson in 1776, was not the only major document produced that year. The Scottish philosopher Adam Smith published a book entitled *The Wealth of Nations* that over a generation's time revolutionized the way educated persons thought about economic affairs and the relationships between government and business. Smith summarized what some scholars and men of affairs (the two were often the same in the eighteenth century) were thinking about mercantilism and its faults, and his ideas influenced Thomas Jefferson, Alexander Hamilton, and other American revolutionary leaders, as well as subsequent generations of American business owners and politicians. The new American government never followed Smith's prescriptions exactly, but his ideas were so powerful that for more than two centuries they influenced how Americans thought about government policy toward business.

✳ Adam Smith's Ideas

Adam Smith rejected mercantilist thought and practice at a time when other philosophers were beginning to question it. In France "physiocrats" developed the notion of laissez faire—a belief that governments should keep their hands off the economy because government regulations inhibit the growth of wealth, which always comes from the soil. Smith adopted their idea of discouraging government regulations, added his own keen insights, and argued that the proper goal of economic policy was the material well-being of citizens, not an increase in state power.

Smith viewed the economy as dynamic. Individuals who tilled the soil, manufactured useful articles, or engaged in trade created wealth. The "invisible hand" of the market (the unstructured system through which individuals bargained for the production and exchange of goods and services), not governmental edicts, would regulate relationships among persons. Smith envisioned only a minimal role for government: the provision of police forces to keep the peace, military forces for national defense, and educational institutions. Smith reasoned that the laws of supply and demand best governed business relations by determining the prices and production of goods through the demands of purchasers and the supplies of goods and services. Smith thought that allowing the interaction of supply and demand would result in a self-regulating economic system capable of producing larger and larger amounts of wealth. The free interplay of the "invisible hand" of the market, moreover, should occur among nations as well as within a nation if economic well-being were to advance. Under international free trade, Smith reasoned, each nation would specialize in what it could do best (a concept known today as that of "comparative advantage"), and the efficiency and productivity of the economies of nations throughout the world would rise. Free trade, Smith asserted, would benefit everyone.

The Significance of Smith's Ideas

Smith's ideas confirmed the notions of individualism and democracy that the American political revolution expressed, and they were very attractive to Americans. If the individual was entitled to certain political freedoms and a certain form of government, so too should he be free from government or other institutional restrictions on his business life, and this freedom would provide the greatest wealth for human society. Thus, laissez faire in economics and democracy in politics came to be coupled in a framework of thought that the Americans and British in the nineteenth century called "liberalism."

Much of the amplification, explication, and adoption of Smith's ideas, however, remained for the future. In America, few members of the revolutionary generation, whether farmers, planters, merchants, or politicians, quickly cast off the old mercantilist habits of thought. Some leaders, including Thomas Jefferson and Alexander Hamilton, read *The Wealth of Nations* and found that it helped them comprehend the workings of the economic system. Most Americans agreed with Smith's proposition that the purpose of the business system should be to enlarge the wealth of the people, not the power of government—which, in the American view, came from the people in any case. Nevertheless, they continued to think that government policies directing the economy were desirable in order to augment the numbers of propertied, independent citizens. In fact, Americans never consistently and systematically applied the core ideas of laissez faire to government-business relations.

ESTABLISHING THE TRADITION OF GOVERNMENT-BUSINESS RELATIONS

The revolutionary decision to break with England and its empire was emotionally difficult for Americans, most of whom thought of themselves as British subjects. The Declaration of Independence was one matter; ahead lay great problems of statecraft. The American revolutionaries still had to decide on the appropriate form the Republic should take, the proper roles of the state and federal government, and the kind of political economy best suited for a nation with diverse interests.

The Creation of the New Government

The men who gathered at the Continental Congress in Philadelphia to announce their independence from Great Britain and form a new government demonstrated their hostility to the policies of British rule by creating a weak central government for the United States. The first American constitution, called the Articles of Confederation (finally ratified by all thirteen states in 1781), left most authority in the hands of separate states. The Articles of Confederation permitted the federal government to provide for the armed forces and international relations. The federal government also established a postal system, issued a currency (which quickly became worthless), and began a program for the sale and settlement of western lands.

However, the federal government lacked many important powers, and this situation soon distressed many businessmen. It had no power to levy taxes and depended largely on assessments voluntarily contributed by state governments, assessments not often paid in full. Lack of funds made it difficult for the federal government to support a navy, something merchants wanted so as to protect their ships from piracy. Nor did the federal government have the power to regulate commerce among the various states, and, to the dismay of business entrepreneurs operating beyond the boundaries of their own states, some states enacted tariff laws to protect and promote local manufacturing. Individual state governments also passed their own navigation acts in attempts to direct overseas shipping to their ports and issued their own paper currencies, again distressing entrepreneurs seeking to operate in more than one state.

A number of important American leaders came increasingly to see this first federal system as unsatisfactory. These men, who by the end of the 1780s called themselves Federalists, had during the Revolutionary War developed a vision of a strong central government capable of asserting American interests against the self-serving practices of European mercantilism. The Federalists envisioned their new nation as a great free-trade area, an arena in which all Americans would be free to engage in commercial activities with one another under common sets of rules and a common currency. The Federalists were especially concerned with financial matters: the establishment of a stable and uniform currency for the conduct of business, government assistance in the creation of capital needed for funding new ventures or expanding old ones, and the financing of naval protection of merchant ships. By 1784, the debt of the federal government stood at $40 million, and there was little revenue coming in to retire it, much less to conduct current governmental activities. By then, merchants had established banks, one each in Philadelphia, New York, and Boston, to provide short-term credits for overseas trade. But those three banks had neither the will nor the resources to support capital expenditures within the nation or to fund the national debt. Congress, in the meantime, had to borrow additional funds just to pay interest charges on the outstanding notes.

The dissatisfaction with the Articles of Confederation thus revolved to a considerable extent around questions of political economy. The Federalists were, for the most part, wealthy men of affairs—merchants from the seaboard cities, ambitious entrepreneurs, and planters from Virginia—who sought a new federal system able to meet the needs of business and commercial agriculture. A nationalist vision bred during the war tied this elite group of men together. Eventually, they met in Philadelphia, ostensibly to discuss revisions in the Articles of Confederation. Instead, they drafted an entirely new Constitution, which was debated in each of the states by specially elected conventions and finally ratified in 1788. The new federal government, divided into executive, judicial, and legislative branches, began to oversee the country from New York City, the provisional capital, in 1789.

The new Constitution included a number of provisions important to the development of American business. One provision granted Congress the power to impose import duties and raise revenues. Funds thus were potentially available for naval protection on the seas and military security for westward expansion. Congress assumed the sole authority to impose tariffs and conduct foreign relations, and its ability to adjust tariff rates could be a powerful weapon for encouraging foreign powers to allow American businesses to penetrate their markets. The Constitution also granted the federal government the exclusive right to coin money and issue currency, thus making possible a national medium of exchange. (However, states could still charter banks that issued notes that circulated as money.)

In addition to its fiscal and foreign relations measures, the Constitution provided the political framework for the creation of a national market. States were prohibited from restricting the flow of commerce or from passing laws that impaired contracts between businesses. Bankruptcy laws had to be uniform, assuring creditors that state bankruptcy laws would not be used against them. A postal system, guaranteed by the Constitution, provided all citizens (and business firms) with a reliable means of communication. Patent and copyright laws were authorized that eventually would serve to protect the rights of the pioneers of new technologies. Under the new Constitution, both investment capital and labor (except for slaves) were free to move within the United States according to the needs of the market. Nowhere in the world in 1789 was there a basic legal framework more conducive to the free flow of goods and people over such a large area—a framework, in other words, favorable to entrepreneurial activity.

The decision for a new governmental structure still left many questions unanswered. Differences of judgment regarding federal economic policy, differences rooted in conflicting political theories as well as in varying business interests, soon appeared. By the 1790s, those differences centered on the personalities of Thomas Jefferson and Alexander Hamilton. In part, they involved disputes over how the new, more powerful federal government should best use its resources for the expansion of the American economy. Both Hamilton and Jefferson used the insights of Adam Smith to explain how the economic system functioned; but, unlike Smith, they were unwilling as practical politicians to follow a consistent program whereby invisible market forces alone determined the destiny of American business.

Alexander Hamilton and American Business

The ideas, ambitions, and energetic leadership of Alexander Hamilton led to the first major conflict over government-business relations in the new national government. Born in the West Indies in 1755, Hamilton grew up in an impoverished family, but his aunts arranged for him to go to New York in 1772. In 1773, he entered King's College (now Columbia University), and in 1774, at the age of nineteen, he wrote widely read pamphlets attacking the British Parliament. Hamilton received an artillery commission in the Continental Army in 1776, and the next year George Washington appointed him his personal secretary. In this post, which he held until the battle of Yorktown in 1781, Hamilton served as an important manager for the American army. After the war, he became a lawyer and settled in New York City, where he established a successful practice. Hamilton was one of a group of war leaders dismayed by the weakness of the federal government, and in 1787 he arranged for the state of New York to approve the calling of a constitutional convention, to which he won appointment as a delegate. He played a small role in the convention, but afterward was instrumental in persuading the state to ratify the new Constitution.

Hamilton earned recognition as one of the ablest men in the young nation, and George Washington appointed him the first secretary of the treasury in 1789. In this position, which he held until 1795, Hamilton provided bold initiatives for the federal political economy, initiatives that sparked much of the political controversy of the 1790s. Disputes over his policies helped divide Americans into their first political parties.

Hamilton was primarily interested in strengthening the nation through the promotion and preservation of both private property and the means of accruing wealth. The main purpose of government, he thought, was not just to protect property but to provide a legal structure for its expansion. Hamilton had little trust in democracy. He believed the success, even the very survival, of the new government and the American nation depended on its wealthiest citizens' identification of their economic interests with preservation of the government.

Hamilton believed that the linchpin of political economy—the key to ensuring that the rich and well-born tied their fortunes to the survival of the government—was government credit. The failure of the government under the Articles of Confederation to pay even the interest on the national debt was a complaint that attracted men to the idea of writing a new Constitution in the first place. So Hamilton worked quickly and ably to develop a proposal for the funding of the national debt and for assumption by the federal government of the state revolutionary war debts. If government credit was good, he believed, wealthy men would support the government. If merchants, manufacturers, and bankers believed that the government really would make good on its notes, then they would trade in government securities. Such confidence would provide a medium of exchange and, most important, substantially enlarge the supply of capital for the financing of new business ventures.

Hamilton also proposed the creation of a Bank of the United States. Under his plan, which Congress adopted, the bank combined public and

The First Bank of the United States issued this ten-dollar bank note in 1796. The crosses probably mean that the note was redeemed or turned in for gold or silver. The holder's name and the date were written on the note. (John Carter Brown Library)

private ownership, with the federal government holding one-fifth of its stock. Because the remainder of the stock was sold to wealthy men, the personal economic interests of these men were linked to the stability of the new government and to its promotion of economic growth. The bank provided a place for the government to deposit its funds, and through the establishment of branches (eventually there were offices in eight important commercial cities), it created a mechanism for transferring money from one place to another. The bank's notes circulated as part of the nation's money supply, thereby easing commercial transactions. The Bank of the United States also acted as a general commercial bank, accepting deposits from and making loans to businesses.

Hamilton's economic policies proved highly controversial. They were intentionally designed to attract the wealthy merchants in the eastern seaports to the support of the government and did not reach out directly to the small property holders, who were in the majority, or to the southern planters, who used the services of the merchants to export staple crops. Many Americans thus viewed Hamilton as a politician advancing the interests of one privileged class.

Moreover, Hamilton favored a pro-British foreign policy. He worked and developed close personal ties with merchants who had made their fortunes exporting American materials to England in exchange for manufactured goods. Hamilton wanted to preserve and promote that trade. This commerce was essential to his economic program, for the British trade provided the largest source, some 80 percent, of the tariff revenues needed to service the national debt and operate the government.

Hamilton's desire to promote the export trade, as well as his personal and political ties to the wealthy merchants of the eastern seaports, became clear in the last of his great proposals for the American political economy, his famous report "On Manufactures." This report, which had a long and tortuous history, was first drafted by Tench Coxe, a wealthy Philadelphian who served as assistant secretary of the treasury. Coxe called for a vigorous government program to foster a new surge of internal manufacturing so as to enable Americans to compete successfully with British manufacturers. Hamilton, however, reformulated the report to recommend governmental provision of funds to his merchant friends to produce items for the export trade.

Although Hamilton discussed manufacturing enthusiastically in his report, he offered no program to help manufacturers obtain the needed capital to expand or start industries. He offered little in the way of help to develop the domestic market for home manufacturers. And he opposed tariff barriers lest they reduce the income of the government so essential to retiring its debt. The report "On Manufactures," unlike Hamilton's other recommendations, was never adopted by Congress, and the men, including Coxe, who were most interested in establishing a political economy favorable to manufacturing and internal business development eventually opposed Hamilton politically. They turned to Hamilton's opponent, Thomas Jefferson, to provide the leadership for using government to enlarge business opportunities for the development of domestic commerce.

⍦ Thomas Jefferson and Agrarian Democracy

Thomas Jefferson's background contrasted sharply with Hamilton's. Jefferson was born in 1743 in Virginia, where his father was a large landholder on the western fringe of settlement. In 1757, Jefferson inherited 2,750 acres of land and an established position in his community. As a young man, he developed wide literary, scientific, and architectural interests, but emotionally he remained rooted in the agrarian community from which he had come. He was a slave owner, and his plantation, Monticello, produced, among other goods, tobacco for the export trade.

Deeply involved in the independence movement and the Revolution, Jefferson served as governor of Virginia from 1779 to 1781. After the war, from 1784 to 1789, he was the American minister to France, where one of his main goals was negotiating a free-trade treaty between America and France. He had read *The Wealth of Nations* and agreed with Adam Smith's ideas about free trade. The theory of free trade fit in with Jefferson's democratic beliefs because it was, in effect, evenhanded. Free trade, after all, meant the absence of policies benefiting particular nations or special interest groups within a nation. The American Revolution gave France access to markets previously closed by the British Navigation Acts, so Jefferson saw France as a logical trading partner of the United States. After the French Revolution of 1789 created a republic similar in some ways to

America's, Jefferson saw France as a potential partner in establishing free world trade.

In his hope of achieving a commercial treaty with France, however, Jefferson was frustrated. The United States eventually negotiated a commercial treaty with Prussia, but that small German state was of little consequence to American merchants. The weakness of the American government under the Articles of Confederation made it impossible to bring any significant pressure to bear on the European powers during negotiations, and Jefferson's awareness of the situation led him to support the writing of a new Constitution that established a stronger federal government.

In 1789, Jefferson returned to America to accept the post of secretary of state under President Washington. As secretary of state, Jefferson almost immediately clashed with Hamilton. The two men held fundamentally different views on important questions of political theory, federal economic policy, and foreign policy. Jefferson's ideas about economic policy were less clear-cut than Hamilton's, and over his long political career they changed as circumstances changed. Although poorly focused at times and inconsistent on occasion, Jefferson's ideas embodied democratic values that contrasted sharply with Hamilton's aristocratic tendencies. The clash between the two men eventually led to the formation of the nation's first political parties and, after Jefferson became president in 1801, to a reversal of some of Hamilton's most cherished accomplishments.

Jefferson served as Washington's secretary of state from 1789 to 1793. His main responsibility was foreign policy, but because the United States was a trading nation whose well-being depended on overseas commerce, Jefferson inevitably confronted questions of political economy. He was deeply disturbed by Hamilton's desire to link the wealthiest class of merchants to the fortunes of the federal government and by Hamilton's insistence that the new nation maintain friendly relations with its most important trading partner, England.

Jefferson had a preference for an agrarian society. This preference did not mean that he believed agriculture to be the source of all wealth but, rather, that the bulwark of a republic consisted of independent farmers. Jefferson's observations of the factory system in Europe led him to fear that it encouraged rulers to engage in tyranny in order to control the underpaid workers. He was convinced that manufacturing centers were a source of corruption in Europe, and he was afraid that industrial workers, unlike independent farmers capable of self-sufficiency, would become dependent on the caprices of the marketplace.

Jefferson was also appalled by what he saw as Hamilton's favoring of Britain. Hamilton's close ties with the mercantile establishment seemed to result in a pro-British foreign policy and a fiscal policy favoring the wealthy. The two prongs of Hamilton's bias were, of course, interrelated, and they rankled the Virginian, who strongly believed that America should retain her hard-won independence from the British.

❦ Conflict Between Jefferson and Hamilton

Jefferson's dispute with Hamilton grew more bitter in the first years of the Washington administration, especially their disagreement over tariff policy. To Hamilton the tariff was an essential element in raising the revenue without which his entire fiscal program would collapse. Hamilton therefore wanted to encourage trade with England through the commercial ties that were already established. Jefferson, on the other hand, wanted to use the tariff as a political weapon in diplomatic negotiations. His objective was free trade; his means toward that objective were negotiations of reciprocal trade agreements that would break down old mercantilist barriers. Jefferson was thus willing to have the United States impose tariff barriers, even mercantilist-style restrictions, on foreign trade as weapons to persuade European nations to negotiate reciprocal trade agreements.

The Bank of the United States, so important to Hamilton's program, was another point of bitter dispute. Jefferson was dismayed by its creation, his complaints kindled by his suspicions about the handling of higher finance and his dislike of public debt. He disapproved of the speculation and fraud he observed and thought it was only the speculators, the creditors, and the wealthy bank stockholders who benefited from a public debt that, in the final analysis, wrung its repayment from the sweat-stained shirts of honest taxpayers. The bankers, claimed Jefferson, had no stake in general prosperity or public well-being except insofar as they generated tax revenues to pay the interest charges that enriched them. The bank and Hamilton's entire fiscal program seemed to Jefferson to have been created to serve merchants and speculators, not those Americans who invested capital and toil in the improvement of land and buildings.

Constitutional as well as economic issues separated Jefferson from Hamilton. The Tenth Amendment to the Constitution stated that any power not specifically granted to the federal government was reserved to the states or the people. Jefferson interpreted this measure as restricting the power of the federal government. He said, for instance, that the federal government had no power to charter the Bank of the United States. Hamilton, on the other hand, interpreted the amendment more broadly, believing it gave more power to the federal government. Jefferson's views on these matters eventually proved more popular than Hamilton's program. The rivalry between the two men resulted in Jefferson's resignation as secretary of state in 1793. (Hamilton left his treasury post in 1795.) In the late 1790s Jefferson and his supporters formed a Democratic Republican party (not to be confused with later parties), and in 1800 Jefferson was elected the nation's third president.

As president, Jefferson showed his practical side. With the Louisiana Purchase, which added vast tracts of western land to the United States, and the dispatch of the Lewis and Clark Expedition to the Pacific Coast, he helped open the North American interior to development. Those actions were consistent with his background as a nationalist and with his advocacy of an agrarian society. His policy of free trade, however, changed according to the practical realities of world politics. In 1805, with Europe in the turmoil of the Napoleonic Wars and American commerce threatened, Jefferson advocated tariff protection. In 1807, in response to British attacks on American ships and to restrictions imposed on neutral American ships by both England and France, Jefferson and Congress ordered an embargo on the export of American foodstuffs and the import of British manufactured goods. By this time, Jefferson was seeking a domestic equilibrium among agriculture, commerce, and manufacturing so that America could be more self-sufficient in a world fraught with dangerous warfare.

As a politician, Jefferson attracted the support of those Americans who wanted to develop the interior of the country and local manufacturing. The nation's leading advocate of a political economy favorable to manufacturing, Tench Coxe, who once served under Hamilton as assistant secretary of the treasury, eventually became a Jeffersonian. Coxe realized that Hamilton would retard the development of American industry, because Hamilton feared that domestic manufacturing might reduce imports to the United States and therefore lessen the federal government's tariff revenues. In 1811, the Jeffersonians, under the leadership of President James Madison, allowed the charter of the Bank of the United States, one of Hamilton's most prized creations, to expire.

THE LEGACY OF THE
REVOLUTIONARY GENERATION

The death of Hamilton's Bank of the United States and the pragmatic response of the Jeffersonians to the issues of tariff protection and domestic manufacturing may appear to have closed a chapter in the history of the American political economy, with one side victorious over another. In one sense, this was the case, but in another, more important historical sense, it was not. The dispute between Hamilton and Jefferson was superficially a debate between conflicting personalities, but more fundamentally it involved recurring questions of federal policy.

Enduring Ideas and Principles

The principles underlying Hamilton's program appeared in later debates concerning the political economy. Although Hamilton left public service in 1795 and died in 1804, his ideas of using the federal government to expand the capital resources of the nation and of creating a Bank of the United States to stabilize and direct the allocation of capital resources continued in succeeding generations. So too did the notion of benefiting the nation through policies that directly helped its leading businesses. "Hamiltonianism," as this philosophy has been termed by historians, lived on in a general body of ideas supportive of strong federal intervention in the economic system to assist the expansion of business.

If Hamilton's vision eventually became a shorthand description of a particular political economy, so too did Jefferson's reaction. While Hamilton seemed to advocate policies enhancing the wealth and power of a merchant aristocracy, a myth arose of Jefferson as a great democrat (even though he was a wealthy slaveholder). Jefferson sought policies to promote free trade and a fiscal system that was evenhanded. Those were democratic ideals. So too, in a sense, was his later support of protection for American manufacturing, for in the nineteenth century a persuasive ideology emerged in support of federal economic policies designed to grant Americans the ability to develop their own industries and business firms, free from ruinous foreign competition.

Institutions

If the revolutionary generation left a legacy of dispute in the American political economy, it also left institutional factors basic to the future development of the American business system. The most important result for American business of the formation of the United States, especially after the adoption of the Constitution in 1789, was the gradual creation of the world's largest internal market. At the end of the eighteenth century, the United States was already a wealthy nation by world standards, but unlike the nations of Europe it embraced a huge geographical area—an area that was later to become even larger, of course. In the 1790s, the internal market, still largely unreachable and underpopulated, existed only as an exciting possibility whose time had not yet come.

A second legacy of the revolutionary generation was the creation of a political system that sanctioned private investments. Under the Constitution, individuals were free to invest in business enterprise, although some ill-formed ideas were expressed about the need for occasional regulation. The freedom to lend money at interest went unchallenged. Under their new government, Americans could hold land or other property for appreciation. The basic features of capitalism were protected by the same political system that provided what became the world's largest market.

A third legacy was occupational freedom. The wealthy merchants and planters occupied the top niche of society, but social groups were less sharply defined in the United States than in Europe, where they were made more rigid by ancient, inherited feudal customs and prejudices. In America, people could rise (or fall) in their social standing according to their acquisition of wealth. White males were free to move from one occupation to another. Talented Europeans could bring their skills to mills, shops, offices, and farms in the United States and thereby enrich the nation. This freedom, this geographical and occupational mobility, was a basic policy upon which all political factions agreed, and it provided a fluidity of human resources in the conduct of business. The absence of occupational and political freedom for black Americans, however, would increasingly rack the nation's conscience and divide its politics. Moreover, the decisions of entrepreneurs to invest in new ways of manufacturing goods in the nineteenth century would eventually destroy the artisan class.

INTO THE NINETEENTH CENTURY

Later generations of Americans took for granted the gifts bestowed by their revolutionary forebears. The freedom from distant mercantilist restrictions, the ability to influence governmental policy through institutions of representative democracy, the high esteem for the rights of property, and a geographically large and wealthy internal market provided a framework within which American business institutions changed, entrepreneurs adapted to new opportunities, business prospered, and wealth increased over the course of the next two centuries.

Furthermore, while Jefferson, Hamilton, and the others were debating fundamental features of the new political economy, important, but as yet unappreciated, changes were beginning to occur that would prompt unprecedented entrepreneurial opportunities and vitally affect the American business system. Those features included technological innovations, the birth of the Industrial Revolution in the United States, and a large expansion of agricultural enterprise. They also included a westward expansion of the American nation, so that within half a century, America was geographically and physically a very different place than it had been during colonial and revolutionary times.

Selected Readings

The importance of economic grievances as a cause of the American Revolution is discussed in Marc Egnal and Joseph Ernst, "An Economic Interpretation of the American Revolution," *William and Mary Quarterly* 29 (January 1972): 3–32; Allison Olson, "The London Mercantile Lobby and the Coming of the American Revolution," *Journal of American History* 69 (June 1982): 21–41; and Joseph Reid, Jr., "Economic Burden: Spark to the American Revolution?" *Journal of Economic History* 38 (March 1978): 81–100. Curtis P. Nettels, *The Emergence of a National Economy, 1775–1815* (New York: Holt, Rinehart & Winston, 1962), provides a useful overview of economic developments. Drew R. McCoy, *The Elusive Republic: Political Economy in Jeffersonian America* (Chapel Hill, N.C.: University of North Carolina Press, 1980), is a sophisticated treatment that explains how important the political economy was to American revolutionary thinkers and politicians. Broadus Mitchell, *Alexander Hamilton* (New York: Macmillan, 1957 and 1962), 2 vols., is a thoroughly researched biography; and Merrill D. Peterson, *Thomas Jefferson and the New Nation: A Biography* (New York: Oxford University Press, 1970), is a balanced, sympathetic account. The standard account of the Bank of the United States is in Bray Hammond, *Banks and Politics in America from the Revolution to the Civil War* (Princeton, N.J.: Princeton University Press, 1957). Finally, for a fresh view of Hamilton and manufacturing, see John R. Nelson, Jr., "Alexander Hamilton and American Manufacturing: A Reexamination," *Journal of American History* 65 (March 1979): 971–995, and Jacob E. Cooke, "Tench Coxe, Alexander Hamilton, and the Encouragement of American Manufacturers," *William and Mary Quarterly* 32 (July 1975): 369–392.

IMPORTANT EVENTS, 1789–1853

1789   Samuel Slater brings plans for cotton textile machinery to America.

1793   Eli Whitney invents the cotton gin.

1807   Robert Fulton operates a steamboat on the Hudson River.

1813   Boston Associates found the Boston Manufacturing Company to produce cotton textiles.

1828   The Baltimore & Ohio Railroad is chartered.

1831   Cyrus McCormick demonstrates the first workable reaper.

1837   Samuel Morse invents the telegraph.

1853   The British study the American system of manufacturing.

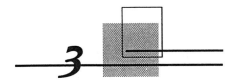

The Expansion of
American Business:
Agriculture,
Commerce, and
Industry

In the autumn of 1784, George Washington departed on a seven-hundred-mile horseback journey through the wilderness into the interior of the United States. Like many other leaders of the revolutionary generation, Washington foresaw the internal development of North America, and he had bought some land near the headwaters of the Ohio River. The fifty-two-year-old planter, now a national hero because of his military leadership during the Revolution, left on the arduous journey to inspect his investments and ensure that trespassers were not falsely claiming his fertile forests and fields. He also hoped to discover and explore navigable waterways between the Potomac and Ohio river basins.

For more than twenty years, Washington had advocated the westward extension of navigation, believing that internal shipping routes were crucial to the development of the country. Washington was convinced that someday a great waterway would connect New York State's Hudson River and the Great Lakes. Such a canal would enormously expand business opportunity in the American North, and Washington believed that a similar canal to the South would have a like effect. He hoped for a commercial route from Mount Vernon across the Appalachian Mountains that would branch south to New Orleans and north to the Great Lakes and Detroit. Now, with the American nation and the peace secured, Washington sought not just to enrich himself but to provide commercial opportunities for other investors as well.

When Washington returned from his travels, he reported his findings and recommendations to the Virginia government. He suggested the chartering of a Potomac Company to construct canals around the falls of the Potomac River, clearing the stream of obstacles to make it navigable, with a road from the headwaters across the mountain barriers that divided East from West. With the cooperation of friends from Virginia and Maryland (the Potomac River runs through both states), Washington secured the necessary charter, invested $10,000 of his personal funds, and embarked on the great project.

Washington lived to serve as the new nation's first president, but he did not live to see the completion of his hoped-for water route. At his death in 1799, entrepreneurs still found most of their business opportunities in overseas commerce. However, Washington's vision, his dream of the westward expansion of settlement and commerce, was realized within three generations.

Between 1800 and 1850, the American economy developed explosively, and with that development came several crucial changes. The general merchant of colonial times disappeared, replaced by many specialized firms serving the needs of an internal market. In 1850, some Americans still looked outward, toward the seas, for commercial opportunities, as entrepreneurs have always done; but many more looked inward at the great prospect of developing business within the continental expanse of the United States. New inventions powered transportation, communication, agrarian, and industrial revolutions of lasting significance. American capitalism bloomed in the early nineteenth century, and Americans worked and prospered as never before. Entrepreneurs increasingly invested in specialized opportunities and thereby helped create a new American business system, one regulated by the laws of supply and demand (Adam Smith's "invisible hand" of the market). The market governed both the allocation of capital to private firms and the flow of goods and services through the system. The government became involved in business activity by developing commercial opportunities, convinced that developmental opportunities helped the entire community.

ECONOMIC GROWTH

Economic growth accounted for the emergence of the specialized business firm in the first part of the nineteenth century, the transition to the second stage in the history of the firm. The general merchants and planters of colonial times had invested their capital in a variety of enterprises because they could not expect a good return on their investment if they sank all their money in one business venture. As the country grew, however, the situation changed, and more opportunities for profitable specialization emerged. The growth of the United States was remarkable. When Congress declared independence in 1776, the new nation had about 2.5 million inhabitants. By 1815, that figure had grown to 8.5 million; by 1860, it had reached 31 million. This dramatic expansion of population caused an equally dramatic enlargement of the domestic market, which in turn created more and more business opportunities.

What caused such dramatic changes in the new country in such a relatively short period of time? Forged in the crucible of an eighteenth-century political revolution, America was further molded in the nineteenth century by three other revolutions: in transportation and communications, in agriculture, and in industry. Each of these revolutions resulted in important changes in entrepreneurial opportunities, and each spurred growth in the nation's wealth. The growth in material wealth was not always steady: there were significant downturns in the business cycle (Americans called them "panics") in 1819, 1837, and 1857. And, as we shall see, the changes associated with the Industrial Revolution sometimes hurt the well-being of the men and women and their families who toiled in the new factories. Overall, however, business publicists and political leaders characterized the period as one of optimism and energy. Between 1839 and 1859, America's per capita real gross national product (the measured amount of all goods and services produced in a nation, adjusted for inflation and deflation, divided by the number of people in the nation) rose by 37 percent. American business success earned the country one of the highest standards of living in the world.

THE TRANSPORTATION REVOLUTION

At the start of the nineteenth century, overland transportation was so difficult that businessmen looked toward the oceans for trading opportunities. As late as 1816, shippers could bring a ton of goods three thousand miles from Europe by sea for about $9, but the same sum would move a ton of goods inland by wagon only thirty miles. George Washington was among the American leaders who recognized that overcoming the barriers to inland transportation was a necessity for the commercial growth of the domestic American market. Therefore, Washington and other entrepreneurs, often in alliance with government officials, set out to lower transportation costs through what they called internal improvements.

Roads

The construction of improved roads was one of the first internal improvements Americans made in the early nineteenth century. Most of the nation's

Roads were primitive in early national times. Pictured here is the Fairview Inn on the Frederick Road near Baltimore. (The Maryland Historical Society)

original roads were nearly impassable: severely rutted, axle-deep in mud during rainy weather, and usually single-lane. Americans made a start in overcoming such obstacles to travel with several major improvements, called turnpikes, constructed in the early 1800s. The most famous road was the National Road, which reached from Baltimore across the mountains to Wheeling on the Ohio River by 1818. However, these roads were still primitive; contractors building the National Road, for instance, were permitted to leave any tree stump less than eighteen inches tall in the roadway. And the roads charged tolls to defray their costs. The roads speeded travel somewhat, but the cost of moving goods over them was still high.

Steamboats

The primitive highway technology meant that most people regarded waterways as the best hope for internal improvement. The interior of the United States contained a vast river system that, once made navigable, could allow plentiful commercial opportunities. But making that river system navigable was not easy. When Americans first settled the transappalachian West, they built rafts and floated cargoes downstream to the port of New Orleans. Traveling upstream, however, was another matter. One technique of ascending the rivers called for twenty to thirty men to pull keelboats—squat, cargo-carrying vessels—against the current by harnessing themselves to long lines and trudging upstream on the riverbank. Under those conditions, the round trip from Pittsburgh at the headwaters of the Ohio River to New Orleans near the mouth of the Mississippi River took 130 days. During

1807, more than 1,800 boats or rafts arrived downstream in New Orleans, but only 11 departed upstream.

The solution, clearly, was to develop some way of moving boats against the river currents mechanically. Robert Fulton successfully demonstrated a steam-driven boat on the Hudson River in 1807, and the steamboat era began. Steamboats were first introduced on the Mississippi River in 1811; by 1860, there were 800 on western waters. During the high water of springtime, enterprising captains even drove their steamboats up small tributaries to earn extra profits.

The successful development of the steamboat provided important new business opportunities in the American interior. Owning and operating the boats was one such opportunity. Entrepreneurs, usually operating singly or in partnerships, could purchase a medium-sized riverboat for about $20,000, the grander versions for $40,000 to $60,000. Some steamboats ran as tramp steamers, stopping for cargo and passengers wherever they were available. Other owners joined together in packet lines to provide scheduled service. As the number of operators increased, competition among them drove down the cost of service, allowing farmers and manufacturers along the nation's rivers, lakes, and bays more opportunities to reach customers profitably.

The river system and the mountain barriers to overland transportation from the eastern seaboard prompted the early development of manufacturing in the interior. For instance, in Pittsburgh, favorably situated at the confluence of two major rivers, merchants began investing in manufacturing, so that by 1810 the city was producing goods worth more than $1 million. Iron was the main industry. Local entrepreneurs established smelters, where the area's plentiful iron ore was melted down using coal mined from the local hills. In 1811, the city's first rolling mill was built. It produced iron bars for sale to local artisans and blacksmiths, who fashioned iron goods and tools that were then shipped to customers downstream. There were many other examples of productive opportunities along the navigable waterways. Along the Ohio River at Cincinnati, for instance, a few businesses specialized in brewing, purchasing 40,000 to 50,000 bushels of barley from the countryside annually. As a center of the meat-packing industry in the Ohio Valley, Cincinnati also became known as "Porkopolis."

Canals

As important as steamboats were, the realization of Washington's dream of canals linking the Midwest with the Atlantic seaboard was a more dramatic development. Washington correctly surmised that a logical route existed across New York from Albany to Buffalo.

The Erie Canal inaugurated east-west commerce when the *Seneca Chief*, carrying Governor De Witt Clinton, entered it from Lake Erie on October

*These pictures of Cincinnati graphically illustrate how transportation improvements
helped spur economic growth and business development in the United States during
the nineteenth century. Steamboats plying the Ohio and Mississippi rivers connected
the city to other regions in the United States. (Above: The Cincinnati Historical Society.
Right: From the Collection of the Public Library of Cincinnati and Hamilton County.)*

26, 1825. A steamer took the boat in tow at Albany, and when the *Seneca
Chief* arrived in the port of New York on November 4, the governor poured
a keg of lake water into the sea. He and the crowds of well-wishers who
greeted him at every stage of the trip well knew that significant new commercial opportunities had appeared.

The Erie Canal was an instant success. Even before it was finished, hundreds of thousands of barrels of flour, bushels of grain, gallons of whiskey,
and millions of board feet of lumber began arriving in New York's port
annually. Entrepreneurs built flour mills, sawmills, distilleries, and other
enterprises in towns along the canal route, and farmers opened new fields
to commercial cultivation. Other persons entered the shipping business. In
1831, for example, one small entrepreneur built a 49-ton canal boat for
less than $1,500, operating it with two horses along the towpath. Boat
operators paid tolls for their passage, and the revenues soon covered the
construction and maintenance costs of the Erie Canal.

The success of the Erie Canal in opening commercial opportunities
sparked a flurry of canal building elsewhere. In the 1820s, for instance,
Ohio launched two projects to connect the Ohio River and Lake Erie. By
1840, the United States had more than 3,000 miles of canals. In 1833, a
firm in Nashville, Tennessee, reported that it received New York goods

most cheaply via sailing ship to New Orleans and steamboats chugging upriver on the Mississippi, Ohio, and Cumberland rivers. However, the same goods arrived most quickly when sent across the Erie Canal and Lake Erie, down the Ohio Canal to Portsmouth, and then by steamboat on the rivers. After 1833, canal rates fell, and more and more trade followed the interior route. By 1852, it was cheaper for Cincinnati entrepreneurs to ship tobacco through the Erie Canal to New York than by the longer route on the river and seas, and the goods arrived in better condition.

Railroads

Speed of passage was the major advantage of the east-west route that the Erie and other canals provided. Still, overland travel was slow. When Abraham Lincoln retired from Congress in 1849 and returned home to Springfield, Illinois, he left Washington, D.C., on a new device, the railroad. He traveled 178 miles to Cumberland, Maryland, where he caught a stagecoach on the National Road, which he rode about twenty-four hours to Wheeling on the Ohio River. Then he went by steamboat, first down the Ohio River and then up the Mississippi River, finally reaching home on another stagecoach. The entire trip took eleven or twelve days. Twelve years later, in 1861, Lincoln left Springfield for his March inauguration as president and made the entire trip by rail. He stopped en route to greet

Map 3.1 Major Canals in 1860 (SOURCE: From The Transportation Revolution, 1815–1860, by George Rogers Taylor. Copyright 1951 by George Rogers Taylor. Reprinted by permission of Mrs. Mary L. H. Taylor.)

well-wishers, but if he had gone directly, he could have reached the capital in a little more than two days. The trip by river was impossible, in any case, because in March the nation's northern waterways were icebound.

Lincoln's two trips illustrate why American entrepreneurs favored the railroad for overland transportation. Railroads came into use in England in the early 1800s, first to carry coal and somewhat later for general transportation. In fact, the first locomotives used on American railroads were constructed in England. As early as 1828, Baltimore merchants, lacking a good water route to the West, chartered the Baltimore & Ohio Railroad, the nation's first major line. They saw that the railroad offered potential advantages of speed, reliability, and flexibility over water transportation. By 1840, American business firms had laid 3,000 miles of track. The first routes fed passengers and freight to and from navigable waterways, but by the 1850s, railroads were linking one region to another with trunk lines, which were the major railroads connecting East Coast cities to Chicago. By 1860, the country had more than 30,000 miles of track.

The advantages of railroads lay not only in their speed and all-season reliability but also in the fact that builders could locate tracks in many places where streams were not navigable or canals were impractical. Unlike waterways, railroad technology did not allow small-scale ventures into the transportation business, but the railroads did create an expanding horizon of commercial opportunities for nineteenth-century Americans. For instance, as we shall see later in this chapter, it was the transportation improvements resulting from a great railroad network that enabled Cyrus McCormick to sell reapers (mechanical devices used to harvest wheat), produced in his Chicago factory, to farmers throughout the Midwest. By 1860, Americans had invested about $188 million in canals and $1.1 billion in railroads. The next five decades would see additional investment in the construction of an eventual total of 254,000 miles of track. The development of the railroad network in the 1850s and thereafter, as we shall see in Chapter 5, ushered in a new era for American business.

Communications

Improvements in the transportation network allowed corresponding improvements in the communications system of the country. In 1790, there were only 75 post offices serving about 2,000 miles of routes. Although most mail was still carried by stagecoach or on horseback, steamboats began to carry some as early as 1813, and the first railroad mail car was introduced in 1837. By 1840, there were 13,468 post offices serving 155,739 miles of routes. However, mail service was still slow and expensive. It took seven days to complete an express delivery between New Orleans and New York in 1825, and until 1845 it cost at least fifty cents to send two sheets of paper

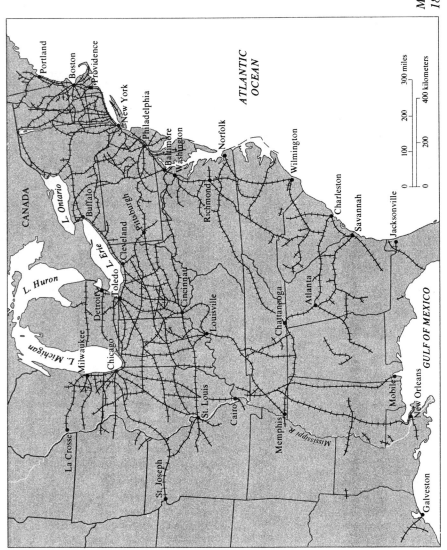

Map 3.2 Major Railroads in 1860

over 400 miles. By 1851, however, rates were reduced to three cents for letters going under 300 miles, and in 1863 free city delivery began.

A second major development in communications was the telegraph. Invented by Samuel F. B. Morse in 1837, the telegraph provided rapid communication between most of the eastern states by 1846, and its wires reached all the way to California in 1861. Although significant for all Americans, the telegraph was especially important for business. By the 1840s and 1850s, railroad executives were using the telegraph to schedule the movement of trains. Within one or two more additional generations, many other types of business people came to see the telegraph as essential in coordinating the operations of their companies. The speed of the telegraph in transmitting messages helped bring predictability to America's business world.

THE AGRARIAN REVOLUTION

The transportation revolution opened up the American interior and made possible the development of its vast agricultural potential. From the early days of colonial settlement, as we have seen, entrepreneurs invested in opportunities to harvest the agricultural resources of the continent. The opportunities to sell grain and other produce profitably in European markets that had arisen in the colonial period continued to seem attractive to American farmers. George Washington wanted to open a water route to the Ohio River valley—not just, as he reported to the Virginia governor, "for the fur and pelting trade" but also "for the produce of the country." The first cargo carried on the Erie Canal to New York was agricultural produce and liquor manufactured from grain. Clearly, the midsection of the country was a resource just waiting to be tapped.

It was not long before commercially minded American farmers tapped the rich resources of the transappalachian frontier. To expand their wealth, farmers made tremendous efforts to clear the forests that dominated the landscape of the region. The dominant belief was that the acquisition of wealth, especially as expressed in the ownership of land, was desirable. At first, farmers tried to be as self-sufficient as possible, to save cash for further land purchases. In the northern states (outside the thin and rocky soils of New England), market opportunities for farmers steadily expanded, so that by the 1850s a market-oriented agriculture, in which most farmers thought of themselves mainly as small business owners selling farm commodities for manufactured goods, had become the dominant type of farming.

The business system of the southern states deviated from the northern pattern with the expansion westward of the plantation system and slavery to take advantage of new opportunities in cotton growing. Cotton was the commercial crop that had the largest impact on the American business system in the first half of the nineteenth century. Cotton cultivation expanded westward from the sea islands off the Carolina and Georgia shores in the 1790s, through the belt of rich black soil in Alabama and Mississippi, and on into Louisiana and Texas by the time of the Civil War. In this period, cotton was the largest American export item in both volume and value, and the organization of the cotton trade, made possible in part through the transportation revolution, changed the way many Americans conducted business. In the South something of a dual economy developed. Large economically productive cotton plantations were complemented by smaller, often subsistence white family farms (only 25 percent of white southerners owned or used slaves in 1860).

Eli Whitney, the Cotton Gin, and the Plantation System

The agrarian revolution in the South owed much to an inventor-entrepreneur from New England named Eli Whitney, born in 1765. During the American Revolution, Whitney manufactured nails and knife blades at his family's Massachusetts farm workshop, only to have cheaper British imports challenge his thriving business with the return of peace. A versatile person, Whitney shifted to the production of hatpins and walking sticks. However, bored by the drudgery and isolation of farm life, he left the farm for an education at Yale. There Whitney moved in polite society, met socially prominent people, and made personal connections that would help him later in life. In 1792, he graduated from Yale and, now twenty-seven, used his connections to win appointment as a tutor to the children of a planter in South Carolina.

Whitney invented the cotton gin in 1793 while at this post. There was a large and growing market for cotton at that time in Britain, but American farmers could not profitably supply it. The problem was the type of cotton that could be grown in the American interior: it had short fibers that were expensive to remove from the seed when done by hand. Whitney's invention changed that situation. The cotton gin removed the seeds from the cotton fibers mechanically. In doing so, the gin greatly reduced the cost of processing the raw cotton, making possible the profitable cultivation of cotton, which soon became the major crop of the South.

To satisfy the ever-growing market for cotton, plantations and the slave system they depended on spread westward across the South into Alabama and Mississippi to exploit virgin soils. The emphasis on cotton production led the plantations to become much more specialized than those of colonial days. Most of the cotton came from plantations using twenty or more slaves, with plantations along the Mississippi River using a hundred or more. About half of the slaves worked for farmers who owned fewer than twenty. Planters continued to grow food or to purchase foodstuffs from neighboring farmers, and some slaves continued to work as artisans, fabricating goods for use on the plantation or for sale elsewhere; but concentration on cotton production tended to occur, and most manufactured items were purchased from entrepreneurs located elsewhere, in Europe or the North. Southern spokesmen referred to the crop as King Cotton because it was the basis of the region's business system.

Northern Merchants and the Organization of the Cotton Trade

The emergence of cotton as the nation's largest export provided new opportunities to organize and profit from its trade. At the time Whitney invented the cotton gin, the South was producing about 3,000 bales of cotton a year; on the eve of the Civil War, production had risen to almost 4 million bales a year (a bale weighed about 400 pounds). The organizing, supplying, warehousing, insuring, and financing of this tremendous output provided new and specialized business opportunities that did much to reshape the nature of the American firm. Northern merchants, especially those from New York, led the way.

Northern merchants were able to organize the cotton trade of the South because they supplied essential shipping and credit services. New York merchants pioneered so-called packet lines of ships that sailed on appointed, scheduled days. By the 1820s, there were regularly scheduled shipping services in the coastal trade between New York, Charleston, Savannah, Mobile, and New Orleans. The availability of packet services meant that shippers did not have to hold valuable cargoes in warehouses while waiting for ships to appear, an important consideration when a single bale of cotton might be worth $50.

Cyrus McCormick and the Reaper

Although cotton was the biggest export from the United States in this period, the agrarian revolution also occurred elsewhere. Commercial farming greatly expanded as a business enterprise, thanks to the lowering of transportation costs brought about by the steamboats and canals but also because of the development of a mechanical reaper by another inventor-entrepreneur, Cyrus McCormick. In a sense, McCormick did for the North what Whitney had done for the South.

From time immemorial, harvesting grain had been a backbreaking, time-consuming task. When a field of grain ripened, farmers had to walk through it, cutting the stalks with hand tools before the kernels spoiled or were ravaged by weather. By 1830, harvest technology had improved only slightly from ancient times; a person could reap only two acres of wheat a day, limiting the acreage planted. Even with those primitive techniques, grain production was important to the American business system. After McCormick's contribution, however, opportunities for expanding the production and processing of grain grew dramatically.

Better communications and transportation systems—such as the railroad and steamboats pictured here at Davenport, Iowa, around 1858—began linking the different regions of the United States even before the Civil War. (Pike Collection, Chicago Historical Society)

Born in 1809, Cyrus McCormick grew up on a farm in Virginia's Shenandoah Valley, a wheat-growing region. He observed both the laborious tasks of harvesting wheat and his father's frustrating efforts to develop a mechanical reaper. The younger McCormick took up the task and in 1831 demonstrated a workable mechanical reaper that he had assembled in the farm workshop. Drawn by a team of horses, the reaper derived its power from a wheel that was turned by coming into contact with the ground. The wheat was then cut by blades arranged on a circular wooden frame that turned constantly as the horses pulled the reaper along. For a time, McCormick diverted his attention to an iron-mining venture, but in the 1840s he began manufacturing and marketing his reaper, guaranteeing that the machine would cut two acres an hour. He moved to Chicago in 1848 and in 1849 made 1,500 reapers; production soared to 4,500 machines just nine years later. Over time, McCormick set up a network of franchised dealers who sold, financed, and repaired his machines. His successful device and his system of producing and marketing machines allowed farmers in the Midwest and, later, on the Great Plains to enlarge greatly the acreage under wheat cultivation. McCormick's skill as both inventor and businessman earned him a fortune; he was a millionaire by 1858.

The expansion of the grain trade, already under way even before the mechanical reaper was developed, created business opportunities in the North and West just as the cotton culture had in the South a generation earlier. Millers located themselves at strategic intersections of navigable waterways to grind the grain into flour. Servicing the farm economy with credit, transportation, and merchandise became significant areas of enterprise for many business people. For instance, lumbering grew to be the second largest industry in the United States. Ships laden with lumber sailing the Great Lakes were second in number only to those hauling grain, as the farmers and townspeople of the Midwest bought lumber to build farms, houses, stores, and workshops. Farming brought people to the interior of the continent; by 1840, 40 percent of the population lived west of the Appalachian Mountains. More people with more money meant a growing domestic market for goods, and entrepreneurs seeking to satisfy that market sparked the third of the three great nineteenth-century revolutions that so transformed the ways Americans worked and lived.

THE INDUSTRIAL REVOLUTION

In 1789, an English mechanic named Samuel Slater arrived in New York, eager to enter textile manufacturing. Slater was a harbinger of the coming of the Industrial Revolution to the United States, a revolution that transformed manufacturing. New technologies for fabricating goods provided significant new business opportunities during the first decades of the nineteenth century. Opportunities to organize industrial production prompted merchants to invest capital in new kinds of factories and encouraged the general trend of specialization in the American business system. By 1850, American entrepreneurs had built one of the leading systems of industrial enterprise in the world. (See Figure 3.1.) While the majority of Americans continued to earn their livelihood on the farm, entrepreneurial decisions were dramatically changing how goods were made and how the men and women who fashioned manufactured commodities lived.

Textiles and the Industrial Revolution

Samuel Slater's arrival in New York was a significant event in American business history because he was knowledgeable in the new techniques of textile manufacture that British entrepreneurs had developed in the second half of the eighteenth century. These entrepreneurs had observed that there was a large market for comfortable cotton clothing to replace scratchy, uncomfortable woolen and linen garments. The problem, however, was that the spinning of cotton thread and the weaving of cotton textiles, when done by hand, was too slow and costly for the products to garner a wide market.

The development of two ingenious machines overcame this problem. The spinning jenny quickly spun thread from cotton fibers, and the power

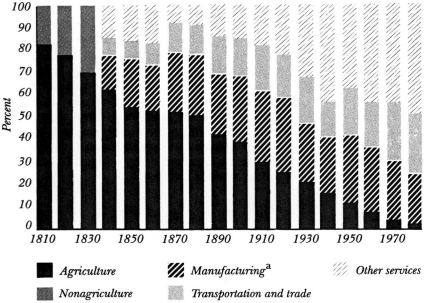

Figure 3.1   U.S. Labor Force Shares by Industry, 1810–1980 [SOURCE: *Economic Report of the President, 1988* (Washington, D.C.: U.S. Government Printing Office, 1988), p. 190, based on data from Department of Commerce and Department of Labor.] ªAlso includes fisheries, mining, and construction.

loom wove the thread into cloth. British entrepreneurs placed those machines, which were driven by giant water wheels, in factories and trained workers to operate them in return for wages. These techniques were successful, and British businesses soon dominated the world textile market with their cheap cotton goods. Their success in organizing industrial textile mills created the great demand for cotton that sparked the agrarian revolution in the American South.

The British sought unsuccessfully to protect their industrial leadership. The London government's mercantilist regulations included bans on the export of advanced machinery and the emigration of skilled mechanics. When Samuel Slater left for America, he violated those rules. After arriving in New York in 1789, Slater contacted Moses Brown, a Rhode Island merchant who had failed to establish a successful textile mill. Brown agreed to provide Slater with the capital to build a spinning jenny to make cotton yarn. Slater completed the machine in 1791, and, tended by nine children, it began to make yarn. The firm put out the yarn to workers who wove cloth in their homes. By 1801, the mill was a success, employing more than

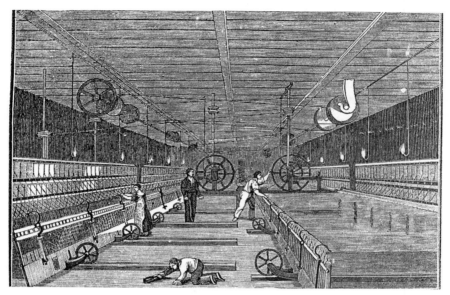

Samuel Slater's cotton mill used machinery to replace hand labor and thus speed up the production process. Each spinning mule—as the machines were called—could do the work of 300 hand spinners. (White's Memoirs of Slater)

a hundred children and adults. The Industrial Revolution was under way in America.

From these early beginnings in Rhode Island, Slater and other New England merchants, such as Francis Cabot Lowell, developed the textile industry further. Lowell came from a trading family, and when Harvard University suspended him for making a bonfire in the university's Yard, he went into business, specializing in trade with Europe. Lowell enjoyed success as a merchant, soon forming partnerships with other Bostonians to trade with China and India. Political events, however, brought their business to an abrupt halt. In 1807, President Jefferson ordered an embargo on imported British goods in an effort to make the London government respect American trading rights. Disputes between America and Britain eventually led to the War of 1812. By cutting off trade with England, the source of most cotton goods that Americans imported, the embargo and war also created a demand for domestically manufactured cotton textiles.

Pushed and pulled by international events, Lowell, like many other merchants, used the capital he had made in trade to enter manufacturing. In doing so, he was joined by Boston merchants whom he knew personally: Patrick Jackson, Israel Thorndike, John and James Lloyd, Nathan Appleton, and others. Later called the Boston Associates, this group set up the

Boston Manufacturing Company in early 1813. The company was capitalized at (had financing of) $400,000, a very large sum in those days. Lowell had visited British textile mills in 1810, and he used the information he picked up then, together with his own ideas, to establish the Boston Manufacturing Company's factory at Waltham, Massachusetts. By 1815, the Waltham mill was using water power to turn out cotton cloth. From the outset, the company was a success, making money on the sale of both the cloth (which was marketed through another firm controlled by Appleton) and the textile machinery made in its machine shop. By 1817, the Boston Manufacturing Company had sales of $34,000 and paid its investors a dividend of 17 percent.

The Boston Associates reinvested their profits and founded America's first new factory town, Lowell, Massachusetts. Completed in 1823, the manufacturing center consisted of six factory buildings grouped together to integrate, or link, the different steps in making textiles. In this one center, machines spun yarn, wove the yarn into cloth, and finished the cloth through bleaching and printing. The firm made and maintained its own machinery as well, and wherever possible the owners substituted machines for hand-labor. The firm provided boarding houses, attracting women from the surrounding countryside to work in the mills with wages higher than those in any other occupation open to them.

So well put together was the Lowell enterprise that it prospered, even under competition from British mills. In fact, cotton textiles proved to be the largest manufacturing opportunity in the United States prior to the Civil War. Entrepreneurs like the Boston Associates made fortunes from the business and reinvested their profits not only to advance textile manufacture but also to further the emerging railroad, insurance, and banking industries.

The Nature of the Industrial Revolution

The textile industry illustrates some of the changes in the organization and technology of manufacturing that characterize the Industrial Revolution. Before the Industrial Revolution, men and women made yarn and cloth at home, with simple, hand-powered machinery; the industrial production of textiles used complex machinery tended by men, women, or children working in factories. Water wheels drove the first textile machines; by the 1840s, American entrepreneurs were using water turbines and steam engines to provide power.

The social system that accompanied the industrial production of textiles also changed. The business leaders who formed the textile industry reorganized the ways in which humans worked. In the preindustrial manufacture of textiles, a worker at home might card wool, spin it into yarn, and weave the cloth from which he or she made clothing. The worker would then use the clothing or would market it through the local area's system of merchants. In the industrial processes at Lowell and elsewhere, however, work was organized much differently. Individual workers earned wages, paid to them by the owners, in exchange for accomplishing specialized, and usually routine, tasks of tending machines. The firm organized the individual workers into groups and employed foremen to supervise those groups, which accomplished just one part of a much larger task. The Industrial Revolution tended to separate the individual worker from the finished product and to reduce his or her ability to control the pace, technology, and quality of production.

Other industries took similar advantage of technological advances. The steam engine, greatly improved by James Watt in Scotland in 1769, was initially used to pump water from mines, utilizing coal for fuel instead of horses for power. As steam-engine technology improved, entrepreneurs used steam engines to drive machines in factories. Other technological innovations included the widespread use of the mineral resources of the earth. Men began to substitute iron for wood in machinery, and later they began using iron and steel instead of timber to support buildings. Iron became a symbol of the new industrial age.

Thus industrialization changed the way goods were produced in three fundamental ways. First, machines—tireless, precise, and rapid—replaced hand-labor in making things. Second, new raw materials and new sources of power gained importance in the production process. Finally, workers became concentrated in factories away from their homes. The new industrial organization of manufacturing eventually eliminated independent artisans as persons who played an important role in the economy.

One dominant characteristic connected the industrial, transportation, and agrarian revolutions: the availability of customers, the market. Americans desired cotton textiles. The American population was large enough by the 1820s, and linked well enough together by a transportation system, to justify the expansion of industry that Lowell represented. Industrial manufacturing drove down the cost of textiles and thereby enlarged the number of customers who could afford them. Moreover, the mills created a demand for raw cotton that merchants and planters could supply. The development of the domestic market created the opportunities for Americans to organize the industrial revolution in textiles, and that market would do the same for other industrialists as well.

Merchants and Manufacturers

The success of the Boston Associates illustrates a common trend in the development of manufacturing: merchants were central figures in organizing industrial processes. The pattern usually followed one of two routes. One was the direction that Lowell and the Boston Associates took as wealthy merchants risking their personal funds in a new textile venture because they saw an opportunity to seize a market. New York City's merchant elite followed this pattern, supplying craft entrepreneurs with the credit necessary for organizing industrial factories. One result was that New York became the most productive manufacturing city in the United States by 1850. The other direction was for an individual versed in mechanical innovations to observe the opportunity for lower production costs through the use of machines and to turn to merchants for assistance in financing factories and distributing their products. In either route, bankers were seldom involved at the early stages of industrialization, for their resources went into funding the nation's trading system.

The industrial transformation of shoemaking in Lynn, Massachusetts, was an important example of the changes that took place in the first half of the nineteenth century as merchants invested capital to reorganize the fabrication of goods. The merchants' investment decisions changed the lives of individuals and families, and even the dynamics of an entire community. Shoemaking was originally a handicraft operation conducted in a multitude of household businesses. Working in small shops, master shoemakers owned their tools, organized production from raw materials to finished products, and controlled the pace of their work. Production occurred in family units, with wives and children joined by journeymen and apprentices in small work teams. By 1800, there were two hundred master shoemakers in Lynn turning out 400,000 pairs of shoes annually. The shoemakers sold some of their output to Lynn shopkeepers and distributed shoes to a growing regional market in the Northeast through a network of small consignment merchants and retailers.

The industrialization of shoemaking that changed this production system occurred in three stages, during each of which merchants were the principal innovators. First, after 1814 the master shoemakers lost their autonomy to the shopkeepers. Opportunities to market shoes were expanding, but the shoemakers lacked the capital needed to purchase the larger volumes of raw materials and to employ more workers to seize those opportunities. The Lynn shopkeepers, however, enjoyed access to capital, credit, and markets, enabling them to begin reorganizing shoe production to take advantage of expanding markets. The shopkeepers used their resources to take control of shoemaking, contracting with skilled artisans for production.

In the second stage, completed by 1830, the merchant organizers sought to standardize production. They moved shoemakers out of their workshops into central shops and broke down shoemaking into separate steps. One worker now performed just one step in producing a shoe, and the capitalist organizer controlled the fabrication of the finished product. As the artisans lost control of the work process to the merchants who ran the central workshops, the family unit lessened in importance in the workplace. By

1830, the central workshops typically employed fifty to one hundred people. With the centralization of production, output soared. Lynn's shoemakers made mostly women's shoes. In 1790, the town's master shoemakers had sold one pair of shoes for every 10 white females in the United States, but in 1837, with the successful reorganization of production by merchants, the shoe workshops sold one pair for every 2.5 white females.

The third stage, which occurred in the 1850s, transformed the central workshops into factories. The introduction of sewing machines powered by steam engines provided a major advance in productivity. The efficiencies thus gained displaced skilled workers almost entirely. The industrialists who organized shoemaking further and further subdivided the production process, so that by the early 1860s, there were forty distinct steps in shoe-making. With the introduction of new machinery and the further subdivision of the work process, the shoe factories became larger enterprises; by the 1850s, they typically employed 300 to 500 persons. With the refinement of industrial shoemaking in the second half of the nineteenth century, shoe output per worker tripled over what it had been in the preindustrial system. In fact, between 1855 and 1875, employment in the shoe industry fell by 2,000 workers, but output rose by 7 million pairs.

A second type of relationship between merchants and manufacturers involved a knowledgeable mechanic or artisan striking up an alliance with a merchant, as in the case of Slater and Brown. These alliances were of great mutual benefit, because each member needed something the other had.

Artisan entrepreneurs who wanted to grasp a market opportunity by organizing a new industrial enterprise required both long-term and working capital. Long-term capital provided resources to acquire land, construct buildings, and buy machinery. Working capital was necessary to purchase raw materials and pay employees until sales of the factory's products began to earn revenue.

However, it was difficult to secure capital in the early stages of the Industrial Revolution. The United States had an established banking system, and banks provided credit to farmers, shipowners, merchants, and the like. But, for some bankers, new factory processes seemed too risky to make the sizable loans required, when trade provided surer profits. So entrepreneurs were forced to turn elsewhere: to the merchants who had accumulated capital from the profits of more traditional trade.

The formation and early growth of the Jones & Laughlin Company proved how workable an alliance between mechanics and merchants could be. Neither Benjamin Jones nor James Laughlin was especially familiar with iron making; yet a successful firm bore their names. The firm began in 1850 when mechanics started a rolling mill on the south bank of the Monongahela River in Pittsburgh (a rolling mill shapes raw iron or steel into products). They had developed an ingenious process that produced a high-quality iron rail, but a shortage of capital soon thwarted their efforts.

The mechanics began to solve their capitalization problem in 1853 when they struck an alliance with two merchants, including Jones, who had bought and sold iron products in Pittsburgh and Philadelphia. Jones was an able financier, and his capital was vital to the firm's success, but more was still needed. Jones arranged a partnership with Laughlin, who had made a fortune as a pork packer and by selling provisions to migrants moving west through Pittsburgh. Laughlin enjoyed considerable personal credit, which he used to supply the steel business with working capital. He became the firm's financial backer, although he played no active part in its management. By 1857, because of reinvested profits and Laughlin's infusions of capital, J & L, as Pittsburghers called the firm, owned blast furnaces to make pig iron, other furnaces to refine and prepare the iron, five rolling mills, and twenty-five nail-making machines.

Artisans as Entrepreneurs

Although artisans often acted in concert with merchants, they also worked on their own to bring industrialization to the United States. Some craft-oriented artisans found themselves unable to compete with businesses using new production methods, whereas others successfully made the transition to industrial production.

In some communities, large numbers of artisans in a broad range of crafts shifted to industrial modes of production. This transition occurred in Newark, New Jersey, America's leading industrial city in 1860. There artisans making saddles, shoes, jewelry, trunks, leather goods, and hats moved from handicraft to industrial production. These artisans were well educated for their time and self-confident about the benefits of technical innovations for their work and lives. They banded together in cooperative institutions such as the Newark Mechanics Association for Mutual Improvement in the Arts and Sciences and the Mechanics Bank of Newark, and were innovative and flexible in their approach to business. They embraced steam power: in 1840 no Newark factory used steam power, but by 1846 more than one hundred did. By 1860, the artisans had turned their shops into factories; in Newark twenty-two firms in six fields had at least $50,000 in capital and employed at least one hundred workers. Of those substantial enterprises of 1860, three-fifths had begun as artisans' workshops.

In other locales, artisans sometimes specialized in one type of manufacturing. In the Connecticut Valley, for instance, craftsmen made cutlery. The craftsmen began applying steam-powered machinery to production in the mid-nineteenth century, and they were inventive in acquiring capital and opening markets to take advantage of the opportunities that new technologies afforded. By remaining flexible in their production techniques and by changing their cutlery to take advantage of market niches, the Connecticut Valley companies remained industry leaders until World War II.

In yet other cases, individual artisans industrialized. One was Charles Chickering. Beginning as an apprentice in several Boston piano-making establishments, Chickering struck out on his own in 1826. At first he depended on the marketing and financial skills of a merchant to help his fledgling firm get started, but within a decade he had bought out the merchant's share in his business to become an independent manufacturer. Chickering changed piano making from a craft to an industrial operation by building a factory that in 1850 employed 100 workers to turn out 1,000 pianos worth $200,000. Within the factory Chickering divided work into twenty different departments, each devoted to a single step in making pianos. Outside the factory an additional 100 men made cast-iron frames for the pianos. In contrast to skilled artisans, no workers in Chickering's factory understood all the steps involved in making pianos.

With many industrial businesses originating in the workshops of artisans, it is not surprising to find that small enterprises dotted America's industrial landscape as late as 1870. In most industrial fields, large plant size was simply not needed to capture the economies of scale available with the machinery then in use. Although average plant output rose dramatically during the antebellum years in a few industrial fields, such as the cotton textile and iron industries, it increased only modestly in others, such as lumber mills. Factories generally remained small in most fields until technological developments in production made it feasible for entrepreneurs to introduce greater economies of scale by constructing big industrial firms.

Industry in the South

Although the economy of the South remained primarily agricultural throughout the nineteenth century, in the 1840s and 1850s about 20 percent of the capital invested in American industry was in the South. After 1850, it was there that about 5 percent of the total slave population worked in industry, typically located in small facilities in rural sites. Although southern industrial entrepreneurs typically owned slaves directly, a few masters earned income by hiring out their slaves to industrialists. One of the most significant industries was coal mining in eastern Virginia, which supplied most of the bituminous coal in the coastal trade until the opening of Pennsylvania coal fields in the 1840s and 1850s. The Virginia mines used slaves, who numbered 150 or more in the largest of them.

THE INVISIBLE HAND OF THE MARKET

The expansion of commercial and manufacturing activities made possible by the transportation, agrarian, and industrial revolutions caused significant

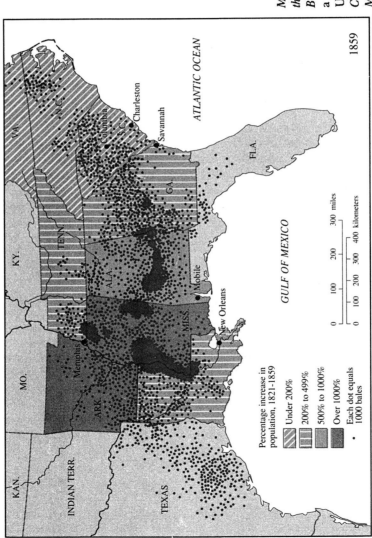

Map 3.3 Cotton Production in the South (SOURCE: From Mary Beth Norton et al., A People and a Nation: A History of the United States, Brief ed., 2nd ed. Copyright © 1988 by Houghton Mifflin Company.)

changes in the American firm, as we have seen. A complex web of business transactions developed, created by the enlarging internal market and transportation system, and presented many opportunities for providing specialized business services. The number of specialized firms grew accordingly. By the 1840s, the general merchant had all but disappeared, replaced by firms that engaged in a much narrower range of tasks than was the case in colonial times.

Specialization by Merchants

By the mid-1800s, thousands of specialized mercantile establishments were operating in the American business system. As most were relatively small, no single firm controlled its field of business. Despite the progress made in industrialization, the output of industrial products remained low enough in volume for merchants to handle directly. Moreover, most of the early industrial goods were technologically simple enough for the merchants to demonstrate, sell, and service themselves. Market forces—Adam Smith's "invisible hand"—proved to be adequate guides for determining the prices and quantities of goods produced and distributed in the United States. Only in the 1880s did the business network established before the Civil War break down, changed by the processes set in motion as manufacturing and its products became technologically more complex and industrial output soared.

The complexities of the increasingly large cotton crop initiated the shift toward specialization. Traveling merchants called "cotton factors" scouted interior plantations, marketed the planters' crops, and, in turn, provided them with credit and supplies. The factors either arranged sales of cotton to representatives of manufacturers or, more commonly, sent cotton to merchant firms in large cities such as New York or New Orleans that specialized in marketing cotton. (Many of the firms also had branches in Europe.) Only rarely did the firms assume ownership of the cotton. Rather, they took the cotton on consignment. They sought to sell the cotton for the highest price possible for the planters. The factors and other middlemen received a commission, usually around 5 percent, for their services. By 1840, some 381 commission houses were doing business in Louisiana, and 1,044 were open in New York. In the largest port cities, the amount of trade justified the development of yet another specialized institution: the brokerage house. For a fee, brokerage houses brought together buyers and sellers of cotton. An elaborate credit system based on advances from one middleman to the next, using the traditional financial instruments of promissory notes and bills of exchange, grew up to service the cotton trade.

Developments in the trade of other agricultural goods, such as wheat, roughly paralleled those in the cotton trade. The trend, again, was toward increased specialization. Farmers sold their grain to local merchants in country stores; the merchants, in turn, arranged storage and shipment to millers. With the opening of the Erie Canal, these local midwestern merchants shipped the grain and flour to specialized commission houses in Great Lakes cities such as Buffalo for sale and transshipment to points farther east. As in the cotton trade, the commission houses took the produce mostly on a consignment basis and found buyers for it in the eastern United States or abroad. Like the cotton trade also, the grain trade relied on a complex system of financial transactions based on advances in credit carried out through bills of exchange and promissory notes.

Specialization also occurred in the selling of manufactured goods, whether imported or made domestically. Leading merchants in large port cities concentrated on importing or exporting. Most merchant houses left retailing to specialize in wholesaling, where greater profits were available, and many came to specialize in handling just one line of goods. The same trends were apparent in the marketing of consumer goods, items bought directly by consumers, and producers' goods, products sold by one manufacturer to another. Both cotton textile manufacturers and pig-iron producers, for instance, relied on wholesale merchants to find markets for their growing outputs.

After short-lived and generally abortive efforts to sell the products of their mills directly to retailers (since mill owners lacked the knowledge of market conditions needed to make their selling successful), cotton textile manufacturers turned to wholesale merchants for help. The New England mills sold their textiles to wholesale commission houses, usually located in New York City. Because these firms specialized in the cotton textile trade, they became known as textile "selling houses." J. W. Paige & Co. was the first modern selling house, established to dispose of the output of four New England mills in 1828. Paige became the sales agent for the entire production of the mills, receiving a 1 percent commission on most sales. It assumed all risks on credit sales, thus relieving manufacturers of a major source of unpredictability in their business. Paige sold the cotton textiles to other merchants and to consumers on credit. If any purchaser defaulted on paying his bill, Paige—not the textile mills—bore the loss. This type of arrangement dominated cotton textile marketing in the years before the Civil War. Manufacturers welcomed it; for, in addition to taking the output of the mills, the selling houses often supplied them with sorely needed capital as advances on goods received for sale.

A new type of merchant—the "jobber"—connected the selling houses with the thousands of country stores and other retail outlets across the nation. Retailers found it time consuming and tiresome to visit all the cotton textile selling houses looking for bargains. For their part, the selling houses did not like to break up their bales of textiles into the small quantities desired by the retailers and often charged large fees for doing so. Jobbers filled the gap between the selling houses and the retailers, buying in large quantities from selling houses and selling in small amounts to the many retailers. Retailers, whether country stores in villages or small shops in large cities, then sold the textiles to consumers.

Roughly the same situation prevailed in producer-goods industries. Specialized merchants served as crucial links joining separate segments of these industries. They proved essential, for instance, in the expansion of the iron industry. During the colonial period, iron makers either sold their wares directly to consumers or relied on general merchants to handle their goods. These simple marketing arrangements, however, became inadequate for the rapidly increasing output of iron products that poured from American smelters and foundries in the early and mid-1800s, and they gave way to a multilevel marketing system run by specialized iron merchants.

Despite a large increase in output, iron making was largely an unintegrated industry in the pre–Civil War period. Firms like Jones & Laughlin, which combined all or most of the steps of a manufacturing process under one company, were the exception. Usually, several different companies were involved in the various stages of the manufacturing process. Furnace companies smelted pig iron; foundry companies cast the pig iron into stoves, hardware, simple machinery, and merchant bars (undifferentiated bars of iron); blacksmiths and toolmakers turned the merchant bars into finished products. Moving the iron from one stage of the manufacturing process to the next was a major problem, for the iron makers lacked the resources and market knowledge needed to produce the iron at the proper times and ship it to the right places. Specialized iron dealers arose to rationalize the flow of iron goods from furnace to foundry. They usually acted as commission merchants, taking the pig iron on a consignment basis and supplying it to finishers. City merchants or iron jobbers, in turn, often disposed of the outputs of the foundries. These merchants, especially the iron dealers, provided the credit and capital, as well as the marketing services, required by the iron makers—particularly the furnace owners, whose business was capital-intensive. (A capital-intensive business is one whose major expense is the cost of capital—money—needed to build expensive plants and to purchase machinery for those plants.) With large blast furnaces and other works, iron making was capital-intensive.

The pattern whereby manufacturers sold to commission merchants or selling houses that, in turn, sold to jobbers, who then dealt with retailers, was repeated in industry after industry. Most pre–Civil War industrial ventures, such as the cotton textile and iron companies, lacked the resources to handle all phases of their operations by themselves. As a result, merchants' knowledge of the country's diffuse markets, combined with their control over scarce capital, gave them dominance over large segments of the American economy during the pre–Civil War years.

Specialization in Service Businesses

Some merchants specialized by leaving the buying and selling of goods altogether and entering new fields of endeavor. During the first half of the nineteenth century, they took the lead in providing banking, insurance, shipping, and credit-rating services for America's expanding economy.

Some of the larger sedentary merchants in America's leading seaports dropped most of their earlier mercantile activities and specialized in granting credit to other merchants. John Jacob Astor, Stephen Girard, and Alexander Brown were among those who turned from trade to finance. They were particularly important in financing interregional and international commerce, especially the cotton trade. Brown is an especially vivid illustration of this particular process of specialization. A successful linen merchant in Ireland, he emigrated to Baltimore in the 1790s and there founded a new firm to deal in linen goods. His firm quickly prospered and as it did, the House of Brown (all of Alexander's four sons entered the business) moved into a wide range of commercial activities in Philadelphia, New York, and Liverpool. In the 1820s and 1830s, however, the Browns began to specialize. From general merchandising they turned to buying and selling on commission only. Finally, in the 1840s, the House of Brown developed into the most important international banking house financing the commercial segment of the American economy. As early as 1830, its capital of more than $3 million surpassed even that of Baring Brothers & Co., a British firm and the Browns' chief rival in the financing of Anglo-American trade.

In smaller towns and cities, local merchants and other business people entered commercial banking as a moneymaking proposition. Hundreds of small commercial banks operated at the state level during the years preceding the Civil War. Many of these banks were chartered and regulated by state governments, but a large number, called private banks, were regulated by no one. Whether chartered or private, the banks made loans to local businesses and farmers, using real estate, crops, business securities, and personal promissory notes as collateral.

Additional forms of banking began to develop in the early and mid-1800s. First started in 1816, savings banks were originally operated by merchants in a few large cities to help the poorer classes, but they were soon taking deposits from people of all incomes. They invested in federal government securities and made personal loans. Savings bank deposits rose from $1 million in 1820 to ten times that amount fifteen years later and continued to increase in subsequent years.

The bare beginnings of investment banking may also be traced to the early and mid-1800s, although the term "investment banker" did not come into common use in the United States until the early 1900s. Investment banking began as part of the efforts of merchants to finance international and interregional trade and took on a new life with the selling of railroad stocks and bonds starting in the 1850s. Investment bankers served the users and suppliers of capital by providing the means by which savings could be moved into long-term investments. They were essentially specialized middlemen providing links between companies with surplus capital and others needing that capital. Merchants in New York organized a "stock exchange office" in 1792, and the New Stock Exchange opened for business twenty-five years later. It was at these exchanges that the investment bankers met, or worked through brokers, to sell the stocks.

Merchants had engaged in primitive types of shipping and mercantile insurance during the colonial period (sea captains and ship owners bought shares in one another's voyages so as to spread losses in the event a ship sank), but insurance did not develop as an independent enterprise until the early and mid-nineteenth century. The first company formed specifically to insure ships and their cargoes came into existence in 1792; by 1807, forty such firms were doing business. Fire and life insurance were slower to develop, but by 1860, the United States possessed eighty-one general insurance companies, many of which wrote fire insurance, and forty-three life insurance companies, including the "Big Three" that dominated the industry in the late nineteenth century: New York Life, Mutual of New York, and Equitable Life. By 1860, the life insurance companies had policies worth $205 million in force and possessed assets of $25 million, most of which they conservatively invested in real estate mortgages rather than in the more speculative securities of railroads and industrial enterprises.

The Conduct of Business

In the conduct of business the specialized business people of the nineteenth century showed both important similarities to and striking differences from their colonial counterparts. As in colonial times, most businesses were family enterprises, and a single individual could supervise most firms' operations. The largest American industrial firm in 1860 was the Pepperell textile mill, which employed about eight hundred people, and even it could be toured and understood by a single manager in a matter of a few hours. Management, therefore, tended to be informal. Partners might divide responsibilities, with one, say, handling sales and the other finances, and with coordination between them occurring in informal conversations. Elaborate managerial hierarchies for the most part did not exist in pre–Civil War commerce and manufacturing.

This informality, however, began to change in some manufacturing concerns before 1860. In the largest industrial firms of the textile industry, the merchants who set up the mills did not always participate in their routine operation. Instead, the owners appointed a company treasurer and factory agents to take charge of daily affairs. Samuel Slater, for instance, found that he and his closest associates could not personally supervise his textile empire, which by the time of his death in 1835 had grown to include ten cotton textile mills, two machine shops, and a wholesale and commission firm, spread across Massachusetts, Rhode Island, and New Hampshire. Instead, Slater hired salaried managers to run his businesses and devoted his attention to coordinating the work of the mills and planning for the future. Thus, as the industrial business advanced, entrepreneurial functions began to separate from daily management.

Another change that the early industrialists had to face involved workers. Industrial work differed from preindustrial work and therefore posed new sorts of problems for the business executives who organized it. Trading firms had few employees, who were easily supervised through personal contact, but industrial firms employed many more men and women. Moreover, industrial work depended on the routines of machines, not the rhythms of nature that governed occupations such as farming or fishing. Thus industrialists had to devise ways of recruiting and disciplining workers for the new industrial mills and workshops; they had to devise a new managerial function.

The organizers of industrial work devised managerial schemes that mixed paternal concern for their workers with harsh discipline. The founders of the Lowell mills tried the paternalistic path first. They sent recruiters into the countryside offering employment to young women, who would live near the factories in carefully supervised dormitories. By the 1840s, however, the owners were experiencing difficulty recruiting workers for their mills, because the women found the industrial life harsh, with long hours and low pay. The women complained of "the yoke which has been prepared for us." A common response of the early industrialists was to demand regimented performance by workers and to dismiss those who refused to accede to the dictates of management. "I regard my work people," one factory agent said, "just as I regard my machinery. So long as they do my work for what I choose to pay them, I keep them, getting out of them all I can."

The new management problems of dealing with workers were not, however, a major source of change in the conduct of business before 1860, simply because industrialism was not yet fully developed. In 1860, America still had more slaves than factory workers. The organization of most firms, therefore, was still informal. And there were other similarities to the ways business had been conducted for centuries. The pace was still slow. Until the advent of the telegraph in the 1840s, communications depended on animal or wind power. A large ship, for instance, took about eighteen

The factories of Lowell, Massachusetts, were the nation's largest when they were built. As this label shows, the owners of the Merrimack Manufacturing Company were not only proud of their product—printed cotton whose colors would not run when wet— and guaranteed it, but they also displayed their workers and their industrial equipment. (Museum of American Textile History)

days to sail the 1,700 miles from New Orleans to New York. In addition, merchants kept their accounts using the Italian double-entry method, and they were only beginning to call counting houses "offices."

Although vestiges of the past remained, the future—in the form of a larger, more impersonal business environment—was clearly at hand. As a consequence of the transportation and communications revolutions, farms, villages, plantations, seacoast towns, and interior cities became interconnected. Personal business networks disappeared. Instead, the world of the specialized businesses of pre–Civil War America was governed by the unseen forces of supply and demand. The prices that entrepreneurs received for their goods depended on the demands of customers and on how many rival firms were seeking to supply those demands. One result was that business people cared less about their past experience in their line of trade than about immediate and future prospects. The profits received from, say, moving barrels of whiskey across the Erie Canal depended not so much on the costs of production as on the uncertain demand in the city market. Knowledge of the market demand—fresh news—was the key element of entrepreneurial success. Consequently, entrepreneurs paid scant attention, in keeping their accounts, to the costs of production. Advances in accounting techniques much beyond those developed by medieval Italian merchants awaited the rise of modern big business firms.

A BUSINESS IDEOLOGY

Along with the growth in the number of business firms in America, the atomization of the business system, and the vulnerability of businesses to unseen market forces came changes in the ways that Americans thought about themselves, their entrepreneurial activities, their families, and their society.

Individualism

The development of the economy, the growth of specialization, and the increase in wealth that resulted from increased agricultural and industrial production changed the social milieu. Colonial merchants and planters and their families had belonged to a relatively well-ordered, cohesive society in which they had accepted roles to play. Europeans had first settled the colonies as members of group enterprises. After 1790, however, this well-defined society crumbled and fragmented. Those who seemed to develop the nation, to increase its wealth, were those who risked their fortunes in hopes of gain. The business opportunities the nation now presented seemed to call for strong-willed individualists, and the expansion of opportunities seemed to be producing a nation where commercial values were ascending.

Alexis de Tocqueville, a French political figure and historian who traveled through the United States in the early 1830s, was the most widely read of many European observers who wrote about the young nation. De Tocqueville observed this individualistic enthusiasm for private gain; he also noticed that an exploitative attitude toward natural resources was widespread among the American people. When he informed pioneers in the Michigan Territory that he wanted to visit the wilderness for pleasure, they thought he was quite mad. Most Americans viewed the wilderness as an obstacle to be overcome in wrenching a living from the earth and as a source of raw materials for humans to put to use. "In Europe people talk a great deal about the wilds of America," de Tocqueville wrote, "but the Americans themselves never think about them; they are insensible to the wonders of inanimate nature and they may be said not to perceive the mighty forests that surround them till they fall beneath the hatchet."

Americans clearly sought to gain individual wealth through this kind of exploitation. George Washington was among those who purchased unsettled western lands, speculating that in time their value would rise as population and commerce advanced. Nor was the optimism that Washington typified confined to real estate. In the winter of 1839–1840, Jay Cooke, who eventually became one of the nation's millionaires, told his family about the bank in which he worked. "My bosses are making money fast," Cooke wrote. "Among our customers are men of every age and every position in society, from the hoary miser to the dashing buck who lives upon his thousands. Through all grades I see the same all-pervading, all-engrossing anxiety to grow rich."

When American speculators and entrepreneurs thought about their pursuit of wealth, they expressed not only a desire for personal gain but a faith in Adam Smith's precepts in the working of market forces as the best route to human progress. Entrepreneurs were confident, when they reflected upon the matter, that they were achieving larger results. Profits, in this view, not only were individual but added to the store of material plenty to which all citizens, if they chose to do so, could contribute, and in which they could share. One of the partners of John Murray Forbes, an early railroad magnate, observed that Forbes "never seemed to me a man of acquisitiveness, but very distinctly one of constructiveness." Forbes seemed driven by a "dominant passion for building up things."

The faith in "constructiveness" involved more than accumulating personal wealth. It included the notion that business built character and improved the individual. Business success seemed to depend on self-discipline; trade seemed to sharpen a person's faculties. In the atomized business system of the time, successful people, in this view, needed to develop personal characteristics of honor, trust, and integrity. Commercial people could not deal with one another and promote the greater good of American society without those attributes. Nor did the belief in building character end at the counting-house door or the steamboat gangplank. Hard work was a virtue that business people encouraged. Discipline extending into the lives of industrial workers was essential for the operations of industrial factories powered by machines.

Exceptions

The victory of individualism and the admiration of commercial activity was far from complete, however. Just as the business system became more complex with the expansion of the American economy in the first half of the nineteenth century, so the diversity of views and social situations among Americans increased. The individualism that became so large a part of American rhetoric in the first half of the nineteenth century, and that seemed to many observers to define the American character, was often rejected by workers, once in control of their craft but now increasingly subjected to the authority of the business people who organized manufacturing. Individualism seldom extended to women and minorities, who were excluded from full participation in the nation's business opportunities. Social customs and family traditions prevented women from realizing their full potential as participants in the world of business, and the continuation of slavery meant, of course, that black Americans seldom enjoyed any economic opportunity.

The growth of the commercial economy altered economic opportunities for women and American ideologies concerning them. There were two main trends. On the one hand, as work left the home for the factory and artisans became workers whose activities a factory manager controlled, women usually found themselves relegated to lower-paying, routinized jobs. The Boston Associates, for instance, were famous for their recruitment of New England farm girls to leave their homes and work in the mills of Lowell. In that sense, the specialization that swept through economic life lowered the status of women, who seldom found themselves in positions of authority. On the other hand, successful business owners began to idealize and elevate women as "ladies" who should not soil themselves with business. This concept fully flowered in the middle of the nineteenth century as the "cult of true womanhood." While American rhetoric was promoting individualism for white men, it was idealizing women as the pure, pious, gentle keepers of the home who nurtured children and comforted husbands.

There were exceptions to the general rule, of course. Women continued to work in family businesses. For instance, Rebecca Lukens assumed managerial control of an iron mill on Brandywine Creek in eastern Pennsylvania when her husband died in 1825. During the twenty-two years that she ran the company, it grew from a small craft operation serving a local market to a large industrial firm reaching a substantial regional market. Occasionally, too, women emerged as business entrepreneurs in their own right, not just as family members, by running shops and taverns, for instance. In New Orleans, Eulalie d' Mandeville Macarty, a freed black slave, owned a wholesale mercantile and dry goods store worth about $155,000. Macarty bought manufactured goods from Europe, stored them in a warehouse she owned, and distributed them through a network of slaves to a number of retail outlets.

As in the colonial period, women were vital participants in the family farm's operation as a small business. In addition to taking care of the home, farm women made and repaired clothing, prepared medicines, made soap, candles, and cheese, raised vegetables, and fed animals. Blankets, shawls, tablecloths, and undershirts were made from raw flax and wool spun on their spinning wheels. In times of peak labor demand—such as planting and harvesting—women might also have worked alongside their husbands in the field.

If the business achievements of a few women were exceptional, those of black Americans were remarkable. Commercial values spread in the black population even while slavery was a thriving institution before 1860. Most blacks served white masters as slaves. Yet some slaves engaged in business. In rural areas, slaves sometimes raised vegetables, livestock, and staple crops to trade with their masters or to sell to nearby merchants. In towns and cities, slaves sometimes bought their time from their masters on a semi-annual or annual basis and hired themselves out as workers. A few slaves even owned businesses. For example, Frank McWorter of Kentucky set up a saltpeter works, Benjamin Montgomery operated a drygoods store in Mississippi, and Benjamin Turner of Alabama owned a livery stable. All three shared the proceeds with their owners.

Most of those blacks who owned businesses were, however, freedmen. In 1860, free blacks constituted about 10 percent of America's black population of 4.5 million. By that time there were about 2,300 black-owned businesses in the United States. A few black businesses had existed during colonial times, and in the decades before the Civil War ended slavery, black entrepreneurs entered additional enterprises, especially in the region from South Carolina to Texas. Black businesses were typically small and engaged in merchandising, manufacturing, or providing services. A few blacks, however, achieved substantial success. Between 1830 and 1865, twenty-one black business owners accumulated at least $100,000 in wealth. William Leidesdorff, a San Francisco merchant, became America's first black millionaire, worth $1.5 million at his death. Like their white counterparts, these entrepreneurs often benefited from inherited wealth, family connections, and apprenticeships in family enterprises. Some blacks even owned slaves. John Carruthers Stanly was one. An emancipated slave, Stanly was the son of a white merchant-shipper and an African-born Ibo woman in North Carolina. He received an education and opened a barbershop while still a slave. After he was freed, Stanly turned his barbershop over to two trusted slaves and spent his time speculating in real estate and slave labor. By the late 1820s, he owned three cotton and turpentine plantations along with 163 slaves. His assets amounted to $68,000.

Social Responsibility

Some of the entrepreneurs who so greatly developed America's opportunities saw themselves as stewards, trustees, or essential leaders in other areas of American society. An elite group of Boston merchants and industrialists went the furthest in this regard. Called Brahmins because of their emphasis on family background and cultural ideals, they sought to improve their city and American civilization in a variety of ways. They hired architects to design attractive offices and homes for themselves. And they patronized the arts and funded libraries, scholarships, and scientific projects, making

Boston the showplace of American civilization. One of the Brahmins, Nathan Appleton, so important in organizing the industrial revolution in textiles, once wrote, "The truth is that my mind has always been devoted to many other things rather than money-making."

The idea of social responsibility was not confined to the entrepreneurs of Boston. For instance, the Tappan brothers, prominent New York merchants, provided sorely needed finances to the antislavery movement. And Amos Kendall, who advocated individualism while serving as a close adviser of President Andrew Jackson (1829–1837), later made a fortune in the new telegraph industry and eventually retired from business to found Gallaudet College for the deaf, the first such institution in the world. The list of benefactions in pre–Civil War America was long. Businessmen also served society as political leaders, just as they had in colonial and revolutionary times.

AMERICA'S CHANGING BUSINESS SYSTEM

The business system of the United States underwent vast changes in the seventy years following independence. George Washington would have been astonished by the enormous growth of business activity and the market that supported it, the many specialized firms, and the machine technologies that eased travel, manufacture, and farming. During this period as well arose new ways of conducting business that presaged the methods of the big business firms that were to come. American railroad executives, especially, who did so much to overcome the barriers of time and space that had hindered entrepreneurs in Washington's time, were facing and solving unprecedented business problems with new techniques of organization and management.

Washington was prescient in observing the great possibilities for internal improvements. Successive political leaders continued to call for and receive governmental assistance in the financing and construction of roads, waterways, and railroads to open even greater opportunities than Washington had imagined. Ultimately there remained widespread political consensus regarding the desirability of having government encourage entrepreneurial opportunities and provide the necessary legal framework for their full fruition.

Selected Readings

Douglas C. North, *The Economic Growth of the United States, 1790–1860* (Englewood Cliffs, N.J.: Prentice-Hall, 1961); Charles Sellers, *The Market Revolution: Jacksonian*

America, 1815–1846 (New York: Oxford University Press, 1992); and Diane Lindstrom, *Economic Development of the Philadelphia Region, 1810–1850* (New York: Columbia University Press, 1978), examine the expansion of America's business system. George Rogers Taylor, *The Transportation Revolution, 1815–1860* (New York: Holt, Rinehart and Winston, 1951); Albert Fishlow, *Railroads and the Transformation of the Ante-Bellum Economy* (Cambridge, Mass.: Harvard University Press, 1965); and Cynthia Owen Philip, *Robert Fulton: A Biography* (New York: Franklin Watts, 1985), look at transportation improvements. Paul Gates, *The Farmer's Age: Agriculture, 1815–1860* (New York: Harper & Row, 1960), and Clarence H. Danhof, *Change in Agriculture: The Northern United States, 1820–1870* (Cambridge, Mass.: Harvard University Press, 1969), are classic studies. And on farming as a business, see Jeremy Atack and Fred Bateman, *To Own Their Own Soil: Agriculture in the Antebellum North* (Ames: Iowa State University Press, 1987).

David Hounshell, *From the American System to Mass Production 1800–1932* (Baltimore: Johns Hopkins University Press, 1984), and Thomas Cochran, *The Frontiers of Change: Early Industrialism in America* (New York: Oxford University Press, 1981), survey the process of industrialization. Alan Dawley, *Class and Community: The Industrial Revolution in Lynn* (Cambridge, Mass.: Harvard University Press, 1976); Robert Dalzell, Jr., *Enterprising Elite: The Boston Associates and the World They Made* (Cambridge, Mass.: Harvard University Press, 1987); and Gary Kornblith, "The Craftsman as Industrialist: Jonas Chickering and the Transformation of American Piano Making," *Business History Review* 59 (Autumn 1985): 349–368, are useful case studies.

Glenn Porter and Harold Livesay, *Merchants and Manufacturers: Studies in the Changing Structure of Nineteenth-Century Marketing* (Baltimore: Johns Hopkins University Press, 1971), present a penetrating analysis of business changes in America during the 1800s. The classic account of the cotton trade can be found in Robert G. Albion, *The Rise of New York Port, 1815–1870* (New York: Charles Scribner's Sons, 1939). For an introduction to the plantation, see Eugene D. Genovese, "The Significance of the Slave Plantation for Southern Economic Development," *Journal of Social History* 28 (November 1962): 422–437. Morton Keller, *The Life Insurance Enterprise, 1885–1910* (Cambridge, Mass.: Harvard University Press, 1963), introduces the early years of the life insurance industry. Claudia Golden, "The Economic Status of Women in the Early Republic: Quantitative Evidence," *Journal of Interdisciplinary History* 16 (Winter 1986): 375–404, examines women in business, focusing on Philadelphia. And, finally, Juliet E. K. Walker, "Racism, Slavery, and Free Enterprise: Black Entrepreneurship in the United States Before the Civil War," *Business History Review* 60 (Autumn 1986): 343–382, reveals the remarkable story of black business achievement in the age of slavery.

IMPORTANT EVENTS, 1784–1861

1784   George Washington requests Virginia's assistance in connecting the Ohio and Potomac river valleys.

1789   Congress enacts the first tariff law.

1803   Ohio is admitted to the Union.
Congress authorizes construction of the National Road.
Thomas Jefferson arranges the Louisiana Purchase.

1808   Albert Gallatin calls for a national program of internal improvements.

1811   The Bank of the United States' charter expires.
New York passes the first general incorporation law.

1816   Congress charters the Second Bank of the United States.

1824–1838   The General Survey Act provides assistance for planning roads, canals, and railroads.

1825   The Erie Canal is completed by the state of New York.

1832   Andrew Jackson vetoes the rechartering of the Second Bank of the United States.

1844   A telegraph line between Washington, D.C., and Baltimore is completed with federal funds.

1850   Congress authorizes the first federal land grant in support of railroad construction.

1861   Eleven Southern states secede from the Union.
California is linked to the East by the telegraph.

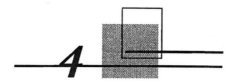

Government and Business

After George Washington explored possible routes to connect Virginia with the Ohio River valley in 1784, he appeared before the Virginia Assembly to request the state's assistance. The legislators agreed to help. Virginia appointed an official commission to survey routes, chartered the Potomac Company to begin clearing the Potomac River of obstructions, and offered to help finance the venture. The project eventually failed because the available technology and capital were insufficient to maintain navigation on the Potomac River. Thirty-three years later, however, the legislature of New York passed a law to finance, construct, and operate the Erie Canal. On July 4, 1817, De Witt Clinton, then mayor of New York City, ceremoniously lifted the first shovel of earth, and the great project was under way.

The stories of the abortive Potomac Company and the successful Erie Canal illustrate the extent of government involvement in the development of the young nation. In fact, one major aspect of the relationship between government and business after 1789 was developmental. There was considerable agreement among American leaders that the government should assist private entrepreneurial enterprises. This agreement differed from European forms of mercantilism. The mercantilist policies, against which Americans had rebelled, were impositions by a government upon the people it ruled. In the new United States, by contrast, there was no sense that the government was somehow separate from its people. The propertied men who ran the American government were not part of an aristocracy ruling on the basis of ancient feudal privileges. Thus, governmental policies intended to promote business were not policies to benefit some separate ruling class, or some entity called the state, but instead were seen as policies of the people to help the people. The result was a series of initiatives that promoted entrepreneurial opportunity.

If there was general consensus about a developmental political economy, however, there was much disagreement concerning its particulars. We have seen how bitter those disagreements were in the 1790s, and more disputes followed. The growing diversity of specialized business enterprises also meant a growth in competing business interests. The clash of interests meant that local interests tended to prevail over visions of uniform national policy during the nineteenth century. After 1820, the racial and economic institution of slavery loomed over all other political considerations until 1861, when slavery's Southern defenders, in the most extreme form of localism, felt compelled to secede from the Union. Nor was slavery the only issue in which local and particular interests disjointed the nation. American entrepreneurs and their political representatives disagreed about important internal-improvement, tariff, banking, and land policies as well. These grave conflicts notwithstanding, the overall characteristic of government-business relations during the nineteenth century was developmental, as all levels of government actively promoted business opportunity.

INTERNAL IMPROVEMENTS

When Thomas Jefferson was inaugurated president for the second time in 1805, he pointed proudly to the success of his fiscal program. "Because of the elimination of internal taxes," Jefferson observed, "it may be the pleasure and pride of an American to ask, what farmer, what mechanic, what laborer, ever sees a tax-gatherer of the United States." A growing revenue surplus from the tariff on imported goods was retiring the debt and freeing the federal government to use its resources for improving "rivers, canals, roads, arts, manufacturing, education, and other great objects." And there was a lot of country to improve now. Concerned about ensuring American access to the seaport of New Orleans at the mouth of the Mississippi, the president had greatly enlarged the size of the United States with the Louisiana Purchase of 1803. Much internal improvement appeared necessary if America was to fulfill Jefferson's promise as a republic resting on a productive, independent citizenry.

The Federal Government

In matters of planning for internal improvements, Jefferson's most brilliant adviser was Secretary of the Treasury Albert Gallatin. Born in Switzerland in 1761, Gallatin emigrated to America in 1780. In 1786, he moved to southwestern Pennsylvania, where he attended the convention of 1788 that discussed the ratification of the new Constitution, and he became a member of the state legislature in 1790. As a member of Congress from 1795 to 1801, Gallatin was part of the faction opposing the military and fiscal policies of President John Adams. Gallatin's proposals for financial reform, to have

Congress more cautiously appropriate money, made him Jefferson's logical choice for the important cabinet post of treasury secretary.

As secretary of the treasury, Gallatin became the nation's first economic planner in matters of internal improvement. Whereas Hamilton had looked outward toward overseas commerce as the key to the nation's economic health, Gallatin the Jeffersonian looked inward. With the movement of population westward across the Appalachian Mountain barrier, the need for overland transportation and communications links was clear. Shortly after 1803, when Ohio was admitted as the first state from the Northwest Territory, as the Great Lakes basin was then called, Congress authorized the building of a road west from Baltimore, Maryland, to provide an overland route to the Ohio River. In 1807, the Senate also instructed Gallatin to draw up a comprehensive report on the need for further public improvements.

Gallatin issued his *Report on Roads, Canals, Harbors, and Rivers* in 1808. In it he described both the needs of the nation and the problems of meeting those needs. According to his national plan for transportation and communications, the country should have "from north to south, in a direction parallel to the seacoast," both "a great turnpike road" and "canals opening an inland navigation for sea vessels from Massachusetts to North Carolina." From east to west, similarly, roads would cross the Appalachian Mountains and extend as far as Detroit, St. Louis, and New Orleans. Waterways, built to improve the navigation of rivers and combine them with canals, would connect the eastern seaboard with the transappalachian interior. At places where there were natural bottlenecks, such as Niagara Falls or the falls on the Ohio River near Louisville, canals would be built to allow boats to pass. Thus, Gallatin planned to open "navigation from Lake Ontario to the upper lakes as far as the extremities of Lake Michigan," with Lake Ontario connected by canal and river to New York City. He estimated this plan would cost $16.6 million. To make it politically palatable to regions that would not directly benefit from improved connections to the interior, he suggested the expenditure of another $3.4 million on "a number of local improvements," which would "do substantial justice and give general satisfaction." The total cost of $20 million, he believed, could be paid in ten years' time from surplus tariff revenues.

When Gallatin presented his sweeping program, he explained why it was necessary for the federal government to embark on internal improvements. He observed that there were two types of projects. *Exploitative* projects went through populated countryside. Private investors saw profitable opportunities for capital improvements in such cases. *Developmental* projects such as those he proposed were different. They were based on the anticipation that, upon completion, settlements and business would arise along their paths. Private investors were often reluctant to engage in developmental projects, which promised only remote and uncertain profits. Individuals and private enterprise simply did not have the resources, or the incentive,

Cincinnati, situated on the Ohio River, bustled with commerce along its waterfront even after the railroad came. Merchants and merchandise crowded the levee, and steamboats docked in the shadow of the new railway bridge. (Courtesy of the Ohio Historical Society)

to embark on such projects, however desirable they were from the viewpoint of the national interest. Gallatin made a key point: "The General Government can alone remove these obstacles."

Gallatin's report came to naught after 1808. The warfare between Britain and France made his scheme for financing improvements impossible. President Jefferson felt compelled to order embargoes on the importation of British goods, and the tariff revenue surpluses upon which Gallatin had based his projections disappeared. The need for internal improvements continued, and the obstacles to private development that Gallatin had noted remained, but the financial and political ability of the federal government to act evaporated in the foreign policy crises that resulted eventually in the War of 1812. The actual construction of internal improvements after the war ended in 1815 fell mostly to state and local governments.

Although the federal government did not build the canals and roads that Gallatin envisioned, it did provide essential help in planning both state and private ventures. In 1802, the army created the Corps of Engineers, located at West Point on the Hudson River upstream from New York City. The establishment of the United States Military Academy, run by the corps as an engineering school until the outbreak of the Civil War in 1861, provided the government with a cadre capable of providing valuable assistance in laying out the routes for roads, canals, and railroads. In 1816, army engineers began to survey western rivers and lakes and to help state and local projects along the Atlantic seaboard.

The federal government enlarged this service under the General Survey Act of 1824. Between 1824 and 1828, a Board of Engineers for Internal Improvements investigated the links essential for the nation's transportation system. President John Quincy Adams thought this work was of "great importance," and the army engineers began to help build the nation's first railroad lines. When the Baltimore & Ohio Railroad was chartered in 1828, it asked for a government survey, and the army lent three surveying brigades, each told to follow the company's instructions. Army engineers, led by Major William J. McNeill, supervised the construction of the first Baltimore & Ohio line. Eventually, McNeill worked for eight other railroads. After 1828, the government paid only the salaries of the engineers whose services it lent to the railroads, and the companies assumed their other expenses. Under this arrangement, army engineers had made at least ten railroad or canal surveys by 1830, and by 1835 at least twenty railroads were receiving vital federal engineering assistance. This policy lasted until 1838, when Congress repealed the General Survey Act. By that time, army engineers had helped build 1,879 miles of track.

Congress repealed the law because after the general economic depression that began in 1837, there seemed a sufficient supply of civilian engineers to complete the necessary work. But only eleven years later, when Americans began to think about crossing the Great Plains and the formidable Rocky Mountain barrier with iron rails, Congress again began making annual appropriations for military and geographical surveys west of the Mississippi River. In 1853, the government began the Pacific Railroad surveys, which examined four major routes. Actual construction of the first transcontinental railroad was delayed, however, until after the start of the Civil War.

This limited federal assistance for internal improvements was hardly the fulfillment of Gallatin's grand plan. The need for internal improvements remained, and the federal government commanded sufficient fiscal resources to help fund them, but the political will to engage in internal improvements dissipated in the face of the slavery controversy. As the plantation system of the South expanded westward, southern political leaders came to see every national policy issue in the light of its potential impact on the institution of slavery. Much of the South was blessed with rivers that flowed to ports on the Gulf of Mexico. High-value, compact bales of cotton could be sent to market on rafts, barges, or steamboats without resort to expensive improvements. Internal improvements sought by northerners were largely east-west ventures, and the southern planters did not want to pay the higher tariff duties needed to fund them. Southerners saw the tariff as a tax on the South for the benefit of the North and West, and they thought it would serve only to augment the wealth and therefore the power of the sections that were antagonistic to the continuation of slavery. Then, too, debate over a constitutional issue helped limit federal aid for internal improvements. Those opposing federal involvement argued that the Constitution did not give such far-reaching powers to the federal government, that they were reserved, according to that document, to the state governments. In this view, federal funding of internal improvements was simply unconstitutional.

Presidential encouragement of federal support of internal improvements waned in the face of the bitter intersectional rivalry. John Quincy Adams, who served in the White House from 1825 to 1829, was the last of the pre–Civil War presidents to support the idea of federal aid for transportation improvements. His successor, Andrew Jackson, ended sizable federal expenditures for roads and canals, arguing that those projects, under the Constitution, belonged to state and local governments. He turned over the completed sections of the National Road to Maryland, Virginia, Ohio, and Indiana. By the 1830s, Gallatin's integrated plan was no more. In its place stood the more decentralized situation of individual, state, and local government action; localism had triumphed.

There were two significant exceptions to the general pattern of federal retreat from support for internal improvements before the Civil War, however. Both involved the newest technologies of transportation and communication: the telegraph and the railroad. As we saw in Chapter 3, the federal government subsidized the development of communications through the reduction of postal rates and the expansion of postal routes. It went a step further after the invention of the telegraph in 1837. Private investors were unwilling to support the risky venture of building an experimental telegraph line, so Congress appropriated $30,000 to complete a line from Washington to Baltimore in 1844. Some consideration was given to making the telegraph part of the postal system, but instead, once the practicality of the new technology was demonstrated with public funds, it was left to private exploitation. By the end of 1846, most of the eastern states were connected by telegraph line, and California was linked to the rest of the country by telegraph in 1861.

Federal subsidies for railroad construction were even greater than those for the telegraph. Western interests had asked for federal help in expanding railroad mileage in their region, but a combination of southern and northeastern congressmen, who saw no immediate advantage in transferring wealth to the West, had stopped them. That situation changed in 1850 with the proposed construction of the Illinois Central Railroad to link the upper Mississippi River valley and Chicago with the port of Mobile, Alabama. Investors in Boston and New York saw the advantages of such a line connecting to ones they owned running eastward toward Chicago. The result was the first federal railroad land grant, passed by Congress in 1850. This measure granted federal land to Mississippi, Alabama, and Illinois, which they could turn over to the railroad, and which the railroad could then use to back its bonds. The railroad received a two-hundred-foot-wide right of way and a checkerboard of sections of land in a six-mile-wide swath along its path, land which the railroad could either sell or use to secure private loans. In effect, the federal government underwrote the original capital costs of the Illinois Central. In return, the railroad was obligated to carry the troops or property of the United States government free from any toll or other charge, and Congress had the authority to set the rates for carrying mail.

This subsidy provided enormous help for the entrepreneurs building the new railroad. The cost of construction and equipment for the Illinois Central was $23 million, only one-sixth of which came from private stockholders. The rest of the funds came mostly from mortgages secured by the lands granted by the federal government. Not only was this policy instrumental in speeding the construction of an important north-south carrier, but it also set a precedent for the future. Once the political power of the South was broken by the Civil War, the way was clear to extend the land grant system for the support of the construction of transcontinental routes. The first transcontinental railroad, created by linking the track of the Central Pacific building eastward from Sacramento and the Union Pacific building westward from Omaha, was completed under federal incentives and support, including land grants, in 1869.

State and Local Governments

Although the federal government before the Civil War played an important role in planning internal improvements but was thwarted in executing their development by constitutional and political disputes, no such factors retarded state and local government action. In an era when business firms were small and specialized, merchants, manufacturers, commercial farmers, and land speculators tended to influence state and local governments, viewing them as logical entities to meet the needs of economic development. Unlike the situation with the federal government, within each state there were no restrictions imposed by strict constitutional construction on economic activity. Nor were state politicians, often ambitious entrepreneurs themselves, encumbered by laissez-faire theory. Whenever the needs of economic development were critical, state aid was enthusiastically given. Missouri, admitted to the Union in 1820, perhaps best expressed this spirit in its constitution, which stated that "internal improvement shall forever be encouraged by the government of this State." In the absence of legal and theoretical restrictions, it was the state and local governments, responsive to local entrepreneurial ambitions, that gave the most aid to internal-improvement projects in the period before the Civil War. This assistance did not follow the national plan laid out by Gallatin but, instead, helped projects intended to improve or create local economic advantages.

State and local government aid was instrumental in hurdling the Appalachian Mountain barrier. The aid took several forms, all of which involved available transportation technologies, from roads to steam railroads. Some railroads and canals were built as public works. Others were mixed enterprises that combined public and private funds. The first commercially important east-west transportation link was the Erie Canal. The total original cost of the Erie Canal was $7 million, by far the largest sum ever expended on an internal improvement and one that exceeded the capitalization of the nation's largest manufacturing firm by ten times. The state of New York financed the canal because private entrepreneurs were unwilling to engage in such a difficult and speculative venture. So the state held lotteries and sold bonds to pay for the venture and operated the canal as a public work. The Erie Canal was an immediate commercial success and, as noted in Chapter 3, sparked a veritable craze for canals elsewhere. But most of these other canals failed to generate enough toll revenues to pay for both their capital and maintenance costs.

Since state funds were by far the most important source of capital for canals, the failure of canals to generate revenues sufficient to repay the state caused serious problems. By 1841, for instance, Indiana was carrying more than $9 million of debt attributable to internal improvements. These investments were simply not recoverable from canal tolls, and the states that had to pay the bill from tax revenues legislated against any such future investments. After Ohio lost money on its canals, for example, its new 1851 constitution forbade the state or any of its cities, counties, or townships from owning stock, making loans, or raising funds for any internal-improvement companies.

This was an extreme reaction to the canal debts, however. There were innumerable instances of states, cities, counties, and towns funding railroad projects in anticipation of diverting or developing trade and thereby enhancing local entrepreneurial opportunities. The best-known example of government support for railroad construction was one of the nation's first lines, the Baltimore & Ohio Railroad, which was a joint public and private venture. The business and political leaders of Baltimore realized that the success of the Erie Canal threatened their long-term prospects, for the canal drew trade to New York City, which rapidly eclipsed its rival ports. Baltimore's leaders wanted to counter this competition by the construction of a railroad west to the Ohio River valley, in effect fulfilling George Washington's earlier vision. The city provided capital for the construction and hoped eventually to reap the rewards of dividends and interest. (Profits were too far in the future to attract the necessary private capital.) The City of Baltimore held a financial interest in the Baltimore & Ohio until 1890 and in another line, the Western Maryland, until 1902.

In the South, as well, much of the investment in railroads came from governments. Southern agricultural production was capital-intensive: that is, it required large monetary investments. Cotton farming exhausted the soil, necessitating investment in new land, and the requirements of the slave system, although generally profitable for its owners, soaked up capital. Private financiers used their resources to fund the short-term needs of agriculture. The result was that southerners often turned to public sources

The building of the Erie Canal was a mammoth enterprise for its time period. The Erie Canal and many other important canal projects were funded by state governments. (Cadwallader D. Colden, Memoir prepared for the celebration of the completion of the N.Y. Canals, 1825)

of capital for building railroads. Georgia led the way in 1836 when it launched the Western & Atlantic Railroad as a state enterprise. Between 1841 and 1850, up to one-third of Georgia's budget went to railroad construction. The main line of the Western & Atlantic went to the northwestern region of Georgia, up to then a landlocked and sparsely populated area, and in 1849 it reached Chattanooga, Tennessee. The line carried thousands of cotton bales to market in Savannah during the 1850s, and freight revenues soon began to repay the state's investment. The plan of the Western & Atlantic was not that it would compete with private facilities—they were not being constructed—but that it would provide a focal point for a rail network. Shorter lines constructed by towns and private investors connected to the trunk line, and the Western & Atlantic provided terminals in Savannah and Atlanta for goods originating on them.

Public Investment in Private Enterprise

Georgia and the other states that were building railroads and other improvements did so to expand opportunities for private enterprise. The projects, thus, were not manifestations of mercantilism in the traditional sense, or precursors to modern socialism, but developmental planning ventures intended to foster business and agricultural opportunities for private citizens.

Much of the railroad investment came from residents along the lines who hoped not so much for a profitable return as for the benefits of using the facilities.

Public investment in internal improvements was substantial. In the years between 1815 and 1860, about 60 percent of the total investment in transportation facilities came in the form of government public works. More than half of this investment was concentrated in the seven states that either faced or included parts of the Appalachian Mountain range. In canal construction, about 73 percent of the funds came from public investment; the federal government granted about 4 million acres of land and $3 million to Ohio, Michigan, Indiana, Illinois, and Wisconsin for canals. For railroads, 25 to 30 percent of the investment before 1861 was public, not including land grants. All these funds were required, as Gallatin had predicted, either where capital costs exceeded the resources of private entrepreneurs or where profits were too far in the future to entice private developers, given the absence of prior social and economic development.

The results of the public investments were sometimes chaotic. Towns feared, rightly, that if they lacked rail service they might die as viable economic entities, so excessive and wasteful construction occasionally ensued. In retrospect, the shortcomings of relying on state and local government planning for internal improvements, in contrast to Gallatin's national scheme, were clear. In the decentralized system, there were no workable criteria for selecting projects or for assigning particular projects to different levels of governmental responsibility. Nor did governments have effective means of supervising projects. Just as the nation lacked an engineering cadre at the start of the nineteenth century, throughout the period it had no body of public experts and no system of legal agencies capable of overseeing the usage of public funds. Sometimes waste and fraud were the result, although the worst scandals occurred after the Civil War, when the first transcontinental railroad was completed.

BANKING AND THE TARIFF

Although there were areas of strong collaboration between government and business in the pre–Civil War years, as in the funding and building of internal improvements, there were also areas of intense conflict. Controversies over the appropriate use of the federal government's power to levy import duties racked national politics after 1789, as businessmen with competing and changing interests wrangled over questions of tariff protection for domestic manufacturing from foreign competition. Disputes over banking policies, on the other hand, arose not just from the competing economic interests of businessmen but also from the need of officials to provide an adequate currency system for the operation of the government.

Banking Policies

Just as there was a fragmentation of the political economy on policies of federal support for internal improvements, so there was a similar situation in banking policy before the 1860s. As we have seen, the chartering of the Bank of the United States was the most controversial subject in the political economy of the 1790s. That controversy deepened and grew more complex by the 1830s. The charter of the Bank of the United States ran for twenty years, and the Jeffersonians, ever suspicious of the concentration of so much power in the hands of a few private individuals, refused to renew it in 1811. During the War of 1812, the United States had no federally chartered bank, but the ensuing difficulties in maintaining a sound currency led prominent businessmen and financiers, including John Jacob Astor and Stephen Girard, to encourage Congress to charter a Second Bank of the United States in 1816.

Businessmen like Astor and Girard wanted a Second Bank of the United States, and Congress agreed, because the absence of such an institution had led to chaos. State governments chartered banks, so-called state banks, in which the federal government deposited its funds after 1811. Both businesses and the government borrowed from the state banks, which issued notes redeemable in specie (gold or silver) that circulated as currency. When borrowing increased, as it did during the War of 1812, the amount of currency flowing into the economy rose. When the economy boomed, optimistic bankers freely loaned money, liberally printing more notes, sometimes without regard to their ability to redeem them in specie. Bank notes—the nation's currency, in other words—became suspect, adding to the risks of conducting business.

Congress tried to correct this situation when it created the Second Bank of the United States. The Second Bank was like its predecessor, except that the government appointed five of its twenty-five directors, and the directors enjoyed considerable power to control the nation's currency. When the federal government collected revenue (mostly from tariff duties) in bank notes, it deposited them in the Bank of the United States. The bank, in turn, could require their redemption in specie and thus provide a powerful brake on state banks that might otherwise overexpand their credit. In other words, the Bank of the United States indirectly regulated the supply of credit and the volume of currency available. The new scheme worked well for a time, but by the 1830s, the Bank of the United States encountered vociferous complaints from agrarians, who suspected all banks and all paper money, and from optimistic financiers, who wanted to promote rapid economic expansion.

The Bank of the United States, especially after Nicholas Biddle became its president in 1823, was very helpful to established businesses. Business people could count on the value of the currency they received because Biddle, from his office on Philadelphia's Chestnut Street, tried to ensure that the state banks did not extend their credit beyond their assets. Moreover, the Bank of the United States supplied about a quarter of the nation's currency, and its branch offices—twenty-nine by 1830, all in commercial centers—facilitated interregional monetary exchange. The Bank of the United States also operated as a commercial bank, accepting deposits and making loans.

If Biddle's policies were helpful to the conduct of business, however, agrarians, especially in the West and the South, and many state bankers questioned them. Agrarians, eventually championed by Andrew Jackson, who was elected president in 1828 and reelected in 1832, were suspicious of all paper currency and the power of so few men to manipulate its value. Jackson denounced the bank for its failure to establish "a uniform and sound currency," by which he meant an entirely metallic currency whose volume of circulation and value would not fluctuate. Some bankers, on the other hand, denounced Biddle's policies as "coercion" and "oppression." Calling themselves "Democrats by trade," they promoted the virtues of free enterprise and laissez faire and exalted the rugged individualism of the entrepreneur and the pioneer. Alexander Hamilton's son, ironically, was a leading Democrat who sought the destruction of Biddle's power in order to gain more freedom for a large bank on New York's Wall Street, controlled by him and his friends.

The controversy, sometimes summarized as one between Wall Street and Chestnut Street, concluded in the 1830s with the New Yorkers and the other Democrats victorious. President Jackson vetoed the rechartering of the bank in 1832, complaining that it made "the rich richer and the potent more powerful." Then the federal government withdrew its deposits from the Bank of the United States. The result was a bonanza for state banks, which increased in number. The Wall Street bankers seized this opportunity to increase their power, expecting that the assets of the American business system would begin to concentrate in the nation's leading port and largest city. Lending policies were liberal in the absence of any central control, and, true to the expectations of the New Yorkers, assets began to concentrate in their banks. Efforts on the part of some western states to allow only a metallic currency proved futile. It was not until the 1860s that the federal government devised a new banking policy. Until then, Americans often had to question the worth of the notes they received in payment of goods and services.

These developments in banking were an important part of the larger American business scene of the pre–Civil War decades. They were evidence of sentiments that reflected the growing diversity of the American business

GENERAL JACKSON SLAYING THE MANY-HEADED MONSTER.

"General Jackson Slaying the Many-Headed Monster." The cartoonist here depicts the Bank of the United States as evil by portraying it as a snake. Clearly the evil bank had already appeared in many places and thus was difficult to exterminate. (Library of Congress)

system. The nation's political leadership was unable, in banking as in transportation, to develop uniform, consistent, long-range policies that brought together the divergent economic interests of western farmers, southern planters, cotton factors, nascent northern manufacturers, and Wall Street bankers. The net effect of the transportation and banking policies, however, was the promotion of speculative, optimistic business enterprise.

Tariff Controversies

The longest-running controversy in the political economy of the nineteenth century concerned the tariff. This controversy resulted in a further retreat by the federal government from intervention in the free flow of goods among markets. The retreat was the product of a concern with holding the Union together; it was a political compromise, not the result of any growing consensus regarding free-market economic theory. Federal tariff policy came to reflect not so much the needs of domestic industries as the potent political power of commercial agriculture, especially of the southern planters. As in the other areas of political economy before the Civil War, the growing size and diversity of the American business system prevented agreement in favor of planned federal intervention.

At its simplest level, the debate about the tariff raged between those Americans, led before the Civil War by the planters in the South, who were consumers of manufactured products and exporters of raw materials and foodstuffs, and those who saw the tariff as essential for the encouragement of manufacturing within the United States. The debate involved Adam Smith's idea of comparative advantage and was complicated by the fact that the tariff was the principal source of revenue for the federal government at that time. The issue of the tariff affected the outcomes of elections and helped separate Americans permanently into two political parties. By the end of the 1850s, the Democratic party, with deep southern roots, generally stood for a tariff "for revenue only," while the new Republican party argued for a protective tariff to promote industrialization.

The first piece of legislation enacted by the new Congress that met after ratification of the Constitution was the Tariff Act of July 4, 1789. It established precedents for both future legislation and heated debates on the subject. One purpose of the law was to raise revenue for the new government. The tariff generally placed a tax of 5 percent on the value of items imported to the United States (so-called ad valorem duty) and, for special items listed, specific duties regardless of their value. Boots, for instance, were taxed at fifty cents a pair. But this first legislation expressed more than the desire to raise revenue for the government. Among its declared purposes was "the encouragement and protection of manufactures." The specific rates selected for items like boots were intended to protect American producers from foreign competition. The protective features of this first tariff act were ineffective, but they marked the beginning of heated dispute that saw political leaders trying to shape American development and individual business people or their organizations seeking special favors through legislation.

Disputes over the tariff grew more vociferous and more complex as American merchants invested their capital in manufacturing. Manufacturers, when having to compete with more advanced firms abroad, especially in Great Britain, claimed the high patriotic ground of protecting the internal American market for American producers. Their opponents, usually agrarian or other business interests who bought manufactured goods, promoted Adam Smith's arguments that it was best to allow self-interest to operate through the invisible hand of the free market. Advocates of protection dismissed those arguments as "abstract and theoretical" ideas spoken by "foreign speculative writers."

The shifting needs of producers and consumers complicated tariff politics and divided business leaders. For example, the burgeoning railroad network used large quantities of iron rails. Before 1860, the British exported rails to the United States at prices American manufacturers could not match. Thus, one of the battles over tariffs involved conflict between the railroads, as consumers of rails, and the American iron makers who wanted to produce them. The iron makers, led by Abram S. Hewitt, began petitioning Congress in 1849 for protection; although they could raise money for publicity and lobbying, they could not translate those funds into the necessary popular voting strength to change legislators' behavior. The railroads struck an alliance with western and agrarian interests that sought the expansion of their regional railroad facilities and kept the duties on British rails low. As manufacturing businesses appeared west of the Appalachian Mountains, however, politicians from states like Ohio sometimes took up the protectionist cause.

The result was a welter of confusion in national politics, exceeded in emotion prior to the Civil War only by the slavery controversy. Congress passed deliberately protectionist measures in 1824, 1828, and 1832; but in 1833, after Vice President John C. Calhoun dramatically resigned and returned to his native South Carolina to lead resistance to the protectionist tariff, a compromise was reached to achieve a tariff for revenue only. When the new Republican party took power in 1861, it launched the nation on a determined course of using the tariff to help American industrialists.

LAW AND BUSINESS DEVELOPMENT

These conflicts over banking and tariff policies were due in part to the country's federal system of government, in which power is separated into different branches and levels. Groups gaining access to political power in these different areas might have very different business interests, depending on their region or local forms of business development. Within the welter of conflict, confusion, and diversity, however, two factors stand out as important for the development of American business institutions. First, there was a tendency in the federal law, especially as it was clarified by court decisions, to give individuals wide latitude in using their entrepreneurial talents. Second, there was support for the rights of individuals to gain, hold, and use property in order to earn profits. The chief exception to the second factor was the antislavery movement. The abolitionists, however, proposed not to destroy capitalism as the basis of the American economic system but, rather, to place the ownership of humans outside the boundaries of what was acceptable.

The Supreme Court and Business Development

In the first half of the nineteenth century, two great chief justices of the Supreme Court of the United States left an indelible stamp on American constitutional law and vitally affected the framework in which American business institutions developed. John Marshall, the first of these justices, served on the court from 1801 to 1836, when he was succeeded by Roger Taney, the other greatly influential justice. Marshall matured during the American Revolution and expressed the federalist viewpoint of the men who wrote the Constitution. His decisions protected federal supremacy over the states. Taney, in contrast, was embroiled in the Jacksonian politics of a later era. His decisions tended to reduce the power of government to restrict business enterprise and, thereby, to enlarge business opportunities.

Marshall's main contribution to American constitutional law was the care he took to assert the Supreme Court's right of judicial review—the Court as the final authority on the Constitution—and its independence from the legislative and executive branches of government. With respect to the development of the American political economy, three of his decisions stand out. In the case of *McCulloch* v. *Maryland* (1819) the Court ruled against the effort of the state of Maryland to impose a tax on the Second Bank of the United States, and Marshall asserted his famous dictum that the power to tax was the power to destroy. Not only did this decision protect the bank from an important source of opposition but it also provided a doctrine that allowed the federal government, if it so chose, to create instruments such as the bank to govern or promote business enterprise. The second case, *Dartmouth College* v. *Woodward* (1819), involved the question of the states' power to change corporate charters. Dartmouth College was a corporation chartered by the British crown in 1769. When New Hampshire sought to change the charter to make it a public institution, Marshall ruled that corporate charters were contracts that the states could not "impair." Rather than preventing state regulation of corporations through charter changes, however, the effect of the decision was to encourage the states routinely to place clauses in corporate charters stating that they could be changed. Such action, in effect, made the possibility of change part of the contract. *Gibbons* v. *Ogden* (1824), a case involving the commerce clause of the Constitution, which grants the federal government exclusive authority to govern business among the states, was even more significant. Aaron Ogden was a steamboat operator who enjoyed a monopoly, granted by the state of New York, to operate a ferry service across the Hudson River between New Jersey and New York City. Thomas Gibbons set up a competing line, and Ogden sued. Marshall decided the case in favor of Gibbons. A state, the chief justice said, may regulate commerce within its boundaries but not transactions that cross state lines. In such matters, national authority prevailed. This decision affirmed the commerce clause and asserted the importance of the national market over the states' more parochial desire to promote their self-interests. Marshall's ruling would have far-reaching consequences in the future, both for the development of a national market, which businesses could tap without state government restrictions, and, eventually, for allowing federal regulation of business. Neither result occurred immediately, however, as legal disputes and political wrangling lasted over a century.

Marshall's successor on the bench, Roger Taney, brought conservative convictions of hard money and respect for private property to the Court. His most significant decision for the expansion of the American business system conformed to a growing spirit supportive of free enterprise. In *Charles River Bridge Company* v. *Warren Bridge Company* (1837), the Court attacked monopolistic privilege. It was common in the earliest days of internal improvements for states to grant monopoly privileges to corporations in order to encourage private investment. The Charles River Bridge Company, which operated a toll bridge across the Charles River at Boston, had an implied monopoly privilege. When a free bridge threatened its investment, the toll bridge company sued. Taney ruled against it. The charter for the toll bridge was, he said, no insurance against competition. Taney's opponents worried that he was in effect ruling against private property rights, but such was not the case. Taney was concerned with promoting entrepreneurial opportunity. For instance, in 1848 Taney upheld the right of the states to use their power of eminent domain to take property for public use, which meant, in practice, enlarging public facilities, such as railroad rights-of-way, so as to create greater entrepreneurial opportunity. Taney's most controversial and famous decision came in 1857, when he protected the slave investments of the planter class.

One further development important for business growth occurred while Taney was chief justice. After the new government was first formed in 1776, English common law became American common law in the states, but it was left for the federal courts to formulate a national common law. In one decision, *Swift* v. *Tyson,* written by Associate Justice Joseph Story in 1842, the Court enunciated a doctrine important for the conduct of business on a national scale. The justices ruled unanimously that in civil suits the federal courts could ignore state precedents in favor of developing their own rules. This doctrine stopped state courts, which reflected local prejudices and interests, from preventing out-of-state creditors from recovering their debts. Businesses, in other words, could now enjoy a reasonable assurance of their rights when they made contracts and loans across state lines. Eventually, as we shall see, the court's decision allowed corporations to escape state governmental restrictions by settling disputes in the federal courts.

Corporation Law

Other laws passed by other levels of government also aided business. The use of the corporate form of business organization, for example, quickly became much more widespread in the United States than it was abroad, as the state governments chartered corporations to achieve public goals. Corporations were legal entities created to bring individuals together for a specified purpose. Between 1776 and 1800, some three hundred companies were incorporated by state governments. About 60 percent of these corporations were located in New England, with an additional 15 percent in New York and Pennsylvania.

Businesses organized as corporations possessed advantages not held by single-owner proprietorships or partnerships. Most important, the corporation had a life of its own under law, separate from that of its owners who held shares of stock in it. When a shareholder died, his stock could be sold to someone else without affecting the affairs of the corporation. A partnership, in contrast, had to be dissolved and reorganized whenever a partner died or withdrew from the business, a costly and time-consuming process. Moreover, incorporation sometimes granted limited liability to investors in a business, though this situation became more common in the mid- and late 1800s. That is, shareholders were not held personally responsible for the debts of a corporation and could lose only the amount of their investment in a company that failed. Partners, however, were personally responsible for any debts incurred by their partnerships and could have lost their homes and personal possessions if their businesses failed. Indeed, they might have ended up in debtors' prison! The promise of limited liability served as a strong inducement for investment in corporations. This situation made it easier for corporate businesses to raise the capital needed for their expansion, just at the time that larger markets were inducing such growth. Finally, the state charters possessed by corporations gave the business some promise of immunity from governmental interference in their affairs, and this circumstance also appealed to potential investors.

In return for these advantages and privileges, the American public initially expected corporations to serve the public interest as well as the interests of their private stockholders. The concept that the corporation would serve the public interest originated in the Middle Ages, when towns granted the privilege to incorporate had some degree of political and economic freedom from feudal lords. In England many of the chartered joint-stock companies of the 1500s and 1600s took the corporate form and were set up with the mercantilist goal of increasing that nation's strength. In colonial America, some towns, church groups, and educational organizations such as colleges and universities incorporated, thereby gaining rights of self-governance. Of the business corporations organized in the early United States, two-thirds consisted of transportation firms, toll-road companies, bridge companies, and canal businesses (banks and insurance companies constituted most of the remainder), all of which had the clear public purpose of enlarging commercial opportunities for citizens.

However, as the nineteenth century progressed, the public-service aspect of the corporation gradually dissipated in favor of policies that enhanced individual business opportunities. The corporation became simply a legal device, available to more and more Americans, to mobilize capital for business enterprise. Instead of implying public restraint, incorporation became a way to free the company from public or governmental control. The gradual adoption of general incorporation laws by the states opened these paths. Originally, an individual act of each state legislature chartered each corporation. Not only was the process cumbersome, but fears grew that the process enhanced the privileges of the wealthy. New York legislators, who desired to foster economic growth, responded in 1811 to these concerns by passing the nation's first general incorporation law for manufacturing firms. Under this law, no special legislative act was needed; certain types of companies could incorporate whenever they met a few simple requirements. Between 1811 and 1848, 228 textile manufacturers, 63 metal products firms, and 15 glassware companies incorporated under the law's administrative procedures. Other states emulated New York with general incorporation statutes. Connecticut passed a general incorporation law for all types of businesses in 1837. By 1870, nearly every state had some type of general incorporation law.

The willingness of the states to sanction the corporate form of business was evidence of the widespread desire for governmental support of business development. The passage of general incorporation laws, especially, demonstrated the eagerness of Americans to use legislation to encourage business growth. The state legislature intended the laws, at least indirectly, to augment the general prosperity.

Contract Law

The states also gradually changed contract law in the early nineteenth century in a way that fostered business development. In the more traditional society, the community had maintained its right to judge the fairness of contracts. Thus, if a jury felt that a price charged for something was higher than its objective value, the jury had the power to redress the grievance of the buyer. But by the 1840s the courts had begun moving to a new doctrine, *caveat emptor:* let the buyer beware. Under this new doctrine, the community could no longer intervene in the determination of prices. Business entrepreneurs now had the advantage in selling scarce goods, because the new court doctrine disallowed suits from purchasers claiming that prices were too high. The effect was thus to allow entrepreneurs opportunities to reap large rewards in developing the country's economy.

Property Law and Eminent Domain

American law also helped entrepreneurs to establish new ventures for the creation of wealth by removing some traditional property rights that stood in the way of growth. This form of assistance became even stronger after the 1820s as the states developed the legal doctrine, called the right of eminent domain, that permitted them to take a person's land for some public purpose.

The use of the right of eminent domain varied from state to state, but the general pattern promoted industrial development and new technologies at the expense of vested farming interests. By the 1820s, the states generally held that sovereignty included the right to eminent domain but that this right could not be exercised without some clear public purpose and without "just" or "fair" compensation. Eminent-domain powers were important both for state-promoted internal improvements, such as canals, and for private projects. States often granted private corporations, in their charters, eminent-domain powers for the construction of roads, bridges, and railroads. The use of the power of eminent domain to help manufacturers spread in the 1830s.

THE POLITICS OF GROWTH

The use of eminent domain was but one indication that public policies deliberately fostering the growth of private business opportunities were widespread in the United States in the first half of the nineteenth century. All three branches of the federal government promoted business, but governmental aid was especially pronounced at the state and local levels. Government supported private entrepreneurial action to produce burgeoning agricultural growth, an internal system of transportation and communications, the beginnings of an industrial system of production, and the spread of an urban network.

Although government at all levels tended to support business enterprise in general, particular policies were often controversial. As the United States experienced economic growth, it also witnessed the appearance of diverse economic interests, each of which made different demands on the government. Any particular government economic policy inevitably involved taxing some citizens for the benefit of others. Gallatin's hope that the "General Government" would be able to make internal improvements in the national interest proved futile in the face of the growing number of special and local interests.

As a result, the growth of American agricultural, industrial, and commercial enterprise in the pre–Civil War period took place without any overall direction or planning from the national government. Through the middle decades of the nineteenth century, Americans struggled to define more precisely the nature of their federal system and the appropriate powers of the national government versus the state governments. By midcentury this constitutional question had crystallized around the slavery issue, and that issue was settled only by a civil war. The relationship between the national government and the nation's economic development was part of the constitutional contest, and misgivings that powerful federal intervention with the intent of fostering economic growth might lead to tyranny at worst—or, at best, was inappropriate for a nation with striking regional differences—restrained the national government. Unlike the federal government, states and municipalities were not restrained from economic intervention by constitutional questions of federalism, and their political economies were often frankly interventionist and developmental.

The American political economy changed after the Civil War. Government policies fostering business opportunities continued, but as new business institutions emerged to mobilize capital and organize the flows of production and distribution, new tensions appeared in American society that were reflected in the political economy. The development of a managerial revolution fundamentally changed the American business system.

Selected Readings

Stuart Bruchey, *Roots of American Economic Growth, 1607–1861* (New York: Harper & Row, 1968), is a good description of America's political economy. Carter Goodrich, *Government Promotion of American Canals and Railroads, 1800–1890* (New York: Columbia University Press, 1960), remains a standard reference on the role that government played in the development of internal improvements. E. A. J. Johnson, "Federalism, Pluralism, and Public Policy," *Journal of Economic History* 22 (December 1962): 427–444, examines the importance of federalism in the fragmentation of government economic policy. John Lauritz Larson, " 'Bind the Republic Together': The National Union and the Struggle for a System of Internal Improvements," *Journal of American History* 74 (September 1987): 363–387, illuminates the political considerations behind the failure to adopt a national plan for internal improvements. Robert A. Lively, "The American System: A Review Article," *Business History Review* 29 (March 1955): 81–96, reviews the studies that demonstrate the great extent of government support for business development. And Carter Goodrich, "Internal Improvements Reconsidered," *Journal of Economic History* 30 (June 1970): 289–311, evaluates the scholarship that appeared after the publication of Lively's essay.

Bray Hammond, *Banks and Politics in America from the Revolution to the Civil War* (Princeton, N. J.: Princeton University Press, 1957), provides a solid overview of the politics of finance and banking. John Dobson, *Two Centuries of Tariffs* (Washington, D.C.: United States Trade Commission, 1977), is a brief, readable account of the tariff controversy and legislation. James Willard Hurst, *Law and the Conditions of Freedom in the Nineteenth-Century United States* (Madison: University of Wisconsin Press, 1967), argues that legal decisions created opportunities for business in the nineteenth century. On the changing nature of the corporation and corporate law, see James Willard Hurst, *The Legitimacy of the Business Corporation* (Charlottesville: University Press of Virginia, 1970). Finally, Donald J. Pisani, "Promotion and Regulation: Constitutionalism and the American Economy," *Journal of American History* 74 (December 1987): 740–768, includes a treasury of citations to scholarship regarding the relationships between law and economic development and regulation.

IMPORTANT EVENTS, 1855–1901

1855   Daniel McCallum of the New York & Erie Railroad issues a statement on the "general principles" of management, one of the first efforts to standardize management practices in a big business.

1869   The Union Pacific–Central Pacific, America's first transcontinental railroad, is completed.

1872   Montgomery Ward is founded.

1876   Alexander Bell first demonstrates the telephone publicly.

1880   Nonfarm jobs employ more workers than farm jobs.

1882   John D. Rockefeller founds the Standard Oil Trust.

1886   Richard Sears organizes Sears, Roebuck.

1895–1904   The first major merger movement in the United States occurs.

1898   Blacks form the North Carolina Life Insurance Company.

1900   General Electric establishes the first industrial research laboratory in the United States.

1901   J. P. Morgan organizes United States Steel, the first billion-dollar U.S. corporation.

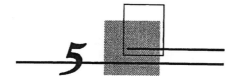

The Emergence of Big Business

On October 5, 1841, as a result of a scheduling error, two trains collided in western Massachusetts. One conductor and one passenger were killed; seventeen other passengers were injured. This accident horrified the public and provoked an investigation by the Massachusetts legislature. Clearly the great promises of overland travel by steam power also held the potential for human tragedy. In response to the accident, officials of the Western Railroad, responsible for operating trains along a 150-mile line between Massachusetts and New York State, began to define a new approach to business—what scholars would later call the managerial revolution. It was apparent that the old informal business practices had become unsuitable. Business executives now realized the necessity of having firm, exact, human control over the new railroad technology, and this realization led to a gradual unfolding of new methods of doing business. The managerial revolution that began in the railroad industry after 1841 changed forever the way business was conducted in America and began the process known as the rise of big business.

An event that occurred six decades later in New York City symbolized the second grand theme in the rise of big business in America. In 1901, J. P. Morgan, America's best-known and most powerful investment banker, purchased Carnegie Steel and combined it with other firms in the steel industry to form United States Steel, capitalized at over $1.4 billion. The establishment of the world's first billion-dollar corporation was a signal that big business had achieved a permanent institutional status on the American scene. Morgan organized United States Steel from firms that had earlier competed in the marketplace. Now those firms could cooperate; and through their combined size, control of iron ore, and efficiencies of production, Morgan expected they would dominate the nation's steel industry, reducing if not ending price competition. With the rise of giant companies such as United States Steel in the post–Civil War years, the personal management of earlier years gave way to bureaucratic management (management through organizations such as committees), as big business executives designed new corporate structures capable of controlling the vastly enlarged outputs of their companies' plants and factories.

The nature of economic decision making in the United States experienced major changes with the rise of big business. Decisions previously made through the free play of market forces came to be internalized within the new, gigantic business firms. The invisible hand of the market gave way to the visible hand of business management in ordering and coordinating parts of the American economy. In some key industries, oligopoly developed and competition lessened, as big businesses grew in importance. (In an industry characterized by oligopoly, a few companies are so large and powerful that they can influence the market, especially the prices, for their products.) In fact, the United States began developing a dual economy in which big businesses dominated the center of the economy, with smaller firms at the periphery—a trend that continued well into the twentieth century.

RAILROADS: PIONEERS IN BIG BUSINESS

By the 1850s, individual railroads had become the biggest businesses of their day. Even before the Civil War, the trunk-line railroads controlled about 500 miles of track each and employed hundreds, sometimes thousands, of workers. During the late 1860s and early 1870s, trunk-line railroads such as the New York Central and the Pennsylvania established control over through routes to the West, and entrepreneurs completed America's first transcontinental lines. Building these lines was an expensive task; the trunk-line railroads connecting the East with the Midwest were capitalized at from $17 million to $35 million each. Other pre–Civil War businesses paled by comparison. Even the largest textile mills employed fewer than a thousand people, and only a handful were capitalized at more than $1 million.

Railroads and the Problems of Growth

Railroads continued to grow in size and complexity after the Civil War. Hungry for capital before the war, they became voracious after it; for example, the Pennsylvania Railroad issued $78 million worth of securities to help finance its expansion in the 1870s. In the 1880s, Americans built an annual average of 8,000 miles of track, so that by 1890, the nation had 166,000 miles of track, and a growing number of large cities were linked by a national transportation network. The construction of more than 254,000 miles of track finished the system by 1916, but even by the end of the 1880s, an integrated, nationwide railroad network was available to farmers, manufacturers, merchants, and passengers. In 1883, railroads (not the government), responding to pressures from scientists, established the four time zones in the United States as a way of standardizing their schedules, and three years later, railroads in the Southeast joined those in other regions in adopting a standard-gauge (uniform width) track, thus allowing car interchanges and through freight traffic between different sections of the nation.

New or improved forms of communications accompanied the development of the railroad network. The relationship between the railroad and the telegraph evolved symbiotically in the 1840s and 1850s, with the telegraph serving to help managers schedule trains and with the railroads allowing the telegraph to use their rights-of-way for its poles and wires. In 1866, the nation's three leading telegraph companies merged to form Western Union, and by 1915 this company had 1.6 million miles of wire in operation. The use of the telegraph quickly spread beyond railroad executives, as business leaders across the United States used it to control their own far-flung business empires and to communicate with managers in other firms. Similarly, the telephone, first publicly demonstrated in 1876, came into use as an instrument of business in the late nineteenth and early twentieth centuries. The Bell Company, which grew to dominate the industry, had 8.3 million telephones in use by 1920, and independent companies operated an additional 5 million.

Because of their rapid expansion, railroads faced unprecedented managerial problems. They were much larger in terms of people employed, regions served, and capital invested than any other companies of the period, even the biggest textile mills. Moreover, their operations were more complex and much faster than those of other businesses. Canal traffic, for example, was much slower, and each canal boat was individually owned. Unlike railroads, canals did not need to be run as unified, coordinated systems. Decisions that affected the lives of people over ever-larger regions needed to be made quickly and accurately in the railroad business, and suitable ways of making such decisions had to be developed, as the 1841 disaster on the Western Railroad demonstrated. Even more complex were strategic problems: problems of financing expansion and problems in meeting competition. The unparalleled demands for capital by their lines meant that top railroad executives found themselves spending much of their time arranging for financing. Moreover, as America's railroad network expanded, railroad officers had to deal more and more with the question of how to anticipate and respond to the moves of their competitors.

Railroads and the Beginning of Modern Management

Clearly, business executives could not run railroads in haphazard ways and hope to survive very long. The complexities of both the operating and the strategic problems called for systematic management methods. Railroad

Women entered factory work forces in large numbers after the Civil War. (Pennsylvania Historical & Museum Commission)

executives solved their problems through the establishment of business bureaucracies, the first in American history. For the most part, railroad officers acted as innovators in setting up new management systems in response to specific business problems. To a degree, however, some railroad executives were influenced by the example of another bureaucracy, the United States Army. By the 1820s and 1830s, the army had a fairly sophisticated structure in which there was a separation between staff officers, who made strategic decisions at headquarters, and the widely scattered line officers, who carried out decisions in the field. Precise recordkeeping allowed headquarters to stay abreast of events in the field. Whether working on their own or influenced by the army, railroad executives changed the nature of business management in America.

The Western Railroad was one of the first to institute bureaucratic management practices. Both military officers and civilians had surveyed and built the Western Railroad in the 1830s, with the military engineers in the technical positions and the civilians in charge of business matters, and the system of reporting and accounting later adopted by the railroad closely resembled that used by the army. A bureaucratic structure developed, in a process hastened by the accident of 1841, that comprised three geographical divisions whose operations were coordinated by a headquarters in Springfield, Massachusetts. Each division had an assistant master of transportation,

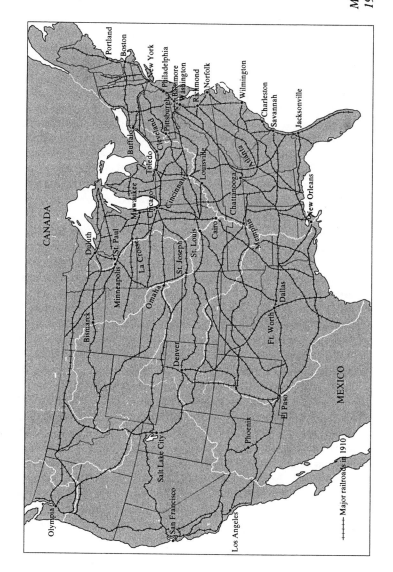

Map 5.1 *Major Railroads in 1910*

a roadmaster, and a senior mechanic, all reporting to headquarters. New regulations tried to eliminate ambiguities in daily operations by laying out definite lines of authority and responsibility. Employees were required to file frequent, detailed reports about their work for the central office.

Like the Western Railroad, the Baltimore & Ohio Railroad was aided in its development by the military. The army engineers who surveyed its route introduced army accounting and reporting techniques during the 1830s, and their military experience enabled them to advise the railroad's management on how best to define the specific duties and responsibilities of the firm's officers. Although it was important in the Baltimore & Ohio's early years, army influence became less significant in the late 1840s, when Benjamin Latrobe, the line's chief engineer and a man without military experience, organized his own bureaucratic structure to run the railroad. Latrobe set up an administrative structure that separated the responsibility for activities into two parts: a finance department to handle the internal and external financing of the line and to take care of other matters of grand strategy, and an operations department to run the trains. The operations department was separated into geographic divisions. Each geographic division, in turn, possessed three managers—one in charge of transportation (scheduling and running the trains), a second in charge of constructing and repairing the roadbed, and a third in charge of repairing machinery. All three functional managers reported to their respective functional superiors in the central office, where the railroad's general superintendent coordinated the work of the different managers.

Daniel McCallum of the New York & Erie added still further refinements to railroad management. Taking over as the Erie's general superintendent in the 1850s, he sought to cut the railroad's soaring operating expenses. In doing so, he issued "general principles" of management, which stressed the clear definition of responsibilities for each railroad officer, and drew up one of the first organization charts in the history of American business. McCallum emphasized that lines of authority should also be lines of communication within his company and required daily reports from his conductors, agents, and engineers. Monthly statements prepared from these reports allowed McCallum to assess accurately how his railroad was doing financially and proved very useful in setting its rates.

The Pennsylvania Railroad became known as the "standard railroad of the world" because of its good management. Herman Haupt, a West Point graduate, helped develop its bureaucratic organization during the 1840s and 1850s in his position as the railroad's superintendent of transportation and as its general superintendent. This structure was then more fully developed by J. Edgar Thomson, the railroad's president. In 1857, Thomson enlarged the central office of the line by separating the accounting from the treasury department and by creating a secretary's office and a legal department. Thomson also clarified relations between the head office and the railroad's operating divisions and began moving in the direction of fully demarcating the duties of its officers. In the 1860s and 1870s, he completed the task of separating the responsibilities of the executives in the central office from those of the managers in the railroad's three regional divisional offices, and he installed financial controls by which the executives in the central office could monitor and coordinate work throughout all of the divisions.

Three hallmarks of modern business management stand out in the steps taken by these railroad executives. First, they began to separate policy making from operations—that is, they began to divide strategy and tactics. Different groups of executives were in charge of overall planning and of operational details. It came to be the job of top management to plan for the future of the lines and to coordinate the functions of different parts of the lines. Second, and directly related to the first point, the railroads began to build bureaucratic organizations staffed by middle managers. These middle managers were essential to the development of the railroads as big businesses. While the top management in the central office concentrated on grand strategy, the middle management in the divisional offices attended to the operational details. These middle managers received reports from conductors, station managers, and the like, digested them, and then made their own reports to the top management, forming a chain that connected the various levels of the railroad bureaucracy. And if they were the chain, better financial reporting—the third hallmark of modern business management—was one of the major links. Railroad executives developed new types of accounting methods to hold together and analyze the work of their complex business empires. These new accounting techniques were of three types.

In *financial accounting,* railroad officers moved beyond the relatively simple profit-and-loss statements of double-entry bookkeeping to the use of operating ratios to analyze their companies' profitability, the first American business managers to do so. Operating ratios relate companies' earnings to their volume of business and even today are the basic standard by which profitability is assessed.

Before the advent of the railroad, America possessed few capital-intensive businesses. That is, for the vast majority of businesses the cost of labor, not the cost of capital, was the major expense. Railroads, with their enormous demand for funds, reversed this situation. Not surprisingly, then, railroads were the first companies to develop systematic *capital accounting.* By the 1870s, railroad executives were charging the repair and replacement of equipment against their operating revenues, an early form of depreciation.

Finally, railroad executives developed *cost accounting.* They divided their companies' costs into various categories of fixed costs (such as those of roadbeds and tracks) and variable costs (such as that of labor). Because their fixed costs were much higher than their variable costs, railroad managers sought to run as many fully laden cars as possible. And they used cost accounting to pinpoint problems in their companies' operations and to aid in setting profitable railroad rates. The men responsible for railroad accounting thus pioneered in administering prices, as opposed to allowing invisible market forces to determine them.

The adoption of bureaucratic methods by railroads marked a fundamental shift in how American business people conducted their affairs. The personal business world of the merchant gave way to the more highly organized and impersonal world of modern big business, a trend that continued in the late nineteenth and twentieth centuries and came to characterize many firms beyond the railroad industry.

Railroads and the Rise of Big Business

The changes occurring in railroad management were important not only for the railroad industry but also for a vast array of other businesses and industries in the United States. As their companies grew in size and complexity during the 1870s and 1880s, America's industrialists sought new management methods and structures by which they might control them. They found these methods and structures, in part, in their nation's railroads. The general idea of bureaucratic rather than personal management and specific methods of accounting and statistical controls spread from the railroads to other industrial ventures.

As railroads increased in size and their executives perfected new techniques of business management, the railroads became the first businesses in the United States in which the visible hand of management replaced the invisible hand of the market. What the managers of railroads decided to do became more important than market forces in determining what happened on the railroads. Here, too, the railroads provided a model for other businesses.

Railroads were important to the rise of big business in the United States in yet another way. Economic growth created new opportunities for businesses to expand the scope of their operations, and the building of America's railroad network lay at the heart of this business expansion. As we saw in Chapter 3, the transportation revolution spurred business development in the pre–Civil War years, and the completion of the national railroad system continued to power business expansion after the Civil War. The internal development of a vast land rich in natural resources was far more important than foreign trade in America's economic growth in the late nineteenth and early twentieth centuries. Central to the exploitation of these resources was the railroad, for it created a large domestic market for industrial goods. By 1890, railroads carried twice as much freight as all other forms of transportation in the United States, and railroad freight traffic more than tripled over the following twenty years.

In the late nineteenth century, most U.S. factories were powered by steam. This source of power required elaborate systems of belts to transmit energy to the machines. It was not until the twentieth century that electric power, which was easier to use in many situations, replaced steam power in most factories. (Library of Congress)

THE SPREAD OF BIG BUSINESS

The growth of the U.S. population and its concentration into cities linked by the railroads was an important change that allowed entrepreneurs to construct big businesses. The population of the United States rose from 31 million people in 1860, to 63 million in 1890, to 106 million in 1920, and most of that growth occurred in the cities. In 1860, 16 percent of Americans lived in towns or cities greater than 8,000 in population; in 1900, the proportion had risen to 33 percent. The growth in population combined with the railroad system to create unprecedented business opportunities.

Andrew Carnegie and Carnegie Steel

The story of Andrew Carnegie and the steel industry illustrates the importance of railroads and expanding cities to the rise of big business. Carnegie benefited directly from the example of the railroads in organizing his steel business; the railroads and urban construction projects provided significant markets for his steel mills. A Scottish émigré who moved with his family to Pittsburgh in 1848, Carnegie owed much of his success to what he learned in the railroad business. In Pittsburgh, Carnegie held several low-paying menial jobs, including that of bobbin boy in a textile mill, before becoming one of the city's leading telegraph operators. While he was working as a telegrapher in 1852, Carnegie was hired by Thomas Scott, the superintendent of the western division of the Pennsylvania Railroad, as his personal telegrapher and secretary. When Scott became a vice president of the line seven years later, Carnegie succeeded him as superintendent of the railroad's western division, a position he held until he resigned in 1865 to pursue other business interests.

Introduced to the world of high finance by Scott, Carnegie became an investor in numerous enterprises: a railroad sleeping-car company, an oil company, and a bridge company, among others. Benefiting from inside information about many of these enterprises from his railroad contacts, Carnegie became a very rich man. As early as 1863, Carnegie's investments were bringing him $45,000 annually, and Carnegie could tell a friend triumphantly, "I'm rich, I'm rich." Over the next decade, however, Carnegie's outlook changed. He still wanted to make money, but wealth alone could not satisfy him. "The amassing of wealth is one of the worst species of idolatry," he wrote in 1868. He wanted to create something of lasting importance, and it was this desire that led him to forsake his career in finance and enter the steel industry.

When Carnegie entered the steel business in 1872, he brought with him several important lessons from his railroad experience. He was aware of the large and expanding market for steel that railroads were creating with their requirements for track, bridges, and locomotives. In fact, one of his first major sales was steel track to the Pennsylvania Railroad. Moreover, in managing his steel company Carnegie took to heart the obsession of railroad executives with low-cost, high-volume operations. Like the railroads, steel was a capital-intensive business, and Carnegie sought always to lower the costs and increase the volume of production of his steel mills. Like the executives of the Pennsylvania Railroad, he installed sophisticated cost-accounting and recordkeeping systems in his company, systems he used both to locate production inefficiencies and to reward (or penalize) his plant managers. Take care of the costs, Carnegie believed, and the profits would take care of themselves.

Carnegie's policies proved successful. He created the largest steel company in the world and, with bankers and other American steelmakers, established the United States as the leading steel-producing nation. By 1900, America's output of pig iron had risen to 15 million tons, surpassing Great Britain's. The output of steel in the United States soared from 70,000 tons in 1870 to more than 4 million tons just twenty years later, as steel went into America's expanding railroad network and into skeletons for the buildings of the nation's growing cities. By 1900 American steel production had leaped to nearly 12 million tons, and in 1920 it reached 47 million tons. By the latter date, the United States was producing about 60 percent of the world's steel.

Big Business in Industry

Big business developed in American industry when some entrepreneurs took advantage of the new national market and improvements in technology to combine mass production with mass distribution. A few entrepreneurs did so even before the Civil War. Cyrus McCormick set up a large factory to mass-produce reapers in Chicago in 1848, and he established a nationwide network of franchised dealers to demonstrate, sell, and service them in the 1850s and 1860s. Most big businesses, however, had to await the integration of the national market by the railroad and the development of new technological processes in production. When they did develop, big businesses grew up quickly, in just one or two generations. In 1860, no single American company was valued at $10 million; by 1904, some three hundred were.

Mass Distribution

The creation of a national market through improvements in transportation and communications revolutionized the marketing and distribution of goods in the United States. Major changes occurred in wholesaling and retailing, and these alterations affected the handling of both agricultural and industrial products.

The use of the telegraph and the railroad led to significant alterations in the organization of the wheat and cotton trades. Commodity dealers using "to-arrive" contracts and working through established exchanges came to dominate both businesses during the 1850s and 1860s. (A to-arrive contract, which was paid for in cash, detailed the amount, quality, price, and future delivery date of the items bought, such as wheat or cotton. This type of contract was a step in the evolution of futures trading. The to-arrive or future-delivery contract required standard grades and language, which helped regularize and stabilize transactions by making them more routine and less subject to negotiations and disputes between different layers of merchants.) These institutions were further developed in the late nineteenth and early twentieth centuries. Futures trading grew out of the to-arrive contract, and large commodity firms and dealers supplanted the traditional merchant in the trade in agricultural goods. By 1921, some 60 percent of the cotton crop of the United States was handled by only twenty-four firms. The establishment of the New York Cotton Exchange by New York cotton merchants in 1871 regularized trading in cotton by setting up formalized channels for the necessary transactions.

Still more dramatic changes occurred in the marketing of manufactured products. Jobbers increased in importance as a link between manufacturers and retailers. Instead of working on a consignment basis as they had before the Civil War, jobbers now bought the goods they handled. And to a greater extent than in earlier times, they set up extensive purchasing networks throughout the nation and established close relations with retailers, such as country stores in farming areas and specialized retail outlets in big cities.

The jobbers soon found their control over marketing in America challenged by mass retailers, firms that saved money by purchasing directly from manufacturers and by emphasizing speed and volume, rather than high profit margins, in making their sales. Mass retailing developed first in the large cities, the biggest markets. Department stores appeared in cities across the nation, especially between 1860 and 1890: Macy's, Bloomingdale's, Marshall Field, Abraham & Strauss, Wanamaker's, Lazarus, and I. Magnin were leading examples. Big-city department stores pioneered a new way of selling. Traditional retail establishments were often dingy and crowded, and carried only a limited line of goods; haggling over prices was common, and clerks harassed customers to make purchases. In contrast, the new department stores created inviting public places filled with attractive displays of tempting merchandise. One-price shopping replaced haggling and harassment. Customers flocked to the department stores, which became a business institution symbolizing American urban life for the prosperous.

Meanwhile, for small-town and rural Americans, mail-order companies with national distribution systems appeared, capable of selling goods advertised in attractive catalogues: Montgomery Ward in 1872, and Sears, Roebuck about fifteen years later. Chain stores also began to bring the products of America's industries and farms to customers. In variety goods, beginning in 1879, F. W. Woolworth pioneered the Five-and-Ten-Cent stores that came to both small towns and urban districts. In 1905 Woolworth's sales volume exceeded $15 million, and in 1913 the Woolworth Tower graced New York's skyline as the world's tallest habitable building.

With the evolution of mass-marketers, marketing in America entered a new stage of development that would last until after World War II. The department stores, mail-order houses, and chain stores gradually replaced the older merchants, large and small, in distributing goods throughout the American economy. The merchants, from colonial times into the mid-nineteenth century, had emphasized making high profits on a low volume of business. They sold commodity products such as unbranded coffee, tea, and cloth in local, restricted markets. The coming of the railroad and the telegraph allowed the new mass-marketers to dramatically change this situation. The mass-marketers prospered by handling high volumes of transactions on which their profit margins were low. By organizing workers in centralized distribution facilities to handle a growing quantity of goods, mass-marketers were able to lower their unit costs and widen their markets. Volume and speed of sales came to dominate distribution in the increasingly urbanized American economy.

The mass-marketers also differed from the earlier merchants by selling mainly name-brand (not commodity) goods—items ranging from Uneeda crackers to Coca-Cola to the Model T Ford. And they advertised these products extensively in big-city newspapers and national magazines. The mail-order houses used catalogues sent out through the mail, as did some of the department stores and chain stores. They encouraged a consumer culture in America by making shopping an exciting and pleasurable activity, a trend that would reach maturity after 1920. Increasingly, Americans valued goods for more than their tangible attributes. Products came to be desired as symbols of a new lifestyle based on consumption.

Mass Production

Mass production evolved nearly concurrently with mass distribution, and for much the same reason. The opening of the national market enticed manufacturers into boosting their production, and the development of new technological processes made increased output feasible.

Mass production first appeared in industries processing liquids, where the application of new heat and chemical processes made it possible to turn out more product in less time with fewer workers. The use of enlarged stills, superheated steam, and catalytic cracking permitted the development of large-batch or continuous-process production in the oil, sugar, fats, and alcohol industries during the 1870s and 1880s.

Breakthroughs in machinery designs brought mass production to a number of mechanical industries at a slightly later date. The use of a machine to make cigarettes transformed that industry in 1881. By the mid-1880s, one machine made 120,000 cigarettes per day, many more than the 3,000 that could be made by hand. The adoption of similar continuous-process machinery also remade the match, soap, and grain-milling industries, bringing mass production to them in the 1880s and 1890s.

Finally, the establishment of mass production in the metalmaking and metalworking industries occurred in several steps. First, more complex and expensive machinery was installed to make and work the metal. Using new steel alloys as cutting edges on machine tools greatly sped metalworking processes. Even more important, entire plants were designed to ensure as continuous a flow as possible from the suppliers of raw materials through the various production processes to the shipment of goods to market. Inefficiencies and bottlenecks in production were eliminated. As Figure 5.1 shows, the rise in U.S. manufacturing production was dramatic.

Restructuring the Business Firm

As companies began combining mass distribution with mass production, they became very different from earlier American business firms. As we have seen, the new companies were much larger; they were the nation's

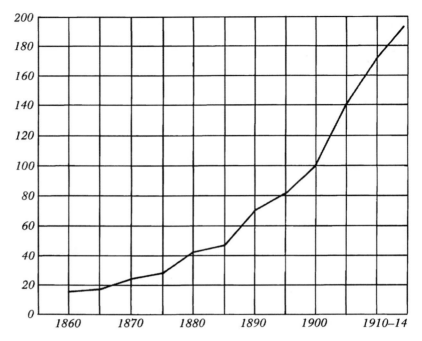

Figure 5.1 Growth of U.S. Manufacturing Production, 1860–1914
(Indexes based on the year 1899 = 100) [SOURCE: Based on data from U.S.
Bureau of the Census. *Historical Statistics of the United States, Colonial Times to 1970*, pt. 2
(Washington D.C.: U.S. Government Printing Office. 1975), p. 667.]

first industrial big businesses. In addition to their increase in size, the late-
nineteenth-century companies differed from their predecessors in other
ways.

More of them were corporations as incorporation became increasingly
widespread after the Civil War, especially among manufacturing companies. Manufacturing concerns needed to raise vast amounts of capital to
build new factories and modernize old ones. The corporate form of organization, with its promise of limited liability for investors, proved particularly
attractive to industrialists. As in earlier times, the legal aspects of the incorporation—the fact that, unlike single-owner proprietorships or partnerships, corporations did not have to be dissolved and reorganized if one
investor left the business—also appealed to late-nineteenth-century business
people. As a result, corporations accounted for three-quarters of all of
America's industrial production by 1904.

As they grew larger, the big businesses of the late nineteenth and early
twentieth centuries developed internal structures different from those of
most earlier enterprises. These structures evolved in response both to the

opportunities of the new national market and to the increasing complexity of manufacturing processes and goods. The national market offered glittering possibilities to American business people, but it also presented them with previously unknown perils. The nationwide transportation network broke down local monopolies, intensifying competition across the United States and demanding changes in business methods. At the same time, the tremendous increase in the output of their factories and the growing complexity of goods their factories produced raised additional difficulties for industrialists, giving rise especially to problems in marketing the increasing numbers of technologically sophisticated products.

Vertical Integration

In an attempt to reestablish control over their economic destinies, business executives restructured their companies. Vertical integration was one common response to the problems and opportunities of the new national market and became a hallmark of big business in America. In vertical integration a company that initially engages in only one stage of the production and sale of its goods may acquire control of its sources of raw materials and/or the making and sale of its finished products.

Andrew Carnegie's desire to control fully his costs of production while taking advantage of the opportunities offered by the national market for steel led him to construct a self-contained, vertically integrated business empire. Initially, the Carnegie Steel Company depended on other firms for many of its raw materials—iron ore, coking coal, limestone, and the like. This situation displeased Carnegie, because he thought he was being charged too much for the raw materials and, even more important, because he could not always secure enough of them during times of peak production. To lower his costs and ensure adequate supplies, Carnegie moved to control his sources of raw materials. In the 1880s and 1890s, Carnegie gained control of the Frick Coke Company (a producer of coking coal), the Mesabi iron-ore range, and numerous limestone quarries. Moreover, to carry the raw materials to his smelters near Pittsburgh, Carnegie acquired a fleet of Great Lakes ore ships and put together a railroad system of about a thousand miles of track. He also took steps to control the making and sale of finished steel products. In the 1890s, Carnegie began production of a wider variety of finished goods than in early times, and he set up his own sales offices in major cities in the United States and Canada. Figure 5.2 illustrates vertical integration at Carnegie Steel.

The development of vertical integration at Carnegie Steel and other steel companies marked a fundamental change in the way the iron and steel industry was organized. As we saw in Chapter 3, the pre–Civil War iron industry was mainly unintegrated: different companies controlled different stages of the manufacturing process and depended heavily on independent merchants to move their products from stage to stage. As men like Carnegie

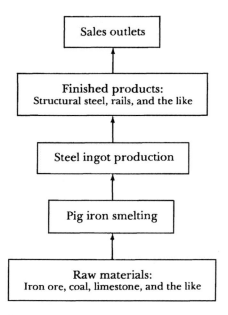

Figure 5.2   Vertical Integration at Carnegie Steel

reorganized the industry, however, the merchants became much less important, and giant companies emerged that coordinated all the steps in making and selling goods. Market forces began giving way to managerial decisions as the controlling factors in the American iron and steel industry. Vertical integration, as at Carnegie Steel, was a major method by which business owners sought to exploit new marketing opportunities in the late nineteenth century. Business executives used vertical integration to try to insulate their firms from market forces and to keep all the profits within one company.

Some entrepreneurs also found in vertical integration a solution to problems they encountered in trying to sell their goods through America's network of merchants. Business people who used continuous-process machinery in their factories found that the nation's established network of jobbers and retailers could not adequately market the rapidly growing output of their plants, for they proved incapable of handling the impact of the explosive growth rate of America's post–Civil War factories. As a consequence, manufacturers in some fields—matches, cigarettes, flour, and canned products—moved, almost of necessity, to set up their own nationwide marketing outlets. Producers of perishable goods—beer, meat, and citrus fruits—also set up their own sales systems when the nation's established marketers either refused to handle their goods or proved unable to do so. Finally, the manufacturers of technologically sophisticated products ranging from sewing machines to elevators moved into sales because jobbers could not adequately demonstrate, install, or service the goods. A variety of reasons, then, led industrialists to link manufacturing with sales through vertical integration.

Horizontal Integration

Horizontal integration provided a second mechanism by which industrialists tried to restructure their companies. In horizontal integration, a number of companies combined forces to control one step in the production or sale of their products. As in vertical integration, the goal of horizontal integration was to bring order to an unstable, highly competitive business situation. Horizontal integration sought to lessen competition, thus reducing the risks to the capital invested in America's new industrial enterprises. John D. Rockefeller's Standard Oil Company was a classic example of horizontal integration, as Rockefeller and other oil magnates sought to control their rapidly expanding industry.

The growth of the oil industry, like that of the steel industry, was explosive. In Pennsylvania in 1859, E. L. Drake sank the first commercial oil well in America. This strike led to oil booms throughout the East and Midwest during the late nineteenth century, as Americans substituted kerosene for whale oil and candles. Oil discoveries in Oklahoma, Texas, and California in the 1890s and early 1900s further expanded the petroleum industry. In the early twentieth century, oil began gradually supplanting coal as a source of energy for railroad locomotives and some industrial plants. And with the development of the automobile, gasoline emerged as the major oil product in the 1910s and later. Spurred by the growth of new markets, crude-oil production in the United States rose from 5 million barrels in 1870 to 64 million barrels in 1900, and to 378 million barrels in 1919.

Rockefeller was a pioneer in the oil industry. Born in Richford, New York, in 1839, he had moved to Cleveland, Ohio, by the time he was sixteen years old. There he entered the business world as a bookkeeper in the firm of a commission merchant, earning a salary of fifty cents per day. Using his own savings and a gift from his father, Rockefeller became a jobber of hay, grain, and meat in 1859. Rockefeller took his work very seriously. "Don't be a good fellow," he later warned people. "It is my firm conviction that every downfall is traceable directly or indirectly to the victim's goodfellowship, his good cheer among his friends." Not surprisingly, he was viewed as solemn and humorless. "Oh, young Rockefeller—he's a stick!" noted the son of the Cleveland merchant who first hired Rockefeller. But Rockefeller was successful, and he soon used the earnings made in trade to go into the oil business.

Rockefeller entered oil refining in 1863, just four years after Drake drilled his well. By 1867, he owned a large refinery in the Cleveland area

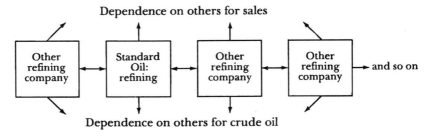

Figure 5.3   Horizontal Integration at Standard Oil

and purchased oil for it from well-owners in Pennsylvania and other eastern states. Needing capital for further growth, he incorporated his company in 1870 as the Standard Oil Company. The anticipated expansion occurred. However, oil refining was a very competitive industry, and Rockefeller and his rivals soon found themselves battling fiercely over the national market for kerosene and other oil products. No one really wanted to engage in this competition, which threatened to disrupt operations and lower profits.

To lessen competition, the owners of the Standard Oil Company and forty other oil-refining companies entered into a trust agreement in 1882. They turned over the common stock in their companies to nine trustees. The nine trustees then operated the companies in ways that avoided competition among them. In return for the stock in their original companies, the shareholders received trust certificates, and each year the nine trustees distributed what they thought were equitable shares in the earnings of the refining companies to the shareholders. By the 1890s, Standard Oil controlled more than 90 percent of the petroleum refining capacity of the United States. Figure 5.3 illustrates horizontal integration at Standard Oil.

Additional changes soon took place in Standard's structure. In 1889, New Jersey amended its incorporation law to become the first state allowing one company to own stock in another company—to become a "holding company." Many large corporations took advantage of this provision to become holding companies by incorporating in New Jersey. Standard Oil was one of these firms. In 1899, Standard incorporated under New Jersey law and purchased the stock of the other members of the trust. In the early 1900s, Standard emerged as a single operating company. Its management sold or closed inefficient plants and rationalized the work of the corporation by uniting offices, such as sales offices, previously operated separately. Once horizontally integrated, Standard turned to vertical integration. In the 1880s, Standard had begun securing its own supplies of crude at a reasonable cost. Somewhat later, Standard began operating long-distance pipelines to transport its oil and sales outlets to market it.

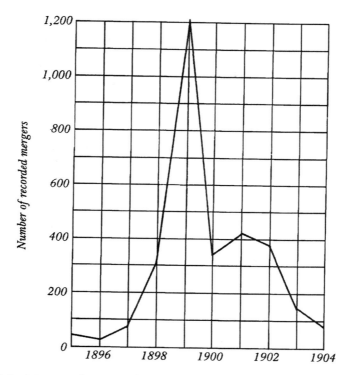

Figure 5.4 Mergers in Manufacturing and Mining in the United States. 1895–1904 [SOURCE: Based on data from U.S. Bureau of the Census, *Historical Statistics of the United States, Colonial Times to 1970*, pt. 2 (Washington, D.C.: U.S. Government Printing Office. 1975), p. 914.]

America's First Merger Wave

Business integration, both vertical and horizontal, took place more through mergers of formerly independent companies than through the growth of individual companies. From the 1880s on, mergers became increasingly common, culminating in America's first major merger movement during the years 1895 through 1904. (See Figure 5.4.) More than 2,000 firms disappeared into consolidations in this period. Truly gigantic combinations resulted. When the United States Steel Corporation was formed in 1901 by the purchase of Carnegie Steel and the merger with competing steel firms, United States Steel consisted of 213 different manufacturing establishments, 41 mines, more than 1,000 miles of railroad track, and 112 ore ships. The company controlled 43 percent of the pig-iron capacity and 60 percent of the steel-making capacity in the United States.

There were many motives for these mergers. A search for efficiency and predictability in all facets of his business led Carnegie into vertical integration, just as the need to demonstrate and service new, technologically sophisticated products led other manufacturers to integrate vertically, sometimes by merging with established firms. However, a quest for market control lay behind many mergers. In fact, in half of the mergers, the consolidations absorbed more than 40 percent of the manufacturing capacity of their industries, and in a third, more than 70 percent of that capacity. Manufacturers in capital-intensive, mass-production fields were especially eager to form consolidations to escape the severe price competition they faced during the depression years of the mid-1890s. Their companies had expanded rapidly in the 1880s and, as a result of their extensive capital investments, had high fixed charges. To cover those charges, manufacturers operated their plants at full capacity. However, since their competitors were doing the same and manufacturing companies in any given field were usually evenly matched, the result during the depression years was rampant competition, overproduction, and low prices. It was the desire to dampen this competition and control markets that led to the merger wave.

Events in the telephone industry illustrate the complexity of the motives often involved in mergers and integration. Formed in 1877, American Bell originally relied upon agent licenses and equipment leasing for its revenues, but competition with Western Union quickly led Bell to extend financial support to, and administrative control over, its agents. In 1879, Western Union and Bell agreed not to compete (Western Union abandoned voice communications, and Bell left telegraphy), but despite the lessened competition, integration continued at Bell. The need to centralize switching centers and long-distance services, combined with a key business decision in 1882 favoring consolidation, spurred both vertical and horizontal integration throughout the 1880s. When its patent monopoly expired in 1894, American Bell faced renewed competition and responded with a reinvigorated integration drive. A variety of motives in different time periods thus interacted to speed consolidation and integration at American Bell.

The results of the merger movement soon became apparent to Americans in the form of lessened price competition in many industries. Whereas in the depression years of the mid-1890s there had been severe price competition as production outran demand, the recession year of 1907 brought fewer instances of price cuts, even though production again surpassed demand. In the steel and paper industries, for example, price reductions were few, for these industries had come to be dominated by combinations formed during the merger movement: United States Steel and the International Paper Company. Those companies exercised price leadership over their industries, significantly dampening price cuts.

Not all mergers were successful, however. Only about half of the mergers lasted for more than a few years. The list of failed mergers was long indeed:

American Bicycle, National Starch, U.S. Leather, American Glue, National Salt, National Cordage, United Button, and a host of others. Two elements were often present in those mergers that succeeded. First, the combination achieved production efficiencies as great as or greater than those of the firms remaining outside the merger. Second, the consolidation erected nonprice barriers to entry into its industry. For instance, United States Steel bought up much of the high-grade iron ore in the United States during the opening decade of the twentieth century, making it difficult for any new firm to compete with it on equal terms.

The Persistence of Small Businesses

The rise of big business was a trend limited to some industries, not suddenly a fact of life that encompassed all of the American economy. Small firms persisted as an important part of America's business system. In farming, retail sales, and service industries, small firms remained the norm. Even in manufacturing, small businesses continued as viable entities. In 1914, a third of America's industrial workforce found employment with firms of 100 or fewer laborers. More than half still worked for companies employing fewer than 250 workers. Some 54,000 little businesses with 6 to 20 workers remained in manufacturing on the eve of World War I.

Those small manufacturing firms that survived and prospered followed several strategies. In some fields—such as leather working, furniture making, and lumber milling—few economies of scale existed and big businesses did not develop. In the manufacturing industries where big firms emerged, successful small industrialists adapted by providing goods and services in smaller, "niche" markets—markets for products not susceptible to efficiencies of vertical integration. These firms did not mass-produce large quantities of homogeneous goods for American consumers. Rather, they turned out smaller quantities of products for various specialized audiences. This response by smaller industrialists to the growth of big manufacturing firms lasted throughout the twentieth century as small entrepreneurs avoided competing head-on against big companies, instead finding ways to differentiate their products from those turned out by large firms. By making specialty goods or by providing special services, small firms were frequently able to prosper. Small manufacturing firms were especially successful when they employed intelligent, innovative workforces able to use advanced, flexible manufacturing techniques.

The evolution of the textile industry provides a good example of how small manufacturing firms could coexist with larger companies. In New England a handful of large factories at Waltham, Lowell, and other locations employed large numbers of unskilled workers to turn out standardized goods for the mass market. The mills were fully integrated, combining spinning, weaving, and printing of fabrics under one roof. In Philadelphia a very different system developed. There hundreds of entrepreneurs, many of whom had been skilled artisans, set up small companies employing skilled workers to make a wide range of textiles for seasonal and niche markets. In 1850, 326 Philadelphia firms with 12,400 workers, two-thirds of which had 25 or fewer, coexisted with the much larger New England mills. By the early 1880s, 849 textile companies in Philadelphia employed 55,000 workers, the largest such concentration of firms and workers in the nation. In 1907, 728 Philadelphia textile firms were capitalized at a total of $100 million and employed 60,000 workers, and additional textile companies operated in Philadelphia's suburbs.

The Philadelphia firms prospered well into the twentieth century by stressing specialization and flexibility in production and marketing. Their owners looked not to manufacture standardized goods for mass markets but, rather, to the niches provided by changing seasons and fashions. Few were fully integrated. Instead, most specialized in just one of the steps involved in making textiles, which they did very well, using the most modern machinery and employing skilled workers, usually men at high wages. The location of spinners, weavers, and printers near each other in one city made integration unnecessary. With skilled workers and up-to-date equipment, the Philadelphia firms were able to respond rapidly as market demands, seasonal or long-term, changed. In 1910, for example, a carpet maker celebrated its twenty-fifth anniversary by bringing out its 25,000th pattern. These were profitable companies. In 1890, a typical year, Philadelphia textile companies earned an average 23 percent return on their capital; those in New England earned only 6 percent.

A similar story developed in Pittsburgh's iron and steel industries. Carnegie Steel (and later United States Steel) came to dominate important segments of the steel industry there. Using large-batch production methods, they turned out vast quantities of homogeneous steel products, such as rails and structural steel. Nonetheless, many smaller independent iron and steel mills continued to thrive. In 1901 forty remained, with a combined production capacity considerably larger than that of United States Steel. In 1920, fully three-quarters of the independent mills in existence two decades before were still doing business.

The independent Pittsburgh mills survived and prospered by specializing. Rather than compete directly with Carnegie Steel, most coexisted with the larger firm by turning out products for niche markets, in a manner similar to the way Philadelphia's textile makers coexisted with the larger New England firms. Oliver and Phillips, for instance, went into the making of nuts and bolts, wagon hardware, and barbed wire; and Vesuvius Iron emphasized producing bar and sheet iron, rods, hoops, and nails.

Common themes ran through the successes of those small companies—in textiles, iron and steel, and other fields—which proved capable of coexisting with big businesses. Their owners adopted a growth strategy that would remain one of the keys to success in small business into the late twentieth century: they developed specialty products that they then sold in niche markets. To make this growth strategy work, the firms usually adopted or developed the most advanced production technologies of the day. Far from being backward workshops, the small companies were among the most advanced industrial establishments of the nineteenth century. Running the companies were managers deeply committed to their success. Most of the companies were operated as family enterprises, devoid of managerial hierarchies. A sense of personal satisfaction, almost a sense of craftsmanship, remained an animating force for workers and owners. In a letter to his wife in 1908, the president of a small steel company captured this feeling when he observed, "We have had hard times to bear, but surely we should not care to have our lives easy, for there would be no accomplishment, no development."

The New Corporate Business System

As their companies grew in size and became fully integrated enterprises, the decisions of the managers of big businesses played ever-larger roles in determining how the business system of the United States functioned. In those parts of the nation's industrial economy dominated by big businesses, the visible hand of management replaced the invisible hand of market forces in controlling production and distribution of industrial goods and services. Decisions once made in thousands of independent market transactions became concentrated in the hands of managers of relatively few big businesses. By the opening decade of the twentieth century, in fact, key segments of U.S. industry were characterized by oligopoly. That is, in some fields of manufacturing, a handful of companies dominated their markets. Oligopoly was particularly characteristic of the metal, oil, rubber, chemical, tobacco processing, electrical machinery, transportation equipment, and sugar refining industries. As early as 1904, a few major companies controlled at least half the output of seventy-eight industries in the United States. During the opening decade of the twentieth century, the structure of much of American industry assumed its modern form: oligopolist and concentrated.

The emergence of big businesses in some fields, combined with the vigorous persistence of small businesses in other fields, illustrates a key fact about America's business system in this period: it was fast becoming a dual system. The big businesses, "center firms," were at the center of the nation's new business system. Center firms were capital-intensive companies, such as Standard Oil and Carnegie Steel. They often used continuous-processing or large-batch production methods to achieve important economies of scale. Center firms were also usually vertically or horizontally integrated (or both) and frequently exercised some degree of control over their markets. As large ventures in manufacturing, communications, and transportation, the center firms were of tremendous importance to America's emergent industrial economy; the fortunes of a single center firm often had a ripple effect on the nation's economy as a whole. "Peripheral firms," on the other hand, were smaller, for no production efficiencies resulted from increasing their scale of production. They were likely to be labor-intensive rather than capital-intensive and usually had no control over their markets. Small businesses in the aggregate remained very important to the American economy, but what happened to any single peripheral firm had little impact upon the national economy.

Business Executives Begin Organized Research and Development

A major distinction between center firms and peripheral firms lay in their degree of commitment to industrial research. Center firms set up the first U.S. industrial research laboratories during the opening two decades of the twentieth century. Company executives tended to engage in research and development, which had high fixed costs and represented large capital investment, to ensure that their factories would have a stream of goods to produce in the future. Only in this way, they reasoned, could high-volume production be maintained and burdensome fixed charges be paid off. Peripheral firms, by contrast, typically lacked both the incentives and the resources for setting up research laboratories.

There was, however, another important reason for the establishment of research laboratories by the large center firms: center firms used the new products, processes, and patents developed by their laboratories to maintain or increase their market share. Just as many mergers resulted from attempts to control markets, so did the creation of research laboratories. General Electric set up the first such laboratory in 1900 to advance the technology that would maintain the company's domination of the U.S. electric lighting market. Only after the laboratory successfully fended off threats to the company's markets through the development of the ductile-tungsten light filament in 1911 was it allowed to move on to a broader range of projects. Similarly, American Bell set up its research laboratory in 1911 to increase the company's lead in telephone communications through the development of an electronic repeater. The same product, the company's executives hoped, would allow their firm to control radio technology.

Corporate research laboratories took root in the United States between 1900 and 1920. Counting only the 18 companies employing the greatest numbers of scientists, the number of Ph.Ds employed by industry rose from 4 in 1900 to 172 twenty years later. In 1900, only a tenth of the new physics Ph.Ds trained in the United States chose industrial employment; twenty years later, a fifth did. By 1920, some 300 American companies claimed to have industrial research laboratories. Nearly all of these were large center firms: Standard Oil of Indiana, DuPont, Kodak, General Motors, B. F. Goodrich, and the like. Almost none of the small peripheral firms had

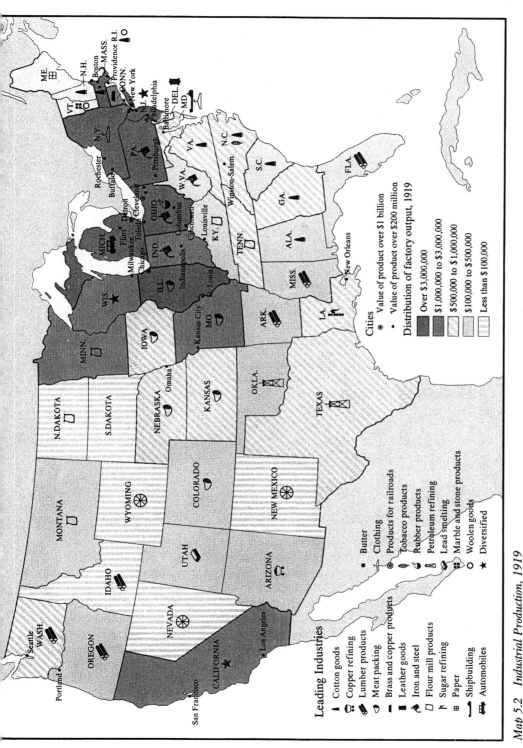

Map 5.2 *Industrial Production, 1919*

(SOURCE: © American Heritage Publishing Co., Inc., *American Heritage Pictorial Atlas of United States History*; data from U.S. Bureau of the Census, *Fourteenth Census of the United States, 1920, Vol. 9: Manufacturing* [Washington, D.C.: U.S. Government Printing Office, 1921].)

By the early twentieth century a growing number of large industrial companies were opening research laboratories—such as this DuPont lab around 1900—as a way of ensuring the development of new products. (Hagley Museum and Library)

such laboratories. Nonetheless, smaller enterprises continued to make many product innovations well into the twentieth century.

SERVICE INDUSTRIES: POST–CIVIL WAR EXPANSION

The growth of the national market and the emergence of giant firms that manufactured for and sold to that market provided new entrepreneurial opportunities for service businesses, companies that provided services for other businesses. Large capital-intensive ventures required help in selling their stocks and bonds, insuring their properties, and learning about market conditions. Specialized businesses that could perform these functions—banks, insurance companies, and credit-rating agencies—matured rapidly after the Civil War and continued to develop in importance during the twentieth century.

Banking and Financial Institutions

First started as independent businesses in the late eighteenth and early nineteenth centuries, banks continued to expand in the late nineteenth century. The number of commercial banks (banks lending money to farms and businesses) rose from about 2,000 in 1860 to nearly 25,000 by 1910. Unlike many European nations, America possessed a decentralized banking system, with no central bank. The expansion of commercial banks was paralleled by that of other types of financial institutions. The 149 savings banks in existence in 1860 grew to nearly 2,500 by 1900, a sixteenfold increase. Investment banking, through which businesses sold stocks and bonds, attained maturity in the late nineteenth and early twentieth centuries. Established stock exchanges like the New York Stock Exchange broadened their range of interests as time progressed. First developed to serve the voracious capital needs of railroads in the mid-nineteenth century, they began to handle industrial securities (stocks and bonds) in the 1890s. Insurance companies also grew in numbers and significance. The United States possessed 81 general insurance companies in 1860 but almost 500 by 1900. The growth in numbers of life insurance companies was even more rapid. Reaching out to new customers by offering new kinds of policies, they increased from 24 in 1860 to more than 1,700 by 1900.

As an increasing number of businesses began to operate on a national scale, credit-rating companies increased in importance. In the new national market, business managers were simply unable to gather their own information about companies across the country, and they began to rely on specialized credit-rating agencies for their information. These agencies advised companies about the creditworthiness of other firms, thus allowing the companies to reach rational decisions on whether or not to extend credit or make loans to those firms. Two companies came to dominate this field after the Civil War. By 1880, the credit-rating agency run by R. G. Dun had 69 branch offices in major cities and employed 10,000 credit investigators. The Bradstreet Agency, its main competitor, also operated throughout the nation. These two firms later merged to form Dun and Bradstreet and continued to supply credit information.

Commercial banks, savings banks, investment banks, stock exchanges, insurance companies, and credit-rating firms played important roles in America's expanding business system by helping to channel funds from the general public to the nation's rapidly growing railroads and industrial companies. Nor did the financial intermediaries simply provide capital for new railroad and industrial ventures; they often also played active roles in managing them.

Investment Bankers and Corporate Management: The House of Morgan

The House of Morgan was the most important but far from the only investment banking house that grew up to supply the tremendous capital needs of America's rapidly expanding railroads and industrial enterprises. As it did so, the House of Morgan became involved in the management of some of the companies it funded as a way of safeguarding its investments in them.

Junius Morgan founded what would become the world's leading investment banking house in the mid-nineteenth century. Of mercantile New England background (and the Morgans always thought of themselves as *merchant*-bankers), Morgan moved to London in 1854 to become a partner in a well-established private banking house. He built up this establishment as one of London's major private bankers, nearly on a par with the Barings and Rothchilds. In the years after the Civil War, Junius' son, the fabled J. P. Morgan, began private banking operations in New York City, making his "house," as the firm was called informally, a power of national importance by the 1880s and 1890s. Through personal ties, these houses, both in London and in New York, were allied with banking houses in Philadelphia and Paris as well. The growing Morgan empire financed loans for the British, American, and continental European governments. Ultimately, its financing of American railroads moved the House of Morgan ahead of other private bankers to become the undisputed leader in world finance.

In the 1890s, the investment banking firm controlled by J. P. Morgan (Junius died in 1890) became deeply involved with the railroads whose debts it funded, to the extent that Morgan's efforts to end competition between these railroads became known as the "Morganization" of the railroad business. A severe depression in the middle of the 1890s left many railroads in bankruptcy and threatened many others with failure. Morgan stepped in to consolidate and reorganize the lines in an attempt to make them profitable again and thus insure his own investments. Moreover, Morgan envisioned a risk-free, harmoniously operating business system. Chaotic competition, railroad rate-cutting, and business failures had no place in Morgan's scheme, and he tried to eliminate them.

The involvement of investment bankers like Morgan in the affairs of railroads set the stage for their engagement in the activities of industrial companies in the opening decades of the twentieth century. The House of Morgan itself became involved in financing for United States Steel, General Electric, International Harvester, and other ventures. In return for their help in arranging financing for industrial enterprise, investment bankers demanded and received seats on boards of directors and could thus oversee and influence the decisions of corporate management. By 1913, just four investment banks—J. P. Morgan & Company, the National City Bank, the First National Bank, and the Bankers' Guaranty Trust Company—held 118 seats on the boards of directors of 34 banks and trust companies, 35 seats in 10 insurance companies, and 193 seats in 68 nonfinancial firms. Such concentration of influence probably lessened competition in American industry and may also have dampened innovation. Indeed, investment bankers were generally not risk-takers. They wanted steady returns from their investments and so were most interested in order and stability, not new departures. Thus, for example, the House of Morgan refused to fund General Motors, then a fledgling company.

THE NEW CONDUCT OF BUSINESS

As business firms grew in size and complexity, business executives developed new management methods and structures to control their operations. As we have seen, railroads led the way in substituting bureaucratic for personal management. Other businesses soon followed. Companies became too large and complex to be managed as one-man shows. The systematic division of authority became increasingly urgent.

Taylorism: Scientific Management

Management attempts to control industrial firms in new ways were often initially apparent at the plant level. A method that came to be known as scientific management or Taylorism, after its creator, Frederick Taylor, offered new methods of organizing work processes and controlling workforces in factories.

Taylor attended Exeter Academy in New Hampshire as a young man, but he soon left to go to work at the Enterprise Hydraulic Company and later at Midvale Steel as a machinist and engineer. Even as a boy, Taylor was interested in efficiency, experimenting with the most efficient strides when hiking and the most efficient strokes when playing croquet. Appalled by the chaotic situations he found at his workplaces in the 1870s and 1880s, Taylor set out to make them orderly and efficient. Using a stopwatch, he measured the time it took workers to accomplish tasks on the factory floor. He tried to redesign the jobs so that they might be done more efficiently.

Taylor soon moved beyond examining individual tasks to redesigning the physical layout and the flow of work in entire factories. In doing so, he stressed three factors: the logical positioning of machinery in a plant to move material from point to point in an efficient fashion, accompanied by the minute subdivision of labor; strict recordkeeping to speed the flow of materials through the factory; and detailed internal cost accounting to keep track of exactly what went on in a plant. Taylor spread his ideas through talks and books and by working as one of America's first management consultants. His concepts were well known throughout the United States and the world by the early 1900s. Few companies adopted all of Taylor's ideas, but many, especially in the metalmaking and metalworking industries, used some of them.

Through scientific management, plant managers were at least partly successful in removing bottlenecks standing in the way of mass production.

As scientific-management practices spread, workers correspondingly lost to managers the control they once had over the pace and nature of their work.

Company Management

More far-reaching than changes at the level of the individual plant were changes in the methods by which entire companies were run. The most widespread managerial change in the late nineteenth century, a change especially common among big manufacturing businesses, was the movement toward the establishment of strong central offices (or corporate offices, as they might be called today) to oversee the operations of the company. These head offices were departmentalized by function. Different people or, more commonly, different committees in the headquarters were in charge of handling different functions for a company. There were typically separate committees in the head office for production, transportation, and sales. No single person tried to take charge of all those functions. At Standard Oil Company, which set up a functionally departmentalized central office in 1886, the head office consisted of committees dealing with domestic commerce, foreign trade, containers for oil, manufacturing (refining), and transportation. An executive committee composed of Standard's top officers coordinated the work of these different committees.

This type of management was less personal than that of the past. The large industrial enterprises of the 1880s and 1890s required more administrators to run them than even the largest mercantile concerns of fifty years before. A major consequence of this requirement was the sudden growth in the numbers and importance of middle managers after the Civil War. By the opening years of the twentieth century, Singer Sewing Machine, for example, had 1,700 branch offices across the United States staffed by middle managers. No longer could most business executives personally know their customers, employees, and fellow managers. The personal business world of the merchant had given way to the organized and bureaucratic business world of the railroad magnate and industrialist.

Business Cooperation

Just as business executives sought to rationalize the administration of their individual companies, their desires for profits and stability in a rapidly changing economic environment led them to try to restructure relations with one another. They sought to replace competition with cooperation as they grappled with the effects of the new national market on their businesses. Pools and trade associations were the major tools by which business executives sought to achieve industrial peace.

As in so many other areas, railroads pointed the way. From the point of view of railroad officials, America's railroad system was overbuilt by the late nineteenth century. There was not enough traffic for all of the lines to remain profitable. To attract more traffic, weak railroads often lowered their rates, setting off rate wars that could injure the profits of all of the lines, even the strong ones. This situation first appeared during the depression years in the mid-1870s, and it occurred again as traffic fell off during a recession in the mid-1880s. In 1887, an extreme example took place. Because of a rate war between the Southern Pacific and Santa Fe railroads that year, passengers could travel from Texas to California for only one dollar! To dampen competition, railroad managers resorted to a form of cooperation called pooling.

Albert Fink of the Louisville & Nashville Railroad led the attempts to set up pools. In 1875, Fink established the Southern Railway and Steamship Association to control traffic in the Southeast. Fink later helped set up regional pools in the Northeast and trans-Mississippi West. Each of these pools tried to limit competition by fixing uniform railroad rates, establishing standard freight categories, and setting freight quotas for member lines. But none of these pools worked as well as their founders had hoped, for they lacked the force of law. No railroad could be required to join or remain in a pool. Since there was almost always some railroad willing to stay out of or withdraw from a pool and cut its rates to win short-term increases in traffic, the pools did not end the rate wars.

Business executives in a wide variety of fields emulated railroad officers in seeking to limit competition through the formation of pools. As in the case of railroads, however, these pools did not usually achieve their goals. In most instances, someone was willing to break ranks and cut prices. In the steel industry, for example, Carnegie joined pools just long enough to gain information about his competitors. He then left the pools and, using the information obtained from them, engaged in all-out competition with their members.

Failing in their efforts to create workable pools, many business executives turned to the establishment of trade associations as a way of regulating or limiting competition. Trade associations consisted (and still consist) of firms from the same or different industries working together for common purposes. Some early trade associations set prices and production or sales quotas for member companies. More commonly, trade associations tried to limit competition in indirect ways, by spreading market information through newsletters, for instance. Active at both the regional and national levels, trade associations lobbied politicians vigorously for business interests. A few, most notably the National Association of Manufacturers, worked with officials of the federal government to expand markets for U.S. products overseas.

While trade associations were more successful than pools in achieving some goals, trade associations, like pools, could not stop competition between member companies. As we have seen, it was in part the failure of business executives to limit competition through cooperation that led them to try to create fully integrated business firms. Only through the establishment of integrated business empires, many business executives thought, could they take advantage of the riches offered by the national market while avoiding competition with other companies.

THE CHARACTER OF THE BUSINESS LEADER

For many late-nineteenth-century Americans, the leaders at the helm of the integrated business empires were heroic figures—industrial leaders to be admired for their fame and power, not simply for the wealth they had acquired. Popular magazines of the day and widely read novels depicted business leaders as achieving success by virtue of their strong-willed individualism. The ideology of individualism in business, which had become entrenched in the American mind during the pre–Civil War years, continued to dominate, even as business became more bureaucratic and impersonal.

Social and Economic Backgrounds

The 135 pieces of fiction written by Horatio Alger were among the most widely read works of the era. All of these books have the same basic plot. A young man, usually an obscure person of lower-class origins, moves from the farm to the big city to seek his fortune. There he gets ahead through hard work, a morally upright life, and luck (such as rescuing the boss's daughter from a fire). In short, through a combination of "pluck and luck" an individual could, according to Alger, rise from "rags to riches." Writers for popular magazines put forward essentially the same ideas; most described business leaders as farm boys from lower- or middle-class backgrounds.

What the writers described and what the American readers wanted to believe was not reality, however. Only a few business leaders rose from rags to riches. Andrew Carnegie, who came to the United States as a penniless immigrant, was the exception, not the rule. More than two-thirds of America's business leaders of the late nineteenth and early twentieth centuries had fathers who were businessmen or professional men. Most of the men who led the business system came from middle-class or upper-class families and were well educated by the standards of their day. Few were immigrants or the sons of immigrants. Moreover, most spent all of their lives in large cities; few had grown up on farms. The heads of the large center firms in America's emerging industrial business system were white and male.

Women found white-collar positions as clerical workers, department store buyers, and saleswomen, and took blue-collar jobs in such sex-segregated industries as textiles and clothing production, bookbinding, hatmaking, and tobacco and food processing. As in earlier times, most of those few

Lydia Pinkham's face, which appeared in advertisements and on boxes containing her patent medicine, was one of the most widely distributed images in the United States. Patent medicine companies advertised more heavily than any other type of firm before the Progressive Era. (The Schlesinger Library, Radcliffe College)

women who made it to the top as managers succeeded in family businesses. Kate Gleason, for instance, began her career in her father's manufacturing firm. Gleason learned the trade of machinist and worked for the company as a saleswoman. After a falling-out with her father and brothers in 1913 over business matters, she struck out on her own, first as the president of the First National Bank of East Rochester and later in a variety of businesses, including housing construction. Like many men heading peripheral firms, some women exploited markets ignored by large center companies. Lydia Pinkham succeeded by developing a tonic designed to cure "the ills of women" and marketing it nationally.

The expansion of large businesses with many levels of management opened up new opportunities for women as secretaries, previously a male preserve. Between 1890 and 1930, the share of all female workers in the clerical sector rose from 4 percent to 21 percent (the proportion of all employed men in the clerical sector increased from 3 percent to 6 percent). The clerical sector was 50 percent female by 1930, up from only 15 percent in 1890. Most of the women who joined the clerical ranks had just finished high school and in earlier years would have gone into factory or retail work if they sought employment at all. Now they looked for office work in surroundings more pleasing than factories.

The nature of clerical work changed in the late nineteenth century, to the detriment of women. Previously, clerks were trusted employees with diverse tasks, and secretaries were close to company presidents. Both clerks and secretaries knew all of the operations of their firms and could hope for promotion to senior management ranks. But a revolution in office communications altered this situation. When typewriters and other types of office machinery came into common use beginning in the 1870s, the women hired to operate them were not given knowledge of their firms' overall operations. Instead, they were considered specialized office workers with little chance for advancement. Typists, stenographers, and office-machine operators were hired directly out of high school, and these occupations quickly became feminized.

The system of racial segregation that characterized American society provided few business opportunities for black Americans. Blacks eagerly seized those that they could, mainly opportunities in peripheral businesses. When white-owned insurance companies initially turned down black applicants for policies or charged them excessive rates, black entrepreneurs formed their own insurance companies. Commonly, black entrepreneurs used their profits to establish additional businesses of great benefit to black communities. Most influential was the North Carolina Mutual Life Insurance Company, started by three black entrepreneurs in Durham in 1898. Those forming the company combined a quest for private profits with a desire to use business institutions for the advancement of their race. From their base in insurance they branched out into banking, printing, and cotton milling in the years before World War I. With assets of nearly $120 million in 1970, North Carolina Mutual remained a leading black business in the years following World War II.

Black entrepreneurs also promoted the formation of new black towns as business enterprises after the Civil War. Altogether, they started forty-two new towns, many of them located in the trans-Mississippi West. Like towns founded by white entrepreneurs in the same time period, the black towns were begun mainly for economic reasons. From Nicodemus, Kansas, to Allensworth, California, the black towns were designed to bring profits to their promoters and economic progress to the blacks choosing to live in them. Thus, the newspaper of Langston City, Oklahoma, one of the black towns, promised its residents "cheap homes, unrestricted privileges, and paying investments."

Still, the obstacles to black success in business were many, and black-owned businesses generally remained small. Faced by competition from knowledgeable white business owners eager to sell to them (even in the insurance field by the twentieth century), blacks had a difficult time starting or expanding their businesses. As had been the case before the Civil War, most black businesses were small-scale affairs: retail shops, hauling outfits, restaurants, and the like. Even in the field of insurance, black businesses were usually small. North Carolina Mutual was just one of a host of fraternal insurance organizations that blacks founded between 1880 and 1910. Few lasted long or became large firms. By 1927, the thirty-two largest black

Black entrepreneurs formed businesses to take advantage of market niches ignored by white-owned firms. The Liberty Life Insurance Company of Chicago, whose head office is pictured above, became the third-largest black-owned life insurance company in the U.S. by 1965. (Supreme Liberty Live, now Supreme Life, commenced business, incorporated in the state of Illinois, on July 25, 1921. Its Home Office is located at 3501 S. Parkway, now known as King Drive.)

insurance companies, which accounted for 85 percent of all the black-held insurance written by black-owned businesses, had $316 million worth of policies in force. That same year a single white-owned company had $900 million worth of insurance in force on blacks, and by 1940 one white-owned company had a greater value of policies in force on blacks than the top forty black insurance companies combined.

For other minorities as well, small businesses provided a way to get ahead. The commercial spirit was widespread in America. Chinese and Japanese immigrants established retail outlets, especially grocery stores, and service businesses, such as laundries and restaurants. Here they succeeded by creating market niches for their small firms. Few white business owners either wanted to go into their lines of work, as in laundries, or had the necessary knowledge to do so, as in the operation of stores or restaurants specializing in Asian food—a situation in marked contrast to that faced by black business owners, who often encountered fierce competition from their white counterparts. Some Chinese and Japanese immigrants also established various forms of insurance companies and banks to serve their compatriots. Here, where they did face white business competition and hostile state legislation, they proved less successful. For example, none of the ten banks started by Japanese in California survived the 1920s.

There was a wide gap, then, between popular conceptions about the social and economic backgrounds of business leaders and reality. The reason for this discrepancy is that Americans wanted to keep believing they could achieve success in the business world as individuals at the very time when the spread of business organizations with managerial hierarchies was decreasing their chances of doing so. Believing deeply in individualism, and especially in the ability of the individual to get ahead economically, some Americans had (and still have) a difficult time coming to grips with the giant corporation. They found it hard to realize that the personal business world of the merchant was being replaced by the organized world of the industrialist and that in the business bureaucracies of the twentieth century there would be less room for individuals to become independent entrepreneurs.

The Business Leader and American Society

While most Americans viewed their nation's business leaders as captains of industry who had achieved success through the exercise of their will power, the business owners were less certain of their dominance over the economy of the United States. Many felt insecure in the face of the economic forces that were transforming their country. Far from controlling the course of events, business executives—like other Americans—were often bewildered by them, particularly during times of depression and financial panic. A leading California insurance broker expressed sentiments felt throughout the nation when he observed in 1904 that although "business was constantly changing," at the present time "the changes are revolving with such velocity that some of us are made dizzy by the mere contemplation of them."

The same feeling of insecurity that led business executives to restructure their companies and industries also encouraged them to look for stability in society. This quest led them into many avenues, some heavily traveled, some less so. The railroad barons Commodore William Vanderbilt and Leland Stanford turned to mystics and seers as they tried to understand the present and future through spiritualism. (Vanderbilt once even tried to call upon the spirit of Jim Fisk, a notorious stock-market manipulator, for advice on business affairs.) For others the Bible, with its timeless verities, offered solace. For many business people, "natural laws" of economics, whether learned from reading the works of Adam Smith or more commonly from personal observations, provided a rudder in the perilous seas of economic change. Despite the growth of oligopoly in many fields of industry, most business executives continued to believe that the invisible hand of supply and demand could and should determine economic transactions. Even as they formed giant corporations and sought to control competition through pools and trade associations, business executives emphasized the importance of the free play of economic forces in determining how the American economy functioned. Yet for them, no less than for other Americans, the realities of big business were unnerving and difficult to understand.

Perhaps because of their sense of insecurity, some executives resorted to what the American economist Thorstein Veblen labeled "conspicuous consumption" as a way of winning social acceptance for themselves. They spent their money lavishly in attempts to become members of the social elite of America. Those entrepreneurs who made their fortunes in railroads and industry after the Civil War felt this need most acutely, for they faced two interrelated problems. First, they wanted to show people that they were wealthy, no mean feat at a time when large fortunes were becoming more common. (The United States possessed 4,074 millionaires by 1892.) Second, they yearned for acceptance by America's established social elite—an elite whose inherited wealth was based on trade and commerce and who looked down on new wealth derived from industrial pursuits. Aping the aristocracy of Europe, the newly rich industrialists built houses that were castles and constructed fifty-room "cottages" at oceanside retreats. They used private railroad cars and yachts to travel from place to place. Their parties and dinners, which featured rarities like peacock tongues, were ostentatious. And they wore clothing to these functions that made them stand out in a crowd. A gown worn by Mrs. Jay Gould, the wife of the railroad financier, had $500,000 worth of jewels sewn onto its cloth.

More than just a desire for social recognition motivated these business leaders, however. Nineteenth-century American business leaders believed in the virtues of capitalism and were confident that their efforts added to their nation's plenty and to the well-being of all Americans. "I saw a marvelous future for our country," John D. Rockefeller noted, "and I wanted to participate in the work of making our country great. I had an ambition to build." Or, as the railroad president Charles Perkins asked rhetorically in 1888, "Have not great merchants, great manufacturers, great inventors done more for the world than preachers and philanthropists? Can there be any doubt that cheapening the cost of necessities and conveniences of life is the most powerful agent of civilization and progress?"

Andrew Carnegie best typified this sort of business leader. He took personal pride in the accomplishments of his business and viewed that business as an extension of himself. Carnegie abandoned a very successful career selling stocks and bonds to enter the steel industry because he wanted to build an establishment of permanent value. Once in it, Carnegie identified himself closely with the steel business. When he constructed one of the world's largest blast furnaces in the early 1870s, he named it the Lucy furnace after the wife of his brother. He valued his business for its efficiency and productivity, for its ability to build up America. Carnegie, in effect, equated the development of his steel company with the progress of the United States.

Carnegie Steel owned mammoth production facilities, such as its steel mill at Braddock, Pennsylvania. (Library of Congress)

The same desires to improve the United States and to leave monuments of lasting value led business leaders to engage in philanthropy. In a very paternalistic fashion, they believed that they knew what was best for the majority of Americans, and they were determined to use their wealth to change the lives of everyday people. Under the flood of contributions from business leaders, charity was transformed into philanthropy; its aim became less the relief of the immediate ills of the poor than the improvement of the whole quality of life in America. "The best philanthropy," observed Rockefeller, "is constantly in search of finalities—a search for cause, an attempt to cure evils at their source."

Business leaders supported those philanthropies they thought best embodied the values in which they believed. Like other Americans, most business leaders thought that anyone could rise in status through hard work and the acquisition of knowledge. Not surprisingly, they funded educational institutions as a way of making knowledge, especially technical knowledge, available to enterprising young people trying to move ahead. Andrew Carnegie, who had attended night school as a young man, gave millions of dollars to found thousands of libraries across the nation. He believed that libraries would do more to help the poor than direct aid, for they would build character by rewarding those taking the initiative to use them. For much the same reason, other business leaders gave large sums to colleges and universities. Johns Hopkins, a merchant banker, donated $3.5 million to establish the university bearing his name. Leland Stanford gave $24 million to found Stanford University, named after his son who had died as a young man. And Rockefeller donated $34 million to remake the University of Chicago.

❧ *Robber Baron or Industrial Statesman?*

While most Americans looked up to business leaders as heroic figures, many disapproved of some of their actions. Big business leaders were blamed for financial panics and recessions, for breaking labor unions and keeping wages lower than they might have been, for engaging in "unfair" forms of competition that destroyed small businesses, for controlling the prices of consumer goods through monopolistic actions, and for many other misdeeds. As early as 1869, the editor of the *Nation* labeled big business leaders "medieval barons." And by the 1890s, business leaders were commonly being referred to as "robber barons," by which it was meant that they controlled crucial production processes and communications networks for their own profit rather than for the good of society as a whole.

What of these accusations? Were business leaders robber barons, as their critics charged? Or were they industrial statesmen dedicated to building up the economy of the United States, as they and their defenders asserted? Or should they be viewed in yet another manner?

There can be little doubt that late-nineteenth-century business leaders often engaged in what would today be viewed as unethical practices from which they benefited personally. Competition was ruthless and did drive some small businesses to extinction. Big businesses were often able to secure secret rates from railroads lower than those given small businesses, and this situation gave the large enterprises a competitive advantage over the smaller concerns. Indeed, as we have seen, big businesses often sought to control their markets. Big businesses operating on a national scale sometimes engaged in selective regional price cutting designed to drive local rivals out of business. Money lost in lowering prices in one area was made up by raising prices in other regions where less competition existed. The Standard Oil Company was notorious for employing this tactic. George Rice, an independent refiner in Marietta, Ohio, was one of many who complained about Standard's methods. "They could cut only my customers' price, and below cost, leaving the balance of the town, nine-tenths, uncut," Rice observed in 1899. "This they can easily do without any appreciable harm to their general trade, and thus effectually wipe out all competition."

Big business leaders did corrupt politics. At both the state and national levels they used money to buy favors for their companies and, less frequently, to win election to office for themselves. At one point, Andrew Carnegie tried to bribe the Pennsylvania legislature to get that body to lower railroad rates. But he was outbid! The Pennsylvania Railroad offered larger bribes, and railroad rates stayed high. Business people also used their power, backed up by the courts, to break unions.

As their critics charged, big business leaders did benefit from these actions. When he died in 1893, the railroad magnate Leland Stanford left an estate valued at $100 million. And Carnegie retired from the steel business in 1901 with a fortune of $300 million. When judged by the standards of their day, however, big business executives appear less deserving of blame. Concepts of business ethics and conflicts of interest were not as well developed as they would become later, and business leaders were groping to redefine their relationships to the rest of society in the wake of disruptions caused by the rise of big business.

The emergence of oligopolistic big business had a mixed impact on the general public. Price competition decreased between different businesses in many fields. However, the trend toward oligopoly does not appear to have retarded economic growth in the United States, at least not in the late nineteenth and early twentieth centuries. Between roughly 1870 and 1920, the nation's gross national product (GNP) increased by a factor of eight, and per capita GNP tripled. (See Table 5.1.) Big businesses contributed to this growth by helping to mobilize capital and by providing organizational leadership for America's expanding industrial enterprises. Moreover, the prices of many industrial products dropped, as the larger, more fully integrated, and more efficient manufacturing concerns passed on some of their gains to consumers. Between 1866 and 1894, for example, the price of a gallon of kerosene fell from thirty cents to five cents.

The view of America's business leaders of the late nineteenth and early twentieth centuries as either robber barons or industrial statesmen may be

Table 5.1   Gross National Product (GNP) in the United States, 1869–1921

	1929 Prices	
	Total *(in billions of dollars)*	*Per capita* *(in dollars)*
1869–1873	$ 9	$223
1872–1876	11	254
1877–1881	16	327
1882–1886	21	374
1887–1891	24	388
1889–1893	26	405
1892–1896	30	434
1897–1901	37	496
1902–1906	47	569
1907–1911	55	608
1912–1916	63	632
1917–1921	72	683

SOURCE: U.S. Department of Commerce, *Historical Statistics of the United States* (Washington, D.C.: U.S. Printing Office, 1958), p. 139.

misleading. It probably attributes more power to them than they actually possessed. They were not in command of events to the extent that most Americans imagined they were. More often, business executives understood only partially and incorrectly the growing complexity of the economic situation in the United States. Rather than mastering circumstances, they were frequently mastered *by* circumstances. Instead of thinking of Rockefeller, Carnegie, and Stanford as either robber barons or industrial statesmen, then, it is more accurate to see them simply as business executives searching for opportunities in a difficult and rapidly changing economic situation. Like other Americans, they found it hard to comprehend fully the spread of industry and the rise of big business in their land.

AMERICA'S BUSINESS SYSTEM TRANSFORMED

Although American business executives may have had a difficult time understanding the economic changes occurring in the late nineteenth and early twentieth centuries, the actions they took to deal with those changes permanently altered the nature of business in the United States. Big businesses with managerial bureaucracies replaced many small businesses run directly by their owners. Vertically and horizontally integrated companies supplanted single-unit firms, thus leading to concentration in industry and to the creation of oligopoly in many fields of manufacturing. These developments, in turn, influenced the nature of economic decision making in the United States. With the rise of big business, decisions about the production and distribution of goods that had previously been made by the free interplay of market forces came to be internalized within the business firm. The visible hand of management replaced the invisible hand of the market in determining the functioning of part of the American economy.

The rise of big business also altered the nature of government-business relations in the United States. Federal, state, and local governments continued their developmental policy of aiding businesses as a way to build up their economies—a policy begun in the pre–Civil War years. But after the Civil War, a new element appeared in the realm of government-business relations. Governments, especially the federal government, began regulating business practices. Starting with railroads in 1887, the federal government expanded its regulatory powers over other businesses in the early 1900s.

Selected Readings

Alfred D. Chandler, *Scale and Scope: The Dynamics of Industrial Capitalism* (Cambridge, Mass.: Harvard University Press, 1990), offers a survey of the rise of large industrial firms in the United States, Great Britain, and

Germany. His *Visible Hand: The Managerial Revolution in American Business,* cited at the end of the Introduction, examines the emergence of big businesses in America. Glenn Porter and Harold Livesay, *Merchants and Manufacturers: Studies in the Changing Structure of Nineteenth-Century Marketing* (Baltimore: Johns Hopkins University Press, 1971), remains valuable on the same topic. Naomi Lamoreaux, *The Great Merger Movement in American Business, 1895–1904* (New York: Cambridge University Press, 1985), examines America's first business merger movement. And Richard S. Tedlow, *New and Improved: The Story of Mass Marketing in America* (New York: Basic Books, 1990), surveys the development of modern marketing methods by leading companies.

For overviews of the continued importance of small business, see the essays in Stuart Bruchey, ed., *Small Business in American Life* (New York: Columbia University Press, 1980), and Mansel Blackford, *A History of Small Business in America* (New York: Twayne Publishers, 1991). John N. Ingham, *Making Iron and Steel: Independent Mills in Pittsburgh, 1820–1920* (Columbus: Ohio State University Press, 1991); Philip Scranton, *Proprietary Capitalism: The Textile Manufacture at Philadelphia, 1800–1885* (Cambridge: Cambridge University Press, 1983); and Scranton, *Figured Tapestry: Production, Markets, and Power in Philadelphia Textiles, 1885–1941* (New York: Cambridge University Press, 1989), are valuable studies on the importance of small firms in the textile and the iron and steel industries.

Two good studies of Andrew Carnegie are Harold Livesay, *Andrew Carnegie and the Rise of Big Business* (Boston: Little, Brown and Company, 1975), and Joseph Frazier Wall, *Andrew Carnegie* (New York: Oxford University Press, 1970). Allan Nevins, *John D. Rockefeller* (New York: Charles Scribner's Sons, 1940), 2 vols., and Ralph and Muriel Hidy, *Pioneering in Big Business, 1882–1921* (New York: Harper and Brothers, 1955), look at the history of Standard Oil. Alfred D. Chandler, Jr., ed., *The Railroads: The Nation's First Big Business* (New York: Harcourt, Brace & World, 1965), investigates new managerial practices developed by railroads. Leonard Reich, *The Making of American Industrial Research: Science and Business at GE and Bell, 1876–1926* (New York: Cambridge University Press, 1985), and David A. Hounshell and John Kenly Smith, Jr., *Science and Corporate Strategy: Du Pont R&D, 1902–1980* (New York: Cambridge University Press, 1988), are pathbreaking studies.

Benjamin J. Klebaner, *American Commercial Banking: A History* (Boston: Twayne Publishers, 1990), looks at the development of commercial banking in the United States, as does Larry Schweikart, "U.S. Commercial Banking: A Historiographic Survey," *Business History Review* 65 (Autumn 1991): 606–664. On the development of investment banking, see Vincent Carosso, *Investment Banking in America* (Cambridge, Mass.: Harvard University Press, 1970), and Carosso, *The Morgans: Private International Bankers, 1854–1913* (Cambridge, Mass.: Harvard University Press, 1987). Morton Keller, *The*

Life Insurance Enterprise, 1885–1910 (Cambridge, Mass.: Harvard University Press, 1964), examines the history of life insurance.

William Miller, ed., *Men in Business* (Cambridge, Mass.: Harvard University Press, 1952), and Edward Kirkland, *Dream and Thought in the Business Community, 1860–1890* (Ithaca, N.Y.: Cornell University Press, 1956), investigate the relationship between business and society. And Walter Weare, *Black Business in the New South: A Social History of the North Carolina Mutual Life Insurance Company* (Urbana: University of Illinois Press, 1973), is an excellent case study of black business development, as is Kenneth Hamilton, *Black Towns and Profit: Promotion and Development in the Trans-Appalachian West, 1877–1915* (Urbana: University of Illinois Press, 1991).

Claudia Golden, *Understanding the Gender Gap: An Economic History of American Women* (New York: Oxford University Press, 1990), is a valuable survey. Margery Davies, *Woman's Place Is at the Typewriter: Office Work and Office Workers, 1890–1930* (Philadelphia: Temple University Press, 1982), examines the entrance of women into business offices. JoAnne Yates, *Control Through Communications: The Rise of Systems in American Management* (Baltimore: Johns Hopkins University Press, 1989), examines the office revolution that occurred in American business during the late nineteenth and early twentieth centuries. Finally, see Olivier Zunz, *Making America Corporate* (Chicago: University of Chicago Press, 1990), for an insightful study of the growth of corporations and a new middle class of employees.

IMPORTANT EVENTS, 1864–1897

1864 Congress establishes a system of chartering national banks.
Congress uses a land-grant system to help fund the first transcontinental railroad.

1869 Entrepreneurs and workers complete the first transcontinental railroad.
State regulation of railroads begins.

1872 Scandal besets the Union Pacific Railroad.

1876 The U.S. Supreme Court begins to ban state restrictions on center firms.

1877 The Supreme Court upholds state regulation of railroads.
Railroad strikes disrupt service and alarm the nation.

1886 The Knights of Labor membership peaks at more than 700,000.
Union Leaders found the American Federation of Labor.
The Supreme Court restricts state regulation of railroads.

1887 Congress establishes the Interstate Commerce Commission to regulate the railroads.

1890 Congress passes the Sherman Antitrust Act.
The Supreme Court assures center firms of their ability to operate in a national market.

1894 The Pullman strike highlights "the labor problem."

1895 The Supreme Court allows the "Sugar Trust."

1896 Inflationist campaigns culminate with the defeat of Populism.

1897 The Supreme Court forbids railroads to collaborate in fixing rates.

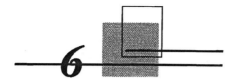

Government and
Business in the Gilded
Age

Mark Twain and Charles Dudley Warner, in their 1873 novel *The Gilded Age*, coined a phrase that came to characterize the period from the end of the Civil War in 1865 to the dawn of the next century in 1901. Twain and Warner portrayed not just a national enterprising spirit but what they saw as a veritable rampage to make money that tainted American institutions and democratic customs with materialistic values. Changing business institutions, especially the rise of big business and the emergence of an urban-industrial society, produced new problems in Americans' daily lives and new issues in the nation's political economy. With the emergence of powerful center firms, the localism of the American political economy during the first half of the nineteenth century began to recede after 1850, to be replaced by national policies of the federal government. The federal government remained weak, however, compared to what it would later become. Nevertheless, federal policies regarding tariffs, currency and banking, industrial labor, and especially access to a national market had the overall effect of promoting a business system dominated by large, dynamic center firms, which by 1900 operated on a scale vaster than any entrepreneur had envisioned at midcentury.

One result of the emergence of the new business system of center and peripheral firms was a fiery debate over the very nature of the U.S. political economy. Some Americans began claiming that the growth of corporate power threatened democracy itself. Protest movements aimed at the business system sought to strengthen the power of government to direct the behavior of business people, their firms, and business organizations. By the end of the nineteenth century, the country began taking its first hesitant steps toward federal regulation of business, while a political movement,

Populism, advocated outright government ownership of center firms in the railroad and communications industries.

A second result of the increased diversity of the time was a changing stance by some business leaders toward the government. Business groups were traditionally interested in policies that promoted economic growth. Those developmental policies continued in the Gilded Age, but another set of concerns arose: the need for regulation. The burst of economic growth that occurred after the Civil War led Americans with varied outlooks to try to control economic circumstances. They sometimes turned to the government—local, state, and federal—to enact laws; some wanted laws designed to achieve greater stability in an uncertain business environment, and others desired laws to check the power of large corporations.

The Gilded Age was a period of considerable political and social turmoil. The rise of big business and the continuing reorganization of work caused by the spread of industrialization were two critical changes faced by Americans. Other problems seemed to abound. In the nation's cities, mill towns, and mining camps, the social sores of human poverty and degradation contrasted starkly with the opulent lifestyle of the successful. Despite the country's spectacular economic growth, farmers and small business owners sometimes felt that their commercial opportunities were diminishing and that they were losing control of their enterprises to banks and corporations headquartered far from their own communities. The traditional patterns of localism in government remained, even in the face of nationwide innovations introduced by the center firms in railroading, communications, and manufacturing. Governmental institutions did not keep pace with economic changes. In the 1890s, for instance, the Vanderbilt family employed more workers on one estate than the total number of employees in the U.S. Department of Agriculture. Governmental agencies capable of paying expert, continuous attention to business and social problems awaited the twentieth century.

SOCIAL CHANGE AND SOCIAL THOUGHT: THE FLOWERING OF LAISSEZ FAIRE

The rapid technological, social, and economic changes that occurred in the United States in the decades after the Civil War were unprecedented in human experience. The mushrooming of factories, the shifting relationships between human beings and machines that newer technologies required, and the reorganization of daily life that the modern city entailed happened within one or two generations and represented a tremendous uprooting of traditional patterns of human behavior and economic interaction. Americans living during this time turned to laissez-faire economic theory to explain and justify what was happening.

The Gilded Age saw the full flowering of laissez-faire economic thought in America. It permeated judicial decisions (especially in the federal courts), appeared in the writings of social theorists and college professors, and was popularized by thoughtful journalists. In the courts, laissez faire was part of a long heritage of protecting liberty. Judges wanted to prevent those holding governmental power from using it to benefit one group or person at the expense of others. Like Adam Smith a century earlier, these jurists and theorists thought that the best system of political economy allowed for the free interplay of natural economic laws, unimpeded by state interference. Governmental services that benefited everyone, like education or the postal system, met with approval. But on the great questions of the day relating to labor conditions, the tariff, currency, and the "trusts"—the word used then to describe "big business"—the theorists advocated laissez faire.

For business executives, to the extent that they paid attention to economic theory at all, laissez faire provided a theoretical justification for preserving the status quo in social relations, especially in the issues that divided business and labor. Laissez-faire theorists preached that the free market should set wages, hours, and working conditions. If a business manager abused workers, so the theory went, the workers could exercise their freedom and obtain employment elsewhere. Any law protecting the rights of workers or imposing the eight-hour day was seen as an infringement on the individual freedom of the workers to enter into contracts. When industrial workers tried to guard their interests by forming unions, business executives objected on the grounds that workers' collective action impeded the operation of market forces. For business owners fighting unionization and seeking lower production costs through new work rules, or trying to survive in a competitive marketplace by lowering wages and providing substandard working conditions, the laissez-faire theory held an obvious appeal.

Unencumbered by the necessity of maintaining logical consistency, business people could advocate laissez faire with respect to labor laws and at the same time ask for tariff protection from foreign competitors. Always pragmatic in their approach to government, they saw no inconsistency in seeking government aid for the development of their firms while denying such help to workers trying to form unions or secure protective labor legislation.

Although promoters of business interests and even judges used laissez-faire doctrine inconsistently, it nevertheless remained part of a deeply held faith in the virtues of the republican government established by the American Revolution. During the nineteenth century, judges embedded laissez-faire theory firmly in the law, a development that held particular significance for business interests. In 1842 the U.S. Supreme Court, in *Swift* v. *Tyson,* had asserted the right of federal courts to ignore state precedents in developing federal doctrines. At first, the decision had prevented the states from prohibiting out-of-state creditors from the recovery of debts, but in the decades that followed, the policy combined with judges' laissez-faire convictions to provide corporations with a federal bastion against unfriendly state laws and regulations.

POLITICS AND PARTISANSHIP

A predominant political theme in the nineteenth century was the conflict between localism and the vision of a unified national policy. Within that context, the second half of the century witnessed considerable change in favor of national power, especially as the Civil War ended slavery and established the supremacy of federal authority. Less dramatic, yet critically important for the institutional development of the business system of center and peripheral firms, was the ability of business firms faced with hostile state legislation to obtain redress in the federal courts. The center firms were dramatically changing how the American economy functioned, and they needed the assistance of the federal courts. By 1890, the U.S. Supreme Court had ensured center firms the ability to reach a national market, unfettered by local regulation. In short, the localism that had prevailed in the federal system no longer fit the national and international business system that entrepreneurs were establishing.

Problems of Politics

Although the entrepreneurs organizing the new factories and railroads, and the financiers who assisted them, had a reputation for enormous political influence, they often felt abused by and mistrustful of politicians. Americans whose lives were still rooted in patterns of local economic organization continued to wield enormous influence. Industrialists and financiers faced movements by farmers and local merchants seeking governmental economic policies to protect their interests in the face of more modern and more efficient systems of production, distribution, and transportation. Financiers wanted a currency whose value was stable; but other, more numerous Americans, who were debtors seeking rapid growth for their own enterprises, desired inflation. In that setting, business leaders developed techniques of political influence that corrupted traditional American egalitarian institutions.

The uncertainty that business leaders faced from the legislative branch of government and the corruption in which some business leaders were willing to engage became clear in the course of events associated with particular policies. The great issues of the political economy concerned tariffs, money labor, trusts, and internal improvements; as these issues were or were not resolved, the fabric of the political economy was woven.

The Tariff

The tariff once again became a subject of lively controversy in the late nineteenth century. As a major point of contention between the theorists of laissez faire and the practitioners of politics, the issue divided major party platforms and fueled campaign rhetoric. Despite the bitter complaints from some consumers and the attempts, especially of the Democrats led by President Grover Cleveland, to have Congress lower duties, the general trend of American tariff policy remained protectionist. By the end of the 1890s, the Republican party had gained majority standing, in part because it championed the cause of a protective tariff as part of a stronger federal government that fostered economic growth, high wages, and substantial business profits. In the meantime the Democratic party, although it contained important congressional representatives who supported tariff protection, generally asserted the benefits of a tariff for "revenue only."

Underlying the partisan debates over the tariff were conflicting business interests similar to those that had divided American opinion before the Civil War. During the Gilded Age, however, the context of those debates was more complicated. Price deflation was occurring all over the world, partly because the cost of producing many goods was declining with new industrial techniques. In addition, some American manufacturing firms were maturing and seeking export markets for their products; those firms feared that high American tariffs might prompt foreign governments to retaliate. Also, as center firms began to dominate some industries, entrepreneurs in smaller firms complained that the tariff was the "mother of trusts"—the tariff's protective shield allowed big business to avoid competition and grow even more in wealth and power.

There were numerous examples of shifting sentiments concerning the tariff. Railroad magnates had once opposed protective duties on foreign-made rails, but after American producers, led by Carnegie Steel, became low-cost producers they lost interest in avoiding tariff duties on British rails. Similarly, when Carnegie was establishing his steel firm, he favored protecting the American market from foreign competition, but when he became the leading low-cost producer in the world, the lowering of trade barriers was to his advantage. In any case, iron makers who favored protection always advocated free trade in raw materials. In the tariff politics of the nineteenth century, then, there was much intellectual inconsistency. Business people wanted tariffs that were to their advantage, regardless of theoretical principles. As the Democratic senator from Indiana, Daniel W. Voorhees, said in 1883, "I am a protectionist for every interest which I am sent here by my constituents to protect." (Just a year earlier, his party had condemned tariff protection as "unjust.")

The intellectual inconsistency that arose over the tariff was a product, of course, of immediate economic interest. Indeed, there was widespread support for tariff protection. In general, industrial workers believed that the protective tariff allowed employers to pay higher wages with free trade, and the workers feared that low-wage workers in foreign factories would take away American jobs. Moreover, there were American industries—the woolen, hemp, flax, and sugar industries were examples—that depended on tariff protection for their very survival. On the other hand, farmers and other business owners who purchased manufactured commodities believed that free trade was to their advantage, doubly so when they searched for export markets for American goods. The conflicting economic interests involved with the tariff issue meant that politicians were unable to arrange either fully satisfactory compromises in the law or strategies on election day.

The Currency Question

If the recurring battles over the tariff provided more heat than light, issues relating to currency eventually exceeded them in the intensity of political emotions. The currency question arrayed hard money against soft money, a creditor class against a debtor class, and established business people against those interested in new entrepreneurship and speculation. By the 1890s this issue, along with the rise of center firms and the growing wealth and power of eastern banks and businesses, had contributed to a major movement of political protest called Populism, which sought to break up the control of the big corporations to create better opportunities for aspiring entrepreneurs.

The currency controversy arose initially because of the Civil War, when the Union government issued a paper currency called greenbacks to help pay for the war's extraordinary costs. The government required the acceptability of greenbacks; that is, they became legal tender for all debts, public and private, except customs duties and interest payments on the national debt. For those obligations, specie—gold or silver notes—were still required, so that the government could accumulate hard currency. By the end of the war there were $462 million worth of greenbacks outstanding.

After the return to peace in 1865, the continued existence of the greenbacks became controversial. As was the case with the tariff, the debate revolved around the special interests of rival groups of business people. Established manufacturers and merchants tended to favor "hard money"— the abandonment of greenbacks and a return to a currency backed by specie. For instance, New England textile producers, by now established for three generations, wanted both hard money and lower tariff duties, as they operated in an international market. These textile manufacturers imported raw materials, including coal from Nova Scotia and some raw cotton from India, on which they did not want to pay a high tariff. (Their British competitors imported raw materials free of duty.) The New England textile producers, furthermore, disliked the greenbacks, for although they received them as payments, they could not use them to pay customs duties.

A lowering of customs duties and a return to hard money, they felt, would help the American textile industry. Other American business executives—importers, wholesale grocers, commission brokers, and the like—agreed with this hard-money sentiment. Aspiring entrepreneurs, on the other hand, tended to favor "soft money"—the continuation of the greenbacks—to expand the supply of capital available to boost the opportunity for investment. These entrepreneurs of the late 1860s and 1870s were typified by the Pennsylvania iron men. Their spokesman, Republican Pennsylvania Congressman William D. Kelley, whose nickname was Pig Iron, summarized their view: "The contest is between the creditor and debtor class—the men of industry" and the financiers. Entrepreneurs tended to want soft money, such as greenbacks, which had the effect of enlarging the supply of available capital. They believed that soft money led to a desirable inflation, allowing them as debtors to pay back loans with a currency lower in value.

In the late 1870s, the federal government finally resolved the greenback controversy by limiting their number. Soon a new controversy arose, however, not over the printing of paper money but over the question of expanding the money supply and reversing the deflationary trend in the economy (prices generally were falling during the Gilded Age), by declaring silver as well as gold an acceptable currency base. The complex question of using silver, which affected American politics until the end of the nineteenth century, arose because American silver production was increasing and silver mining interests began demanding its use as a currency base along with gold. Wanting a market in the federal treasury, the miners launched a twenty-year campaign to establish a bimetallic coinage, the "free and unlimited coinage of silver" at a ratio of sixteen grains of silver to one of gold.

The campaign of the silver producers, obviously rooted in self-interest, was significant because it was heard sympathetically by discontented farmers and small business operators, mostly in the West and South, who desired an expansion of the money supply and saw bimetallism as the most feasible course. As the discontented westerners and southerners mounted the wide-ranging critique of American business and politics called Populism, they took up the free-silver cry as part of their reform program. The Populists demanded government ownership of the railroads and telegraphs and inflation through free silver in order to redistribute the wealth and power of eastern bankers and manufacturers to aspiring entrepreneurs. In the eyes of the protesters, deflation operated to the advantage of eastern creditors while it hindered the ability of indebted, independent operators of small businesses and farms to seize opportunities.

The emotions surrounding the silver issue ran high, reaching a climax in the presidential campaign of 1896. The issue resonated most clearly among wheat farmers of the Great Plains and cotton farmers of the South. The farmers who protested in the Populist movement were trying to organize cooperatives that would wrest control of the distribution of farm products from merchants and railroads. The protesting farmers knew that

William Jennings Bryan (1860–1925) spent much of his life advocating the rights of the ordinary citizen to invest in small business. Bryan traveled widely on the nation's lecture circuit and published popular columns expressing his views against those Americans who, he believed, enjoyed too much wealth and power. Here he is shown delivering his famous "Cross of Gold" speech. (Library of Congress)

inflating the currency would facilitate the retirement of mortgages and thereby, they believed, ensure the viability of the family farm in the larger economy. The popularity of the Populist rhetoric in the cotton and wheat belts of the South and Great Plains, and the movement's victories at the polls in several states, frightened investors whose fortunes were tied to the railroad industry. Populism's call for government ownership and inflation threatened to destroy the very fabric of the American business system that had evolved after the Civil War. In 1896, silver-inflationist Democrats captured control of their party and nominated William Jennings Bryan of Nebraska for president, as did the Populist party. The Republican platform and its candidate, William McKinley, favored maintaining the gold standard. Inflation, silver versus gold, was a main topic in the campaign that year, and established bankers and corporations rested easy only after Bryan's sound defeat. McKinley's victory, the return to prosperity after 1896, and the opening of new gold mines in Alaska and elsewhere caused the high emotions surrounding the coinage issue to recede more quickly than they had flared.

A National Banking System

During the Civil War, Congress established a new national banking system. The creation of national banks and the subsequent evolution of the financial system were key features of the political economy, although they did not provoke the emotional, long-running disputes of the currency question. Nevertheless, banking and currency policies were obviously related, and the bank laws led to a concentration of financial power in New York City. Thousands of farmers, merchants, manufacturers, and bankers outside of the eastern seaboard centers believed that the banking system operated as a kind of conspiracy of plunder or, more moderately, that it provided unfair advantages to firms and banks that constituted an "eastern establishment."

Salmon P. Chase, secretary of the treasury in the administration of Abraham Lincoln, was the father of the national banking system of the Gilded Age. Responsible for raising the large sums needed by the Union during the war, he considered the system of state-chartered banks and the consequent uneven value of state bank notes to be undesirable. So he set out to devise a system of federally chartered banks (but without a main bank, such as the old Bank of the United States, which had proven so controversial in the 1830s). In statutes enacted in 1863 and 1864, Congress provided for the chartering of national banks as a means of financing the war. In this system the government printed national bank notes that a new Treasury Department official, the comptroller of the currency, received in exchange for government bonds. The Treasury Department then used the paper currency to pay the government's bills. The law declared the notes legal tender for all transactions except the payment of custom duties. Meanwhile, an 1865 law taxed state bank notes and drove them out of existence. The result, along with the greenbacks, was the establishment of a new national bank-note currency secured by the debt of the federal government. By 1865, there were nearly 1,300 national banks whose resources included almost $400 million in federal bonds, with a commensurate flow of currency into the economy. Government banking policy thereby encouraged the growth of an important service industry.

The federal government provided little administrative control over the national banks, but it did place requirements on them intended to ensure their soundness. The banks earned profits from lending funds at interest, but bankers could keep only enough cash on reserve to meet withdrawal demands. The law required country banks to maintain a 15 percent reserve against deposits, three-fifths of which could be kept in either reserve or central-reserve cities. Banks in reserve cities had to keep 25 percent, half of which they could deposit in a central-reserve city. New York was the only central-reserve city until 1887, when Congress added Chicago and St. Louis. Banks in the central-reserve cities had to maintain 15 percent of their money on hand to meet depositors' demands.

This system pleased the bankers, but it did not always serve business well. When one bank deposited reserve funds in a reserve bank, it earned interest on the deposits, but the bank that held the money had full use of it. The banks in the central-reserve cities, especially those in New York, thus received enormous deposits that they lent at call. To maintain the ability to repay, those loans were customarily secured by stock securities that could

This illustration depicting the panic that swept Wall Street in the spring of 1884 indicates just how fragile the banking system was during the Gilded Age. If a rumor or development prompted suspicion of a bank's soundness, then great "runs" would occur, with depositors frantically trying to withdraw their funds before the bank went under. Such panics periodically reverberated through the U.S. economy, triggering depressions, business failures, and unemployment. (Library of Congress)

quickly be sold on the Wall Street exchange. This situation operated well during prosperous times, but after the Civil War the economy experienced the ups and downs of business cycles, which the banking system aggravated. At the peaks of the business cycle, with demand for loan funds high, the banks had trouble supplying sufficient credit. And when that occurred, depositors, worried about the health of the bank to which funds were entrusted, sometimes made withdrawals. As those withdrawal demands filtered to New York, banks there called in loans based on stock securities, and panics struck the securities exchanges. Wall Street panics in 1873, 1884, 1893, and 1907 helped provoke sharp downturns in the business cycle, as investors in corporate securities encountered a shortage of capital and scaled down their spending on new buildings, plants, and machinery.

The banking system not only aggravated downturns in the business cycle but also poorly served the more sparsely settled and agricultural regions during this period. The government had placed a number of restrictions on the banks. For instance, fairly substantial amounts of capital were required for the issuance of corporate banking charters, making it difficult to found banks in small towns and remote regions. Further, the law forbade banks from making loans secured by land, the main asset in agricultural areas. This situation, added to the ambitions of western and southern entrepreneurs and their demands for currency inflation, evoked political complaints about a "money power" entrenched in Wall Street that seemed to manipulate credit and banking to work against the interests and desires of farmers and business firms that were not well established. After the Panic of 1893 fueled the nation's worst-yet economic depression, complete with bankruptcies and widespread unemployment, pressures mounted for reforms in the banking system. None, however, were immediately forthcoming.

Industrial Workers and the Political Economy

In addition to these crucial tariff and banking issues were concerns regarding government policy on conditions of work and the relations between employers and employees. In fact, the pain experienced by so many workers and their families in adjusting to the new factory conditions led sometimes to violence and at other times to union agitation and demands for redress from the government. In fact, between 1876 and 1896, there were more strikes and more persons injured or killed in labor protests than in any other nation. The conflicts that occurred between workers and management, "labor" and "capital" in the language of the day, prompted widespread alarm over "the labor question" in the minds of many Americans, including prominent politicians, clergymen, educators, and journalists.

Rapid industrialization left both employers and workers groping for the power to control the conditions of work. Generally during this period, business enjoyed the upper hand in defining the limits of government intervention in controlling hours, wages, safety, and other conditions of work, but that control caused considerable dispute, even violence. The Gilded Age witnessed antagonism between social and economic classes, with industrial workers convinced that employers were intent on exploiting their talents and energies so that investors and managers could live in splendor.

Much of the worker agitation arose from this underlying class antagonism between labor and business. Most hurtful in labor's view was the "wages system" through which the privileged few managed the work of the multitudes. The largest organization giving expression to this complaint was the Knights of Labor, whose leaders wanted to alter the way the industrial process was organized. The Knights attracted large numbers of industrial workers and other Americans interested in reforming the industrial system. They envisioned cooperative enterprises in which workers owned and controlled the facilities of production, distribution, and communication. At its peak in the mid-1880s, the Knights of Labor had at least 700,000 members (and many more sympathizers) and owned and operated a coal mine, 62 grocery and retail stores, 11 newspapers, and 55 workshops and factories.

The railroad strike of 1877 was the first nationwide strike in the United States. Striking railroad workers sometimes resorted to violence to prevent strikebreakers from taking their jobs. Although he wished for an amicable settlement of the conflict, President Rutherford B. Hayes ordered troops of the U.S. Army to intervene and preserve order. (Library of Congress)

The Knights' resources were inadequate for more substantial cooperative enterprises, however, and by the 1890s they had waned in influence, as other groups were attracting the allegiances of workers and reformers.

In addition to the alternative ways of organizing production the Knights of Labor had explored, some workers organized trade unions to protect their interests from the practices of industrial capitalists. These unions—formed mostly by skilled, white, male workers—were less concerned with rejecting the wages system than with improving the workers' lot within the prevailing industrial order. In 1886, the trade unions organized the American Federation of Labor (AF of L), whose purpose was to support existing unions and help found new ones (it was, and is, a kind of union of unions) so that more and more workers could act collectively in negotiating contracts with employers. This development, and especially the determination of generations of men and women to have unions, provoked ideological and economic conflicts that affected the political economy in both theory and practice for a long time.

The emergence of the trade union movement in the Gilded Age provoked a major confrontation between labor and management. Laissez-faire theory, which most business people professed to believe in, called for contracts between individual workers and individual employers. If workers did not agree with terms of the contract, including the wages, hours, and working conditions, they were free, employers argued, to seek employment elsewhere. The workers' freedom should serve as a self-correcting mechanism to ensure that businesses offered fair terms of employment. Workers, however, realized that in reality they were neither free agents nor on equal terms with employers and that in the impersonal setting of modern industry businesses all too often had incentives to lower labor costs by replacing skilled workers with machines. Workers saw their interests from the perspective of class, or craft, as distinct and often opposite from the interests of employers, and their trade unions wanted to redress the balance of power in labor contracts by insisting on collective bargaining (workers negotiating as a group with their employer). Unions therefore tried to develop power independent from business, government, or other institutions to allow workers to negotiate agreements for higher wages, shorter hours, and improved working conditions as a group. As Adolph Strasser, president of the Cigar Makers' Union, explained to a Senate committee in 1883, "We are fighting only for immediate objects that can be realized in a few years."

When workers tried to gain those "immediate objects," however, they clashed with business interests and goals. Unions, for instance, sometimes demanded work rules designed to protect traditional crafts, while business executives, wanting to control and cheapen every aspect of production, insisted on breaking up old craft prerogatives in favor of newer techniques and machines. When managers introduced scientific-management principles into their factories in the late nineteenth and early twentieth centuries, as discussed in Chapter 5, they shifted control over work routines from the workers to management, with the workers sometimes becoming mere appendages to their machines. Partly because of management's drive to have tradition yield to efficiency, skilled workers rebelled, a situation that was a major cause of strikes. Moreover, in a deflationary setting, with some industries suffering from overproduction, businesses often lowered labor costs by paying "starvation wages." These were a major bone of contention, but worst of all in the minds of industrial workers were the long, grinding hours of work. Carnegie's steel firm, for instance, demanded that production workers be on the job for twelve-hour shifts seven days a week when the mills were running at full capacity. The cry for the eight-hour day and the forty-eight-hour work week was the most popular rallying point for the union movement in this period.

The clash between labor and management complicated American politics. Officials in local communities and state capitals often sympathized with the struggles of workers who seemed victimized by powerful capitalists who did not reside in the local mill towns or mining camps. There were thus occasions when unionized workers found that local governments aided their cause. At the very least, union leaders wanted government to remain neutral in disputes. Business managers, on the other hand, frequently complained that work stoppages violated the law, and they demanded forcible government intervention. (Here was one case in which business leaders deviated from their belief in laissez-faire ideas.) Powerful corporations succeeded in obtaining help from local and state officials, and they did not hesitate to turn to federal authority when doing so was necessary to suppress a strike. In general, especially as the federal courts assumed more authority to check state and local regulation of economic affairs, the weight of government power in labor-management disputes operated against the interests of trade unions.

The Pullman Strike of 1894: A Case Study in "The Labor Problem"

There were many strikes during the Gilded Age, and many more would follow in the first four decades of the twentieth century. Their causes varied from straightforward economic grievances to more subtle conflicts, as managers tried to increase their control over the work process. Usually, the basic issue was the right of workers to have unions and to engage in collective bargaining. Typically, strikes ended when the government applied its power against the unions. One strike in particular, the Pullman strike of 1894, highlighted several of these aspects of "the labor problem," as it was then called.

The Pullman Company, owned by George Pullman, was a major producer of railroad rolling stock, including the sleeping cars that made the name Pullman a household word. The company manufactured the railroad cars in a company-owned town on the outskirts of Chicago and contracted with the major railroads to attach them to passenger trains. Pullman publicized his company town as a model community filled with contented, well-paid workers. But events proved that the Pullman workers disagreed. In response to the depression that began in 1893, the company sought to preserve its profits by lowering labor costs. When the firm slashed its work force from 5,500 to 3,300 and cut wages by an average of 25 percent, the Pullman workers rebelled. (Pullman did not cut his stock dividend or the salaries of his managers.) The workers joined the American Railway Union (ARU) led by Eugene Debs, which was trying to organize rail workers all across the country. The ARU had won concessions from the Great Northern Railway early in 1894, and the Pullman workers looked to it as a chance to weaken Pullman's control over their lives and to restore their wages. To bring pressure on the firm, the ARU asked workers operating trains to which Pullman sleeping cars were attached to stop work and thus halt the trains. The union told the railroads that their trains could operate without the Pullman cars, but the railroads insisted that they had contracts with the Pullman Company requiring them to haul the sleeping cars. The result was an impasse, with railroad workers in and around Chicago refusing to operate passenger trains.

The strike ended with the intervention of the United States Army. The passenger trains also hauled mail cars, and although the workers promised to operate mail trains so long as Pullman cars were not attached, the railroads refused. Pullman and the carriers informed federal officials that violence was occurring and that the mail was not going through. Attorney General Richard Olney, who disliked unions, heard their claims of violence (but not the assurances of local authorities that there was no uncontrolled violence) and arranged to send federal troops to ensure the delivery of the mail and to suppress the strike. The union leader, Debs, was jailed for not obeying an injunction that a judge had issued against the strikers.

The Pullman strike was representative of similar, lesser-known events elsewhere during this period, when business executives commonly turned to government for assistance in defeating strikes and breaking unions. The use of the federal army was a dramatic exception to the more usual use of state national guard units and local police forces. Most strikes were broken by firms obtaining court injunctions against the unions from friendly local judges. When strike leaders refused to obey the court order, the police and courts intervened, jailing union leaders, destroying union documents, and bleeding union treasuries.

The class conflict and attendant violence that had appeared in American life in the 1890s led to a search by some religious, labor, business, and public leaders for common interests between business and labor. That search would eventually produce reforms and new policies, but such changes had to await the twentieth century, when they would include some of the reforms associated with the Progressive Era.

GOVERNMENT PROMOTION AND REGULATION OF BUSINESS

The government not only sided with business in breaking labor unions during the Gilded Age but also continued to help in other ways. As we have seen, the government provided significant help for internal improvements before the Civil War. Government aid was especially significant in conquering the Appalachian Mountain barrier during the first half of the nineteenth century. During the second half of the century, government assistance was also important in helping the railroads cross the vast western expanses. Government aid for railroad construction during the Gilded Age was somewhat less important than it had been in the earlier period, when canals and the first railroads were being built, but it nevertheless proved an important factor in linking the Pacific Coast with the rest of the nation.

Tradition and Innovation

Even as the government continued to assist the development of business during the Gilded Age, new issues concerning the control of business began to surface. These new issues related to the use of the railroads, not their construction, and to the emergence of the new "big business" firms. The center firms, which included the railroads, struggled to set prices administratively and to their advantage, while injustices in the eyes of the users of the railroads began to appear. Similarly, the rise of center firms in manufacturing prompted resistance from Americans accustomed to more traditional forms of enterprise.

When Americans began to search for innovative ways of regulating the conduct of the large railroad and manufacturing firms, they did so against a background of a weak national government that lacked a tradition of applying independent, public expertise to private affairs. This tradition revealed itself in a spectacular scandal associated with the construction of the Union Pacific railroad, part of the nation's first transcontinental line. The government subsidized the Union Pacific with land grants that the promoters used as collateral for loans to provide the required capital. When those promoters obtained more capital than necessary, Congress threatened to investigate the financing of the road in 1867. The promoters successfully averted the investigation by bribing high officials, including Vice President Schuyler Colfax. When the scandal broke out anew in 1872, revelations ruined the careers of several politicians, including that of Colfax, and tainted the Grant administration, giving the Gilded Age its aura of speculation, chicanery, and bribery.

The Union Pacific scandal revealed an important weakness: the inability of existing federal institutions to regulate such a crucial business event as the building of the nation's first transcontinental railroad. Thus, when political leaders began to take their first hesitant steps toward a new regulatory state during the Gilded Age, they did so in the absence of a tradition of strong government empowering independent experts to define and watch over the public interest. Eventually the American regulatory state was refined and expanded in the twentieth century.

State Railroad Regulation

The practice of applying independent public expertise to the affairs of the nation's railroads began only after they were built. Responding to the materialistic values of the Gilded Age and fearful that they might overwhelm the public good, Massachusetts established in 1869 the first significant commission for the "general supervision of all railroads." A board of three members, led by Charles Francis Adams, grandson of one president and great-grandson of another, exercised an investigatory function for the railroads. The commissioners investigated the affairs of the railroads, including charges for hauling freight and passengers, in the expectation that public exposure would cause the carriers to redress wrongs voluntarily. The idea of using a commission to investigate and publicize the affairs of the railroads spread to other states. In general, their purpose was not to regulate what

The completion of the building of the nation's first transcontinental railroad linked the Mississippi Valley to the Pacific Coast in 1869. (Courtesy of Union Pacific Railroad Museum Collection)

the carriers actually charged their customers but to focus publicity on the lines.

State railroad commissions with stronger powers, able to instruct the railroads as to the rates they were allowed to charge, came into existence with the so-called Granger laws enacted by the states of Illinois, Iowa, Minnesota, and Wisconsin between 1869 and 1874. Merchants and small business owners in the upper Mississippi River valley, supported politically by farmers in the hinterland who were organized in the Patrons of Husbandry, more commonly called the Grange, pushed for these new regulations, which revealed a change in popular attitudes toward the railroad. When railroads first entered a region, local farmers, merchants, and real estate speculators usually welcomed them as beneficial agents of local prosperity. With the passage of time, however, railroad corporations grew larger, their management more remote from the local scene, and their owners more interested in consolidating rate structures that ensured steady usage of their capital plant than in stimulating area prosperity. These occurrences caused local populations to view the carriers as evil dark powers whose tentacles reached out to corrupt the legislative process, endanger the prosperity of the general population through financial manipulations, and damage the well-being of individual farmers, merchants, manufacturers, and towns with discriminatory rates. The response, first expressed in the Granger laws, was to insist that the carriers were a business "clothed with a public interest." According to this view, the railroads served the public, and because that service was vital to the well-being of the community, the public had the right to regulate railroad affairs.

These laws launched a long series of bitter legal disputes, with attorneys for the railroads insisting that they deprived railroads of their private property and therefore violated the Fourteenth Amendment to the Constitution, which guaranteed the property rights of all persons, including corporations. The U.S. Supreme Court upheld the constitutionality of the Granger laws in its famous 1877 decision, *Munn* v. *Illinois*. But in 1886 the Court reversed itself in *Wabash Railway* v. *Illinois* and forbade the states from regulating traffic that either originated in or went outside the state (so-called interstate traffic). Under this doctrine, only Congress could control the interstate affairs of the railroads.

The Birth of Federal Regulation

Pressures to have the federal government begin regulating the railroads had been mounting well before the *Wabash* decision in 1886. These pressures were a response to the maturation of the American railroad industry in the 1870s and 1880s. When railroads were first built, the lines, at least by later standards, were relatively short ones over which traveled small locomotives and lightweight equipment. Freight rates were accordingly high. After the Civil War, railroad managers interconnected their lines and provided long through routes for hauling freight. At the same time, the introduction of steel rails and, later, air brakes, automatic car couplers, and improved signaling devices allowed longer trains of heavier cars pulled by more powerful, faster locomotives. The costs of operating such trains diminished on a per-mile or unit-of-freight basis, and freight rates for the long haul declined, especially for bulky goods such as grain. In contrast, short runs still produced relatively higher charges on a per-mile basis, because the railroads had to recover terminal and switching charges, regardless of the distance the goods were shipped. The result was a chorus of complaints about long- and short-haul rate discrimination from shippers and communities who believed the rate structure placed them at a competitive disadvantage. By the late 1870s, farmers and merchants in upstate New York, for instance, grimly watched trains laden with western grain rumble through their region; the midwestern shippers had to pay little more for transportation than their New York competitors. New York City merchants, earlier favored by location, saw their advantage disappear with the growth of cheap, long-haul freight trains and concluded that it was time to initiate federal railroad regulation to prevent the carriers from charging less, per-mile, for a long haul than for a short haul.

The advent of through railroad systems capable of making long hauls introduced another element into the picture: competition. When several railroads were able to provide through connections between distant points, each sought to maintain a steady, high volume of business. The result was a competitive pressure that drove prices downward. By the 1880s, for instance, several systems were competing for business between Chicago and the eastern seaboard. One of them, the New York Central, granted to favored shippers six thousand special rates, prices that were well below its published rates. To prevent price wars from endangering the financial well-being of railroad stock and bondholders, railroad managers experimented with pooling, a system by which—as we saw in Chapter 5—they could agree among themselves to stabilize rates at profitable levels. When voluntary pooling proved unsuccessful, however, some railroad executives looked to the federal government for help. Railroad men and many shippers alike pressed for the creation of a governmental body that would stabilize the rate structure and protect their profits.

Neither group received exactly what it desired when Congress enacted the Interstate Commerce Act in 1887 and established the Interstate Commerce Commission (ICC) as the country's first federal independent regulatory commission. (Independent regulatory commissions are agencies separate from the legislative, executive, and judicial branches of government.) The law was the result of a compromise between the competing shipper and carrier interests that left the new commission with little power. Much to the dismay of some railroad executives, it outlawed railroad pools, but its prohibition of long- and short-haul discrimination included an enormous loophole that allowed the practice to continue. The law told the commission

The Pullman Company provided sleeping and dining cars to trains in the late nineteenth century, adding a touch of luxury to first-class passenger service. (Brown Brothers)

to see that freight rates were "reasonable and just" but gave the ICC no enforcement powers. In the 1890s, the U.S. Supreme Court declared that the commission had no authority to set rates and ruled that the railroads could practice long- and short-haul discrimination as a response to competitive conditions. In its early years, the ICC had little impact on the business system; it served mainly as an information-gathering agency. Fulfillment of the vision that somehow it should assert the "public interest" over the behavior of the nation's railroad corporations had to await another generation.

✳ The Antitrust Movement

The concerns that led to railroad regulation in the 1870s and 1880s emerged from the needs and interests of particular business groups. In contrast, the

The ideology of the antitrust movement commonly portrayed big businesses as undesirable institutions that manipulated economic forces in evil ways, and which rested on the back of the common American. (Culver Pictures)

antitrust movement of the Gilded Age and the enactment of the Sherman Antitrust Act of 1890 were deeply rooted in all Americans' conceptions of liberty and political economy. They were the expression of a generalized fear that business developments threatened the very fabric of the country's liberty. Enormous economic growth, the rise of the first giant vertically integrated firms, and the spread of horizontal integration had appeared within the lifetimes of Americans who had matured in a simpler, earlier period when the interactions of thousands of small independent firms governed the marketplace. The emerging business system of center and peripheral firms, in contrast, seemed somehow undesirable, for both the growth of center firms and the alliances among small firms denied traditional opportunities for individual entrepreneurship. In the words of the president of the Grange, spoken at a conference on the trusts in 1899, "the right to acquire, own, control and enjoy the use and income of property, is an inalienable right, that should be enjoyed by each individual." Combinations of firms and vertical integration seemed to threaten that inalienable right.

When Americans voiced complaints during the nineteenth and early twentieth centuries about the "trusts," they used the term in a special way. As we have seen, business owners used a variety of techniques to create greater productivity and security for their firms and investments. Politicians and the general public alike, however, lumped the pools, trusts, and holding companies under the generic term "trusts," which in more modern usage translates roughly as "big business."

The popular dislike of the trusts was clearly rooted in the traditional business system of small independent firms. When center firms appeared in manufacturing, they competed with small enterprises that operated in traditional ways in local markets. For instance, when Chicago meat packers established efficient big businesses that purchased livestock, processed meat in large factories, and distributed products cheaply across wide territories and in large cities, they drove established local butcher firms out of business. The displaced butchers sometimes urged politicians to restrain the "trusts." Other manufacturers established their own company distributors instead of using the services of traditional wholesalers and retailers; I. M. Singer & Company, for instance, employed agents who commanded the technical expertise needed to sell and service complex sewing machines. Rather than applaud the competition, local firms typically turned to local and state governments for regulations, license fees, and taxes to thwart it.

Enjoying influence with their local and state governments, the merchants being squeezed by center firms experienced considerable if short-lived successes. Missouri used a prohibitive tax to keep Singer's agent out of the state until the U.S. Supreme Court outlawed the practice in 1876. And Virginia tried to use license fees in effect to require center firms to distribute goods through independent local wholesalers and jobbers. Again, in 1880 the Court forbade the practice. More dramatic was the formation of the Butchers' Protective Association, comprising firms unable to compete with the Chicago meat packers, which resorted to the tradition of localism in American law. The butchers proposed laws prohibiting the sale of dressed mutton, pork, or beef unless state officials inspected the live animal within a day of slaughter. In 1889, Colorado, Minnesota, and Indiana passed inspection laws to protect local butchers from national competition, and at least a dozen other states considered such proposals. Although the Butchers' Protective Association claimed that such inspection was required to protect the public health, the U.S. Supreme Court saw the measures as a scheme to protect local butchers from competition and in 1890 ruled the laws unconstitutional. The ruling capped a trend, begun in 1876, whereby the Court consciously protected the rights of nationally organized center firms to reach a national market.

While the U.S. Supreme Court was protecting businesses from hostile state regulations and fees and weakening the tradition of localism in American politics, Congress was beginning to assert its authority over big business by passing the Sherman Antitrust Act in 1890. In the debate preceding passage, congressmen expressed concern about the impact of the new business forms on the nation's politics and social character. The trusts, they thought, threatened American traditions of democracy and liberty. Congress should act, according to Senator John Sherman, as the law's sponsor, in order to protect "the rights of individuals as against associated and corporate wealth and power." If present business trends continued, he warned, it would not be long before Americans would face "a trust for every production and a master to fix the price of every necessity of life." In Sherman's view, the accumulation of wealth entailed in the formation of trusts produced a concentration of power that threatened the tradition of free, independent, individual action. Such concentrated power, he believed, affected the social character of Americans in undesirable ways. According to Sherman, the beauty of the invisible hand of the market was that it was diffuse, that it could be located in no particular place, and that it operated impartially to grant every American an equal chance of economic success.

Although the Sherman Antitrust Act expressed those general ideological concerns, the statute was inexact. "All that we, as lawmakers, can do," Senator Sherman noted, "is to declare general principles." In general, sweeping language, the law declared "restraints of trade" illegal but gave no precise guidelines for the executive and judicial branches of the government to follow. Congress left it to the president and his Department of Justice to decide whether or not to prosecute a particular business combination for hindering the free exchange of goods.

No great flurry of antitrust prosecutions followed the enactment of the Sherman law. The attorneys general of the 1890s were men generally sympathetic to the needs of business firms to establish control over the market's competitive jungle. They were also hostile to trade unions; in fact, of the ten cases initiated under the new law between 1892 and 1896, five were against unions, which the administration, and eventually the courts, viewed as restraining trade. For those Americans who wanted a vigorous application of the new law, the first decision of the United States Supreme Court was discouraging. In 1895, in *U.S.* v. *E. C. Knight Co.*, the Court majority ruled in favor of the "Sugar Trust," formally known as the American Sugar Refining Company. This firm dominated its industry and was reaching out to acquire its few remaining competitors. The Court majority saw no violation of the law, which, it observed, applied only to "commerce," not to "manufacture." The Court tried to draw a clear distinction between commerce and manufacturing and ruled that when the Sugar Trust acquired a competing manufacturing plant that did not literally straddle a state boundary, the federal government, authorized only to regulate interstate commerce, had no power to interfere.

Although this doctrine seemed clear in 1895, there remained a large measure of uncertainty. The Court's majority could change, and so it did in 1897 in *U.S.* v. *Trans-Missouri Freight Association*. This case involved railroads, which clearly were engaged in interstate commerce. The decision informed them that they could not collaborate to fix rates. The Sherman law thus remained a potentially powerful weapon against business combinations, and the twentieth century would soon witness highly publicized suits against some of the nation's largest manufacturing firms.

THE DAWN OF A NEW CENTURY

By the start of the twentieth century in 1901, the American political economy had undergone significant changes from that of the mid-nineteenth century. Although the federal government was still minuscule and lacking in power as compared to later developments, the federal courts had successfully prevented the nation's traditional localism from preventing operations by center firms on a national scale. Meanwhile, Congress had asserted its authority, albeit with a negligible impact, over those same big business firms. Passage of the Sherman Antitrust Act and the launching of the Interstate Commerce Commission were harbingers both of augmented federal authority and of a desire to promote public expertise to supervise business. As the new century began, the policies of the federal government were still tending toward development, as in the case of the protective tariff. Similarly, the debates over the banking and currency systems had given evidence that Americans still wanted federal policies designed to promote and reward entrepreneurship. Nevertheless, significant changes had occurred as the Supreme Court forbade local and state restrictions on the national market and Congress established the first federal regulatory commission and asserted its authority over big business.

Regulation and control of a maturing economy were becoming important matters of concern. Sometimes that concern emanated from small business people and farmers who were aggrieved by the practices of the large corporations, especially the railroads. But America's corporate leaders felt some of the same needs. From a variety of sources, then, modern federal government regulation of business began in the Gilded Age, and the experiences of that time period provided a foundation on which a later generation of Americans, living and working in the twentieth century, constructed a more powerful governmental system to regulate the affairs of business.

Selected Readings

Sidney Fine, *Laissez Faire and the General Welfare State* (Ann Arbor: University of Michigan Press, 1966), is a standard account. Herbert Gutman, ed., *Work, Culture, and Society in Industrializing America* (New York: Alfred A. Knopf, 1976), analyzes important changes brought by industrialization. Morton Keller, *Affairs of State: Public Life in Nineteenth Century America* (Cambridge, Mass.: Harvard University Press, 1977), is encyclopedic. Michael Les Benedict, "Laissez-Faire and Liberty: A Re-Evaluation of the Meaning and Origins of Laissez-Faire Constitutionalism," *Law and History Review* 3 (Fall 1985): 293–331, provides a cogent interpretation of the Supreme Court's commitment to laissez faire. Tony Freyer, *Forums of Order: The Federal Courts and Business in American History* (Greenwich, Conn.: JAI Press, 1979) and *Regulating Big Business: Antitrust in Great Britain and America* (New York: Cambridge University Press, 1992), are useful studies of the relationships between legal history and business history. Two essays by Charles McCurdy also stand out in this regard: "American Law and the Marketing Structure of the Large Corporation," *Journal of Economic History* 38 (September 1978): 631–649, and "The Knight Sugar Decision of 1895 and the Modernization of American Corporation Law, 1869–1903," in *Managing Big Business: Essays from the Business History Review,* edited by Richard S. Tedlow and Richard R. John, Jr. (Boston: Harvard Business School Press, 1986), pp. 329–366.

John Lauritz Larson, *Bonds of Enterprise: John Murray Forbes and Western Development in America's Railway Age* (Cambridge, Mass.: Harvard University Press, 1984), explores the attractions and tensions among a business promoter and local merchants and their communities. George H. Miller, *Railroads and the Granger Laws* (Madison: University of Wisconsin Press, 1971), clarifies a complex subject. The Pullman story is told by Stanley Buder, *Pullman: An Experiment in Industrial Order and Community Planning, 1880–1950* (New York: Oxford University Press, 1967).

Finally, Thomas K. McCraw, *Prophets of Regulation* (Cambridge, Mass.: Harvard University Press, 1984), is insightful on government regulation in the Gilded Age and beyond.

IMPORTANT EVENTS, 1900–1917

1900   The National Civic Federation is founded to foster cooperation among business, labor, and the public.

1901   Theodore Roosevelt, an advocate of the supremacy of the "public interest" over business, assumes the presidency.

1902   The National Association of Manufacturers launches a campaign against trade unions.

1903   Congress establishes the U.S. Department of Commerce and Labor.
The Elkins Act outlaws railroad rebates, sanctioning administrative rate making.

1904   The U.S. Supreme Court dissolves the Northern Securities Company.

1906   The Hepburn Act empowers the Interstate Commerce Commission (ICC) to set the railroads' maximum freight rates.
The Pure Food and Drug law bans misbranded and adulterated food and drug products.

1907   Immigration to the United States peaks.

1910   The Mann-Elkins Act requires railroads to obtain prior ICC approval before raising freight and passenger rates.

1911   Ohio pioneers workers' compensation programs.
The Supreme Court breaks up American Tobacco and Standard Oil under the antitrust law.

1912   Woodrow Wilson is elected president, running on a platform of "new freedom" from the power of big business.
The U.S. Chamber of Commerce is founded.

1913   Congress establishes the Federal Reserve system.

1914   The Clayton Act revises the antitrust law.
Congress creates the Federal Trade Commission.

1916   Congress creates the Tariff Commission.

1917   The United States declares war on Germany and Austria-Hungary, and faces the crises of mobilization.

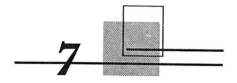

Business in a Democratic Society: The Progressive Era

⋆The dawning twentieth century witnessed the emergence of new issues and new conditions that reshaped the environment of American business. Americans seriously considered new policies toward the growth of big business in the first years of the new epoch. The return to prosperity after 1897 sparked new waves of immigration, which increased not just the size of the population but also the heterogeneity of the labor force. American employers began recruiting larger numbers of female workers than ever before, blacks from the rural South, white migrants from the rural areas, and newcomers speaking many European tongues. Immigration, urbanization, and the growth of big business were not conditions new to the twentieth century, but the problems that emerged from the social changes associated with them came to seem particularly acute to both business executives and social reformers after 1900.

American business faced one especially significant development in the early twentieth century: the rise of social reform movements that acted, sometimes through the governmental system and sometimes through private associations, on business institutions and behaviors. The same era saw the inauguration of a new president, Theodore Roosevelt, who, although not antagonistic to the capitalist social and economic system, asserted the primacy of the "public interest" as represented by the government. At about the same time, other leaders from other walks of life, especially from the churches and universities, began seeking new ways to protect the country against what often appeared the corrupt interests of business. The result was the appearance of a frame of mind called *progressivism*, a set of attitudes and values that optimistically looked toward the erection of new institutions, or the reform of older ones, through which Americans would realize the good society. Among the institutions most affected were business firms and organizations.

Progressivism included a ferment of ideas about policies toward big business, ideas that typically combined a moralistic view with a suspicion that the growth of big business undermined economic opportunities traditionally available. During the early years of the twentieth century Americans seriously discussed various approaches toward big business, a discussion that culminated in the 1912 presidential campaign. Powerful politicians, including President Roosevelt himself, looked forward to establishing a system of state capitalism, wherein big business firms would be required to obtain government approval of their contracts with other firms. Other leaders called for a more vigorous use of antitrust laws to force firms to operate as small units without the benefits of vertical and horizontal intergration. Meanwhile, growing numbers of American workers were coming to believe that a system of public ownership of basic manufacturing, transportation, and communications industries—state socialism—was the only sure route to social justice.

Business leaders were important participants in the activities of progressivism. They played important roles in shaping the national debate about trusts and socialism and, in their roles as church and community leaders, joined and supported private associations seeking reform. More directly, the managers in the headquarters of some of the largest firms became inextricably involved in political affairs. The years between the turn of the century and World War I, called the Progressive Era, saw the emergence of "corporatism" (historians sometimes call it corporate liberalism), a phenomenon in which leading bankers and industrialists sought to achieve cooperation among business, labor, and government—cooperation that, they were confident, would result in harmonious relations among the social classes and ensure prosperity in the general economy. Out of this business involvement with reform came new institutions of government-business relations.

NEW WAYS OF THINKING

A new school of political economists emerged in the United States in the 1880s. This new school comprised young men who, in the 1870s, studied German historical and statistical economic thought. Some German scholars had rejected the deductive reasoning of Adam Smith and his successors in favor of observations of historical and statistical information from which, through inductive reasoning, economists and policy makers believed they could reach conclusions.

A Pragmatic View of the Political Economy

The basis of this new school of economic thought lay in the rejection of the assumption of the classical economists that self-interest always governed the actions of humans. Other factors, it was maintained, also affected human behavior: altruism, national honor, and the like. The economists of the new school thus attempted to combine political economy with ethics and, from their pragmatic observations of the realities of economic life, to determine prescriptions regulating business and achieving the public interest.

The leader of the new-school economists in America was Richard T. Ely, who graduated from Columbia College in 1876 and earned his Ph.D. in 1879 at Heidelberg University in Germany. From 1881 to 1892, he taught economics at Johns Hopkins University in Baltimore, after which he spent more than thirty years on the faculty of the University of Wisconsin. Ely not only wrote numerous books and essays during his long and distinguished career but also lectured widely and served on government commissions.

An essential ingredient of Ely's leadership of the new school was his role in founding the American Economic Association in 1885. This association brought together the younger economists influenced by the German theories. Among the charter members were twenty-three clergymen, most notable of whom was Washington Gladden, the father of the Social Gospel movement in America. The Social Gospel was a Protestant church movement formed to help ease the hardships of life faced by the poor and by workers in the factories and cities of the industrial age. When Ely drafted the platform of the American Economic Association, he unequivocally repudiated laissez faire: "We regard the state as an educational and ethical agency whose positive aid is an indispensable condition of human progress. While we recognize the necessity of individual initiative in industrial life, we hold that the doctrine of laissez-faire is unsafe in politics and unsound in morals; and that it suggests an inadequate explanation of the relations between the state and the citizens." Those words expressed a sentiment that was to have a profound impact on government-business relations in the Progressive Era.

This rejection of laissez-faire doctrine did not mean that Ely or his colleagues believed in state paternalism or socialism. As Ely explained, in a democratic society the government is the people, so when the government acts on behalf of the general welfare, it is acting fraternally, not paternally. In this regard, the role of the economist seemed clear. "In a certain sense," Ely noted, "the political economist is to the general public what the attorney is to the private individual." The economist is a guide, helping the people to determine the public interest. In Ely's view, such guidance should direct policy to some middle course between unbridled competition and state socialism. The prevailing business system had produced social evils of poverty and degradation apparent to anyone who cared to observe them, but in Ely's eyes their amelioration had to involve policies that preserved individual freedom.

Theodore Roosevelt and the Ideology of the Public Interest

Important as the new school of economics was to the environment in which American business functioned, the appearance of its doctrines roughly coincided with other, still more important, intellectual and political developments that shaped the Progressive Era. Among those developments was the assertion of an ideology of the public interest, an assertion in which the new-school economists participated but which was by no means confined to their teachings. There was an old tradition in American thought, extending back to the Puritan founders of Massachusetts, that expressed a belief in the desirability of using the government to promote the commonweal, or public good. That tradition lay behind the economic policy of men like Alexander Hamilton and Albert Gallatin in the nation's earlier years. By the middle of the nineteenth century, there were some who claimed that the best government was one that included good men, men whose personal lives and interests transcended the particular needs of the moment and who were capable of acting for the good of all. In the Progressive Era, political philosophers and social theorists such as Walter Lippmann and Herbert Croly gave formal expressions to this public-interest doctrine, but no one represented the viewpoint better than a man of affairs, Theodore Roosevelt.

Theodore Roosevelt had achieved public prominence before the beginning of the Progressive Era. The son of a well-to-do family that had amassed its fortune before the Industrial Revolution, Roosevelt decided to devote his life to public service. He entered politics in his native New York State over his family's objection that political office was too corrupt for a gentleman and gained public attention by fighting crime and corruption as New York City's police commissioner. After his well-publicized heroism in the Spanish American War in 1898, Roosevelt went on to become governor of New York.

Elected vice president in 1900, Roosevelt assumed the presidency after the assassination of William McKinley in 1901. He served as president until 1909 and then unsuccessfully sought a third term in 1912 on a platform he labeled the New Nationalism. Roosevelt was both a thinker in the tradition of defending the public interest and a practical and powerful politician who acted directly to change American business institutions. As president, he tried to enhance the executive power of the government to safeguard the public interest and to create a more moral and orderly society. He was interested in power not for its own sake but for the public good. He tried to establish the supremacy of the government over business and other

Theodore Roosevelt was an activist president who captured wide public attention. He often spoke of the need for federal government regulation of business. (Library of Congress)

interest groups and to create a governmental system with orderly procedures of regulating business behavior according to the public interest.

Roosevelt wanted to impose federal power on big business. One practical way he could, as president, regulate business conduct was by enforcing the Sherman Antitrust Act. When warring railroad interests in the Pacific Northwest combined under the leadership of J. P. Morgan and James J. Hill to create a new holding company, the Northern Securities Company, to control the stock of the Great Northern, Northern Pacific, and Chicago, Burlington & Quincy railroads, Roosevelt launched an antitrust suit. The Supreme Court ruled in 1904 that the Northern Securities Company constituted an illegal restraint of competition and ordered it dissolved. Roosevelt encouraged a fanfare of publicity about the prosecution and hailed the outcome as a great victory. The significance of the case, for him, was not the practical result—Morgan and Hill found other unchallenged ways to control the Burlington railroad—but its symbolic nature. The ruling was a successful assertion of the supremacy of government over business. When Roosevelt announced the suit, Morgan left New York for Washington to ask if the president had intentions to attack his other interests. Roosevelt assured the financier that he did not, so long as the firms were not guilty of misconduct.

Meanwhile, in 1903, Roosevelt maneuvered a bill through Congress that created a new cabinet-level Department of Commerce and Labor, which contained a Bureau of Corporations whose function was to investigate corporate practices. Soon a series of "gentlemen's agreements" evolved, in which representatives of big business, especially partners in the House of Morgan, collaborated with the Bureau of Corporations. Under these informal gentlemen's agreements, firms granted the government access to information; the government, in return, approved mergers when it found them to be in the public interest. For Roosevelt the importance of these arrangements was the implicit recognition of the supremacy of public power over private interests.

Roosevelt continued to plot for increased supervision of corporations by the executive branch after his election in 1904. Although he considered requiring corporations to obtain approval for their investment decisions from the executive branch of the federal government, in the end he encouraged enactment of less drastic measures of state capitalism. The president supported federal licensing of large corporations and executive branch sanction of horizontal and vertical integration, partly removing questions about reasonable restraints of trade from the courts. His specific proposals, embodied in a bill named for Iowa Representative William Hepburn in 1908, aroused passionate opposition from small business leaders. Although not specifically enacted, the vigorous expression by Roosevelt and his supporters of a clear sense of the rights and wrongs of business behavior endowed the Progressive Era with a character far different from that which prevailed during the Gilded Age.

Efficiency and Corporatism

The notion of the government acting energetically to safeguard the public interest, plus the new economic theories that credited human beings with more altruistic motives than that of profit alone, gave the Progressive Era its unique quality. That was not the end of the story, however. The early twentieth century also witnessed ideological and institutional developments that produced a modern system of government-business relations.

The Progressive Era saw the growth and widespread acceptance of the idea that science and engineering principles held the key to discovering the public interest. The new-school economists thought of themselves as scientists, dispassionately uncovering data about socioeconomic conditions from which the wise, applying Christian ethics, could learn the public interest. Engineers also participated in this trend. Scientific management, first proposed by Frederick Taylor and other mechanical engineers, put forth, as we have seen, principles for changing working conditions inside the factory. Taylor and his disciples believed that scientific management provided efficient coordination among all of the components of a factory, both men and machinery. Through the principles of engineering science, the factory could become a harmonious whole, it seemed. The theory of scientific management extended beyond the factory gates to encompass a social philosophy in which all the components of society could be made to mesh smoothly with one another. According to this ideology, engineering principles, when applied to society, could end conflicts among the social classes and between business firms and industries.

The theory of scientific management, and its concomitant goal of applying engineering principles to all of society, received widespread publicity, especially after 1910. There was general acceptance of the ideology of efficiency, because it conformed to the perceived needs of business people who were attempting to devise new mechanisms of control over their affairs. Financiers, typified by J. P. Morgan, tried to arrange "communities of interest" among firms within industries to restrain unbridled competition in favor of protecting the large sums of capital invested, ensuring the best service for customers, and promoting higher levels of prosperity, including higher wage levels. Within firms, executives developed new systems of accounting and management controls. Small business owners, working in industries that were not susceptible to the merger movement or to vertical integration, organized private trade associations to arrange new systems of interfirm cooperation. By the Progressive Era, the institutional thrust of American business was clear: it was toward control of the uncertainties and instabilities of unbridled price competition by the use of systematic, rational management systems.

The ideology of efficiency and the impulses toward managerial control within industries combined in the Progressive Era to form corporatism, a frame of mind or point of view expressed by some business people, government officials, scholars, scientists, and reformers. The advocates of corporatism looked for a new kind of partnership between government and business and, in some cases, between business and labor, one that emphasized reason and cooperation, not confrontation, to solve practical problems of business strategy. Some spokesmen thought that prices were best determined through management science, not the uncontrollable workings of the market. Similarly, disputes between business firms over such matters as the allocation of available markets or transportation costs were thought to be best resolved through dispassionate, scientific investigation. The result should be not only higher levels of general prosperity but a society of harmony. America, in this vision, could become a nation whose component parts fit together smoothly and efficiently.

Woodrow Wilson and the Ideology of the New Freedom

Vigorous promotion of the public interest and widespread faith in efficiency became significant themes of government-business relations in the Progressive Era. There was, however, another somewhat contradictory theme as well: the desire to strengthen the government so that it could strictly limit the size of business firms and ensure that price competition governed business behavior. Woodrow Wilson, who served as president from 1913 to 1921, most eloquently expressed this view in the presidential campaign of 1912. Sharply differentiating his ideas from the "new nationalism" expressed by Theodore Roosevelt in the same campaign, Wilson ran on a program of "new freedom." In so doing, Wilson not only defeated Roosevelt's attempt to win the presidency again; he also defeated Eugene Debs, running as the Socialist Party's presidential candidate. Debs' defeat proved to be the high tide of the movement for state socialism in the United States, as Americans in 1912 chose not only Wilson but also a middle ground between Debs' socialism and Roosevelt's state capitalism.

Wilson was hostile both to the concentration of assets in fewer and fewer institutions—the "trusts"—and to Roosevelt's policies of allowing that concentration so long as public officials determined that the behavior of giant corporations conformed to the public interest. Wilson feared that the growth of big business tended to undermine traditional American freedoms. The concentration of wealth in a few firms meant that individual entrepreneurs might be squeezed out of business or that they would simply not enjoy the opportunities traditionally accorded to Americans. "I don't care how benevolent the master is going to be," Wilson declared. "I will not live under a master. That is not what America was created for. America was created in order that every man should have the same chance as every other man to exercise mastery over his own fortune." The new freedom, Wilson believed, would result when the government used its antitrust powers to break up big businesses into smaller firms.

Although Wilson expressed a desire to break the trusts and scorned Roosevelt's program of accepting big business upon its good behavior, as president he engaged in little "trustbusting." Center firms, as we have seen, arose from innovative business practices, and it was difficult to prove that their growth resulted from illegal actions. In fact, between 1890 and 1915, antitrust law was actually used less against the new center firms than against combinations of peripheral firms. Although there were well-publicized actions against prominent center firms, most notably court orders breaking up Standard Oil and American Tobacco in 1911, these actions were far overshadowed in number by cases in which the federal government prosecuted small firms for agreeing to fix prices and allocate markets. That pattern began before Wilson became president, and it continued through his two terms.

NEW INSTITUTIONS: ASSOCIATIONALISM

Important institutional developments accompanied the growth of new ways of thinking associated with the Progressive Era. For example, the number, size, and variety of private associations of all kinds, but especially of business associations, proliferated after the turn of the century. Government officials often saw business associations as desirable devices for disseminating information, while business people saw them as agencies through which they could influence government policy.

Business associations, groups of executives, and firms that typically watched over some particular interest were not new in the twentieth century. Business associations of various sorts had promoted their own specific interests on the questions of railroad regulation during the 1870s and 1880s, and individual industries had formed organizations to lobby in Washington for favorable tariff legislation. The national and state bodies of the nineteenth century, however, had usually comprised smaller firms seeking protection from the integrated firms that competed so successfully in the market. Local business associations continued to be important in the twentieth century, but it was then that national associations started to grow in significance. By 1900, there were 3,000 commercial organizations in the United States, at least 100 of which were national bodies. In 1912, the federal government reported the existence of 3,356 local, 183 state or territorial, and 243 interstate business associations. Not only did the number of associations grow, but new types of business societies emerged to bring together business people at the local, state, and national levels to promote their larger interests, as opposed to the narrow interests of particular trade associations.

The National Civic Federation

By the turn of the century, the idea that business leaders should recognize their responsibility toward society was beginning to appear among the ranks of some of the nation's wealthiest, most powerful corporate leaders. This attitude encompassed traditional forms of philanthropy, which expanded in the twentieth century as industrial fortunes enlarged and also involved the idea that corporate leaders had responsibilities for the commonweal. "The larger the corporation becomes, the greater become its responsibilities to the community," observed George W. Perkins, a representative of the Morgan banking interests and a director of both United States Steel and International Harvester.

The National Civic Federation (NCF) was the first important institution that arose to give expression to these desires. After the Pullman strike of 1894, a group of Chicago business and civic leaders began the Civic Federation to bring together corporate officers, conservative union leaders, and public representatives to discuss ways to solve the "labor problem." From its meetings emerged the idea of a National Civic Federation, which was organized in 1900. Marcus A. Hanna, a prominent coal operator who served as a Republican party leader and a United States senator from Ohio, became its first president. The NCF followed a tripartite program of bringing together representatives of capital, labor, and the public. In 1903, about one-third of the nation's largest corporations were members, as were union leaders, most prominently Samuel Gompers, president of the American Federation of Labor, and John Mitchell, president of the United Mine Workers. At one time or another, the NCF executive committee included Grover Cleveland, William Howard Taft, and some of the nation's leading names in education and the professions.

During the Progressive Era, the NCF underwent three periods in which it developed different programmatic emphases. Until 1905, the NCF was most concerned with mediating labor disputes, trying to find ways for unions and corporations to cooperate democratically. It helped negotiate some contracts between industries and unions but was more successful in promoting an ideology of labor management cooperation than in obtaining the acceptance of collective bargaining by the nation's large manufacturing firms. Between 1905 and 1908, the NCF emphasized "welfare work," a form of paternalism in which firms consciously sought a sense of identification between employer and employee by trying to integrate the daily life and leisure activities of workers with the operation of the corporation. NCF leaders saw welfare work as a substitute for the recognition of unions and collective bargaining contracts; if only workers could voice their grievances and air their views, they believed, they would have little desire to join an independent union. Finally, after 1908, the NCF became more involved in legislative activities. It commissioned studies that helped shape revisions in antitrust law and the creation of the Federal Trade Commission in 1914. It also developed model workers' compensation laws and sought to have them enacted by state legislatures.

The most important accomplishment of the NCF, however, was not the achievement of any specific measure. The organization transcended individual firms and industries and brought together some of the nation's most important financiers and industrialists to consider the broader needs of the business system and solutions to some of the social problems that had erupted with the impact of the Industrial Revolution and the growth of cities. The NCF served, thus, as a key instigator of corporatism. In the meetings of its commissions and committees some of the nation's most influential business and professional leaders, politicians, and educators learned from one another and came to realize that the United States needed new agencies and systems of cooperation through which experts could apply their knowledge to the workings of the capitalist order.

The National Association of Manufacturers

In sharp contrast to the activities of the NCF and the ideological expressions of its leaders about corporate social responsibility stood the National Association of Manufacturers (NAM). The NAM was an older organization, founded in 1895 by small, mostly midwestern manufacturers who lobbied for federal policies that would encourage the expansion of foreign trade.

However, the NAM remained a small organization until 1902, when David M. Parry, a militant antiunionist, took over its presidency. The NAM had about 1,000 member firms in 1900, but by 1914, due largely to the popularity of its new antiunion activities, 3,500 firms belonged.

Under Parry's leadership, the NAM began coordinating the antiunion activities of American business. To reduce the power of unions (the membership of the unions affiliating with the American Federation of Labor had risen from 278,000 in 1898 to 1,700,000 in 1904), if not to eliminate their influence altogether, Parry and the NAM embarked on a determined campaign to enforce the open shop, or what the business leaders called the American Plan. The employers in an industry or in a community allied, with the help of locally based Citizen's Industrial Alliances, which were NAM offspring, and agreed to hire only workers who would sign a pledge to refrain from either joining a union or trying to organize one. The firms hired private detectives to spy on workers and developed elaborate systems of keeping track of known agitators. With the help of friendly local politicians, the employers tried to break up unions where they existed. A common technique was to provoke a strike, obtain an injunction from a sympathetic judge against union activities in support of the strike and, upon the union leaders' refusal to obey the injunction, call in the police, who would arrest the offenders and pillage union headquarters. By such means businesses could drain union treasuries in legal disputes and sap their strength.

So in the first years of the twentieth century, two significant national business organizations developed. Both the NAM and the NCF, in very different ways, expressed significant business responses to the conditions of a maturing industrial economy. The importance of the NCF as an organization waned after World War I as more specialized organizations took over its work. The NAM, although it later moderated its record of antilabor excesses, continued to express the interests of a significant portion of American manufacturers.

The United States Chamber of Commerce

The federal government was directly involved in sponsoring the formation of a third association in the Progressive Era, the United States Chamber of Commerce, whose goal was to represent the interests of American business in general. On the local scene, businesses had associated for years in "commercial clubs," "boards of trade," "chambers of commerce," or similarly named groups. But there was no national organization that seemed to voice the views of American business as a whole.

The absence of such an association concerned officials in the new Department of Commerce and Labor, created in 1903, one of whose missions was to "foster, promote, and develop the foreign and domestic commerce." Government officials enjoyed easy access through personal contacts to the nation's large, integrated big business firms. However, there was no simple way for those officials to reach small and medium-sized firms, and it seemed especially important to establish lines of communication with them in regard to foreign trade. American leaders were concerned over the ability of the nation to remain economically competitive abroad, especially in the face of growing German business prowess. Both business leaders and government officials thus saw the desirability of having organized mechanisms through which the Commerce Department and the State Department could transmit information about foreign markets to American business firms. Large firms had their own representatives abroad, but smaller firms depended on the government.

The key figure in solving this problem was Charles Nagel, a St. Louis lawyer and businessman who served as secretary of commerce and labor in the presidential administration of William Howard Taft (1909–1913). Nagel sought to enlarge the role of his department and to provide better service to American business so that it could improve its competitive position in world markets. He especially wanted business support for federal policies that would subsidize the merchant marine and protect firms that were trying to expand overseas operations from antitrust suits at home. He was particularly interested in a national chamber of commerce.

The United States Chamber of Commerce was officially born in 1912 at a national commercial conference called by President Taft. Seven hundred delegates from 392 commercial associations in nearly every state came to the meeting in Washington, D.C. Taft told the delegates that the federal government needed "constant and intelligent cooperation" with "the great industrial forces of our country." Nagel spoke of the need to have sound advice from business leaders if the government was to regulate their affairs intelligently. Regulation, in his view, should involve intelligent cooperation, not adversarial conflict. The delegates responded by writing a plan for organizing the United States Chamber of Commerce and circulating it to 1,250 associations and individuals around the country, who approved it. The national chamber held conferences and issued publications to spread information and ideas among business leaders and between them and government officials in the Department of Commerce. One important function of the organization was to present issues of federal economic policy to its members and to hold referendums on those issues to clarify general business views for both legislative and executive officials.

The National Civic Federation, the National Association of Manufacturers, and the United States Chamber of Commerce gave evidence of a renewed desire on the part of both business leaders and politicians in the Progressive Era to enlarge and institutionalize the ability of business people to help shape desirable public policies. Other national associations played important roles in government-business relations during this period, but these three organizations were particularly noteworthy because they represented attempts to deal with important general concerns about the larger economic system. Associations also formed around more specific needs and interests regarding federal policy that played an important part in devising new systems of federal regulation of business in the Progressive Era.

GOVERNMENT REGULATION OF BUSINESS

In addition to the government-business cooperation symbolized by the associations, new forms of federal regulation of business characterized the Progressive Era. Sometimes this regulation came from administrative agencies in the executive branch, such as the Bureau of Corporations, but more typically it involved some form of independent commission that combined the functions of policy making, administration, and adjudication. The first commission, as we have seen, was the Interstate Commerce Commission. In the years between the turn of the century and World War I, Congress expanded the powers of the ICC and created two important new agencies, the Federal Reserve Board and the Federal Trade Commission. Each was created to deal with specific industries or specific problems, and thus, although their impact was sometimes widespread, none was responsible for the overall regulation of America's business system.

Each specific area of government regulation that emerged in the Progressive Era had complex sources within American society, but in general they were a response to three trends we have already noted as characteristic of the period: the idea of carefully observing economic activity and thereby deriving policies in the public interest, the reassertion of the power of the government to watch over the commonweal, and the growing conviction of the desirability of developing new avenues of government-business cooperation so that America would become more efficient and harmonious. Each area of government regulation was also a product of associational activity—of business people, farmers, and workers expressing their needs and interests and pressuring government officials through associations of various kinds. Finally, the growing role of the federal government in supervising business affairs meant that the tradition of localism, so powerful during the nineteenth century, was beginning to diminish.

Railroad Regulation

The railroad industry was the first recipient of this new form of government regulation in the 1880s, and in the Progressive Era the revival and redefinition of railroad regulation led the way toward establishing what became the fourth branch of government, the independent regulatory commission. Legislation in the Progressive Era enlarged the Interstate Commerce Commission and made it powerful enough to enforce railroad rates and to adjust them after careful investigation.

The growth of the American economy in the Progressive Era complicated railroad politics. Prosperity meant that the carriers faced heavier demands for service, demands that required them to modernize their tracks and equipment. At the same time that the carriers were facing a larger volume of business, price inflation made it more difficult to raise the necessary capital for improvements. While the carriers' costs were rising, the opposition they faced from the powerful shippers' associations made it difficult to raise freight rates and thereby either to generate capital from internal savings or to borrow it in financial markets. The result was a kind of impasse with the railroads, especially after 1908, seeking higher freight rates, and with the farmers and business people, themselves facing higher costs, trying to hold down the carriers' charges.

The Progressive Era legislation regarding railroads initially helped the carriers but then was revised to grant considerable power to the business owners and farmers who depended on railroad service. In 1903, the Elkins Act, written by Senator Stanley B. Elkins, in effect legalized "pooling." The law required the railroad companies to adhere to their published rates and punished railroads and shippers who gave or received rebates. The creation of a rational, administrative—as opposed to market—price structure pleased the railroad corporations but was not satisfactory to shippers, who could exercise little control over the charges. The complaints of business owners and farmers, especially in the South and West, led Congress in the Hepburn Act of 1906 to enlarge the Interstate Commerce Commission to seven members, empower it to control the carriers' bookkeeping, and permit it to set maximum freight rates. This situation still pleased many railroad executives, however, because the law allowed them to set rates administratively. Moreover, the railroad officers could raise charges and collect higher revenues until the ICC rescinded their rates.

Congress completed the Progressive Era system of railroad regulation in 1910. That year saw two important events in railroad politics: the passage of the Mann-Elkins Act and the insistence by the ICC on scientific management before the railroad firms could raise their freight rates. The Mann-Elkins Act made a basic change in the regulatory system by requiring the railroads to demonstrate the necessity of higher freight rates prior to their imposition. This provision pleased shippers, for the burden of proof was now placed on the railroads, and the shippers were convinced that they could persuade the Interstate Commerce Commission to act reasonably and take local and regional interests into account in its decisions.

The result of this legislation was that rates were still set administratively, but the carriers' actions were now supervised by the federal commission. Railroad executives expressed pleasure over the construction of a rational system of ratemaking, but they were displeased by some of the Interstate Commerce Commission's most publicized decisions. When the Panic of 1907 threatened railroad revenues, George W. Perkins, representing the

Morgan bank and investor interests, negotiated an agreement among eastern railroads for a general freight rate increase of 10 percent. Shippers were alarmed, both at the prospect of having to pay higher charges and at the inequities in competitive relationships among industries, regions, and communities that such a general increase threatened.

The two sides were granted a hearing before the ICC that became known as the Eastern Rate Case of 1910. Midwestern shippers organized a new association, the National Industrial Traffic League, to represent them. New England shippers sent Louis D. Brandeis, a prominent attorney who had a reputation as a "people's lawyer," to represent their interests. Brandeis called Harrington Emerson, an efficiency engineer, as a witness, and Emerson testified that with the proper application of scientific-management principles, the railroads could save $1 million a day. This argument persuaded the ICC that no general rate increase was necessary pending a more thoroughgoing attempt to achieve cost savings. The decision, in effect, said that with the application of scientific and engineering principles to business, the public interest could be served and conflict between business firms, as here between railroads and shippers, could be resolved harmoniously.

This hope proved ephemeral. By 1913, it was apparent to the ICC that the carriers, which faced large traffic volumes and burdensome capital expenditures as well as higher operating costs, required additional revenue. Shippers began having to pay higher rates, but always as a result of a decision-making system wherein they had an important voice. By 1917, the railroad unions (called brotherhoods) were sending attorneys to commission hearings, allying with the railroads in the belief that higher rates would mean higher wages. Railroad executives voiced displeasure, of course, when they lost rate cases before the commission. But the railroads, on the whole, did not oppose this Progressive Era system of ratemaking, for it provided protection from the fierce competition that had damaged the industry in the late nineteenth century. The railroad industry set about the tasks of influencing the ICC and, by establishing a new science of public relations, of reaching the general public, the business community, and the politicians with their message of need.

Food and Drug Regulation

Railroad regulation concerned a broad spectrum of Americans, simply because anyone who wanted to travel or ship goods long distances was dependent on railroad service. Food and drug regulation also affected nearly every citizen, although its origins were less obviously rooted in business and farmer associations. Local regulation of foodstuffs extended back into the colonial period, but the modern movement for legislation requiring pure food and drugs stemmed from an increasing dependence on packaged goods sold through impersonal distribution systems.

The problems of adulteration and mislabeling were manifold. Traditional American medicine had not rid itself of quackery; the snake oil salesman with his traveling medicine show was a national institution. Entrepreneurs supplied the market with a large variety of nostrums, usually containing substantial proportions of alcohol, which were supposed to cure all ills. These "patent medicines" may have promised much, but they delivered nothing (except for hangovers and other alcohol-related diseases) and were an affront to the modern sciences of medicine and pharmacy that had emerged in the late nineteenth century. Similarly, food adulteration was a major problem. Some disreputable processors and packagers sought to deceive customers in the interests of quick profits; others who lacked technical expertise used harmful chemicals to preserve meats, fruits, and vegetables.

Harvey W. Wiley, who served as chief chemist in the U.S. Department of Agriculture after 1883, led the campaign for passage of a federal regulatory bill. Wiley conducted experiments that demonstrated the existence of undesirable impurities in foodstuffs and exposed the fraudulent nature of many packaged medicines. He also worked with manufacturers who wanted their disreputable competitors run out of business. By the early twentieth century, Wiley had gained the help of several popular writers, the best known of whom was Upton Sinclair. The 1906 publication of Sinclair's *The Jungle,* which contained graphic stories of noxious practices in the meat-processing industry, produced a public outcry strong enough to allow Wiley to push a compromise measure through Congress.

The 1906 Pure Food and Drug and Meat Inspection laws, which forbade interstate and foreign trade in adulterated and misbranded foods and drugs, were important regulatory achievements in the Progressive Era. The laws relied largely on the power of disclosure for their effectiveness; underlying the laws was the belief that once consumers knew the contents of a product, the good would drive the bad from the marketplace, but they also contained some stringent measures. Federal inspectors employed by the Department of Agriculture henceforth would grade meat before it went on the market. The large meat packers saw such activity as desirable, because it lent an assurance of quality that was especially important in export trade. Similar measures helped protect food canners with substantial investments in factories and brand names from fly-by-night operators. Although the system was far from perfect, its achievements were substantial. These laws seemed to prove that the application of scientific knowledge through government agencies could both protect the public interest and help responsible business firms.

Banking and the Federal Reserve Board

Other businesses also came under increased regulation during this period. Banking and currency policy disputes, as we have seen, had plagued the

Before passage of the Pure Food and Drug laws of the Progressive Era, patent medicines sometimes posed serious threats to consumers. If Hamlin's Wizard Oil really did cure "all pain in man or beast," its powers probably could be attributed to a large dose of opium or alcohol. (Library of Congress)

American political system since the earliest days of independence. The Progressive Era witnessed the major resolution of those disputes with the creation of the Federal Reserve System in 1913. Bankers, other executives, and politicians reached agreement on the proper relationship between the government and banking and on a system for providing both a flexible currency and policies grounded in expert knowledge.

The legislation of 1913 came only after years of disagreement between bankers and other business leaders and among the bankers themselves over the types of assets acceptable as a currency base and the control of the banking system. The controversy over assets arose because the debt of the federal government was shrinking, while the volume of transactions in the economy was growing enormously. The system established during the Civil War had provided for banks to issue currency secured by federal bonds. But now that the number of bonds was shrinking, the bankers were pressing for a so-called assets currency, one in which high-grade corporate bonds, whose quantity enlarged with the economy's expansion, would serve as securities. Country bankers, from those thousands of institutions that had emerged to service the needs of the agrarian economy, insisted that the assets currency should include real estate securities, which were in plentiful supply in rural areas.

Complicating the matter still further was the issue of control. The banking system that evolved in the Gilded Age concentrated deposits in the huge banks located on New York's Wall Street. In fact, this concentration of wealth was so great as to prompt widespread complaints about a "money trust"—the idea that a small, privileged, private group of men with offices in New York and an informal national and international network of communications controlled most of the nation's wealth. Such a concentration was disliked by many bankers and business people outside of New York, who believed that it should be federal policy to disperse control and allow greater influence to bankers in cities like Chicago, Detroit, and Cleveland.

These issues fermented as a result of the Panic of 1907. The banking system created in the Gilded Age turned out to be susceptible to occasions on which depositors withdrew their assets quickly, forcing banks to sell securities suddenly and threatening the entire financial system with collapse. In 1907, when withdrawal demand threatened to wreak havoc on banks and corporations, J. P. Morgan organized resources to shore up institutions faced with bankruptcy. Morgan saved the system but also confirmed the suspicions of the inordinate power enjoyed by a few financiers. The panic led to demands for change: first for an emergency measure to allow banks to issue currency secured by high-grade corporate bonds, and second for the establishment of a National Monetary Commission to study reform proposals and recommend a revamping of federal banking policy.

The studies of the National Monetary Commission, headed by Senator Nelson W. Aldrich of Rhode Island, eventually led to the creation of the Federal Reserve System, but only after a long, tangled political controversy. The commission consulted closely with Wall Street bankers and in 1911 recommended the creation of a central bank in New York City with fifteen regional branches. The private banks would control the central bank, which in turn would be authorized, among other matters, to issue a currency based on high-grade corporate securities. But these recommendations were unacceptable to many bankers and business leaders, for they failed to address the issue of the "money trust." They did not create a decentralized system that granted power to bankers outside of New York or to the business people who depended on banking services. And country bankers disliked the failure to recommend the use of real estate as a currency base.

Finally, Representative Carter Glass of Virginia arranged a compromise that pleased most bankers. The Federal Reserve Act of 1913 created a Federal Reserve Board with five members, each from a different district, appointed by the president. Instead of creating a single central bank, the law established twelve district Federal Reserve banks, each owned by the banks of its region. National banks were required to join the system; state banks might do so. Each district bank had a nine-member board: three members were appointed by the national Federal Reserve Board, three were bankers from the district, and three were nonbankers. The board in Washington directed overall policies. The law met the needs of the banking industry by allowing decentralization and an assets currency. The Wall

Street bankers were the most influential men in the new system. President Wilson made certain that they were represented on the Federal Reserve Board, and all foreign transactions were to go through New York's district Federal Reserve bank. The demand of country bankers for authorization to issue currency based on real estate assets was not met until 1917. Still, the system was so popular that almost all banks rushed to join it.

The Federal Trade Commission and the Antitrust Movement

In 1914, Congress created a new regulatory agency, the Federal Trade Commission (FTC), and passed a new antitrust law, the Clayton Act. Like other forms of regulation, both events involved compromises, and both were a product of agitation and associationalism among different sectors of the business community.

By 1914, the business community had reached a general consensus on the desirability of having a Federal Trade Commission. Small business people—retailers, grain dealers, and the like—desired an agency with broad investigatory powers that could order a halt to the monopolistic practices by big companies threatening to bankrupt their small firms. Big business sought a depoliticization of the trust issue and a structure that would lend continuity to federal trust policy. Partners in the House of Morgan were particularly upset by the breakdown of the gentlemen's agreements they had arranged with the Roosevelt administration. In looking for new federal regulation, they were reacting against the policy of President William Howard Taft.

Unlike Roosevelt and Wilson, Taft was in fact a trustbuster. Under his administration (1909–1913) the Department of Justice launched many new prosecutions and brought others begun under Roosevelt to successful conclusions. In 1911, for example, the Supreme Court ordered the Standard Oil trust and the American Tobacco trust dissolved. Taft also launched a prosecution of United States Steel that especially enraged the Morgan interests. The House of Morgan had secured the approval of Roosevelt's Bureau of Corporations for the acquisition of the Tennessee Coal and Iron Company by United States Steel, an acquisition that gave the Pittsburgh-based firm a dominant interest in the southern steel industry. Taft dissolved the agreement and began an antitrust suit that accused United States Steel of unfairly monopolizing the industry because of this acquisition.

Executives of center firms and large banks wanted to remove such matters from the arena of informal private meetings with administration officials, who might change with the next election and who were always susceptible to the whims of public sentiment. Regulation of business, in their view, was best left to a nonpartisan body removed from day-to-day political considerations. Congress attempted to meet these wishes by creating the FTC in

1914. Each of the commission's five members was appointed for a seven-year term, and these staggered terms ensured long-running policies independent of shifting election results. Congress also granted the commission broad investigatory powers. When the FTC found violations of the antitrust law, it could order them stopped, subject to court appeals.

The Federal Trade Commission Act had a companion, the Clayton Act of 1914, which revised the antitrust laws. The Sherman Act of 1890 had proved to be too vague to satisfy either business or its opponents, so Congress tried to clarify matters in the new bill. The Clayton Act outlawed interlocking directorates in financial firms capitalized at more than $1 million; such firms were not allowed to own stock in other companies if the effect was to reduce competition. The law also forbade "tying contracts" in which large firms prevented their suppliers from doing business with their competitors. And it condemned price discrimination that tended to limit competition. Further, it declared that trade union activities and farm cooperatives did not constitute "combinations in restraint of trade."

Although the Clayton Act gave more clarity and structure to antitrust law, Congress, because of the great diversity of the business interests concerned, was unable to make the law as precise as some wished. The law did not affirm Wilson's earlier call for a "new freedom" for the individual from the center firms; nor did it forbid, as some reformers wished, any firm from capturing more than a specified share of an industry's market. Instead, Congress empowered the FTC to conduct the daily work of trust regulation and the attorney general to seek court rulings to clarify policy.

Tariff Politics and Federal Regulation

The tariff issue continued to plague national politics in the early twentieth century, but during the Progressive Era tariff politics became intertwined with the trust issue. Business associations and reformers began to call for a system of determining tariff rates "scientifically," apart from the pressures of special interests. At the same time, advocates of tariff reform interacted with those who were calling for vigorous antitrust prosecutions.

Some reformers insisted that the tariff was the "mother of trusts" and that adjustments in tariff rates could restore competition to the American business system. The tariff, in their view, contributed to inequities in the distribution of wealth in American society. Some industries that enjoyed protection from foreign competition seemed to enjoy high profits. In the meantime, American consumers paid high hidden taxes when they bought needed imported items. In the eyes of the reformers, a "scientifically" derived tariff schedule designed with the public interest in mind would lower if not eliminate these "regressive taxes" on American consumers. At the same time, the reformers argued that the federal government should impose an income tax on wealthy Americans, a "progressive" tax levied according to the ability to pay.

The ideas of the reformers were not new to the Progressive Era, but they received more publicity and serious attention from politicians than before. The National Association of Manufacturers began pressuring for a system whereby a business-dominated commission would determine tariff rates flexibly, with promises to lower American duties when other nations allowed American goods to enter their markets freely. After it was organized, the United States Chamber of Commerce also took up the call for a flexible system of tariffs designed to ensure greater free trade for American exporters. Even the American Federation of Labor, no longer convinced that high American duties protected high American wages, supported tariff reform.

Tariff reformers enjoyed some successes in the Progressive Era, although the tariff issue was, as always, embroiled in partisan politics. The Payne-Aldrich Act of 1909 provided little relief from existing protective measures, but it did contain some innovations, such as allowing the president to raise American duties by 25 percent when he determined that another nation was restricting American exports. The measure also called for a constitutional amendment to allow Congress to impose an income tax. The law failed to establish a tariff commission to advise the president, however, so President Taft appointed his own Tariff Board to give him expert advice. Congress was reluctant to cede authority over the tariff—and the potential favors to constituents—to a commission, however much the NAM and other business groups advocated the idea.

Tariff reform came only after Woodrow Wilson and the Democratic party assumed control of the government in 1913. Then Congress enacted the Underwood Tariff, which substantially lowered duties. Although it was not a free-trade measure, the Underwood Tariff did reduce rates to the lowest level since the Civil War. With the passage of the income tax amendment in 1913, Congress was able to make up for lost revenue by imposing taxes on the wealthy (the highest tax rate was 7 percent, and there was no withholding tax). But the law also took away the flexibility of the Payne-Aldrich Act, and Congress still declined to establish a tariff commission.

The final Progressive Era contribution to tariff politics came on the eve of the nation's entry into World War I. With the European war disrupting international trade and President Wilson pushing the measure, Congress finally created the United States Tariff Commission in 1916. As with the FTC, the terms of office of the bipartisan commission were staggered to ensure continuity of policy. Under the leadership of its first chairman, economics professor Frank W. Taussig, the commission pursued an advisory role. Taussig believed that elected officials should establish the direction of tariff policy and that the commission should ensure that the policy was put into practice fairly and dispassionately. Congress allowed the commission to work on lowering or raising duties, but elected officials always retained final authority over the tariff.

State Regulation of Business

The creation of the Tariff Commission at the end of the Progressive Era was the last instance before World War I whereby reformers turned to the federally organized commission format for the regulation of business. The use of commissions as responses to the wishes of business associations, the findings of economists, and the complaints of reformers during the Progressive Era also, however, occurred at the state level, where many political leaders looked for fresh ways to shape local business environments.

In the period before World War I, almost all state governments used the commission as a device for regulating business, especially railroad freight and passenger rates and utility rates. By the second decade of the twentieth century, in fact, railroad managers were complaining about their "forty-eight masters." Prior to 1914, state commissions sometimes set rates to benefit local shippers at the expense of distant competitors, but in that year the U.S. Supreme Court clearly forbade states from controlling freight rates so as to have any impact on interstate commerce. After this ruling, the states limited themselves to local rates—some also served as advocates of local shippers before the ICC.

Many national corporate leaders disliked state regulation, not because it was directly hostile to business interests but, first, because it was difficult for a firm doing business in several or even all states to conform to regulations emanating from many different state capitals at once. This was the source of the railroad managers' complaints of "forty-eight masters." And second, state regulation was usually designed to foster the interests of local, and usually smaller, firms and to protect them from competitive pressures from large, vertically integrated, efficient manufacturers and distributors. This situation was particularly acute in the South and the trans-Mississippi West. Up to the middle of twentieth century, those regions suffered from a kind of colonial dependency, sending agricultural goods and raw materials to the cities and factories of the North and East in exchange for finished products. Southern and western entrepreneurs interested in boosting local manufacturing allied with local politicians in attempts to use state regulation to redress the balance.

The use of state antitrust statutes demonstrated this approach clearly. Texas was active in the antitrust field because many of its business and political leaders were convinced that eastern interests were thwarting local development. In the nineteenth century, Standard Oil enjoyed a near monopoly in the oil industry. But subsequent to the opening of vast new oil fields in Texas after 1901, Texas law restrained Standard's activities in the state and promoted the development of two new major oil companies, Gulf Oil and The Texas Company.

State Regulation of Working Conditions

State governments also regulated working conditions during the Progressive Era. The Supreme Court maintained that conditions inside a factory

Bad working conditions—here small boys separate slate from coal—prompted state regulation of work in the Progressive Era. (Library of Congress)

were a local concern, outside of Congress's power to regulate interstate commerce. When Congress outlawed the employment of children, for example, the Court ruled the measure unconstitutional. Nevertheless, many Americans considered unregulated factories undesirable places for the employment of both children and women. Northern states passed laws, for instance, restricting the hours and regulating the working conditions of female employees. They also forbade the hiring of children under the age of fourteen and under the age of sixteen for night work.

Reformers enjoyed notable successes in furthering the cause of industrial safety by the end of the Progressive Era. Economists and other observers wrote about the rates of injury, which were high during this period, and the harmful effects of injuries not only on individual workers but on their families and communities as well. They also worked for systems of state regulation that would effectively force employers to improve safety conditions in plants. The result was the creation of state systems of workers' compensation, either through private insurers or as pioneered by Ohio in 1911.

The workers' compensation reform tied the economic interests of business firms to programs to improve industrial safety. Before the reform, when a worker was injured on the job, he or she could sue for damages in the courts. Businesses were usually able to rebuff their complaints by citing the common law argument that the injured worker had accepted the possibility of injury as part of the job and was therefore responsible for his or her injury. Nevertheless, juries sometimes granted large awards to injured workers. Led by the new-school economist John R. Commons, the reformers created a program designed to give workers a safer environment. Under workers' compensation, the state government insured workers against injury and adjudicated damage claims through an administrative agency (not the courts) according to a schedule of payments rated by types of injuries. Workers' compensation required employers to purchase state insurance, but their premium costs went down when they cooperated with government experts to devise safer working conditions. This program appealed to business as a practical solution to a real labor problem, and associations like the NAM promoted the idea in many state capitals.

State regulation thus became an important factor in the daily lives of many employers and their workers. The problem, from the point of view of business, was that passage of a law in one state could work to the competitive disadvantage of local firms in another state. Federal measures were unlikely to survive a Supreme Court test, given the judicial climate of the day, so the only alternative seemed to be uniform state legislation. One important activity of business associations, thus, was to attempt to have states enact "model" regulatory laws. The idea behind the movement for uniform state legislation was simple: if each state passed the same law and imposed the same regulatory costs, no firm would have a competitive advantage stemming from the fragmented nature of the American governmental system. Business associations spent much time and energy on this matter, but uniform legislation was difficult to achieve in the face of the multitude of special and local business interests characteristic of American society.

The Supreme Court and Reform

The business firms and associations that wanted to resist the efforts of reformers and regulatory agencies often found an ally in the federal courts. Court actions, in fact, had a profound impact on the regulation of business. In the early twentieth century, the Supreme Court often ruled against regulatory measures, especially, as we have seen, those concerning labor. Between 1899 and 1937, the Court used the doctrine of "substantive" due process to strike down state regulatory measures in 184 cases. When the Court found that the "substance" of a law was to deny a corporation its right to life, liberty, or property, it declared the law invalid. This doctrine discouraged both federal and state attempts at regulation.

The Court had an especially profound impact on the antitrust movement. As we saw in the case involving the American Sugar Refining Company in 1895, the Court ruled that a monopoly in manufacturing was not a restraint of trade under the Sherman Act. The Court asserted that a manufacturing monopoly enacted in one state did not "directly" affect interstate commerce even though the factory's products were sold across state borders. This decision caused a furor, and Theodore Roosevelt warned that it would effectively nullify the antitrust law. Not long thereafter, in 1899, the Court ruled that small firms in the same industry could not arrange contracts to control interstate sales. The net effect of these two decisions was to encourage the late-nineteenth-century merger movement, for though it seemed legal for one firm to dominate an industry, it was clearly illegal for smaller firms to control an industry through some arrangement of private associations.

In the Progressive Era, the Supreme Court still retained its prerogative of deciding what "trusts" were legal. In the Northern Securities case of 1904, the Court dissolved the combination of three railroad systems in the Pacific Northwest and thereby asserted the supremacy of federal power. In 1905, the Court ruled against practices of integrated meat-packing firms that amounted to collusion and price fixing. Most dramatically, the Court ordered the Standard Oil and American Tobacco trusts to be dissolved into smaller units in 1911. Rockefeller's firm was required to split into seven smaller oil companies. In these cases, the Court enunciated a "rule of reason" doctrine under which it declared that large firms that did not have an undue impact on competition were allowable. When it applied its "rule of reason" to Standard Oil and American Tobacco, the Court found that those combinations were illegal, because they were so large as to prevent competition. This doctrine allowed the Court flexibility in future cases, and in the 1920s it refused to dissolve other large integrated firms when they operated without monopoly control over pricing in their industries.

BUSINESS, REFORM, AND THE IMMIGRANT LABOR FORCE

American business and its reformers became intimately involved in another important movement during the Progressive Era: Americanization. This involvement came about as a result of the confluence of two major historical trends: immigration and a rising demand for semiskilled and unskilled workers.

With the return to prosperity after 1897, the United States witnessed a flood of new immigrants. During the Progressive Era, the prevailing flow of migration was from southern and Eastern Europe, as Italians, Slavs, Greeks, and Jews sought economic opportunity in America's bustling industrial centers. The immigration reached flood tide in 1907, when 1 million newcomers arrived in the country. Immigration was as old as American history, but these "new" immigrants added to the mixture of cultures in America as never before. The immigrants arrived, moreover, while a second trend was under way: the increasing mechanization and routinization of American factory production. The mines, mills, and factories of the industrial workplace offered numerous opportunities for semiskilled and unskilled workers, occupations for which businesses often recruited the newcomers from Europe.

America's industrial growth attracted millions of immigrants from Europe and Asia in the late nineteenth and early twentieth centuries. (Library of Congress)

The New Immigration

The arrival of the "new" immigrants seemed to pose special problems. To social reformers—educators, nurses, church leaders, social workers, and the like—the problems involved adjustment to American conditions. The immigrants too often arrived in poverty, without the resources and skills necessary to obtain adequate housing, food, and care for themselves. To many other Americans the strangeness of immigrant ways was perceived as a threat to a culture rooted in British traditions. Out of these various concerns arose widespread worries about how American institutions would cope with and care for the flood of newcomers. The immigrants had to be taught the English language, learn American customs and laws, and adapt their traditional lifestyles, which were usually rooted in peasant ways, to the routine and rigor required for survival and advancement in a complex urban-industrial society.

Employers had a special interest in this educational process. Factory work was very different from the agricultural work the newcomers were accustomed to, and they had to be taught its requirements. The immigrants needed instruction in simple matters such as how to take the correct streetcar at the right time to check into the factory at the appointed hour, and they had to learn the importance of punctuality, sobriety, and regular work attendance, no matter what the season or what traditional folk festival might be occurring.

Americanization

The result of these educational needs was the Americanization movement, led by Frances Kellor, a well-educated woman who committed her life to social reform. Kellor edited a magazine devoted to Americanization and enlisted the support of intellectuals and other reformers for her programs. She also worked with the federal government to establish a bureau to promote the education of immigrants and to aid local communities in their own efforts.

Kellor was especially interested in working closely with business firms, both to meet their needs for training and controlling the work force and to satisfy her wish to deal directly with the newcomers. She and other reformers helped the Chamber of Commerce establish its Immigration Committee, which worked to have businesses establish classes inside factories where immigrant workers were being taught English and the necessity of punctuality, regular work routines, and humility toward overseers. The Chamber of Commerce and Kellor recruited volunteer teachers from the YMCA and YWCA to concentrate their Americanization efforts in a so-called industrial zone, the area bounded by the Potomac, Ohio, and Mississippi rivers. In response to this campaign, individual firms provided space for Americanization classes and required immigrant workers to attend.

The paternal spirit that underlay the Americanization movement also led business people to contribute funds and serve on the boards of social-service institutions, to play an active role in reforming public school systems, and to engage in various philanthropic activities. Just as there was an emerging system of government-business cooperation regarding the "trust" question and the control of price competition during the Progressive Era, so was there a growing involvement of business in broader social affairs.

MOBILIZATION FOR WAR

This cooperation reached its zenith when the United States declared war on Germany and Austria-Hungary in April 1917. Suddenly, the nation was confronted with an unprecedented situation: the necessity of rapidly and efficiently mobilizing its industrial resources for a major European war, for America's British and French allies urgently needed its munitions, weapons, and foodstuffs. Peacetime market forces could no longer be permitted to govern the flow of goods and services and the allocation of capital in the American economy. New administrative means had to be found quickly to replace many customary business practices.

The problem with turning from an economy still governed partly by market forces to one operated by administrative agencies was that those agencies did not exist, at least in government. Although government bureaucracies had grown with the reforms of the Progressive Era, they hardly had the resources to administer full-scale economic mobilization. To raise and equip its own armed forces and supply its allies, the federal government had to construct a host of new agencies and then turn to business volunteers to staff them. America's large vertically integrated firms, and to a lesser extent the trade associations, were populated by experienced cadres of administrators. They volunteered for public service, often as "dollar-a-year men" (so called because the government paid them a token salary while they remained on private payrolls).

Wartime Agencies

The new wartime mobilization agencies evolved slowly as business and government leaders struggled to avoid too much government direction while achieving the needed results. Eventually, the intervention of government in business life was extensive. In October 1916, before the American declaration of war, President Wilson formed a cabinet-level Council of National Defense with a seven-member advisory commission. Four of the commission members were prominent businessmen, two were well known in the engineering and medical professions, and the seventh, Samuel Gompers, headed the AF of L. The task of the commission and the council was to recommend policies for improving the nation's preparedness in the event of war. Following the advice of Bernard Baruch, a Wall Street speculator who sat on the commission, the council called on private industry to form cooperative committees for every line of trade, committees with which the government could work in coordinating military procurement. Soon a multitude of committees and subcommittees emerged, each composed of leaders from private industry and coordinated by a designated member of the advisory commission. The committees' original purpose was to make detailed studies of their industries, but when the United States entered the war, they became responsible for coordinating production and sales to the military.

The fairly informal system did not work very well. Soon after the declaration of war, the economy was in chaos, with the armed services competing with one another desperately for supplies and business people trying to position themselves favorably in the new market. Firms tried to arrange rules to their advantage. As the problems mounted, however, the solutions started to come. In the summer of 1917, Wilson appointed a successful mining engineer, Herbert Hoover, who had gained popularity for his work in organizing European food relief, to head a new Food Administration. Hoover's task was to implore Americans to produce and conserve foodstuffs and especially to coordinate the flow of agricultural products to places in desperate need. Then, at the end of 1917, Wilson asked Congress to federalize the railroads and place them under the control of a U.S. Railroad Administration. The nation's transportation system was breaking down, with railroads burdened with large flows of traffic toward seaports. The task of the new Railroad Administration was to sort out the mess, impose efficiencies on an industry whose firms were accustomed to competing for traffic, and coordinate the arrival of freight trains and ships. For this task the government used experienced railroad managers who divided the nation into districts and made certain that equipment and traffic were shared. To coordinate and boost the production of energy, the government also created the U.S. Fuel Administration.

The new mobilization agencies took their final shape in March of 1918 with the appointment of Bernard Baruch as head of the War Industries Board. Under Baruch's leadership, the board avoided issuing commands and encouraged voluntary cooperation. The government worked closely with private associations in allocating contracts and setting production priorities. No believer in an economy operated through free-market forces, Baruch ensured that a close partnership between government and business emerged in which government assisted business people in the private associational activities of administering the economy.

The Wartime Legacy

After the war ended in 1918, most of the special business agencies of coordination and administration began to disband. The values and ideas they represented, however, remained. The American economy had been successfully mobilized in a short period of time to support a large U.S. armed force abroad and to bring critically needed supplies to the nation's allies. This mobilization was impressive, as it was accomplished by cooperation, planning, and administrative coordination. Mobilization had required abandoning the "invisible hand" of market coordination in sectors of the economy still characterized by peripheral firms. The owners of most of these firms believed they had benefited from the wartime partnership with the government as it had involved cooperative planning in allocating and pricing goods and services. As we shall see in Chapter 9, business executives and government leaders thus sought to continue these benefits in peacetime.

TOWARD A MODERN BUSINESS SYSTEM

The American business system changed fundamentally in the years of the Progressive Era and World War I. Those changes did not so much involve the pattern of business organization, which had emerged with the rise of integrated big business firms of the 1880s and the merger wave of the 1890s, but instead occurred in the relationships between businesses and among business, government, and society. Associationalism grew rapidly, peaking during the war. So too did the values of cooperation, not competition. Government regulation of business increased.

In many lines of manufacturing and transportation, the benefits of replacing the invisible hand of the market with the visible hand of management seemed clear, and business managers and prominent politicians sought ways of bringing those benefits to sectors in which economic and technological circumstances had not led to the rise of giant firms. By the start of World War I, they seemed to be reaching their goal. The Supreme Court had announced its "rule of reason," which seemed to grant legal sanction to many big firms. The decades-long controversy over the "trusts" seemed to be ebbing. Even the tariff issue that had so long plagued American politics was, it seemed, susceptible to "scientific" solutions by an expert commission.

It was during this period, too, that business began involving itself with local communities and social problems in new ways. The idea of using the administrative bureaucracy of the business world to deal with social and political problems was deeply implanted by 1917. Business leaders encouraged "efficiency" and the bureaucratic application of expert knowledge to schools, local governments, churches, and other social institutions. Business firms and associations were also instrumental in helping the nation cope with the Americanization of its new arrivals.

The experience of business executives during World War I had a profound effect on the conduct of business in the United States, especially in the center firms. The war disrupted business and the American economy, but it also created new opportunities. After the war, firms supplying consumer durable goods, especially automobiles, came to the forefront of the business system. American executives pioneered in arranging decentralized, diversified big businesses suitable for the new conditions of a more affluent nation.

Selected Readings

Robert H. Wiebe, *The Search for Order, 1877–1920* (New York: Hill and Wang, 1967), is a good introduction to the Progressive Era. More directly concerned with the themes of government-business relations are Samuel Haber, *Efficiency and Uplift: Scientific Management in the Progressive Era, 1890–1920* (Chicago: University of Chicago Press, 1964); Edward Berkowitz and Kim McQuaid, *Creating the Welfare State: The Political Economy of Twentieth-Century Reform* (New York: Praeger Publishers, 1980); and Martin J. Sklar, *The Corporate Reconstruction of American Capitalism, 1890–1916* (New York: Cambridge University Press, 1988).

Other studies that provide insights into this period include Wiebe, "The House of Morgan and the Executive, 1905–1913," *American Historical Review* 65 (October

1959): 49–60; Mansel G. Blackford, *The Politics of Business in California, 1890–1920* (Columbus: Ohio State University Press, 1977); K. Austin Kerr, *American Railroad Politics, 1914–1920* (Pittsburgh: University of Pittsburgh Press, 1968); Robert Cuff, *The War Industries Board: Business-Government Relations During World War I* (Baltimore: Johns Hopkins University Press, 1973); and Thomas McCraw, *Prophets of Regulation* (Cambridge, Mass.: Harvard University Press, 1984).

IMPORTANT EVENTS, 1913–1945

1913–1915 Ford Motors introduces the moving assembly line, used in the construction of the Model T.

1920 More Americans live in cities and towns than on farms and in small villages.

1920–1922 A recession exposes managerial weaknesses in large businesses.

1920–1924 General Motors and Du Pont adopt decentralized management.

1925 Sears, Roebuck opens urban retail outlets.
Black entrepreneurs found the Chicago Metropolitan Assurance Company.

1925–1931 The United States experiences its second merger movement.

1929 The Stock Market Crash signals the beginning of the Great Depression.

1940 Some 110 universities enroll 100,000 students in business courses.

1942 U.S. production of industrial war goods surpasses that of Germany, Japan, and Italy combined.

1945 Henry Ford II becomes president of Ford Motors.

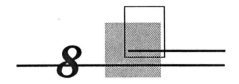

8

The Diversified,
Decentralized Company

Looking back over his long career at General Motors, Alfred P. Sloan, Jr.—who as president reshaped the company's management structure in the 1920s—commented on what he considered his major contribution to the firm and to American business as a whole: "My thoughts . . . have always revolved around one concept which contains considerable complexity in theory and reality—the concept that goes by the oversimplified name of decentralization." Led by General Motors and other firms during the 1920s, 1930s, and 1940s, some businesses moved from centralized to decentralized management systems, especially as they sought to orient their strategies toward available markets. In setting up decentralized management structures, Sloan and his counterparts in other firms were launching a process of restructuring of big firms that would continue after World War II.

The development of new management structures by individual firms was symptomatic of an evolution in business strategy. The business system changed as a result of experiences with markets and profits. After World War I some executives like Sloan were developing an innovative marketing conception of their firms. Prior to 1920, with the rise of big business and the strategy of vertical integration, manufacturing executives tended to view their companies as production units, and they focused attention on lowering production costs and controlling the prices of goods. The route to corporate success lay in controlling direct price competition. Sloan was a pioneer in developing an alternative conception of the manufacturing firm that stressed selling goods as the ultimate goal. The diversification strategy and decentralized structure that Sloan helped spearhead resulted from a marketing as opposed to a production orientation in leading a firm. When the United States experienced the Great Depression that began in 1929 and lasted a decade, the worst collapse of prosperity in history, the firms like General Motors that continued to earn profits tended to be those that had diversified their product lines across a range of markets, and that had reorganized themselves to allow executives to shift resources from less profitable to more profitable markets. In short, in many lines of activity, manufacturing standardized products for a mass market remained profitable; but slowly the most savvy business executives began to think in terms of segmented markets and differentiated and diverse product lines.

Within the phenomenon of the development of a marketing conception of operating a business alongside the more traditional production conception, two trends in the social impact of business developments stood out. First, companies began to spend more heavily on advertising than ever before, attempting to influence the behavior of individual consumers. Businesses thus encouraged the growth of *consumerism*, a set of values that placed a higher priority on the use of goods and services than on their production. Second, the nature of corporate leadership began to shift. As the marketing orientation gained sway, executives with experience in sales and distribution, rather than in production, were more likely to advance to leadership positions in corporations. Also, as the entreprenurial empire builders gave way to a new generation of business leaders, executives with less of a personal stake in their companies rose to power. The separation of ownership from management, which had started in the nineteenth century, accelerated in the twentieth. As the separation of ownership from management proceeded, business executives began claiming the mantle of professionalism. Asserting that they were similar to lawyers, doctors, and clergy, they maintained that their mission was not simply to make a profit but to serve society. They issued codes of business ethics, made corporate contributions to philanthropy, and became involved in professional education for business.

CHANGES IN THE AMERICAN BUSINESS SYSTEM

Business opportunities changed dramatically following World War I, as America evolved from a producer-dominated to a consumer-oriented society. Opportunities also varied with the ups and downs in the general economic climate of the United States.

Economic Growth and Economic Distress

The onset of the Great Depression in 1929 in particular affected every American institution in the decade following. The economic growth rate during this period was much lower than it had been during the previous fifty years. Between 1921 and 1946, America's real GNP doubled, but GNP per capita rose only 79 percent. (See Figure 8.1.) As in the past, economic growth was affected by both domestic and foreign developments.

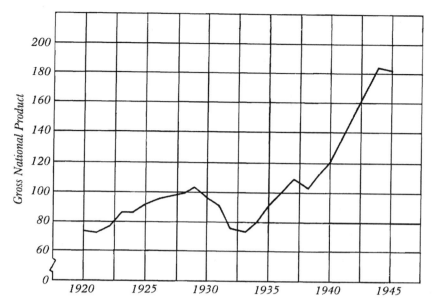

Figure 8.1   U.S. Gross National Product. 1921–1946 (in billions of dollars, 1929 prices) (SOURCE: Based on data from U.S. Bureau of the Census: *Historical Statistics of the United States, Colonial Times to 1957* [Washington, D.C.: U.S. Government Printing Office, 1960], p. 139.)

In foreign trade, the United States became a strong creditor nation during World War I and maintained that position throughout the following three decades. During this period, America's exports exceeded its imports except during the depression years of 1934 through 1940. Reflecting America's emergence as the leading industrial power of the world, the nation's exports came increasingly to be composed of industrial items, while its imports consisted more and more of raw materials.

These changes in foreign trade notwithstanding, the internal domestic market remained, as it had been in the nineteenth century, the most important factor in the economic prosperity of the United States. In the mid-twentieth century, the national market became even more lucrative as it was further unified by new forms of transportation and communications—automobiles, trucks, airplanes, telephones, big city newspapers, and the radio—and as the population rose from 106 million in 1920 to 141 million in 1946. Business institutions continued to develop in order to tap this ever-growing market. Chain stores, for example, greatly expanded. By 1929, A & P had 15,418 stores in America, Woolworth 1,825, J. C. Penney 1,395, and Safeway 2,660.

Structural shifts in the American business system begun in earlier years also continued in the second quarter of the twentieth century. In 1920, for the first time in the country's history, more people lived in towns and cities than on farms or in small villages, and the contribution of farming to the economy declined in relative terms as the United States completed its transformation from a rural agricultural society to an urban industrial one. Manufacturing, which suffered during the depression years of the 1930s, picked up as factories shifted to the production of war goods in the early and mid-1940s. Service industries continued to grow in significance, a trend that would become even more pronounced after World War II.

Sears, Roebuck Exploits America's Domestic Market

The continuing growth of the internal market provided new business opportunities, as the history of the nation's leading retailer reveals. Mail-order houses like Montgomery Ward and Sears, Roebuck, which had grown up in the late nineteenth century to serve the farm market, found it necessary to modify their business strategies as cities became more important. Both companies moved into the rapidly growing urban market by opening retail outlets across the United States, but the experiences of Sears illustrate particularly well this shift in retailing.

Richard Sears founded the company that would become Sears, Roebuck to sell watches through the mail in 1886. Alvah Roebuck, who originally joined him in this venture as a watch repairman, worked to broaden the firm's offerings. In 1893, Sears, Roebuck was incorporated, and throughout the 1890s the company increased its sales, mainly to farmers who could not easily reach urban stores. Farmers selected merchandise from the company's catalogues, placed their orders through the mail (Sears maintained a central warehouse in Chicago from which the orders were filled), and received their goods by railroad.

Sears, Roebuck continued to grow in the early twentieth century, but problems surfaced. Richard Sears was a promotional genius, but he failed to establish the organization needed to run the expanding business. Because of disagreements over how to manage the company, Roebuck left the firm in 1895. Sears then brought Julius Rosenwald, a Chicago clothing merchant, into the business as a source of new capital. Together, Sears and Rosenwald built up Sears, Roebuck into a large national company, with Sears focusing on marketing and Rosenwald on administration. With sales of $10 million, Sears, Roebuck outstripped its rivals to become America's leading mail-order house by 1900. Twenty years later, the sales of Sears topped $200 million. By this time Richard Sears had left the company, and it became a publicly held corporation.

The growing importance of the urban market in the 1920s and 1930s led the managers at Sears to reassess their company's operations. Robert

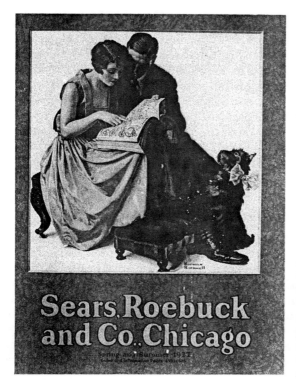

Mail-order firms were an important innovation in the nation's retail distribution system. The 1927 cover of the Sears, Roebuck catalogue featured a painting by Norman Rockwell, who depicted a couple studying a catalogue of the industry's most successful firm. (Sears Archive)

Wood, who joined Sears in 1925 and became president three years later, took the company into the city. Although it continued to serve farmers through its mail-order business, Sears began opening retail outlets in 1925, and over the next three decades the company built its stores at the intersections of busy traffic arteries, where they could be easily reached by automobile, in medium-sized and large cities all over the nation. Montgomery Ward, which continued to emphasize the farm and small-town market, fell steadily behind Sears. Wood complemented his new selling strategy with a new buying strategy: by working closely with its suppliers, Sears was able to provide its stores with a steady stream of high-quality goods designed to the company's own specifications.

The results of Wood's actions were dramatic. By 1929, retail sales accounted for 40 percent of Sears's total sales, and a decade later they composed two-thirds of them. By 1954, when Wood retired, Sears had become the world's largest merchandising operation. The company operated 694 retail stores and 570 catalogue sales offices. These outlets employed 200,000 people and generated annual sales of $3 billion.

The growth of big retailers such as Sears limited opportunities for small businesses in sales, which in earlier years had been a stronghold for small firms. Large department stores and chain stores, such as A & P in groceries, also eroded the importance of small businesses in sales. The growth of chain stores was most dramatic. The number of chains in the United States went from 905 in 1921 to 1,718 seven years later. By 1929, the chain stores were doing 20 percent of the nation's retail business. Most of the nonindependent outlets were considerably larger than those of independent retailers. By 1939, for example, the average chain store had annual sales of $75,000, roughly four times the volume of the typical independent retailer. Also as a result of this trend, thousands of small retailers in towns across America faced new and vigorous competition from large, efficient distributors like Sears.

Manufacturers Stress Consumer Durables

In manufacturing, new consumer goods industries developed, and older ones became more oriented to the production of consumer durables (items purchased by consumers for use over more than a year or two). General Electric and Westinghouse, for example, began producing electric stoves, refrigerators, washing machines, and other appliances in addition to their original electricity-generating equipment. From its pre–World War I base in black powder and chemicals, Du Pont branched out into the making of synthetic fibers such as rayon and nylon in the 1920s and 1930s. The radio industry was born and reached a robust adolescence in the single decade of the 1920s.

Most remarkable, however, was the tremendous expansion of the automobile industry. Henry Ford's success in using the assembly line to produce the Model T greatly lowered the price of automobiles, making them affordable to many farmers and most middle-class Americans and thus bringing "mass automobility" to the nation. In 1915, there were 2.3 million automobiles registered in the United States; by 1929, the number had risen to more than 23 million. The development of the automobile industry spurred the growth of a host of related industries: steel, oil, glass, and rubber. In the rubber industry, for example, B. F. Goodrich, Goodyear, Firestone, and U.S. Rubber (later known as Uniroyal) came of age as big businesses to supply the automobile industry.

As a generalization, it can be said that in the nineteenth century Americans built their factories and that in the twentieth century those factories began turning out an increasing number of products for use by consumers. This redirection involved changes in the American market and in business executives' perceptions of the roles of their firms in terms of the market. Important technological and scientific breakthroughs in chemicals, metallurgy, and other fields allowed executives to think in terms of orienting their firms toward a range of diversified products for different markets. Perhaps most important for the continued industrialization of the United States was the adoption of electricity, a more flexible and efficient power source than steam in many situations in factory work. By 1939, electric motors accounted for 90 percent of the power used in manufacturing.

In short, America began changing from a producer-dominated to a consumer-oriented society, a shift that continued after World War II. Patterns of spending changed. Americans now spent a much greater proportion of their income on consumer durables than ever before. The share of household income devoted to the purchase of major consumer durables such as electric stoves doubled from 4 percent in 1898–1916 to 8 percent during the 1920s. In 1899, more than two-thirds of spending for consumer durables went for household goods such as furniture, china, tableware, and musical instruments; only 7 percent went for transportation goods, mainly horse-drawn vehicles. In 1929, by contrast, household goods, which now included radios, stoves, and the like, accounted for only half of the expenditures. Transportation goods, mainly automobiles, took over a third of all consumer durable spending. Americans dramatically increased their personal debt to finance this spending. Debt per household nearly tripled between 1900 and 1918 and then nearly doubled again during the 1920s. The savings rate correspondingly fell. The share of disposable income (income people could do with as they pleased) that Americans saved nearly halved from 6.4 percent to only 3.8 percent during the opening three decades of the twentieth century.

Nowhere was the new orientation clearer than in the development of a car culture. Like radios and electric appliances, cars became more than luxuries for many Americans. They were increasingly viewed as necessities, and the use of automobiles came to affect nearly all aspects of life. By bringing a new mobility to Americans, cars linked the farm with the city. Urban and rural differences lessened, and life became more standardized throughout the United States. Widespread jokes, especially about the Model T, indicated just how central the automobile had become to American culture. A man about to die, it was said, asked to be buried in his Model T, because he had never yet been in a hole that his car could not get him out of. But not all folklore was so favorable. One ditty declared, "Of all the noises there is none worse than a Model T going in reverse"—a reference to the Ford's transmission.

Business Becomes More Oligopolistic

The trend toward concentration and the growth of oligopoly, which had begun in the late nineteenth century, continued in the twentieth. The United States experienced its second major merger movement in the 1920s (as discussed in Chapter 5, the first merger movement took place between 1894 and 1905). To a greater extent than in the past, the mergers of the 1920s occurred among large and medium-sized, rather than truly giant, companies. There were two important trends in the merger wave of the 1920s. Amost a third of the mergers involved companies seeking to diversify

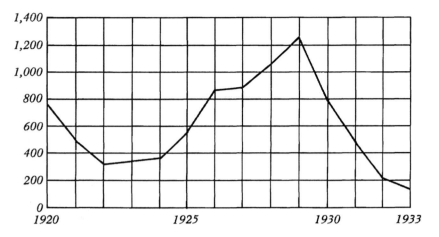

Figure 8.2   Mergers in Manufacturing and Mining in the United States. 1920–1933 [SOURCE: Based on data from U.S. Bureau of the Census, *Historical Statistics of the United States, Colonial Times to 1970*, pt. 2 (Washington, D.C.: U.S. Government Printing Office, 1975), p. 914.]

product lines in pursuit of a market-oriented business strategy. In general, the mergers led not to monopoly, where one firm dominates an entire industry, but toward oligopoly, where a few firms dominate an industry (and behave much like a monopoly). Altogether, 5,846 mergers took place in the years 1925 through 1931. (See Figure 8.2.) As a result, industrial production in America became increasingly concentrated in the factories of big businesses. The 100 largest manufacturing concerns in the United States increased their share of the nation's manufacturing assets from 36 percent in 1925 to 44 percent six years later. These big businesses continued to develop most of America's private industrial research laboratories. In 1933, some 113 of the nation's largest 200 industrial companies operated research laboratories; by 1948, some 164 did. And those laboratories typically were looking for new products to fulfill a corporate strategy of product diversification.

With this growth in the concentration of American industry, price competition between manufacturing firms decreased (competition based on advertising, service, and quality continued). Prices in oligopolistic industries made up of center firms became less flexible, less responsive to market forces. A drop in demand no longer automatically led to a fall in prices. Administered pricing—the setting of prices by managers of center firms—replaced price setting by market forces in many fields of manufacturing. The visible hand of management, already significant in the 1880s and 1890s, grew in importance during the 1920s. This practice of administered prices allowed some companies to survive the Great Depression, for prices generally fell less in oligopolistic industries than in industries characterized by competition. For instance, General Motors, America's largest automobile company in the 1930s, responded quickly to the depression by slashing salaries and wages, laying off workers, and cutting back its production of cars by almost three-quarters. The company was slower in lowering the prices of its cars and, even in the depths of the Great Depression, continued to earn a profit.

The growth of oligopolistic big business, combined with the continued persistence of small business, made the distinction between center and peripheral firms even more pronounced. (While losing market share to larger concerns, some small businesses persisted, as they had since the 1870s, as niche producers in manufacturing.) The differences between large and small enterprises became more noticeable, and America's business system increasingly became divided into separate spheres along those lines. A dual economy developed.

Alterations in farming mirrored the changes taking place in the U.S. economy as a whole. During the first five decades of the twentieth century, two types of farming developed side by side. Small family farms found it increasingly difficult to compete with a growing number of large, highly capitalized farms using the most advanced scientific methods and machinery. Between 1920 and 1945, about 3 million more Americans left farming than entered it. Fewer farmers produced more food for U.S. consumption and for export. Moreover, larger farms produced a greater and greater share of the total farm output. By 1948, the largest 10 percent of America's farms accounted for 24 percent of the nation's farm output; the smallest 20 percent of the farms raised less than 3 percent of the total output.

The Rise of Marketing and Advertising

In the 1920s, a new conception of marketing began to appear that influenced business strategy and led to changes in the structure of American firms. Marketing as an orientation involved conceiving of a company as an institution that sold goods as opposed to simply producing them. Marketing meant setting the firm's strategy according to realistic observations of available customers and then organizing the firm to coordinate production, distribution, sales, and service according to those observations. In the 1920s and 1930s, pioneers in the marketing approach to management learned the importance of differentiating their products from those of their competitors, of having a range of products to offer consumers, and of advertising heavily to influence customers' behavior.

During the 1920s, while marketing was emerging as a conscious business strategy, advertising matured as an important industry. The maturation of advertising in the 1920s and the creation of marketing departments and marketing strategies by major firms both promoted consumer values in American society and reflected the rise of the consumer society. In 1919, advertising costs were 8 percent of total distribution costs in industry; by 1929, the share was 14 percent. In that latter year, advertising costs reached nearly $3 billion.

The content of advertising messages shifted in the early twentieth century. Before 1910, advertisers mostly sought to inform customers about products; after 1910, the main goal was to create a desire to purchase products. By the 1920s, advertising executives recognized that theirs was a business to make consumers want products, and they deliberately sought to break down popular attitudes of self-denial and to foster the idea of instant gratification through consumption. The introduction of new techniques for printing advertisements in color opened new possibilities of suggestion and persuasion. As a result of the growth of advertising expenditures in the 1920s, not only did the magazine business prosper but business executives were better able than ever before to inject attitudes favorable to consumption—even for products for which there was no need. The makers of Fleischmann's yeast, for instance, claimed that the product, in addition to leavening bread, cured "intestinal fatigue" when eaten directly. And one advertisement for Listerine, which promoted fears about a disease newly discovered by copywriters, "halitosis," suggested that "unpleasant breath" was the main "obstacle to pleasant business, professional, and social relations" and urged Americans to use the mouthwash as a way of climbing the social and economic ladder.

At the same time that the advertising industry was flourishing, a few business firms launched innovative programs in "commercial research," or what later generations called marketing. A representative of the *Saturday Evening Post*, a widely circulated weekly magazine, was unhappy with the way advertising space was being sold, because the magazine's space salesmen had no knowledge about their customers' needs or the effectiveness of advertisements. The publisher hired Charles Coolidge Parlin to use social-science techniques to study those questions, the first market research. In 1916 the nation's largest rubber firm, U.S. Rubber, had established a market research department, and the Swift meat-packing concern followed suit in 1917. These efforts pioneered attempts by American manufacturers to integrate systematic knowledge of markets with advertising and the design and production of goods.

In oligopolistic industries, as price competition lessened, marketing techniques and advertising messages became increasingly important ways for companies to differentiate their products and to promote sales. General Motors, for instance, led the automobile companies in instituting annual model changes that were primarily cosmetic in nature (although Sloan insisted that the company improve and differentiate its products through research and technical innovation as well). Style became increasingly important in selling goods. The development of consumer credit accompanied the evolution of marketing and advertising. Paying for goods in monthly installments rather than with a lump sum became more and more common as America's consumer-oriented society expanded. General Motors set up the General Motors Acceptance Corporation in 1919 to help people finance car purchases, and Ford Motors established a similar agency about ten years later. By 1929, installment buying accounted for 90 percent of sewing machine and washing machine purchases, about 80 percent of all sales of radios, refrigerators, and vacuum cleaners, and 60 percent of car sales in the United States.

BUSINESS DIVERSIFICATION AND THE SPREAD OF DECENTRALIZED MANAGEMENT

The changing economic conditions of the United States had a major impact on the nature of the management of the nation's business firms. The broadened range of consumer goods produced by many companies, which resulted from sustained efforts at diversification, required the institution of new management methods. As late as 1910, even the largest American manufacturing companies still produced only one or two major items for a few primary markets. Functionally departmentalized central management systems were adequate for those companies, for officers in the head office could handle the relatively uncomplicated operations of their firms. However, as companies grew in size and especially as they increased the number of goods they produced and the markets they served, centralized management no longer sufficed. A few officers, or even a few committees, in a head office could no longer manage well the growing complexity of their company's work. They could not oversee the daily operations of their firm and simultaneously plan for its future.

Conditions Leading to Decentralization

A sharp postwar recession that began in the summer of 1920 and lasted into early 1922 revealed the inability of centralized management systems to handle complexity and spurred business leaders to revamp their management structures to take advantage of the new consumer markets. This recession showed, above all, that corporate officers were still so caught up in the daily affairs of their companies that they were not preparing for the future. None had any plans for dealing with the drop in demand that their products faced during the recession. Because of this lack of planning, few businesses could adjust to new conditions quickly enough. The consequences were traumatic. Julius Rosenwald was forced to use his personal funds to save Sears, Roebuck from bankruptcy. J. Ogden Armour had to yield control of the meat-packing company founded by his father. And Ford Motors, General Motors, Goodyear, Du Pont, and many other concerns faced severe financial difficulties.

In coping with their problems, some of these companies adopted decentralized systems of management: the head office concentrated on planning for the entire company and delegated authority over most daily operations to semiautonomous divisions organized around product lines. (Decentralized management is sometimes referred to as federalized decentralization. It is also called the M-form of management, with M standing for multidivisional. Centralized management is sometimes called the U-form of management, with U standing for Unitary.) As part of their reorganizations, these firms also greatly improved their market forecasting and financial controls by obtaining more accurate sales information. No longer did a handful of people in the head office attempt to run all aspects of their company's operations. This new form of management gave the companies a flexibility to react to changing situations not present in the older centralized management systems.

As we saw in Chapter 5, many railroads divided managerial responsibility between policy decisions handled by executives in the central office and operational decisions made by executives in the divisional offices. One railroad, the Pennsylvania, developed a fairly elaborate system of decentralized management under the leadership of its president, J. Edgar Thomson. To solve managerial problems caused by a rapid increase in the size and complexity of his company, Thomson divided the Pennsylvania into three regional systems and placed a general manager in charge of each of the regions or divisions. These general managers had direct responsibility for all the operations within their areas: scheduling trains, maintaining the roadbed, purchasing equipment, and hiring personnel. Each of the three major regional systems was further divided into subsystems of trackage. Each subsystem had a manager of operations, who reported to the general manager of his major regional system. The managers of these divisions and subdivisions—known as line officers—handled the routine work of running the trains, and they were given considerable autonomy in accomplishing this task as long as they followed the general guidelines, policies, and procedures of their company. Freed now from the need to make routine operating decisions, the managers in the head office (known as the corporate officers) of the Pennsylvania—the president and three vice presidents—were able to turn their full attention to strategic decision making. They oversaw the work of the regional managers and made plans for their railroad as a whole. They decided where to expand or contract operations, how to deal with competing railroads, and how to arrange financing for their line.

Although the railroads pioneered decentralized management, the executives of industrial companies, led by Du Pont and General Motors, brought it to maturity in the 1920s, 1930s, and 1940s with little reference to those earlier efforts. Instead, each company arrived at a similar solution for a similar problem: how to control complex business operations. The experiences of Du Pont and General Motors illustrate a cardinal point about the history of business in the United States: corporate structure follows business strategy. Those companies that chose to grow through diversification found themselves almost forced to adopt the new structure of decentralized management. Those that expanded without increasing the number or complexity of their products or markets found that centralized management systems could handle their needs and therefore made few changes in their management methods.

The Du Pont Company
Pioneers in Decentralized Management

The Du Pont Company, one of the country's oldest firms, was the first industrial concern to create a plan to decentralize its management, although not the first to implement one. Founded in 1802 on the banks of Brandywine Creek in Delaware as a small gunpowder company, Du Pont remained a producer of gunpowder and other explosives throughout the nineteenth century. Family members ran the company in an informal manner. In 1902 the company's senior partner, Eugene Du Pont, died, and the five remaining family partners, all older Du Ponts, uncertain about what to do, considered selling their firm to a rival company. Alfred Du Pont objected, and with the aid of his cousins Pierre S. and Coleman Du Pont, he persuaded the five elder Du Pont partners to sell out to the three younger Du Ponts.

Pierre quickly emerged as the leader of this trio and soon took the company into a dynamic period of growth and diversification. Du Pont expanded steadily as a producer of munitions and explosives until the outbreak of World War I, when growth soared. Between 1914 and 1918, the number of workers at Du Pont rose from 5,300 to more than 85,000, the gross capital employed by the company climbed from $86 million to $310 million, and net profits totaled $238 million. At the same time, Du Pont started diversifying its production as its officers sought investment outlets for the wartime profits and worried about a slump in demand for munitions once the war ended. As late as 1913, all but 3 percent of the company's sales were in explosives, but over the next six years Du Pont entered new fields. By 1919, Du Pont had moved beyond explosives into chemicals, dyes, paint, and artificial fibers such as rayon.

The management structure of the Du Pont Company lagged behind these changes in business strategy; in 1919 it was still centralized. The company consisted of four major functional departments (production, sales, development, and treasury) and several minor ones whose work was, in theory at least, overseen and coordinated by an executive committee in the head office, which was guided in making its decisions by a flow of financial data from the departments and by advice from personnel, legal, and real estate officers. In the realm of finance, major improvements had been made in cost accounting, and under Pierre the Du Pont Company pioneered in

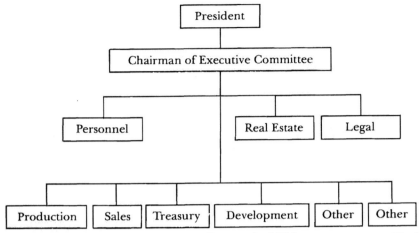

Figure 8.3 Du Pont's Management System in 1919 [SOURCE: From Alfred D. Chandler, Jr., *Strategy and Structure* (Cambridge, Mass.: MIT Press, 1962). Copyright © 1962 by Massachusetts Institute of Technology.]

employing the principle of rate of return on investment in deciding which operations to expand or contract (those that yielded the greatest profits per unit of capital invested were most likely to be expanded). Figure 8.3 illustrates Du Pont's administrative structure in 1919.

Advanced though it was in its day, this management structure broke down, overwhelmed by the combination of rapid growth and diversification. The executive committee in the central office found it difficult to establish broad policies for the diverse company and also failed to provide the needed coordination between key departments. Moreover, problems soon developed within the departments. People in sales, for instance, found it hard to handle a multitude of products designed for different markets. Selling smokeless powder was not like selling paint.

Du Pont's problems deepened with the coming of the postwar recession. In the second half of 1921, the company lost $2.5 million. Of its many products, explosives alone continued to show a profit. It was at this point, in September 1921, that the Du Pont Company adopted a decentralized, multidivisional management system. In the new management structure, the central office was composed of general corporate officers advised by staff officers who were experts in such fields as law and finance. The central office planned for the future of the entire corporation and coordinated the work of its different parts but did not supervise the details of the daily operations of the firm. Those became the province of the company's various divisions. Each division was based on a product line and contained within itself departments responsible for making and selling its own goods. As at

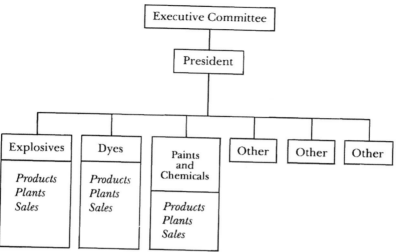

Figure 8.4   Du Pont's Decentralized Management System in 1921 [SOURCE: Adapted in simplified form from Alfred D. Chandler, Jr., *Strategy and Structure* (Cambridge, Mass.: MIT Press, 1962).]

the Pennsylvania railroad in the 1870s, a separation occurred between the duties of the central office and those of the divisions. The head office, now freed from involvement in daily operations, could concentrate on the overall policies—the strategy—of the company. The general managers of each division (who, as noted, were known as line officers) took care of the daily work—the tactics—of producing and selling goods. Figure 8.4 outlines Du Pont's decentralized management system.

The decentralized structure, with divisions based on product lines, served Du Pont well into the 1990s. This structure made it possible for the company's managers to handle the growing size and complexity of Du Pont's operations, something the older centralized management structure had failed to do.

General Motors Provides a Model for Decentralization

Although it was the first industrial company to consider seriously the adoption of a decentralized management system, Du Pont was not the first to implement it. Instead, the General Motors Company, influenced by events at Du Pont, established a decentralized management system eight months before Du Pont, and the General Motors management structure, studied and publicized by business writers, became an important model for other big businesses.

William Durant was the father of General Motors. A carriage maker in Flint, Michigan, Durant first became interested in automobiles in 1904, when he took over the faltering Buick Company in his hometown. Durant redesigned the car made by Buick and built new factories to produce it. By 1908, Buick was the largest automobile manufacturer in the United States, with an annual output of 8,487 vehicles. Excited by the prospects of growth, Durant used Buick as his base to found General Motors. Between 1908 and 1910, he brought together more than twenty-five previously independent companies—including Olds, Oakland, and Cadillac—as the General Motors Corporation. Always more interested in expansion than in profits, Durant failed to provide rational management for his growing agglomeration. When General Motors experienced financial difficulties in 1910, he lost control of the company to a group of Boston and New York bankers, who provided the firm with sorely needed infusions of new capital.

The bankers ran General Motors conservatively over the next five years, liquidating $12.5 million of unprofitable parts of the firm. Although they expanded production to 100,000 cars annually by 1915, they failed to keep pace with the still more rapid growth occurring at Ford Motors. Under their regime, the company's share of the American automobile market fell from 20 percent to only 10 percent.

A resilient businessman, Durant resumed control of General Motors in 1916. He did so by first working with Louis Chevrolet to build and market a light car to compete with Ford's Model T. Durant then used the Chevrolet Company to win back control of General Motors by acquiring a controlling share of General Motors stock. Durant dismissed the bankers and again took over as president of the company. This time, he shared his responsibilities with Pierre S. Du Pont, who acted as the chairman of the board of directors at General Motors. (Looking for investment opportunities for its wartime profits, the Du Pont Company had started purchasing General Motors stock. By early 1918, the Du Pont Company owned 24 percent of the common stock of General Motors, and by the end of 1919 its share amounted to 29 percent.) Caught up in the problems of diversification and reorganization at the Du Pont Company, however, Pierre paid scant attention to the activities at General Motors, despite his firm's growing investment in that company.

Once again, Durant pushed the company into another period of expansion. Between 1918 and 1920, he added Chevrolet, Fisher Body, a tractor company, an electric refrigerator company, and a number of smaller concerns to General Motors. And once again, Durant failed to establish a workable management system for the business. He tried to run the company as a one-man show, making both grand policy and daily operating decisions by himself (as late as 1918 the central office at General Motors consisted of only Durant and several personal assistants). Not even someone as energetic as Durant could adequately oversee such a large company's varied operations. As a result, major decisions on investment, expansion, marketing, and the like often simply were not made. As Alfred Sloan later wrote, "Mr. Durant was a great man with a great weakness—he could create but not administer."

As happened with Du Pont, the postwar recession revealed the managerial weakness at General Motors. Cars continued to sell well during the opening months of 1920, but in September the automobile market collapsed. New-car sales were 21 percent lower in 1921 than in the previous year. General Motors was not prepared for this precipitous decline.

Three related managerial problems surfaced. First, lacking any form of market forecasting, each division continued to invest in new plants to build more cars. The central office, which still consisted mainly of Durant and his assistants, had no criteria by which to evaluate divisional requests for capital improvements, and most were approved with little analysis. In late 1919 and early 1920, the central office approved over $10 million more in capital improvements for Buick, Chevrolet, and Samson Tractor than had originally been scheduled, without any attempt to assess the effect of these extra expenditures on the company as a whole. Second, each division, again without meaningful control from the head office, continued well into 1920 to buy large inventories of raw materials with which to produce cars. By October of that year, the divisions had on hand $209 million worth of inventory, $59 million more than had been approved by the head office. Finally, cash-flow difficulties made these two problems even worse. Each division maintained its own bank accounts, making it very hard for the head office to move funds internally within the company. Buick, in particular, was reluctant to give up its cash to the head office, even when that cash was desperately needed to keep the company afloat.

Underlying these various problems was the basic problem of control. The head office was unable either to plan for the future of the company or to coordinate and supervise the work of its different parts. The divisions were out of control. By October 1920, many General Motors managers were having trouble raising cash to pay invoices and payrolls, and in that month the company had to borrow $83 million from banks in short-term notes. Durant's personal financial difficulties compounded the seriousness of this perilous situation. Trying to support the market price of General Motors stock, Durant had by this time borrowed $30 million from bankers to buy the company's stock. (Durant used General Motors stock as the collateral for his borrowing.) Despite his efforts, the price of the stock continued to drop, and Durant could not repay his debts.

In late November 1920, Durant resigned as president of General Motors, never to return to the company. The Du Pont Company and the J. P. Morgan Company stepped in to assume Durant's debts and to take over most of his General Motors stock. Pierre S. Du Pont, recently retired from the Du Pont Company, became the new president of General Motors.

In saving and then rebuilding General Motors, Du Pont was greatly assisted by Alfred P. Sloan, Jr. A graduate of the Massachusetts Institute of Technology, Sloan went to work in 1895 for Hyatt Roller Bearing, a company making metal antifriction bearings for a wide variety of manufacturers. Something of an engineering and managerial genius, Sloan rescued Hyatt from imminent bankruptcy (aided by an infusion of cash from his father) and became the company's president. As Hyatt began to produce a growing proportion of its bearings for the automotive market, Sloan became concerned about its future independence. Realizing that Hyatt's prosperity depended on the whims of just a few major customers, Sloan arranged to sell Hyatt to General Motors. When this agreement was completed, Sloan became a vice president and major stockholder in General Motors.

Frustrated by Durant's chaotic way of doing business, Sloan prepared an "organization study" that contained a plan to revamp the management of General Motors even before the crisis of 1920. Durant ignored the plan, but Pierre Du Pont and others in top management adopted it at an executive committee meeting on December 30, 1920. This plan introduced a rational system of decentralized management to General Motors by clearly delineating the duties and responsibilities of the head office and the divisions and by providing for effective communications among the different parts of the company. Sloan's goal was to combine divisional autonomy with supervision by a strong central office. Over the next four years, Du Pont and Sloan labored to put this organizational plan into practice, modifying parts of it as they proceeded. By 1924, it was fully implemented.

They began with significant changes in their company's management at the operational level. For the first time, each division—Buick, Cadillac, Chevrolet, and the many others—became clearly defined by a distinct product line. Market segmentation in modern industrial firms, in fact, began at General Motors. As the automobile market matured, Sloan and Du Pont recognized the need to differentiate their cars from each other and from those of their competitors. So they eliminated overlap in the prices, products, and markets of the divisions. No longer did they compete with one another in selling their cars and other goods to the American public; each aimed at a precise market segment defined by price. Advertising and annual model changes identified each make of car. Run by a general manager, each division controlled its own engineering, production, and sales organizations, and each enjoyed a considerable degree of freedom in its daily operations, though not as much as had been the case under Durant. To ensure cooperation and coordination in the work of the divisions, Du Pont and Sloan created the office of group vice president. Freed from specific daily operating responsibilities, the group vice presidents supervised the work of related groups of divisions and helped set policies for the entire company. Four groups were established: accessories, affiliated companies, export, and car and truck. The officers in these divisions and groups were line officers.

Sloan and Du Pont also created a strong central or head office (today called the corporate office) for General Motors. General officers, working through executive and finance committees, coordinated the work of the four groups, made policy decisions for the company, and planned for its future. In doing so, they were assisted by a vastly enlarged staff made up of financial and legal experts. Neither the general nor the staff officers concerned themselves with daily operating matters.

To try to arrive at cooperation and understanding among managers in the divisional and central offices, a number of interdivisional relations committees were established. Officers from all levels belonged to these and met at regular intervals to discuss common problems. Both staff and divisional engineers, for instance, composed the general technical committee that sought solutions for common engineering problems encountered by the different divisions in designing and producing cars.

Finally, Sloan and Du Pont, borrowing from earlier advances made at the Du Pont Company, established solid financial reporting and statistical controls at General Motors. In doing so, they created a model still followed by modern corporations. Like the officers of the Pennsylvania railroad fifty years before, those in the head office of General Motors found the collection of statistical information to be absolutely essential for rational decision making. Three innovations made the collection and analysis of this information feasible. First, the central office received weekly and monthly production reports from each group and division. Under Durant, no such data had been available. Second, the central office received reports every ten days from dealers on how many cars were actually being sold, and this information made market forecasting possible (the ten-day period of reporting sales is still the standard period in the automobile industry). Finally, the work of each division was assessed by the central office, using new accounting techniques that measured its rate of return on investment, making it easier for those on top to decide where to expand or contract the company's operations. Figure 8.5 outlines how this sophisticated system of decentralized management worked.

The decentralized management system instituted at General Motors by Du Pont and Sloan generally worked well. The company's share of the American automobile market rose from 19 percent in 1924 to 43 percent three years later, by which time its annual net profit amounted to an impressive $276 million. The Great Depression provided the acid test for the new organization. Although sales fell by two-thirds between 1929 and 1932, the corporation reacted quickly to the situation and continued to show a profit and to pay dividends every year throughout the 1930s. With only minor changes, the decentralized management structure pioneered in the early 1920s remained the basic administrative framework of General Motors

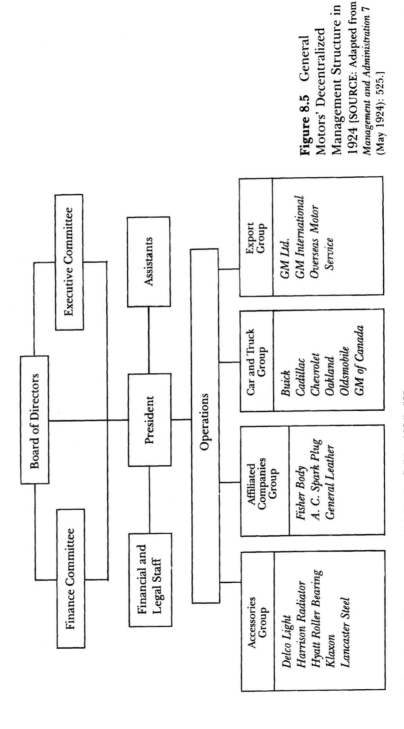

Figure 8.5 General Motors' Decentralized Management Structure in 1924 [SOURCE: Adapted from *Management and Administration 7* (May 1924): 525.]

SOURCE: Adapted from *Management and Administration 7* (May 1924): 525.

through the 1970s. Sloan continued as the firm's president until 1937 and as its chairman of the board for an additional nineteen years, after which he stepped down to devote the rest of his life to philanthropy. He died in 1966 at the age of ninety.

The Spread of Decentralized Management

Both the Du Pont Company and General Motors switched to decentralized systems of management when their operations became diverse and complex, but they were hardly the only ones. The more complex and diversified their products and markets became, the more likely companies were to employ decentralized management systems modeled on those of Du Pont or General Motors. Diversity of operations, not sheer size, was the factor most likely to cause the adoption of decentralized management. As noted earlier in this chapter, structure followed strategy; that is, a company's growth strategy was very likely to influence its management structure.

Companies in three fields most readily established decentralized management systems. In the electrical industry both General Electric and Westinghouse moved beyond making equipment to generate electric power and light by diversifying into the production of a broad range of appliances for consumers. As they entered new consumer markets, they set up decentralized management systems whose divisions were based on product lines. Westinghouse did so in 1934, General Electric in 1950. Growth and diversification in the chemical industry led Hercules and Monsanto to follow Du Pont's lead in adopting decentralized management before World War II; other chemical companies did so after the conflict. The power machinery and automobile industries also witnessed some spread of decentralized management. After investigating the General Motors experience, International Harvester followed suit in 1943. However, only after World War II did other major companies, Chrysler and Ford among them, turn to decentralized management.

Not all big businesses adopted decentralized management systems. Those whose product lines and markets remained relatively simple and few in number usually did not. For them the functionally departmentalized system of centralized management developed by Standard Oil and other companies in the late nineteenth century remained sufficient. Companies in the metals industries, for example, retained centralized management structures. Copper companies—American Smelting & Refining, Anaconda, Kennecott, and Phelps Dodge—and nickel companies such as International Nickel turned out just a few types of products for well-defined markets. With no need to alter their management methods, they kept centralized management systems in place. Steel companies, most notably United States Steel, and aluminum companies, such as Alcoa, did partially adopt decentralized management as they diversified their products, but none went as far as Du Pont or General Motors.

The Model T assembly line became a symbol of American mass production success in the 1920s. (Henry Ford Museum and Greenfield Village)

✏ Henry Ford and Ford Motors

More was involved in decentralization than the logic of products and markets. Personalities played an important role, too, in determining the speed with which businesses set up decentralized management systems. Entrepreneurs who had built up their companies from scratch—people like Durant at General Motors—were often reluctant to share responsibility and authority with others. They continued to try to run their companies as one-man shows long after the complexity of their operations suggested that flexible decentralized management might be more appropriate. Henry Ford was such a business leader.

In technology, Ford was very innovative. Building on the earlier efforts of many industrialists to speed the flow of work through their factories, he brought the concept of assembly-line production to maturity, first applying it to the production of his Model N in 1908. The parts needed to assemble the car were laid out in sequence on the factory floor, the car frame was put on skids and pulled along by a tow rope until the axles and wheels were attached, and the car was then rolled from work station to work station until fully assembled. With the Model N, Ford established the cardinal principle of assembly-line production: the work goes to the worker; the worker does not waste time and energy moving to different places. Ford developed this system fully with the building of the Model T, his most famous car. At his new Highland Park plant in Detroit, he installed continuous conveyor belts in 1913–1915 to carry materials to the assembly lines, and he added still further refinements with the construction of his gigantic River Rouge complex just southeast of Detroit in the early 1920s. Along the assembly lines, single-purpose machines worked the metal in making the parts for the cars. By 1927, when production of the Model T finally ended, 15 million of them had rolled off the assembly line.

His technical accomplishments won Ford renown at home and abroad, and he became a popular folk hero. In 1916, even though he refused to campaign, Ford won the presidential preference primary of the Republican party in Michigan. A few years later, Ford-for-President clubs sprang up spontaneously across the United States; they collapsed only when Ford announced his support of Warren Harding. Ford was equally well known outside of America. Germans referred to mass production as "Fordismus," and Adolf Hitler once remarked, "I am a great admirer of Ford. I shall do my best to put his theories into practice." In the Soviet Union, which purchased 25,000 Fordson tractors between 1920 and 1927, Russians named agricultural communes and even babies after him.

Yet Ford was a complex man. He could be obtuse and irrational. He was a virulent anti-Semite. He associated Jews with bankers, whom he hated, and denounced them in a newspaper he owned. He suspected academics and considered "book learning" impractical; for years no one with a college degree could get a job at Ford Motors. The person most responsible for bringing modern mass production to the world, Ford yearned for what he imagined were simpler times in the past. He built Greenfield Village, a collection of historic shops and homes, near Detroit to bring his version of the past alive. He even tried to revive square-dancing, which he viewed as more civilized and wholesome than the bunny hug, Charleston, and fox trot of the 1920s. (At one point Ford hired a dance instructor for his executives, constructed a ballroom in the engineering laboratory, and kept an orchestra in permanent attendance to play for company officials on his demand.)

Above all, Ford was stubborn. He was determined to run Ford Motors by himself with no outside interference. He bought out minority stockholders, refused to participate in federal plans for industrial recovery during the Great Depression, and violently opposed attempts by the United Auto Workers to unionize his company. (Ford Motors was not unionized until 1941, several years after the other automobile companies.) Ford's stubbornness and his unwillingness to share managerial authority with others nearly destroyed Ford Motors.

The post–World War I recession found Ford Motors, like General Motors under Durant, overextended. Henry Ford was in the process both of building his River Rouge production complex and of purchasing stock the Dodge brothers held in his company. By April 1921, Ford needed $58 million, but he had only $20 million available. To raise cash quickly, he took several steps. He forced his dealers to buy Model Ts for cash, even though they could not sell them, or risk losing their Ford dealerships. He sold every nonessential tool and fixture in the company, including 600 telephones. Finally, he fired half of his middle managers, office force, and engineers. Ford saved his business in the short run, but the steps he took to do so nearly ruined the company in the long run.

By the late 1920s, Ford Motors was a company in decline. The Model T had become outdated, and, lacking enough good engineers, Ford was slower than its competitors to introduce new cars. In addition, the company had marketing problems. Henry Ford envisioned the Model T as a "universal car," good for all people for all times. He did not understand that as the automobile market matured, people would want a broader range of cars to choose from, and so he lagged far behind General Motors in introducing a full line of cars. Moreover, Ford's dependence on single-purpose machines made it difficult for the company to retool for new car lines. When Ford finally ceased production of the Model T in 1927, it had to scrap or change half of its 32,000 machine tools, a situation that helped delay the introduction of the Model A for nearly two years. By way of contrast, General Motors, which relied more on general-purpose machinery, made model changes much more easily.

Even more basic were managerial difficulties. Ford Motors had grown too large and complex for Henry Ford to run by himself, but he was unwilling to share responsibility with others. The result, as at General Motors under Durant, was chaos. There was little coordination among the purchasing, production, and marketing departments. Market forecasting was almost nonexistent, being based on the informal comments of dealers. Asked about the gains Chevrolet was making at one point in the 1920s, Ford characteristically replied, "I don't know how many cars Chevrolet sold last year. I don't know how many they may sell next year. And—I don't care."

These weaknesses deeply wounded the company. Once the industry leader, Ford Motors trailed other companies in new-car sales by 1936. In that year, General Motors had 43 percent of the American market, Chrysler had 25 percent, and Ford had only 22 percent. And, unlike General Motors, Ford Motors incurred losses throughout the 1930s. Difficulties continued into the 1940s. Because of its paucity of engineers and middle managers, Ford Motors experienced more trouble than other automobile companies in converting to wartime production. By 1945, when Henry Ford stepped down as president of Ford Motors in favor of his grandson, Henry Ford II, the company was losing millions of dollars each month.

Henry Ford II reversed the company's decline in the postwar years. He brought in new managers, many of them from General Motors, to rebuild the firm's organizational structure. One of his most effective moves was the hiring of the "Whiz Kids," a group of ten former air force statistical analysts. This group included Robert McNamara, who became president of Ford Motors and, later, secretary of defense under President John Kennedy. These men brought modern management methods to Ford Motors for the first time. Henry Ford II also presided over the introduction of new car lines that caught the imagination of the American public and sold well: Mustang, Maverick, Pinto, and others. Finally, he increased his company's involvement in the world marketplace. Under his leadership, Ford Motors regained second place among America's automobile companies and, at times, challenged General Motors, the industry leader.

Multinationals Grow in Importance

Yet another form of diversification undertaken by U.S. corporations was represented by the spread of multinational operations. A multinational corporation is a company that does business in more than one country. It is usually defined as a firm having direct investments in the form of productive installations, such as plants and factories rather than just sales outlets, abroad. Although U.S. multinationals experienced rapid expansion after World War II, their growth began much earlier.

Even before World War I, the United States had some fairly well-developed multinational enterprises. U.S. multinationals had considerable foreign investments in mining, manufacturing, agriculture, and oil by 1914. In fact, the total direct foreign investment of U.S. companies constituted a sum equal to 7 percent of the GNP of the United States, about the same proportion as in the mid-1960s, although U.S. multinational enterprise had not yet assumed its modern shape. Because of their later start, U.S. multinationals in 1914 still trailed those of Great Britain, France, and Germany in terms of total overseas investments. Moreover, most American investments were in areas close to the United States: Canada, Mexico, the Caribbean Islands, and Central and South America. As yet, United States companies had relatively few direct investments in Europe, Asia, or Africa.

Between 1914 and 1930, U.S. multinationals continued to expand their operations. The United States emerged as the chief creditor nation of the world during and immediately after World War I, and U.S. multinationals began successfully challenging European, and especially British, businesses over growing areas of the globe. The United States' investments in Canada exceeded those of Great Britain for the first time in 1922, and by 1929 the investments of U.S. companies in Latin America had also surpassed those of Great Britain. American investments expanded in Asia and Africa as well, but the most noticeable change occurred in Europe. The direct investments of American businesses in Europe nearly doubled during the 1920s, until by the close of the decade they were nearly as great as those of U.S. companies in Canada or South America and were larger than the sums invested by U.S. firms in the Caribbean. In short, as the economy of the United States prospered, American companies continued to push overseas.

The years of the Great Depression and World War II witnessed a slow-down in the activities of U.S. multinationals. The decline of the world's economy, combined with the destruction of American property overseas during the war, restricted multinational expansion. By 1946, the direct foreign investment of U.S. multinationals had fallen to an amount equal to only 3.4 percent of the United States' GNP, a proportion considerably lower than that of thirty years earlier. Further expansion of multinationals had to wait until the postwar years.

THE PROFESSIONALIZATION OF BUSINESS

Shifts in the character of business leaders paralleled the maturation of big business in America. A separation between management and ownership took place, as many of the original founders—people like Durant, Carnegie, and Rockefeller—retired from the active control of their businesses. In most cases, managers who owned little stock in their companies replaced the owner-managers. This divorce between ownership and management became noticeable in the railroads by the 1870s and 1880s and in many large industrial ventures by the 1920s and 1930s. As early as 1914, Walter Lippmann, a leading American journalist, observed, "The real news about business is that it is being administered by men who are not profiteers. The managers are on salary, divorced from ownership and from bargaining."

The Backgrounds of Big Business Leaders

As the growth strategies of America's leading companies altered, the back-grounds of their executives also changed. Before 1920, executives who had backgrounds in manufacturing ran a majority of the nation's hundred largest companies. By 1949, however, personnel with backgrounds in sales, finance, and general management had largely replaced those in manufacturing as the presidents of the firms, thus reflecting the increasing importance of the domestic consumer market for the companies.

Women and Blacks Find Opportunities in Small Businesses

Not everything changed, however. As in earlier times, white males remained in firm control of America's big businesses. To the extent that opportunities for women to become business owners existed at all in the United States, those opportunities lay mainly in the realm of small businesses, many of which continued to be family enterprises. In big firms, women typically found mainly office work as secretaries or in production-line jobs; and even there a wage differential favoring men in similar positions, first apparent in the nineteenth century, widened in the mid-twentieth century. The garment industry was a case in point. As part of the peripheral economy, the garment industry offered opportunities for advancement to women. Entry into the manufacture of clothing required relatively small amounts of capital. Ida Rosenthal and her husband started Maidenform as a family business in the 1920s to manufacture a new product, brassieres. By the same token, Nell Quinlan, with her husband's support, formed a company to make stylish but inexpensive clothing for women to wear at home under the label of Nelly Don. By the 1920s, the company was grossing as much as $3.5 million annually.

Blacks sometimes found opportunities in small businesses serving markets overlooked or spurned by large center firms. Black and white Americans lived in increasingly segregated communities. In the black communities, retail and service businesses attracted most of the blacks engaged in small business ownership. Very few had the funds needed to found industrial enterprises. At the local level, blacks established grocery stores and dry-cleaning businesses (though in doing so they continued to encounter sharp competition from whites); at the regional and national levels, they formed banks and insurance companies that provided services mostly to black customers.

As in the years before World War I, black businesses often had more than profits as their goal. They also sought to build up the black communities within which they operated. In 1913, Herman Perry of Atlanta founded the Standard Life Insurance Company, developing it as one of the nation's largest black insurance companies in just a few years. From his base in insurance, Perry branched out into real estate, publishing, banking, construction, and many other fields in the early 1920s. Poor management led to the collapse of many of these enterprises in the mid-1920s (Standard Life passed into white hands), but some survived this crisis to form the basis for black business advances in Atlanta in later years. Black entrepreneurs formed the Chicago Metropolitan Assurance Company in 1925. In addition to employing blacks as clerks and agents, this insurance company benefited Chicago's black community through its involvement in the operation of a black radio station, magazine, professional baseball team, and ballroom.

In its collapse, Standard Life typified the fate of many black businesses at the national level. Few survived the Great Depression, which was even harder on black-owned than on white-owned businesses. Hurt by inept management, a lack of funds, and competition from white businesses, most black-owned businesses of regional or national scope ceased to exist as independent enterprises. For instance, only 12 of the 134 banks formed by blacks between 1884 and 1935 remained in operation in 1936, leading one scholar to observe at the time that "notwithstanding the public assertions of many Negro leaders to the contrary, the conviction is growing among them that the future of Negro finance and business is dismal."

The Meaning of Professionalism

The shifts in the management of large companies, especially the divorce of ownership from management, raised questions about corporate goals. Corporations had traditionally been seen as devices to earn profits for their owners, who also ran them. The divorce of ownership from management introduced uncertainties into this way of thinking, especially for the new corporate managers. Since they no longer owned the companies they ran, the managers questioned whether simply trying to earn maximum profits for themselves and their stockholders could serve any longer as their sole or primary goal in business. Searching for new identities and for new sources of approval for their actions, many corporate managers began looking upon themselves as professionals.

When they called themselves professionals, business executives usually had several things in mind. They meant, first of all, that they enjoyed the technical expertise, the competence, to operate successfully the large, complex businesses that were replacing the simpler enterprises of earlier times. A study analyzing the family origins of 9,000 business leaders in 1932 lent some credence to this assertion. It found that 32 percent were college graduates and that nearly 45 percent had taken at least some college classes. The study showed, however, that only 7 percent had received formal business training in college, and it concluded that little correlation existed between a college education and success in the business world. (The study also showed that more than half the business leaders came from families with backgrounds in business or the professions. Rags-to-riches success stories remained the exceptions to the rule for advancement in American business.) A corollary of the belief by business leaders that they had the type of education and training needed to manage the businesses of their day was their contention that the general public, which did not have this education and training, should leave business and economic matters in their hands.

In referring to themselves as professionals, business executives also meant that they were more than money-grubbing profit seekers. They intended, they said, to operate their businesses in ways beneficial to all Americans. Like other professionals—lawyers, doctors, and clergy—they would serve society. For some, service meant simply making available to Americans products of good quality at reasonable prices. Henry Ford exemplified this type of business executive when he promised: "I will build a motor car for the great multitude. It will be large enough for the family but small enough for the individual to run and care for. . . . It will be so low in price that no man making a good salary will be unable to own one." For a growing number of executives, however, service meant more than providing good products at low prices. It meant, as well, mediating the conflicting desires of different interest groups in American society. Elbert Gary, the president of the United States Steel Corporation, took this point of view. In 1921,

IBM trained both men and women to operate its accounting machines, the use of which expanded in business during the 1920s. (International Business Machines)

he defined corporate management as a "position of balance" between "investors, employees, employers, consumers, or customers, competitors, and all others who may be interested in, or affected by, the actions or attitudes of the manager." He went on to observe that "the management of the corporation . . . must have constantly and uppermost in mind the rights and interests of the general public."

Professional Education

Central to business leaders' identification of themselves as professionals was the possession of a professional education. Technical training in finance and business administration gave them, they claimed, the tools needed to manage the complex enterprises of their day. A professional education also, they asserted, broadened their outlook on life and helped them understand the connections between business and the rest of American society. Although, as we have seen, most business leaders remained self-educated in the 1920s and 1930s, they aspired to recognition as professionally educated men.

The University of Pennsylvania established the first collegiate school of business in the United States with the creation of the Wharton School of Finance and Economy in 1881. Other business schools soon appeared at the University of California (1898), the University of Chicago (1898), Dartmouth (1900), the University of Wisconsin (1900), Washington and Lee (1906), Harvard (1908), Northwestern (1908), and Columbia (1916). A tremendous explosion of collegiate education in business followed in the 1920s. By 1928, 89 universities and colleges had enrolled 67,000 students in business courses. And although growth in business education slowed during the Great Depression, by 1940 some 110 business schools had enrolled more than 100,000 students.

These pioneers in business education were probably most successful in imparting technical skills—accounting, finance, and the like—to their students. But few succeeded in giving them a broad outlook on the place of business in society. Most courses were too narrowly conceived and presented. It is hard to imagine, for instance, that New York University's courses on "Principles of Dress," "Hosiery and Underwear," and "Window Display" did much to raise the consciousness of the students who took them.

Professional Ethics

Business executives also sought recognition as professionals by formulating codes of business ethics in which they promised they would act in a responsible manner toward one another and the American public. The most far-reaching of these was the "Principles of Business Conduct" issued by the United States Chamber of Commerce in 1924. Principle 13 of this code expressed the idea of business serving society: "The primary obligation of those who direct and manage a corporation is to its stockholders. . . . Notwithstanding this, they act in a responsible capacity, and in such a capacity owe obligations to others—employees, to the public which they serve, and even to their competitors." Within one year, more than 750 business organizations with 300,000 members had approved these principles.

Business practices did not, however, change strikingly. It is true that cutthroat competition lessened as many industries matured and became oligopolistic. But too often, statements of business ethics, particularly those concerning relations between businesses and their customers, were simply hot air. Investigations into business practices undertaken by the federal government in the 1930s showed that the public had frequently been deceived in the 1920s. The codes were for cosmetic effect, little more. In fact, the development of public relations paralleled the rise of advertising in the 1920s, and both were designed to sell business and its products to the American public. Public relations firms deliberately presented business in a favorable light; their purpose was to convince Americans that their nation's businesses were serving society.

Community Affairs

As self-appointed trustees for society, business leaders and their companies became deeply involved in community affairs. It was during the Progressive

Era and the 1920s that business service clubs such as the Rotary and the Kiwanis were formed and spread across the nation. Also in this period corporate philanthropy began replacing donations by individual business people. Women formed the National Federation of Business and Professional Women's Clubs in 1919. In the 1920s, local welfare federations, community chests, hospitals, and universities started depending heavily on organized corporate philanthropy for the first time. By 1929, some 350 cities had developed community chests to raise funds for philanthropic causes, and these organizations relied mainly on businesses for their support.

The spread of corporate philanthropy raised questions still worth pondering today. For what purpose does a corporation exist: to make a profit, to serve society, or some combination of the two? Does management have the right to give corporate earnings away to charity rather than to reinvest them in capital improvements or to pay them out as dividends to stockholders? Might society not benefit more from a strong economy made possible by capital improvements than from donations by business to charity? Could such donations insidiously influence American values and institutions, since businesses give only to those organizations whose ideals and work they approve? Finally, who decides the priorities of large, wealthy firms, now for the most part under the control of a separate class of professional managers?

The Public Image of Business

During the 1920s, the public generally did perceive business leaders as professionals. The seeming success of the assembly line in bringing material goods to a growing number of Americans won them a high degree of respect. As we have seen, Americans have generally admired business executives, but at no time has this admiration been greater than in the 1920s. One of the best-sellers of the decade was *The Man Nobody Knows,* written by Bruce Barton, a leading advertising executive. A biography of Jesus Christ, the book pictured Christ as a successful businessman who "picked up twelve men from the bottom ranks of business and forged them into an organization that conquered the world." As the public accepted business leaders as professionals, they replaced lawyers, doctors, and clergy on the boards of trustees of universities and on the vestry boards of churches across the United States.

With the coming of the Great Depression, however, this prestige eroded. Americans blamed business people for the hard times, especially when corporate philanthropy failed miserably to help those out of work. Then, too, federal investigations into business practices and ethics revealed that they were not as sound as business leaders claimed. Joseph Kennedy, the father of John, Robert, and Ted, summed up the prevailing mood. Placed in charge of the newly created Securities and Exchange Commission in

1934, he noted that "the belief that those in control of the corporate life of America were motivated by honesty and ideas of honorable conduct was completely shattered."

The prosperity of the war years of the 1940s largely redeemed American business people in the eyes of the public. Most businesses converted fairly smoothly to wartime production, and as unemployment disappeared, Americans became less critical of their nation's business leaders and business system. Business executives regained much of the prestige they had lost in the 1930s, but they would never again be held in the high esteem of the 1920s.

THE NEW MANAGEMENT OF AMERICAN BUSINESS

The 1920s, 1930s, and 1940s were pivotal years in the development of business management in the United States. As large companies diversified their products and markets, their systems of centralized management proved inadequate to handle the growing complexity of their operations. Led by Du Pont and General Motors, some corporations introduced decentralized management systems better suited to their shifting needs and developed further the systems of financial controls, especially cost accounting, first pioneered by railroads in the nineteenth century. As some of their markets matured, these corporations came to depend on market segmentation and new forms of advertising to sell their goods. As management structures and methods changed, so did the nature of the men running America's big businesses. Management was divorced from ownership, and a growing number of business leaders came to think of themselves as professionals who had a duty to serve society.

The crises of these years—the two world wars and the Great Depression—brought changes not just to individual companies but also to government-business relations. Just as they sought rationality and predictability by redesigning their management structures and reworking their relationships with society, the companies also revamped their relationships with the federal government as part of this search for security. A new type of association between business and government emerged, one that has lasted, with some changes, to the present day.

Selected Readings

Alfred D. Chandler, Jr., has written extensively on the historical evolution of the diversified, decentralized company in the United States. His *Strategy and Structure* (Cambridge, Mass.: MIT Press, 1962) analyzes the adoption of decentralized management by General Motors, Du Pont, Standard Oil of New Jersey, and Sears, Roebuck. And his *Pierre S. Du Pont and the Making of the Modern Corporation* (New York: Harper & Row, 1971), written with Stephen Salsbury, provides a detailed look at managerial change within the Du Pont Company. Neil Fligstein, *The Transformation of Corporate Control* (Cambridge, Mass.: Harvard University Press, 1990), is a provocative analysis of these developments. Arthur Kuhn, *GM Passes Ford, 1918–1938* (University Park: Pennsylvania University Press, 1986), compares the development of management systems at Ford and General Motors. Alfred P. Sloan, Jr., *My Years with General Motors* (New York: Macfadden-Bartell, 1965), explains how and why General Motors adopted decentralized management. Mira Wilkins, *The Emergence of Multinational Enterprise: American Business Abroad from the Colonial Era to 1914* (Cambridge, Mass.: Harvard University Press, 1970) and *The Maturing of Multinational Enterprise: American Business Abroad from 1914 to 1970* (Cambridge, Mass.: Harvard University Press, 1974), are the standard histories of American multinationals.

Specific studies examine particular aspects of business enterprise. Allan Nevins and Frank Hill give a detailed business history of Ford Motors in their three-volume account: Ford: *The Times, The Man, The Company, 1865–1915* (New York: Scribner's, 1954), *Ford: Expansion and Challenge, 1915–1933* (New York: Scribner's, 1957), and *Ford: Decline and Rebirth, 1933–1962* (New York: Scribner's, 1963). James Worthy, *Shaping an American Institution* (Urbana: University of Illinois Press, 1984), looks at Sears, Roebuck. And David Mowery, "Firm Structure, Government Policy and the Organization of Industrial Research: Great Britain and the United States, 1900–1950," *Business History Review* 58 (Winter 1984): 504–531, is an excellent examination of research and development efforts.

Several good books examine the relationships between business and society. On the development of advertising, see Roland Marchand, *Advertising the American Dream: Making Way for Modernity, 1920–1940* (Berkeley: University of California Press, 1985). On public relations, see Richard Tedlow, *Keeping the Corporate Image: Public Relations and Business, 1900–1950* (Greenwich, Conn.: JAI Press, 1979). Morrell Heald investigates the professionalization of business in *The Social Responsibilities of Business: Company and Community, 1900–1960* (Cleveland: Press of Case Western Reserve University, 1970). Alexa Benson Henderson, "Herman E. Perry and Black Enterprise in Atlanta, 1908–1925," *Business History Review* 61 (Summer 1987): 216–242, examines the career of an important black business leader. Martha Olney, *Buy Now, Pay Later: Advertising, Credit, and Consumer Durables in the 1920s* (Chapel Hill: University of North Carolina Press, 1991), argues persuasively that a consumer durables revolution took place in the 1920s. David M. Vrooman, *Daniel Willard and Progressive Management on the Baltimore & Ohio Railroad* (Columbus: Ohio State University Press, 1991), is a fascinating account of innovative policies. Finally, Daniel Nelson, ed., *A Mental Revolution: Scientific Management Since Taylor* (Columbus: Ohio State University Press, 1992), examines important changes in management thought.

1918 The Armistice of November 11 ends World War I.

1919–1920 The steelworkers' strike is defeated.

1920 Congress returns railroads to private control.
The U.S. Supreme Court affirms the "rule of reason" allowing oligopoly.

1921 Herbert Hoover is appointed secretary of commerce.

1922 Protectionism reaches new heights under the Fordney-McCumber tariff.

1929 The Wall Street crash triggers the Great Depression.

1932 Congress establishes the Reconstruction Finance Corporation to provide relief to banks and railroads.

1933 Unemployment peaks; the banking system collapses; Franklin D. Roosevelt launches the New Deal with a "bank holiday."
The Glass-Steagall Act regulates banks.
The National Recovery Administration begins "codes of fair competition."
The Business Council is formed to advise the New Deal.

1934 The Securities and Exchange Commission is established.

1935 The National Labor Relations Act grants workers the right to organize and belong to unions.

1936 The Robinson-Patman Act protects small retailers.
John Maynard Keynes explains the causes of the Great Depression.

1937 Sit-down strikes sweep some industries.
The Supreme Court upholds the National Labor Relations Act and ends traditional restrictions on federal regulation of business.

1941 The nation again faces a war-mobilization crisis.

1942–1945 Both trade unions and businesses gain economic benefits from war-mobilization policies.

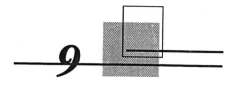

The American Political
Economy in Transition

The crises of world war and severe economic depression affected America's political economy no less than the nation's business system, permanently changing the relationships between the federal government and business. When the United States entered World War I in 1917, the federal government had taken only the first steps toward regulating business. At the end of World War II in 1945, it had instituted a limited welfare state and recognized new responsibilities for promoting the material well-being not only of business firms but of other groups as well.

The steps of this transition were fraught with sharp ideological clashes regarding the proper role of government in controlling business firms. These steps included bitter and sometimes violent conflicts between industrial workers and their employers. The transition began and ended with the U.S. participation in World Wars I and II, crises in which the survival of the nation was at stake. Between the wars was another crisis: the Great Depression of the 1930s, the worst business calamity ever. The depression paralyzed industrial production, destroyed banks, and devastated the nation's workers, who suffered from unemployment and despair. These crises aroused industrial workers to promote their interests: secure wages and jobs. The responses to these crises resulted in a more powerful government and a limited welfare state in which business firms and their executives enjoyed less autonomous power as U.S. public policy tried to accommodate the interests of other groups.

FROM WAR TO PEACE, 1918–1921

The American mobilization effort during World War I had been impressive. The military services had raised an armed force of 4.7 million men and deployed it in time to help defeat Germany. Business and government had devised effective arrangements for retooling industry and redirecting the flow of industrial goods and foodstuffs to the European front. With the return of peace, business and labor both tried to preserve the benefits of that experience in the postwar political economy, and some public officials suggested making permanent the wartime policies of government direction of economic affairs.

Labor and the Postwar Economy

The sudden U.S. declaration of war in 1917 created a crisis of industrial mobilization that presaged what many hoped might become a more powerful position for labor in the American economy. The federal government struck a new arrangement with trade unions: in return for a pledge to refrain from strikes and to cooperate in achieving full industrial production, the unions were to have the right to organize the workers in the nation's industrial plants. This arrangement triggered a chain of events in which workers tried to enlarge their power to influence wages and working conditions permanently. The culmination was a bitter strike in the steel industry, which ended in defeat for the union movement in 1920.

In 1917 and 1918, the federal government empowered the National War Labor Board (NWLB), a special agency set up for the emergency, to oversee this arrangement. The NWLB actively mediated disputes between employers and employees. It prevented employers from continuing their peacetime antiunion policies, and in firms that had a particularly hostile record toward unions, the board established "work councils" in an attempt to prevent disputes from disrupting production. All told, the NWLB mediated disputes in 1,100 plants affecting 711,500 employees during the war. In two well-publicized incidents, when Western Union, the country's largest telegraph firm, and Smith and Wesson, a Massachusetts gun maker, balked at NWLB policies, the agency took them over, installing public officials to manage them for the duration of the emergency.

These wartime policies awakened hopes in the trade unions that the postwar political economy would include an "industrial democracy" in which workers, like businesses, would enjoy the rights of association and the ability to influence wage levels through the process of *collective bargaining*. To try to realize these hopes in the postwar economy, leaders of the American Federation of Labor decided to concentrate their resources on the nation's steel industry. Under the leadership of Elbert H. Gary and the United States Steel Corporation, that industry had successfully eradicated the remaining vestiges of union influence during the prewar years. But the war crisis seemed to promise federal support, for the first time in history, for the union cause.

Union leaders realized that the steel industry was central to the industrial economy, and they thought that if they could establish a union in it, they could proceed to organize other basic mass-production industries that heretofore had also successfully resisted collective bargaining. So in the summer of 1918, encouraged by the policies of the NWLB, AF of L organizers began the slow process of signing up steelworkers for the cause. When the war ended in November, government encouragement ceased. Nonetheless, the union organizers decided to proceed, rallying members with a plea for the eight-hour day and forty-eight-hour workweek. (The twelve-hour day was the standard in the steel industry at the time.) The organizers met bitter, sometimes violent resistance from the steel companies and local government officials sympathetic to them, who equated unionization with Bolshevism. (Lenin's Bolshevik faction had seized power in Russia late in 1917, founding the USSR and threatening to spread the Russian Revolution elsewhere.) As was the case with almost all manufacturers, steel executives adamantly supported the open shop.

When the confrontation occurred in the steel industry, the workers were defeated, and the drive to unionize large industries was turned back for more than a decade. In September 1919, a special steelworker's organizing committee of the AF of L called a strike of the nation's leading steel firms. Steel management bitterly resisted the strikers, refusing to negotiate with them; on several occasions, the firms called on the police, who violently broke up the strikers' picket lines and meetings. The steel firms eventually hired strikebreakers to enter the mills under armed guard, and the firms managed to restore production by Christmas. Finally, on January 8, 1920, recognizing that its resources were exhausted and that the strike had failed, the union asked its supporters to return to work. This outcome ensured that labor-management relations in mass-production industries would remain much as before the war, with management still able to dictate the terms of employment to workers and conflict thus continuing between them. The strike revealed that the peacetime federal government was unwilling to perform a neutral role in industrial disputes or to grant labor the same privileges of associational activity enjoyed by business.

The drama of the steel strike overshadowed another development that threatened, as a result of wartime experiences, to upset the capitalist organization of the American economy. When the nation's railroad firms were unable to coordinate service adequately during the intense mobilization demands of 1917, the federal government had assumed control of the carriers, placing their management under the United States Railroad Administration (USRA). This temporary wartime agency fundamentally altered the economic relationships associated with that vital industry. Underlying federal operation was the theory that disinterested public servants might be better able than private owners to provide the nation's shippers and passengers with efficient, low-cost transportation service. In practice, the USRA, in order to achieve the cooperation of railroad workers, substantially raised wages and, by appointing union leaders to high posts, granted workers' representatives an active voice in determining personnel policies.

After the war, William G. McAdoo, who had served as director-general of the railroads in 1918, proposed that Congress continue government operation to see if the wartime efficiency could be extended to peacetime. The railroad unions countered by proposing the "Plumb Plan." This plan, developed by a union attorney, Glenn Plumb, suggested that a federal corporation, with equal representation from management, workers, and the public, operate the nation's carriers permanently. Supported by workers in other trades, the railroad unions agitated for the plan but were unable to obtain a sympathetic hearing in Congress. The Transportation Act of 1920 returned the railroads to private operation under ICC regulation. Congress also charged the commission with the task of developing a policy for the consolidation of rail firms so that they might operate more efficiently.

The political economy of the postwar decade did not undergo any of the fundamental changes the labor movement favored—not the operation of the railroads along socialist lines nor union recognition nor collective bargaining. The war years saw a rise in union membership that peaked in 1920 at more than 5 million workers. But with the defeat of the steel strikers and the failure of the Plumb Plan, militant union activity receded, and membership declined in the 1920s, ebbing to a low of 3.4 million in 1930, only 6.8 percent of the nonagricultural work force.

Welfare Capitalism

In the 1920s, most business leaders, as we have seen, rejected the idea of bargaining with the labor unions. Instead, under the leadership of the National Association of Manufacturers, they tried to break the unions, with considerable success. Some businesses promoted the concept of welfare capitalism, by which they meant that the businesses, not independent trade unions, should look after the best interests of the workers.

As developed by leading businesses, welfare capitalism encompassed a broad range of activities: housing, educational, medical, religious, and recreational facilities for employees, profit-sharing plans, and retirement pensions. Welfare capitalism often also involved improvements in working conditions, higher wages, and the establishment of company unions. Although company unions were of some help in improving working conditions, they were not allowed to bargain collectively on behalf of workers with management on such fundamental issues as wages and hours of work. Company unions were effectively controlled by management, were limited to individual companies, and mainly provided avenues of communication between management and workers.

From the point of view of management, welfare capitalism was one way to make the business world predictable and rational. It kept workers loyal to their companies while only slightly raising labor costs. Most important, it kept independent unions, which most business executives saw as a disturbing element, at bay. Workers were less enthusiastic. They correctly viewed welfare capitalism as a very paternalistic system that left management in control of their lives. When changes in federal law finally gave workers the chance to form independent unions of their own choice during the 1930s, they gladly did so. In the 1930s, welfare capitalism faded away, as the federal government and newly organized mass industrial unions— the United Auto Workers, the United Steelworkers, and the like—assumed responsibility for the welfare of labor.

Business and the Postwar Economy

Just as labor had sought to preserve wartime changes that allowed a larger role for associational activity and a greater ability to manage economic uncertainties, so too did business firms and their organizations. The federal government had fostered trade associations during the war; it had also suspended the antitrust laws in the interests of achieving rational, managerial coordination of the flow of goods and capital in the business system. The War Industries Board in particular had encouraged trade associations to form in industries where none had existed, so that officials in Washington would have organizations of business firms to help them achieve economic mobilization. The result was the evolution of a system of "open prices" wherein trade associations fixed prices and thwarted competition in the interests of maximum efficiency.

Led by the Chamber of Commerce, American business leaders worked to preserve those arrangements in the postwar world. The War Industries Board lapsed with the coming of peace, but the Chamber of Commerce led an effort to have its price-fixing functions shifted to a new Industrial Board within the Department of Commerce. The president of the Chamber of Commerce observed that it was a foregone conclusion that the regulation of business was in the offing, a fact that deserved "cordial acceptance by organized business." Regulation, in his view, would involve a suspension of the antitrust statutes and result in "agreements between businessmen in the public interest." The Chamber of Commerce wanted a system of cartels, agreements among firms to cooperate and administer prices.

The Chamber of Commerce was unsuccessful in realizing the thoroughgoing cartelization of the American business system. Business leaders, however, were able to prevent a complete dismantling of associational agencies and programs. Business associations thrived in the postwar years even though they enjoyed no formal rights of price administration. Trade association spokesmen adeptly explained to the public and elected officials alike that they represented a "new individualism" of cooperative activity in the service of the public, exchanging information, eliminating waste, fostering labor-management harmony, enlarging the benefits of product standardization, and in general improving the efficiency of the business system and thereby the prosperity of the American people. In their view, cooperation, including price fixing, produced social benefits impossible to achieve under unbridled competition among firms.

This view of cooperation received a boost when the Supreme Court broadened its "rule of reason" doctrine in a 1920 case involving United States Steel. Refusing to break up the steel giant, the Court ruled that it was legitimate, under the law, for a firm to achieve dominance in its industry, so long as that firm did not prevent competition from occurring. In other words, a firm was allowed to remain an oligopoly if it allowed smaller firms to exist in the same industry. The net effect of this ruling was that the tendency toward merger remained largely unchecked in the American business system in the years to come.

HERBERT HOOVER AND THE ASSOCIATIVE STATE

One of the major supporters of business associations in the postwar years, and a significant figure in the American political economy, was Herbert Hoover. The son of a Quaker blacksmith in Iowa, Hoover was orphaned at the age of ten. Sent to live with an uncle in Oregon who later made a fortune in real estate speculation, the young Hoover obtained a degree in geology at Stanford University in 1895. He then went on to make his own fortune in mining engineering projects around the world, earning fame as "the great engineer," and his success convinced him that the key to uplifting and improving human society lay in the systematic application of rational principles to human affairs.

Hoover also became known as "the great humanitarian." The outbreak of World War I in August 1914 had found him in London wealthy but politically uninvolved. The horrors of the war prompted Hoover to organize relief measures for war-torn Europe, and when the United States entered the war in 1917, President Wilson pressed him into government service as his wartime food administrator. Hoover became enormously popular in the United States during the war because he exuded a traditional American faith in the value of every individual and a devotion to humanitarian causes. He was among the American leaders impressed by the accomplishments of the war effort; wartime mobilization taught him that individuals could, of their own accord, act in the public interest.

President Warren G. Harding appointed Hoover secretary of commerce after the 1920 election, and he proved to be an especially adept leader, building the Department of Commerce into a major federal agency and devoting his considerable energy and talent to promoting cooperation among businesses and between business and the government in the name of greater efficiency and prosperity. As commerce secretary, Hoover attempted to put into action his belief in communal cooperation and his commitment to the dignity of the free individual. This attempt confronted Hoover with a dilemma: how to reconcile and preserve the benefits of collective action, through trade associations, giant firms, or other bureaucracies, and guard the right of individual freedom. Hoover solved this problem in part through rhetoric, blending opposites like "cooperative competition" and referring to the "higher freedom." Aside from rhetoric, however, Hoover initiated programs intended to stabilize the economy while maintaining individual autonomy, a political economy that characterizes an "associative state." Hoover expected government officials and trade association leaders to clarify desirable objectives and expected individual Americans to pursue tham voluntarily. In this vein, he worked actively with peripheral firms to have them cooperate in rationalizing their industries.

Hoover and Trade Associations

Trade associations were essential to this conception of a modern political economy; they were the institutions through which Hoover hoped to blend the benefits of collective action with the traditions of individual freedom and achieve the advantages of both worlds. Under Hoover's leadership, the Department of Commerce worked to restructure important features of the mobilization agencies while adapting them to the peacetime economy. Trade associations (especially those of peripheral firms), closely linked to government agencies, were to become the bellwether institutions in the new "cooperative competition" that Hoover, other government leaders, and business spokesmen desired in the new political economy.

Hoover believed that the government should act as a source of up-to-date, scientifically derived business information and use that information to provide leadership for private business action. Under this direction, the Department of Commerce, as well as other economic agencies, developed information of all kinds: data on markets, supplies, production costs, and prices. The development and dissemination of such information was meant to help business conserve resources, eliminate waste, and standardize their products—all of which, when obtained, would result in an efficient business system.

As we have seen, one way in which business persons achieved these goals was through vertical integration and merger. Combinations among business firms thus were a common feature during the 1920s, as the United States experienced its second major merger movement. By the end of the decade, giant firms dominated important industries, and automobile, electrical, communications, and mass-distribution firms joined the list of integrated companies directing operations through managerial, as opposed to market, mechanisms.

Despite the growth of center firms in the American business system of the 1920s, important industries remained in which thousands of small firms interacted through the invisible hand of the market. Coal mining, textiles, clothing, and cement were examples of industries in which vertically integrated center firms did not prevail. Hoover looked to these peripheral firms to help build a new political economy as well. The Commerce Department generated information that individual business executives, in private associations with one another, were encouraged to use in practical ways to bring managerial order out of the chaos and inefficiencies of unbridled competition.

The cement industry illustrates Hoover's belief that it was possible to develop the benefits of cooperation while protecting the autonomy of the independent small firm. The manufacture of cement was geographically dispersed, and the relatively low level of capital investment required for a single cement plant allowed an ease of entry that forestalled domination by center firms. Under Hoover's leadership, the Department of Commerce worked closely with a trade association, the Cement Manufacturers' Protective Association, to analyze costs and set prices. The Supreme Court invoked the antitrust statutes to forbid outright price fixing, however, so the government disseminated cost and price information through the trade association. The system worked so well that when other agencies requested sealed bids for construction projects, the supposedly competing cement manufacturers submitted bids that were nearly identical.

Hoover's vision of new business arrangements was widely shared in the 1920s. State and local governments developed partnerships between executive agencies and private associations that permanently reshaped the political economy. The decade saw an expansion of governmental services, as well as government staffs and budgets, in the cities and states. Highway departments developed close relations with contractors, cities' service departments with real estate promoters, and so on. Especially noteworthy were state and local policies that institutionalized businesses such as real estate, pharmacy, and medicine through licensing laws that set standards, restricted entry, and, among other matters, allowed a system of price controls for essential services.

Hoover and the Economy

In the 1920s, some Americans believed that the nation had developed a new "people's capitalism" capable of generating higher and higher plateaus of prosperity. Business, professional, and government leaders forged new partnerships that narrowed the areas in which unchecked market forces could govern business relationships, convinced as they did so that their actions still preserved the essential attributes of individualism, that they were reducing, if not eliminating, the human hardships that accompanied downturns in the business cycle while ensuring that prosperity would permanently advance.

Although from its inception the American economy had generated ever-higher levels of material wealth, downturns in the business cycle were, as we have seen, inevitable if undesirable realities. Theoretically, government controls could be used to tame the business cycle, but such manipulation ran contrary to the American tradition of private action and individual freedom. Through associational activities, guided by government policies, Hoover and others thought they had found a desirable compromise mechanism for controlling the American economy.

A central idea of this approach was to control the overall fortunes of the American system by influencing individual business decisions. Hoover was confident that private organizations, especially the National Bureau of Economic Research founded in 1920, could show individual businessmen how decisions made with the public interest in mind could smooth the ups and downs of the volatile business cycle. While awaiting this enlightened state of affairs, the trade associations and individual firms should cooperate with social workers and philanthropically minded leaders to devise welfare programs to improve the lives of workers and their families and provide the means for softening the human impact of any business downturns that materialized. Businesses were encouraged to maintain wage rates and share available markets among themselves and available jobs among their employees. Hoover and his advisers tried, unsuccessfully, to have trade associations develop reserve funds to invest in case of a business downturn, thereby stabilizing the business cycle. Governments likewise could invest in public facilities to ensure relatively even economic growth.

Even as the 1920s witnessed Hoover's innovations regarding the business cycle and the trade associations, however, his were not the only policies having an impact on business. Three other features of government-business relations were noteworthy. First, the tariff, traditionally such an important point of contention, reached new heights of protection under the 1922 Fordney-McCumber law. The return to traditional protectionism was mitigated to some extent by a widespread agreement that duties should be adjusted by administrative, not legislative, action. The tariff commission could recommend changes in duties of up to 50 percent after investigating business needs and the nation's trade relations. Second, Secretary of the Treasury Andrew Mellon, one of the world's wealthiest men, worked to have federal taxes on business and personal income, taxes that had risen during World War I, substantially reduced. Mellon and his supporters believed that higher rates of investment and therefore greater prosperity would result. Finally, during the preceding decade would-be reformers had succeeded in enacting a constitutional amendment that forbade the manufacture and sale of alcoholic beverages. By declaring certain business activities—brewing and distilling were major industries—illegal, the reformers expected Americans, aided by enforcement and educational programs,

The experience of human suffering in the Great Depression was so extensive that it inspired artists to give human expression to the failure of the American economy. Reginald Marsh, Bread Line—No One Has Starved, 1932. (Katherine Schmidt Schubert Bequest, Collection of the Whitney Museum of American Art, New York)

to attain the public-interest goal of an alcohol-free society. Prohibition during the 1920s was evidence of a popular willingness to place unprecedented restraints on business enterprise. Although alcohol consumption declined remarkably under the law, some business leaders, especially the Du Ponts of Delaware, who disliked the amendment, successfully obtained its repeal in 1933, arguing in part that prohibition was a dangerous antibusiness precedent.

THE GREAT DEPRESSION

The ideas and institutions of the associative state met their greatest test after the Wall Street crash of 1929, and failed. As the crash evolved into the Great Depression, President Hoover tried to apply his principles of voluntary cooperation. He called on experts from the government and private life to help him identify the public interest and then implored businesses to act accordingly. However, these efforts could not withstand the deepening economic depression that blanketed America from late 1929 through 1932. Banks, many already weak in the 1920s, failed, with customers losing their deposits. As private investment declined, so did employment, and by 1931 the weaknesses in the American economy had contributed to similar crises in Europe. In the United States, people saw a lifetime of careful saving disappear behind the closed doors of banks, millions of workers lost their jobs, and business firms either went bankrupt or had to scramble frantically to readjust payrolls, inventories, and investments in order to survive. As the depression worsened, more Americans, including the very trade associations and business leaders with whom Hoover had been attempting to build a new political economy, repudiated the president's policies.

Shortly after the crash, Hoover called the nation's business leaders to the White House and informed them that the public interest required the maintenance of prices and wages. Although not all businesses were willing to cooperate, the Chamber of Commerce encouraged its members to follow the president. The construction industry, through its trade association, tried to obtain pledges for new or expanded construction projects, while federal agencies speeded up government building projects. But by the end of the year, despite a temporary upturn in business and continuing exhortations from the White House, business activity began diverging from the president's goal. Investments, inventories, and jobs fell off; the collapse of the securities markets and the failure of banks contracted the money supply. Desperate times seemed to call for new approaches.

One new approach was the establishment of the Reconstruction Finance Corporation (RFC) in 1932. Congress, responding to the urgings of the nation's bankers and realizing that large infusions of public capital might alleviate the situation, modeled the RFC on a wartime agency that had helped finance the production demands of mobilization. Congress authorized the RFC to lend up to $2 billion to banks and other credit institutions and to the railroads. As the creditor of last resort, the federal government tried to provide desperately needed relief to American business.

The president agreed to the RFC, as well as to other distress measures, but he did so reluctantly, worrying that individual freedom might become permanently impaired. Moreover, his policies came under increasing attack. There were cries for a return to laissez-faire policies and government retrenchment from traditionally minded business executives and politicians who believed that the economy's natural business cycles had built-in, self-correcting mechanisms that, left to run their course, would eventually result in an upturn. On the other hand, some business groups, especially the Chamber of Commerce, called for a suspension of the antitrust statutes and a revival of the government-directed business planning of World War I. The Chamber of Commerce wanted business to decide on "codes of fair competition" that would allocate available markets, fix prices, and establish minimum wages all under government supervision and enforcement. Hoover, however, rejected both approaches. The Chamber of Commerce's proposal went against his belief in voluntary action, while resorting to unfettered market forces abrogated his responsibilities to act in the public interest.

Meanwhile, the Great Depression deepened. "I know there were students actually starving," remembered one survivor of undergraduate life in the 1930s at the University of Kansas. "There was a biological company that

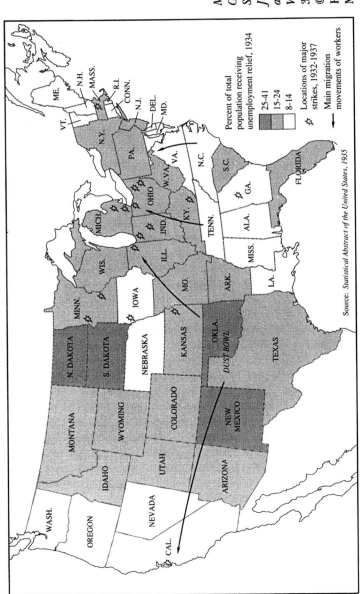

Map 9.1 The Great Depression SOURCE: From John P. McKay et al., A History of Western Society, 3rd ed. Copyright © 1987 by Houghton Mifflin Company.

Percent of total population receiving unemployment relief, 1934

25–41
15–24
8–14

✧ Locations of major strikes, 1932–1937

→ Main migration movements of workers

Source: Statistical Abstract of the United States, 1935

would pay a penny apiece for cockroaches," he recalled, "and some students went cockroach hunting every night." Like this man, most Americans who lived through the 1930s remembered the decade as a period of hard times, and with good reason. Between 1929 and 1932, 110,000 businesses failed in the United States, and industrial production fell by one-half. By the winter of 1932–1933, at least one-quarter of the work force (some 14 million people) were unemployed, with many others employed only part time. In the last weeks of the Hoover administration, the nation's banking system started to collapse when borrowers defaulted and frightened depositors suddenly tried to withdraw funds. In state after state, governors were forced to declare "bank holidays," a suspension of banking transactions altogether, in a desperate attempt to stave off the complete collapse of public confidence and to help those banks that remained sound to solve their own problems.

FRANKLIN D. ROOSEVELT AND THE NEW DEAL

In the midst of economic crisis, the American electorate rejected Herbert Hoover in favor of Franklin D. Roosevelt in the presidential election of 1932. Roosevelt's background was sharply different from Hoover's. Roosevelt, like his distant cousin Theodore, came from a well-to-do family and was by profession a politician. He had served as a member of the New York legislature and as assistant secretary of the navy during World War I before running for vice president on the unsuccessful Democratic ticket in 1920. Especially after being crippled by polio in the early 1920s, Roosevelt had a warmth toward individuals who suffered and a conviction that democracy and capitalism must be made to work. He had been elected governor of New York in 1928, so he entered the White House an experienced politician.

Roosevelt exuded warmth and charm, qualities that Hoover lacked in public. Roosevelt was also flexible, willing to try new approaches to the nation's crises. During the campaign of 1932, he had promised the American people a "new deal" but had been vague about what proposals would be forthcoming either for restoring prosperity or for establishing a new political economy. With his inauguration in 1933, however, Roosevelt and the Democratic congressional majorities brought renewed energy to the public arena, effectively expressing compassion for the millions of Americans who were suffering from the depression. As the new public policies that came to characterize the New Deal evolved in the 1930s, a substantial change occurred in the relationships among business, commercial agriculture, labor, and the federal government. Federal programs eased the human suffering of unemployment, reduced the number of unemployed workers, and restored confidence that the American business system could once again provide for the material well-being of the American people.

Mobilization of the American economy was so important to the nation's success in World War II that President Roosevelt sought personally to inspire workers; here the president inspects an aircraft factory in Tulsa, Oklahoma, in 1943. (Wide World Photos)

Restoring Confidence in the Business System

In his inaugural address, the new president tried to instill hope. Roosevelt's message rang clearly: "The only thing we have to fear is fear itself." In his first action as president, Roosevelt ordered a national bank holiday. Next, working from plans developed by officials in Hoover's Treasury Department, the new administration presented Congress with emergency banking legislation to provide for federal inspectors to examine the closed banks and allow those that were sound to reopen. This action calmed nervous depositors and forestalled further runs to withdraw currency from the staggering banking system. Subsequently, the government instituted a system of federal deposit insurance to assure depositors that even if a bank failed, their personal accounts were secure. These actions were crucial to the effort to restore public confidence in the nation's business system. Now the banks, following federal regulations and supervised by Treasury Department auditors, could make investment capital available without fear of long lines of frightened depositors.

Efforts to restore the banking system meant a new program of federal regulation, which also extended to the securities industry. Widespread suspicion about the manipulation of stock and bond prices by securities dealers and speculators had long existed, suspicions that the Wall Street crash had only increased. An investigation of the banking and securities industries conducted by a Senate committee from 1932 to 1934 showed grounds for those suspicions. The committee's lawyer, a Sicilian immigrant named Ferdinand Pecora, uncovered widespread unethical practices among the nation's most prominent bankers and securities dealers. After the Wall Street crash, for instance, Charles E. Mitchell of the National City Bank secretly made available $2.4 million of bank funds to bank officers, without collateral or interest payments, to enable them to speculate in the market. In the course of this investigation, Congressman Sam Rayburn of Texas expressed the concern of many: "When a people's faith is shaken in a business the business becomes halting and lame. . . . Only one thing can follow in the wake of this destroyed confidence . . . the evils that attend socialism, bolshevism, and communism."

One result of the committee's revelations and the collapse of the banking system prior to Roosevelt's inauguration was the Glass-Steagall Banking Act of 1933. The law, which bankers generally favored, strictly regulated banks by requiring them to keep the Federal Reserve Board informed of the amount and nature of all their loans and investments. To prevent the competition that Congress believed had led banks toward insolvency, the law forbade the payment of interest on checking accounts, and it gave the Federal Reserve Board the power to set maximum interest rates on savings accounts. Commercial and investment banking were separated, and commercial banks were forbidden to underwrite or deal in securities other than those issued by state and local governments. Subsequently, the Banking Act of 1935 gave the Board of Governors of the Federal Reserve System central authority to control interest rates and the nation's money supply.

Other legislation in 1933 and 1934 restored popular faith in the paper instruments so essential to the conduct of the modern American business system. The Federal Securities Act required full disclosure of new securities issues offered to investors and the registration of those issues with the federal government. The Securities and Exchange Commission, set up in 1934, licensed stock exchanges, regulated trading, and prohibited price manipulation. The government began to control the margin rates (the amount of money a person could borrow to buy stocks) in an effort to contain the rapid changes in the prices of securities.

Government officials initiated the reforms, having looked for practical means of making the banking and securities industries function effectively and achieve public favor during the worst crisis in their history; but business leaders helped shape the laws. As the first chairman of the Securities and Exchange Commission, Roosevelt named Joseph P. Kennedy, a successful Boston speculator and father of a future president. Although there was occasional grumbling by business people who now had to confront a new set of regulations issued by a new federal bureaucracy, Kennedy was by and large successful in achieving compliance with both the spirit and the letter of the new regulatory system. "We of the SEC," Kennedy noted soon after his appointment, "do not regard ourselves as coroners sitting on the corpse of financial enterprise. On the contrary, we think of ourselves as the means of bringing new life into the body of the security [*sic*] business."

The National Recovery Administration

The new president and his supporters were willing to go much further than the changes in the banking and securities industries in trying to reform the American business system permanently. One of the first measures of the New Deal, albeit a temporary one, was the creation in 1933 of the National Recovery Administration (NRA). With the NRA, initially conceived as the centerpiece of Roosevelt's new program, the New Deal reformers hoped to reconstruct the government-business partnership that had mobilized the economy during the crisis of World War I and use it to solve the domestic crisis of depression.

This new government-business partnership involved codes of fair competition, a kind of planning. The goal of the NRA was to suspend the antitrust laws and have federal officials cooperate with business leaders from the trade associations to write rules that allocated available markets among firms, fixed prices, and ensured minimum wages and decent working conditions for labor. The idea of the so-called codes of fair competition was to replace competition with price fixing according to plans devised by business and government officials working together. The intended result was to be a planned industrial system involving both center and peripheral firms (there were separate New Deal programs for agriculture).

After Congress established the NRA in 1933, Roosevelt appointed General Hugh Johnson, who had earlier served the War Industries Board, to head the agency. In flamboyant style, Johnson exhorted the various industries to draw up the fair competition codes. Calling for business's cooperation, Johnson explained that the codes would "eliminate eye-gouging and knee-groining and ear-chewing in business. Above the belt any man can be just as rugged and just as individual as he pleases." His call got results: 3,665 codes were proposed (Johnson cut the number to 981). There were codes for major industries dominated by center firms and codes that encompassed peripheral firms in lesser industries. Burlesque theater operators even wrote a code that limited the number of performances. All these codes were designed to prevent the overproduction of goods and services and the consequent pressures for price cutting that threatened to bankrupt firms and increase unemployment.

The NRA was an unprecedented attempt at partnership between federal authority and private business, at least in peacetime. Not only were the codes difficult to write, given the complex networks of economic relationships in the American business system, but any thought of having the government enforce them was questionable on constitutional grounds. So Johnson chose to use the force of public opinion, not police power, to encourage recalcitrant firms to sign codes. The NRA chose a blue eagle as its symbol. Merchants agreeing to a code were to display the eagle, and cooperating manufacturers were to use it as a symbol on their goods. In parades and rallies the NRA encouraged Americans to purchase only items displaying the blue eagle and only from those merchants who showed it. Johnson wanted to arouse a patriotic fervor reminiscent of wartime to stimulate all Americans to a cooperative effort to rationalize and reform the business system so that the nation could recover from its hard times.

The entire NRA effort was soon stuck, however, in a quagmire of disputes that belied the agency's vision of cooperation in the public interest. Patriotic cooperation among business firms with competing interests was not forthcoming. Moreover, opposition arose from consumers, who soon came to view the NRA as a grand exercise in gouging and price fixing. Conflicts also arose between management and labor. The law creating the NRA had guaranteed rights of unionization and collective bargaining, which workers demanded and management resisted; a rash of strikes ensued. By 1934, business executives were beginning to complain about undue federal intervention in private affairs, even though that intervention was intended to save the business system from its worst excesses. By the end of 1934, the NRA was all but dead, a victim of the mistaken belief that it was possible, in the absence of a visible enemy, to rally a diverse nation with a long tradition of individual freedom and managerial prerogative to cooperate in the name of the public good.

Searching for new measures to correct the flaws in the American political economy that had produced the depression, the federal government in 1935 launched a new measure, the National Labor Relations Act (often called the Wagner Act after its sponsor, Senator Robert Wagner of New York), that indelibly changed the relationships between the business community and industrial workers. Meanwhile, deciding on a suit brought by Schechter Poultry Company of Brooklyn, New York, the Supreme Court declared the NRA unconstitutional in 1935. The Court ruled, in part, that the NRA's poultry code could not apply to a local processor under the interstate commerce clause of the Constitution. In those industries where the business leaders involved saw code agreement as desirable, such as coal mining and oil production, separate legislation continued the arrangements begun under NRA auspices.

Labor and the Political Economy of the New Deal

The bargaining relationships between American management and labor began to shift fundamentally in the 1930s, partly because of the militancy of millions of men and women seeking to gain the control over their wages, hours, and working conditions that was possible only through collective action. These changes were also a result of the willingness of New Deal political leaders to respond to the unionization impulse positively. Never before in peacetime had there been an administration willing to place the authority of the federal government on the side of collective bargaining. Because the economic crisis was so deep and threatened to be permanent, politicians, led by Senator Wagner, sought to restore vigor to the business system by granting workers the means, through unions and collective bargaining, of increasing their share of the nation's wealth. In doing so, they would of course be purchasing the products of their own industrial handiwork and would, it was hoped, stimulate a permanent recovery.

In the broadest sense, the new labor relations that emerged in the 1930s resulted from the strong feelings of class consciousness that the depression experience aroused. America's material wealth had always been distributed unevenly, but now, with unemployment a fact and layoffs an ever-present threat, American industrial workers acted on the basis of the reality that their immediate economic interests were sometimes fundamentally at odds with the desire of management to control production costs through low wages and long hours.

One result of these new perceptions and attitudes was the National Labor Relations Act of 1935. This law granted workers the right to form unions of their own choice with leaders and treasuries independent of management, and it required business to agree to collective bargaining. The Wagner Act, as the law was popularly known, established procedures whereby a federal agency, the National Labor Relations Board, could assure workers of their rights and enforce the law against any firm that resisted. Due in large part to the actions of countless industrial workers and the dedication of their union leaders, it now was federal policy to allow workers the same advantages of association as those enjoyed by business.

Not surprisingly, the implementation of this new labor policy occurred only after a protracted struggle. Management resisted the Wagner Act in the courts and, until the Supreme Court affirmed its constitutionality in 1937, argued that it violated the Constitution. In the meantime, large-scale labor struggles broke out, especially in the mass-production industries employing large numbers of unskilled and semiskilled men and women. In those struggles, management typically resisted the unions with every means at its disposal, including the use of armed force in localities where local officials were sympathetic. The most dramatic strikes occurred in 1937, before the Supreme Court's decision, in the automobile industry. Workers there, seeking to have General Motors and Chrysler obey the new Wagner law, occupied strategic factories in sit-down strikes instead of leaving and setting up picket lines. Management could not dislodge the workers without risking the destruction of factories. Finally, in part because of fears of the public relations cost of further resistance, General Motors and Chrysler signed collective bargaining agreements. Ford, on the other hand, faced with the same worker militancy but without a sit-down strike, employed informers and armed guards to keep the union out, with violence

These strikers, members of a union affiliated with the CIO, were typical of American workers in 1937, who were determined to win the collective bargaining rights allowed them by New Deal legislation. (Library of Congress)

if necessary. During 1937, more than 400,000 industrial workers disrupted business by participating in over 450 sit-down strikes.

The movement to unionize mass-production industries remained unfinished by the end of the 1930s. Even where the unions succeeded in forcing management to sign a collective bargaining agreement, management invariably insisted on maintaining the principle of the open shop: contracts applied only to the men and women who had joined the union, and other workers were free to negotiate their own terms. Management hoped thus to weaken the unionization impulse by dividing workers from one another and to assure themselves of a supply of labor in the event of a strike. In spite of management resistance, however, workers established strong unions in virtually all of the nation's mass-production industries. On the eve of World War II, over 8.7 million American workers, or 16 percent of the nonagricultural work force, belonged to unions. More than any other single factor, its labor policy earned the New Deal the animosity of business executives in every region and in every industry.

The New Deal and Small Business

Even though New Deal reformers witnessed the failure of business cooperation through government-inspired codes of fair competition and earned the hostility of employers with the National Labor Relations Act, they did not abandon policies intended to help particular segments of the business community and to restore prosperity. After 1934, the president and his advisers tried to find ways of restricting the power of large corporations within the business system as a means of reinvigorating the economy. While still willing to grant subsidies to important industries and to use the Reconstruction Finance Corporation to assist in the modernization of plants, the government began to focus its interest on helping smaller enterprises survive in a system that had increasingly come to be dominated by giant firms.

Two policies, especially, sought to help peripheral firms. The Robinson-Patman Act of 1936 took aim at the price discrimination that large retailers and chain stores could exercise against independent small merchants by forbidding manufacturers and wholesalers from giving preferential discounts to their biggest customers. Another law strengthened "fair-trade" measures by which manufacturers fixed prices on goods to protect the profits of small dealers. More threatening to corporate America, however, was the renewed vigor with which Roosevelt's administration began to apply the antitrust statutes in 1937. The Department of Justice began to pursue large oligopolistic center firms in the courts. In the end, however, few practical results were obtained before the mobilization demands of World War II called an effective halt to the new antitrust efforts.

Business Opposition to the New Deal

As the new political economy evolved in the 1930s, a growing chorus of complaints began to be heard from American business leaders and their organizations. Prior to the 1930s, business allegiance had been divided between the Democratic and Republican parties, but by the end of the decade, business rested solidly in the Republican camp. Some New Deal measures, especially the NRA, were initially popular among important elements of the business community, and others, such as the regulation of the securities industry, were clearly in the long-range interests of the business system. But because the New Deal responded favorably to the demands of other groups, especially industrial labor, it and President Roosevelt became increasingly unpopular among business executives by 1934 and 1935.

Policies supporting collective bargaining were not the only New Deal programs that affronted business. In 1933, the New Deal launched a major program to develop hydroelectric power in the Tennessee River Valley. The overseeing body, the Tennessee Valley Authority, was a public corporation, and it sparked bitter complaints from privately held utility firms that feared that federal investments in the generation and sale of electricity threatened traditional capitalism. The Roosevelt administration also devised large-scale programs of temporary public employment and work relief. And in 1935, Congress enacted the Social Security law to provide old-age pensions, unemployment compensation, and aid to the indigent and their children. Although these measures did not directly threaten business, the perceived beginning of a limited welfare state went contrary to the traditional beliefs in rugged individualism that many business leaders espoused. Business leaders also opposed the development of a limited welfare state because it interfered with their need for an insecure labor force driven to work for whatever wages, however low, that it could get. Moreover, in spite of Roosevelt's constant concern over unbalanced budgets, the New Deal programs increased federal deficits modestly and threatened business firms with higher tax levies.

Business leaders expressed their opposition to Roosevelt and the New Deal in speeches, editorials, resolutions, and campaign contributions. By the time of the 1936 election campaign, the Liberty League, a political group organized by executives from Du Pont and General Motors, was outspending even the Republican party in trying to unseat the president. In his campaign for reelection, Roosevelt responded mercilessly. The president railed against "economic royalists" who took "other people's money." At the close of the campaign, Roosevelt told a crowd of supporters roaring their approval that the wealthy business interests, "the forces of selfishness and of lust for power," had "met their match" in the Roosevelt White House. "I should like to have it said of my second administration that in it these forces met their master." For the first time in the nation's history, the sharp polarization over the political economy resulted in the reelection of a president (for Roosevelt won by a landslide in 1936) who owed few political debts to business firms and associations and who was in a political position that allowed the possibility of confrontation between the federal government and the nation's largest corporations.

Corporatism Survives

Such a confrontation never really materialized, although Roosevelt did use his power on occasion against business. There were significant exceptions in the general business opposition to Roosevelt, and business still exerted influence on federal economic policy. As vitriolic as were some spokesmen for local chambers of commerce, the resolutions of trade associations, and the private comments of wealthy bankers and industrialists, the tradition of corporatism survived and even expanded during the New Deal. Moreover, the Roosevelt administration felt that receiving the counsel of business leaders on economic policy was desirable. In 1933, the Department of Commerce formed the Business Council, a group of forty to sixty top executives who chose their own membership, to advise the federal government on the best ways of achieving permanent economic recovery. From this advisory relationship there gradually emerged by the middle of the 1940s mechanisms by which leaders of the nation's wealthiest banking and industrial corporations helped shape federal policy toward the economy.

The Business Council became the chief means by which corporate executives influenced policy in the 1930s. Although some executives quit the council in response to the government's new labor policies, others, led by men like W. Averell Harriman of the Union Pacific Railroad and Gerard Swope of General Electric, stayed on, forming committees to advise government officials on particular policies and providing a conduit to the White House. The council was especially influential in framing the Social Security Act of 1935. Business leaders helped to write a self-financing program of old-age pensions that were graduated according to the individual's earnings before retirement. The effects were to ensure that the retirement program did not redistribute income from wealthy to less wealthy Americans (as some reformers proposed) and to create a new social institution—retirement—that would remove older persons from the work force, in favor of creating job opportunities for younger, presumably more vigorous workers. Similarly, the unemployment compensation provisions of the new law, while requiring employers to pay insurance premiums, reduced those costs for firms that enjoyed relatively low layoff rates. Like old-age pensions, unemployment insurance was to be self-financing and thereby kept within strict limits.

❧ Responses to Keynes's Economic Theory

One of the most important influences on attempts to understand and deal with the political economy in the 1930s and later had British roots. In 1936, the British economist John Maynard Keynes published *The General Theory of Employment, Interest, and Money*, a book that challenged widely held convictions about economics. Before Keynes expressed his ideas, classical economists argued that the business cycle contained its own self-correcting mechanisms. Investments produced prosperity as firms built new plants and purchased durable goods. In this view, when a downturn in the business cycle occurred, interest rates eventually dropped and stimulated new investments, returning the economy to prosperity.

Keynes showed that this idea was inaccurate. Investments of capital, he reminded his readers, relied on savings, and the Great Depression had exhausted savings. Without a pool of capital available for investment, and with low levels of consumer demand providing little incentive for investments in any case, it was possible for the business cycle to flatten at an undesirably low level. The only recourse was government intervention with policies aimed at stimulating investment, thereby putting men and women back to work, making it possible for them again to save and provide the private sector with capital. Employed men and women would demand goods and services, thereby providing incentives for businesses to invest.

Keynes outlined three courses of action that government could take. He thought of these actions in an ascending order of desirability. First, government should control interest rates. Once it had control over the cost

of capital, government could adjust interest rates downward
economy was slackening. If controlling interest rates proved insเ
government should follow a second course of using taxes to redเ   .c
income and enlarge the market for goods. Taxing the wealthy to benefit
the poor would make it possible for more people to buy more goods.
When businesses saw sales opportunities and realized that government was
keeping the cost of capital low, firms would invest in new plants or operate
their factories more fully, thus stimulating prosperity. Finally, Keynes argued, when interest-rate controls and income redistribution failed to stimulate desired investment levels, governments must augment private
investments with public investments. In his eyes, traditional notions of
balancing governmental budgets in a depression were misguided; government deficit spending was necessary to make up for insufficient levels of
consumer demand and private investment.

Keynes's ideas about deliberate government deficit spending as a means
of stimulating consumption and moving the economy out of depression
provoked the most controversy. Americans had traditionally relied on private decisions regarding investment, confident that individuals trying to
benefit themselves helped the general economy. In the 1920s, for example,
recognizing the human problems associated with downturns in the business
cycle in a society that was urban and industrial (where few citizens could
be even close to self-sufficiency in sustaining their lives), Secretary of Commerce Hoover had encouraged businesses to increase their investments
when prosperity faded into depression. Now, however, Keynes's ideas
threatened both the faith in private decisions and the economic power
of wealthy men and firms. Public investments for social purposes (dams,
hospitals, housing for the poor, and the like) were seen by those advocating
Keynes's point of view as both desirable in human terms and necessary for
the nation to achieve and maintain prosperity. Keynes's ideas, in other
words, could be, and were, interpreted to challenge the authority and power
of American business, especially the bankers and managers responsible to
the wealthiest corporations.

Disagreements over Keynes's ideas began in the first year of the New
Deal. Observing the calamity of the worldwide depression and recognizing
the importance to recovery of decisions made in the United States, Keynes
on his own initiative tried to influence American opinion and Roosevelt's
policies. He published an open letter to the president, conferred with administration officials, and met with Roosevelt in 1934. The president's
reaction was negative. "He left a whole rigamarole of figures," he told
Secretary of Labor Frances Perkins. "He must be a mathematician rather
than a political economist." Some of Roosevelt's advisers, however, were
more receptive to Keynes's ideas. Business had partly revived under the
New Deal, but when the economy dipped into a serious recession in 1937
and 1938, the advisers were able to persuade Roosevelt to accept a Keynesian
strategy, less on the grounds of economic theory than on the proposition

that government spending would help the unemployed Americans who had suffered for so long. By 1938, however, Roosevelt was having difficulties persuading Congress to follow his lead, and in the end the New Deal never adopted a recovery program modeled on Keynes's ideas. Instead, huge government investments in defense (and later for World War II) began in 1940 to moderate and eventually to end the depression. The issues raised by Keynes resurfaced toward the end of the war, as we shall see in Chapter 11, as American leaders worried about a peacetime return to depression.

The Supreme Court and the New Deal

The judicial branch of the federal government held much of the responsibility for the fundamental shift in government-business relations that occurred in the 1930s. As we saw in Chapter 6, the U.S. Supreme Court had ruled in 1895 that the federal government could not regulate manufacturing. The Court considered manufacturing by itself an intrastate affair and thus not subject to federal jurisdiction. Other Court decisions in the decades after 1895 also discouraged federal attempts to regulate business. In 1935, for instance, it ruled the NRA codes unconstitutional because they also regulated intrastate commerce.

Then in 1937 the Supreme Court dramatically reversed itself in a case testing the constitutionality of the Wagner Act. The Wagner Act provided for government-supervised elections within factories to determine whether or not workers wanted a union and, if so, which union they preferred. Management, resisting the trade union movement with every means at its disposal, challenged the law in the courts, claiming that such elections were entirely local affairs beyond the purview of Congress under the interstate commerce clause. The government lawyers defending the Wagner Act argued that although the elections were local, the affected firms were tied to the national and international economic system. The Wagner Act's defenders expressed the view that the modern American industrial economy was so intertwined that what occurred in one location had an impact in other locations. The strict distinction between intrastate and interstate commerce seemed not to fit modern industrial conditions. The majority of the justices agreed and upheld the Wagner Act. The court's decision meant that a decades-long struggle to define the meaning of the interstate commerce clause was over. After 1937, Court doctrine allowed Congress to pass legislation affecting every aspect of the conduct of business in the United States.

In a sense, then, the most lasting impact of the New Deal on government-business relations was constitutional. As early as the Gilded Age, some Americans had argued that Congress must take steps to govern business in the industrial age. Important new areas of federal regulation were in fact developed, especially in the Progressive Era. But federal power had always been checked by judicial interpretations of the Constitution. After the New Deal court cases, however, Congress was free from the traditional strict interpretations of the Constitution and could choose to regulate nearly every aspect of business behavior. The range of public policy issues potentially affecting business was thereby widened by the end of the 1930s.

BUSINESS AND WORLD WAR II

World War II broke out in Europe on September 1, 1939. President Roosevelt immediately began seeking public support of policies to improve American defenses and ultimately to help defeat Nazi Germany. The United States did not declare war until after the Japanese attack on Pearl Harbor on December 7, 1941. In the meantime, the military services began to prepare for war, Congress began appropriating funds for war goods and enacted a draft law, and Roosevelt called a halt to reform initiatives in favor of gaining the full-fledged cooperation of industrial leaders. By 1942, enormous government expenditures for the war effort were promoting dramatic economic expansion and permanently affecting the structure of the American business system.

Mobilizing Industry

During this second wartime crisis of the twentieth century, the Roosevelt administration evolved a confusing array of executive agencies to coordinate mobilization policies and allocate production priorities. The president apparently preferred to have final decisions made in the White House, and he was unwilling to grant business firms and trade associations the same autonomy to fix prices and set priorities that they had enjoyed under the War Industries Board during World War I.

Nevertheless, the president recognized that the nation required the full cooperation and talents of business executives. Only persons possessing skills and experience in business would be able to arrange the production of materials required by modern warfare. Thus, as was the case in the earlier conflict, Washington was soon crowded with executives staffing new civilian and military agencies whose task it was to arrange a steady stream of supplies and sophisticated equipment for armed forces around the globe. In finding the needed executive talent and establishing the necessary administrative structure, Roosevelt relied heavily on the corporate executives loosely affiliated with the Department of Commerce through the Business Council.

In order to gain the cooperation of business, the Roosevelt administration negotiated policies through the Business Council. This pattern, which started before Pearl Harbor, lasted for the entire period of the war. In these negotiations, business leaders insisted on four basic principles. First, the federal government was not to construct or operate industrial facilities that would compete with private firms. There were to be no wartime equivalents of the Tennessee Valley Authority. Second, and this demand was

World War II not only provided vast opportunities for American business firms but it also created labor shortages that were filled by women. In this photograph, women are assembling the nose section of U.S. warplanes. (National Archives/Records of the Office of War Information)

important only before the attack on Pearl Harbor, corporations wanted to be allowed to continue the production of civilian goods as they geared up for war production. Fearing a return to the depression should the war crisis abate, business leaders wanted to use existing plants; they worried that the costs of heavy capital expenditures for the production of war goods might prove a drain on profits in peacetime. Third, in cases where business did have to invest in new facilities, business leaders insisted that the tax laws allow for their rapid depreciation. In other words, the federal government had to assure America's corporations of their profit margins. Last, in areas like aircraft manufacturing where civilian markets were small, the government must capitalize new production facilities for private firms to operate at nominal rentals. As Secretary of War Henry Stimson, a prominent Republican who had joined the president's cabinet, said, "If you are going to go to war . . . in a capitalist country, you have to let business make money out of the process or business won't work."

Mobilization and the Structure of American Industry

The gargantuan, unprecedented mobilization effort of World War II had major effects on the structure of American industry. Military expenditures greatly accelerated the concentration of production in a few big firms. In 1939, before mobilization began, the one hundred largest American industrial firms controlled 30 percent of the nation's manufacturing output. By 1943, the proportion was reversed: the one hundred largest firms enjoyed a 70 percent share of manufacturing output. This dramatic, sudden rise of giant industrial firms was a direct result of the procurement practices of the military services: the army and navy preferred to work with as few suppliers as possible to ensure a maximum flow of critically needed guns, munitions, and equipment; the benefits of the "visible hand" of large firms reassured the armed services, which were very concerned with the efficient dispatch of war supplies.

When small business owners and their congressional allies realized what was happening, their outcries produced an investigation conducted by Senator Harry S Truman of Missouri. Government policies were amended to mitigate to some extent the tremendous concentration of money and power in the hands of a few giant industrial corporations. Congressional pressure helped secure large sums of federal capital for the aluminum industry, for instance, capital that went to the small Reynolds and Kaiser firms, allowing them to become rivals of the giant Aluminum Corporation of America. The Transportation Act of 1940 and decisions by the Interstate Commerce Commission also brought about freight rates more favorable to small business firms struggling to develop industrial plants in the South and West. Wartime policies ensured that the South and West became important manufacturing regions.

Mobilization and Industrial Labor

The one significant area in which business was unable to negotiate favorable mobilization policies was labor relations. The labor surpluses of the depression had enabled management to maintain the principle of the open shop, even in the face of the militant and growing unionization of industrial workers. With the coming of the war, however, labor was suddenly in short supply, which gave its demands more clout. The unions had also gained political power, for workers and poorer Americans had provided Roosevelt with the margin necessary for reelection in 1940.

The unions believed that once they had won a collective bargaining contract, all of a firm's workers should be required to support and join the union that had won them gains, and that employers should hire only union members (the closed shop). This position seemed reasonable from the perspective of the men and women who had sacrificed to build a union, but it was anathema to business. First, the closed shop took away businesses' right to hire whomever they chose. Second, the closed shop eliminated the possibility that management might be able to play nonunion workers off against union workers and thereby break the power of the unions.

What emerged as government policy during the war was a compromise, called the union shop, which the unions liked more than business did. The government required firms with war contracts to sign "maintenance of membership" agreements with their unions. Under this form of the union shop, management could hire whomever it chose, but after a specified time each employee had to join the union or lose his or her job. The result of this federal labor policy, backed up by its power to require compliance as a requirement for getting contracts for war production, was the firm implantation of unions in American industry. By the end of the war, the number of workers who belonged to a union rose to more than 14 million, nearly 22 percent of the nonagricultural work force.

TOWARD A LIMITED WELFARE STATE

The Great Depression and the two world wars profoundly reshaped the American political economy. The wars in particular forged new partnerships between business and government that indelibly affected attitudes and institutions as the exigencies of the times led to federal encouragement of long-standing business desires to control the market.

If war mobilization in the industrial age affected the political economy, so too did economic calamity, which augmented desires among all groups to improve their ability to control their economic circumstances—their security. The Great Depression was the greatest domestic crisis in the United States since the Civil War. Like the wars that preceded and followed it, the depression redefined the relationships between the federal government and its citizens. Roosevelt's programs failed to end the depression, but the temporary work relief and the Social Security Act created a limited welfare state that softened its effects. Whenever the business cycle turned down after the 1930s, federal programs that originated in the New Deal stood ready to cushion the worst effects of unemployment.

Even though the New Deal did not end the depression, its programs were important for the future security of the American business system. The banking system and the securities industry were able to service the needs of business, again thanks to New Deal measures that salvaged them from the excesses that followed the Wall Street crash of 1929. The federal sanction of the trade union movement after 1935 was also important. Unionized workers received higher wages than workers had before the unions and, thereby, were able to participate more fully in the American economic system as consumers. The entrance of millions of industrial workers into the consuming American middle class was especially important for a business system that was trying more and more to market consumer durable goods.

The search for economic security, however, involved much more than the bargaining relationships between business and labor or the limited welfare state created by the New Deal. In the postwar years, federal policies also were developed to promote and maintain economic prosperity. In the 1930s and 1940s, the federal government greatly broadened its involvement in the American business system. As in the Progressive Era, the government continued to regulate specific industries; in fact, the regulatory work of the federal government widened considerably under Franklin Roosevelt. But for the first time the federal government began assuming responsibility for the economic health of the nation as a whole, a concern that would become still more pronounced after World War II. As Americans continued their elusive search for economic security and the good life in the 1950s, 1960s, and 1970s, the federal government began to play ever-larger roles in their lives.

Selected Readings

Ellis W. Hawley's scholarship is seminal for understanding this period. See especially his *The Great War and the Search for a Modern Order: A History of the American People and Their Institutions, 1917–1933* (New York: St. Martin's Press, 1992) and "Herbert Hoover, the Commerce Secretariat, and the Vision of an 'Associative State,' " *Journal of American History* 61 (June 1974): 116–140. Peter Fearon, *War, Prosperity and Depression: The U.S. Economy, 1917–1945* (Lawrence: University Press of Kansas, 1987), is a readable, up-to-date survey. K. Austin Kerr, *Organized for Prohibition: A New History of the Anti-Saloon League* (New Haven, Conn.: Yale University Press, 1985), explains prohibition as a business-control measure.

Labor historians have supplied much insight into union activity in this period. Two general works are by Irving Bernstein: *The Lean Years* (Boston: Houghton Mifflin, 1960) and Turbulent Years (Boston: Houghton Mifflin, 1970). David Brody, *Labor in Crisis: The Steel Strike of 1919* (Philadelphia: Lippincott, 1965), and Daniel Nelson, "The Company Union Movement, 1900–1937: A Reexamination," *Business History Review* 46 (Autumn 1982): 335–358, are also valuable.

For information on the New Deal years, William E. Leuchtenberg, *Franklin D. Roosevelt and the New Deal* (New York: Harper & Row, 1963), is a standard account. *The Rise and Fall of the New Deal Order, 1930–1980,* edited by Steve Fraser and Gary Gerstle (Princeton, N.J.: Princeton University Press, 1989), offers several important essays. Michael Bernstein, *The Great Depression: Delayed Recovery and Economic Change in America, 1929–1939* (Cambridge, England: Cambridge University Press, 1987), is provocative. *The New Deal and the Problem of Monopoly* (Princeton N.J.: Princeton University Press, 1966) by Ellis Hawley is a classic. Robert M. Collins, The Business Response to Keynes, 1929–1964 (New York: Columbia University Press, 1981), carries the story of corporate liberalism forward. A most interesting account of the World War II years can be found in John Morton Blum, *V Was for Victory: Politics and American Culture During World War II* (New York: Harcourt Brace, 1976). Harold G. Vatter, *The U.S. Economy in World War II* (New York: Columbia University Press, 1985), is also valuable. Finally, Kim McQuaid, *Big Business and Presidential Power* (New York: William Morrow Co., 1982), explains how President Roosevelt and his successors interacted with the leaders of center firms.

1944 The United States leads other nations in setting up the Bretton Woods Agreement.

1947 The United States and other countries enter into the General Agreement on Tariffs and Trade (GATT).

1952 IBM enters the computer market.

1967 The Kennedy Round of GATT talks greatly lowers trade barriers among industrialized nations.

1968 The conglomerate merger movement reaches a high point.

1970 Some 86 percent of America's 500 largest industrial companies are diversified.

10

The Dominance of
American Business,
1946–1971

On a blustery March morning in 1948, a chartered Pan American Airways DC-3 descended across a city that lay in rubble from the ruinous carnage of World War II and landed at Berlin's Tempelhof airfield. Henry Ford II, at the age of thirty an heir to the world's largest industrial fortune and in charge of the automobile manufacturing firm that bore his name, stepped off the aircraft on the final stages of a tour to assess the multinational health of the Ford Motor Company. Ford employees had contributed to the wartime mobilization so recently ended, manufacturing more than 86,000 aircraft among other machines of war. The company at the end of the war was an important multinational firm, with forty-eight factories in twenty-three nations, some of which, like Germany, lay in devastation.

Before landing in Berlin, Henry Ford had observed his company's operations in Britain, France, and the Low Countries, and would conclude his trip with a visit to Spain. Everywhere he had found problems, ranging from a lack of capital to the inability of factory workers to obtain adequate nutrition. Ford left Europe convinced that his company had to make greater efforts abroad. On his trip home he wrote a paper summarizing his thoughts about what he had seen. "I believe the policy of the Ford Motor Company," the young executive concluded, "should be to invest dollars in Europe where such an investment is obviously in the interests of the countries and the people involved. I further believe that in the years ahead, the success of the large American manufacturer will be measured equally on the national and international scales."

This conclusion proved prescient for the future history of the American business firm. The period from 1945 through 1970 was exceptional in the history of American business. In 1945, the American economy dominated the world's production and distribution, and American firms stood poised to take advantage of new multinational opportunities in what Henry Luce, the founder of a publishing empire, had termed an "American century." In the years to come, American products invaded the world's markets as never before, and, like the young Ford, increasing numbers of American business executives began thinking in global terms. Enjoying improved images at home thanks to their participation in the war's mobilization, large American firms—most of them multidivisional, decentralized companies—simply dominated the world economy. At home, the pent-up demand for goods and services soon overcame fears of a return to the conditions of the Great Depression and produced an unprecedented prosperity for Americans and the firms that supplied them goods and services, giving them employment as the consumerism of the 1920s and 1930s continued apace in the postwar years. For the next quarter-century, led by an expanding automobile industry headquartered in metropolitan Detroit, big business grew and prospered, the gaps between center and peripheral firms widened, and American investment came to play ever-larger roles in the economies of other continents. Meanwhile, the American standard of living became the benchmark by which other nations measured their own economic performance.

The prosperous features of the history of the American business firm, with respect to both domestic investments in the United States and multinational investments abroad, were buttressed by important public policies during this period. American political leaders wanted to devise a system of international relations that would prevent a third world war. In 1945, American business executives largely agreed with a policy of removing tariff and other barriers to foreign trade so as to increase the integration of the American economy with those economies beyond the nation's borders. Then, in 1948, within weeks of Henry Ford's visit to Berlin, the attempt of the Soviet Union, once a wartime ally, to blockade the movement of goods in and out of Berlin and generally to enlarge its authority and spread its Communist doctrines even further convinced American leaders of the necessity for rearmament in what became an ongoing cold war. After 1948, continuing government expenditures to rearm the United States and its allies in the face of the Communist threat helped stimulate economic prosperity in important industries. That stimulus was all the greater when in 1950 American troops were sent to South Korea to resist the Communist invasion and later, in 1965, entered the Vietnam War in large numbers.

ECONOMIC PROSPERITY AFTER WORLD WAR II

"Growth" is the word that best characterizes the economy of the United States for the first twenty-five years after World War II. Many Americans feared a recession, or even a depression, after the end of the war, but such worries proved unwarranted. The American economy experienced rapid expansion throughout the 1960s, its growth interrupted by only a few short and mild recessions. Between 1945 and 1960, America's real GNP rose by 52 percent, and its per capita GNP increased 19 percent. Over the next decade the nation's real GNP soared an additional 46 percent, and its per capita GNP rose by 29 percent. And this prosperity was more widely shared than ever before in the American experience. Combined with government tax and social policies, as well as collective bargaining agreements, the postwar prosperity led to a lessening of inequalities in the distribution of income after 1940. Price stability accompanied and contributed to this economic growth. The traumatic experiences of the Great Depression began fading in people's memories as prosperity spread over their land. Prophetically, one of the most popular songs of 1945 was "Let the Good Times Roll."

An increasing share of America's economic growth resulted from the nation's involvement in a global economy. Americans became more involved with foreign countries than before, and the American firm became increasingly linked to the global economy. Urged by American officials, two international agreements designed to increase world trade—the Bretton Woods Agreement and the General Agreement on Tariffs and Trade (GATT)—were especially important. American leaders believed that free trade stimulated both economic growth at home and global economic development, from which they expected international political stability to spring. They also realized that, with so much of the world exhausted and ruined by the war, American firms stood poised to dominate economic activity in a system of free trade.

International Policy and American Prosperity

As the final phase of World War II began, Allied leaders (except those from the Soviet Union) met at Bretton Woods, a resort in the White Mountains of New Hampshire, to plan for what they hoped would be a global financial system to facilitate the development of a prosperous world economy after the war. In the summer of 1944, representatives of the forty-four nations present completed the negotiations. The Bretton Woods Agreement stabilized currency exchange rates among nations by pegging all other currencies to the American dollar—then by far the world's strongest currency—and, in turn, by pegging the dollar to a set value in gold. (One ounce of gold was worth $35.) People in other nations could thus buy dollars with their currencies at a fixed rate of exchange and then use dollars to buy gold at a set price. This system of fixed exchange rates set up a stable and predictable international economic system much desired by business people operating across national borders, a system within which world trade could flourish.

Shortly after they embraced the Bretton Woods Agreement, representatives of most of the same nations sought to reduce trade barriers among themselves, an effort culminating in 1947 with the General Agreement on Tariffs and Trade (GATT), which Japan joined in 1955. The GATT's rules required uniform treatment among nations: the lowest tariffs, the easiest access to markets, and the fewest restrictions granted any one nation had to be given to all nations. (In other words, the "most favored nation" advantages had to be extended to all GATT members.) The nations adhering to the GATT participated in a series of negotiations called "rounds" that lowered tariff barriers on a wide variety of products around the world. For instance, agreements resulting in 1967 from the Kennedy Round (named for President John F. Kennedy) lowered tariff duties by a third on 60,000 items.

American political and business leaders, in addition to their active participation in the Bretton Woods and GATT agreements, took actions designed to increase the prosperity and economic stability of the world. The Marshall Plan, proposed by President Harry S Truman and passed by Congress in 1948, used a combination of American government aid and private technical assistance to promote the economic recovery of Europe. Through various programs, including massive purchases of military supplies for the Korean War in the early 1950s, the American government helped revive the Japanese economy, which lay shattered after World War II.

American businesses benefited from these measures. As we have seen throughout this book, foreign trade has always played a significant role in the economic growth of the United States, but as a large internal market developed in the nineteenth and early twentieth centuries, its importance lessened. The maturing of the national market, combined with the advocacy of free trade by the United States after World War II, altered this trend. Once again, foreign trade grew in volume and economic importance. The value of world trade rose at an annual rate of about 4 percent in the century before 1945, but at a much higher 7 percent over the next twenty-five years. As nations recovered from World War II, world trade expanded by a factor of five between 1950 and 1970! American firms eagerly participated in this expansion. In 1950 American companies sold 9 percent of their production abroad, but by 1970 they sold 13 percent in other nations. America's share in the industrial output of the globe regained the level first attained in the 1920s—roughly 42 percent of the world's total—and stayed there into the early 1970s.

The Cold War and the Structure of American Business

The emergence of the cold war after 1948 also played a prominent role in American prosperity and the evolution of the business structure. Before World War II, the nation's peacetime military forces were kept at low levels. After 1945, U.S. leaders perceived a continuing threat to the very existence of capitalism around the world as a result of the growth of the Soviet Union's power. These perceptions were heightened by the Communist revolution in China in 1949 and the war that broke out in Korea in 1950. In addition, other Asians, as well as Africans and Latin Americans, were beginning to look to China and Russia as desirable socialist models for economic development and national independence. In brief, U.S. leaders faced a continuing cold war between the two economic and political systems, punctuated by "limited" warfare in Korea and, later, Southeast Asia. These perceived dangers to the security and self-interest of the United States and its trading partners gave rise to a policy of partial but continual defense mobilization, a policy that reshaped the relationships among developers of technology, business corporations, and the military services. In 1961, President Eisenhower termed those new relationships the "military-industrial complex," and his phrase caught on because it summarized a new and seemingly permanent set of institutions.

The market for weapons, the increasing technological complexity of weapons systems, and their maintenance involved corporate executives, scientists, and engineers as well as military personnel. During World War II, as we have seen, the military services preferred to arrange contracts with large industrial corporations, and the effect of these procurement policies was to speed up the concentration of assets into fewer and fewer big businesses. The emergence of the military-industrial complex reinforced that trend. One researcher found that "from 1940 to 1965 the fifty largest corporations in the country always received somewhat more than half of all prime military contracts, while small business never received as much as 20 percent."

The continuing expenditures for the military services, and in the 1960s the launching of a major American effort to explore outer space, affected the business system in important ways. The expenditures favored industries located in the South and West: California boomed and became the nation's most populous state in the postwar period in large part because of the defense industries located there. Individual firms organized to take advantage of the military services' need for equipment. And multinational firms invested to export armaments to American allies abroad. In the meantime, thousands of American workers benefited from the high wages typically found in the defense industries.

Toward a Postindustrial Economy

In the United States, structural changes begun earlier accelerated after World War II. The most notable of these was the production of a dazzling array of consumer durables. Cars, television sets, and household appliances poured off assembly lines as America continued to develop a consumer society. With respect to sales within the United States, American businesses initially faced little competition from foreign firms struggling to recover from the war. The lucrative domestic market remained a largely American preserve, despite the GATT, into the 1960s. Even more noticeable was the remarkable expansion in the nation's service industries, as the United States began making the transition into what some observers called a "postindustrial" society. Although the precise nature of the future American economy was unclear, as early as the 1950s and 1960s it was apparent that heavy industry would play a lesser role than it had in the nineteenth and early twentieth centuries.

Despite the growth in foreign trade during these two decades, American businesses found a large part of their sales within the nation's domestic market. Sales of automobiles by foreign firms remained minuscule until the German firm Volkswagen suddenly gained market share between 1958 and 1960. The continued ownership of this market gave American business executives a major advantage over their foreign competitors. In 1950, the American market was nearly ten times as large as the next-largest national market—that of Great Britain. Moreover, it was a rich market. In 1950, the per capita GNP of Americans was 50 percent higher than that of Canadians, three times greater than that of the British, four times larger than that of the Germans, and fifteen times greater than that of the Japanese.

In exploiting this national market American business enjoyed distinct advantages. American workers were more skilled than those overseas. The United States had invented mass compulsory public elementary and secondary education and possessed the world's best system of higher education, which was reaching a larger and larger number of citizens. Americans were leaders in technology, due in part to the educational systems and in part to the investments being made by government agencies and business entrepreneurs alike. And American business managers were arguably the best in the world. Unlike the situation in many other nations, business careers attracted the best and the brightest in the United States.

Marketing and Advertising

Amid the prosperity that characterized the quarter-century following the defeat of the German and Japanese military forces, and as the American business system evolved toward a "postindustrial" society, marketing and advertising took on new roles. The evolution of marketing as a focus of attention among top business executives may have stalled during the production crises associated with mobilization, but marketing and the related advertising aspects of business strategy flowered as never before in the American system after 1945. The most successful manufacturers, from the giant General Motors Corporation to a host of less-known firms, learned to organize their activities around a strategy that integrated careful observation of changing consumer tastes with the design, production, and distribution of products. And the coordination of such activities around a marketing strategy typically involved substantial expenditures on advertising.

The American market underwent basic changes after 1945, evolving from a mass market in many fields to segmented, specialized markets. Following the rise of big business in the nineteenth century, manufacturing opportunities now abounded in the supply of standardized goods to a mass market. Coca-Cola, for instance, grew into a worldwide behemoth by supplying a standardized carbonated beverage—a "universal" drink suitable for all tastes at all times—first across America and then, with the stationing of American troops abroad after 1941, throughout the world. The growth of the multidivisional, decentralized form of big business structure, however, allowed manufacturers to respond to more specialized markets as well. Small companies had persisted in part by focusing on special niches in particular markets. Although the pent-up demand for automobiles and other consumer durable goods in the immediate postwar years required a strategy that emphasized mass production, more and more manufacturers came to realize, as demand was slaked after 1950, that consumer tastes were segmented. The desire for more specialized, less standardized goods had always been present; now rising levels of prosperity allowed consumers to divide themselves into segmented markets.

The evolution of the American mass market to sets of segmented markets was by no means complete in 1970. Nevertheless, awareness of this evolution allowed entrepreneurs new opportunities. Pepsi-Cola was an example. Selling a beverage with a flavor similar to the standardized product of the giant Coca-Cola, Pepsi struggled to devise a strategy to win a larger share of the soft-drink market. For years Pepsi emphasized the lower price of its standardized product, but it failed to win a larger share of the market. However, when Pepsi executive Alfred N. Steele realized after 1950 that beverage consumption was moving from public places such as soda fountains into the home, he gained market share by pursuing sales in grocery stores for home consumption. Finally, the company's ultimate market segmentation strategy hit home in the 1960s, when its advertisements began targeting young people specifically. Whereas Pepsi's net income in 1949 was $2.1 million compared to Coca-Cola's $37 million, by 1970 the gap had narrowed substantially. After 1970, Coca-Cola responded by differentiating its once-standardized product in a variety of formulas and flavors.

Developments in the advertising industry both reflected and promoted the marketing orientation of American businesses. Advertising agencies grew both in number and in size, and often helped their clients study available markets. Spending on advertising had declined during the slump of the 1930s, and the decline had continued during World War II when mobilization commanded attention. In the five years after the end of the war, however, advertising expenditures soared from $2.9 billion in 1945 to $5.7 billion in 1950, or 2 percent of GNP. In 1986, firms spent $102 billion—2.4 percent of GNP—on advertisements directed at American consumers. Although the proportion of advertising expenditures did not grow very significantly relative to the size of the economy, the total volume of advertising messages increased dramatically as expenditures kept pace with the nation's growth. As a result of this trend, combined with the ability in the decades after 1945 to exploit the new medium of television for commercial purposes, advertising became more ubiquitous in Americans' lives.

Advertising remained both a mass and a segmented phenomenon during this period. Television audiences were mass audiences, reached by just a few major networks of broadcasters in that industry's first decades. Skillfully designed advertising campaigns and expensively produced commercial messages bombarded those mass audiences. (Prior to 1970, campaigns in print media were supported by the advertisements in television broadcasts that reached mass audiences, and they were directed at more specialized, or segmented, groups of customers.) In any event, the advertising campaigns allowed businesses to become more and more adept at portraying the consumption of goods and services as important values. The further segmentation of the American mass market—and, with the growth of cable systems, the segmentation of television broadcasting to specialized audiences of consumers—awaited the decades after 1970.

Service Industries

A major area of opportunity for American entrepreneurs in the postwar era lay in service industries, which have always been important to America's economic growth. In the nineteenth century, manufacturing and services had developed together, reinforcing each other. Transportation improvements helped create the national market so necessary for large-scale industrialization, and investment banking houses marketed the securities of the nation's railroads. The pattern of complementary development continued in the early twentieth century. New advertising firms, for instance, allowed manufacturers to reach the growing market for consumer goods in the 1920s.

The service sector—broadly defined to include trade, finance, transportation, and government—accounted for about two-thirds of America's GNP by 1970. By contrast, the contributions of the extractive industries—agriculture and mining—declined substantially. Industry's contribution to America's GNP also fell, from 30 percent of the total in the late 1940s to just 20 percent about forty years later. While some of the service jobs were low-paying, dead-end positions, others could be found in well-paying industries with good prospects for advancement. Exports of service businesses—consulting, telecommunications, and computer services were the most common—also strengthened the foreign-trade picture of the United States.

THE LARGE DIVERSIFIED AMERICAN FIRM

In the years following World War II, earlier trends in the American business system continued. The distinction between center and peripheral firms grew ever-more pronounced as big business continued to dominate the domestic economy and make substantial investments abroad and as the world recovered from the ravages of war. When *Fortune* magazine started its list of the nation's 500 largest industrial firms in 1955, the companies listed had taken in $137 billion, equivalent to 37 percent of GNP. Fifteen years later the dominance of big business in the American economy was even more pronounced: now the gross receipts of the *Fortune* 500 were $445 billion, equivalent to 46 percent of GNP. The list of firms was remarkably stable, furthermore, with few changes in the names on it. The managers of those companies continued to build on successful practices pioneered in the prewar years, planning for the long term and providing secure employment and relatively high incomes for many employees as they satisfied expanding markets for goods.

Diversification and Decentralization

The expansion of the American economy opened new opportunities for business firms. Executives who planned diversified growth strategies increasingly adopted the decentralized structures pioneered at Du Pont and General Motors in the 1920s. By 1970, some 86 percent of the 500 largest industrial companies in the United States were following this pattern. They had diversified into different markets to the extent that each company had at least three different divisions. At the same time, 73 of America's largest 100 industrial companies had adopted some form of decentralized management.

Big business executives who led their firms in a strategy of product diversification worked to perfect decentralized structures. Managing a decentralized firm whose products ranged across more than one industry meant that executives had to develop the ability to judge performance on financial terms. While the focus of top executives at some industrial companies remained production oriented, others stressed the strategies of marketing that had advanced in the prewar period. After 1945, a financial outlook grew increasingly important across the landscape of American big business: executives of diversified, decentralized companies now often looked not to production efficiencies or market shares as a measure of success but, rather, to financial performance. This measure, moreover, typically referred to performance in the short term—namely, in the quarter or the year that the firm reported to investors and government authorities.

Conglomerates

The increasing use of this measure of corporate success contributed to the formation of conglomerates, an extreme form of diversification, in the 1960s. Conglomerates are companies with many different divisions, usually

PacifiCorp was a long-lasting conglomerate that, in the 1990s, operated businesses as diverse as cellular telephone communications and strip-mining of low-sulphur coal in Wyoming. (Telecommunications photo, Kristine Finnegan; Mining photo, Ovak Arslanian)

eight or more, that make and sell mostly unrelated products. Hence conglomerate businesses call to mind the rocks from which they took their name: a conglomerate rock is composed of rounded fragments varying from small pebbles to large boulders, held together by a cementlike mixture such as hardened clay.

Conglomerates became increasingly common in the 1960s as the United States experienced its third major merger movement of the century. Mergers of manufacturing and mining companies reached a peak in 1968, when they totaled 2,500 in number; 715 of these were conglomerate-type mergers. Even so, conglomerates did not become the dominant form of big business in the United States. Even in 1966, at the height of the conglomerate movement, only 46 of the 500 largest industrial companies in America were conglomerates. The merger of firms to form conglomerates sometimes resulted in very large enterprises indeed. Gulf & Western, for instance, expanded its sales through 72 mergers from $10 million in 1958 to $1.3 billion just ten years later.

In the 1960s, the officers of conglomerates often boasted of their ability to manage strictly through financial controls and measurements. They

claimed that a new type of business executive was evolving: a young, ambitious manager with generalized management talents, a person who was versatile, adaptable enough to solve any problem in any business. Trained especially in the techniques of financial management, this new breed could, it was claimed, run a company well without knowing much about its products or production methods.

Whatever the boast, the success of the management of conglomerates varied. On the average, conglomerates performed no better than other types of big businesses in either the 1960s or the 1970s. Management problems limited the success of many conglomerates. Too often, executives in the head offices of conglomerates failed to supervise and coordinate the work of their company's many divisions. Conglomerates frequently lacked the good information flow and statistical controls established at more traditional decentralized, multidivisional companies like Du Pont and General Motors. And sometimes the head offices did not know what the divisions were doing. The conglomerate General Dynamics, for instance, lost $425 million between 1960 and 1962 because the corporate office located in New York failed to place adequate controls on careless work done by the Convair Division, which was making commercial jet airplanes in Los Angeles. A more successful example, on the other hand, was Eagle-Picher Industries, which combined growth through merger with internal growth. Its head, T. Spencer Shore, led the firm out of its historic roots in the lead and zinc industries by acquiring other firms. Eagle-Picher went from five divisions in 1961 to nineteen divisions in 1971. Shore skillfully combined financial controls for the corporate office in Cincinnati with a decentralized structure that allowed operating executives to maintain a focus on production and marketing.

As time passed, the Eagle-Picher experience became typical of successful attempts to follow a conglomerate strategy. Conglomerate mergers were fashionable among some executives and financiers in the 1960s, but the firms that resulted persisted only after top management became aware of the need to allow for strategies of production efficiency, technical innovation, and market penetration.

American Multinationals

Just as the growth in the American economy opened up opportunities for the further diversification of business at home, the expansion of the global economy after World War II encouraged worldwide business diversification. U.S. multinational corporations were among the companies that benefited from this situation. As we saw in Chapter 8, U.S. companies began overseas operations well before World War II. But the return of prosperity after the war brought increased foreign activity. By 1970, at least 3,500 U.S. companies had direct foreign investments in some 15,000 enterprises. The total amount of direct foreign investments came to $78 billion (in current dollars) in the same year, an increase that more than kept pace with the expansion of the American economy. Also by 1970, the direct investments of U.S. companies overseas equaled 8 percent of the GNP of the United States, up from only 3.4 percent in 1946.

As it had since the 1920s, when it replaced mining in importance, manufacturing attracted the greatest share of the investment funds of U.S. multinationals. Also as in times past, the types of manufacturers investing abroad remained the same: those with technological advantages or unique products (such as companies in the electrical, office equipment, and chemical industries) and those already well established overseas. And again as in earlier times, most of these businesses invested in foreign plants and factories to extend the markets for their products, something they discovered they could not do simply by increasing their exports from the United States. Language, cultural, and legal barriers often made it necessary for U.S. companies to set up manufacturing plants, not simply sales offices, overseas. Moreover, cheap foreign labor often made a move abroad very attractive.

As early as the 1920s, U.S. multinationals realized that they had to respect and adapt to the customs and regulations of the countries in which they did business. This concern took on a new urgency in the postwar world, as independence movements in Latin America, Africa, the Middle East, and Asia rearranged the social and political environments of those regions. Increasingly, U.S. companies had to enter into partnership agreements, often as the junior partner, with newly created nationalistic governments if they hoped to continue operating at all (the new governments sometimes confiscated foreign ventures). U.S. oil companies, which replaced the British firms that had dominated the Middle East (and particularly Saudi Arabia) immediately after World War II, made such arrangements with many Middle Eastern governments in the late 1960s.

IBM: A Diversified Multinational

The data-processing industry dominated by International Business Machines (IBM) illustrates the increasing importance of service industries in American daily life. The data-processing industry first developed to serve the needs of the federal government and America's growing number of big businesses. The managers of government and business bureaucracies depended on more and more data supplied at an ever-faster pace as the basis for their decisions. For instance, it was the availability of such data that allowed decentralization to proceed at Du Pont and General Motors in the 1920s. This requirement of business and government created a market for new office machines, such as tabulators and calculators, before World War II and for computers in the postwar period. In the early and mid-1980s, the market for computers broadened, as new types became available for small and medium-sized businesses and found their way into household use. By the late 1980s, computers had become a ubiquitous feature of the American scene.

The origins of the computer industry, and of IBM in particular, stretched back to the founding of the Computer-Tabulating-Recording Company (CTR) in 1910. CTR made time clocks, scales, and—most important for the future—tabulating machines. The federal government used those tabulators in processing census returns, and some railroads employed them in handling their statistics. Thomas Watson, who had begun his business career selling cash registers, joined CTR in 1914 and a year later became the company's president.

Watson remade CTR in the 1920s and 1930s by focusing its resources on tabulators and other office machines. Renamed IBM in 1924, the firm offered electrically powered office machines that were among the most advanced in the United States. IBM based its growth not on technological prowess, however, but on sales and service. Before joining CTR, Watson had worked at National Cash Register, and his experiences there first as a salesman and later as a corporate officer in the company's Dayton, Ohio, headquarters molded his approach to business. National Cash Register stressed sales and service, and Watson took this emphasis with him to IBM. One of his favorite sayings was "We sell and deliver service." This salesmanship, backed up by service, made IBM a leader in the business-machine industry. With earnings of $9 million on revenues of $40 million in 1939, IBM was more profitable than any of its competitors—Burroughs,

Early computers revolutionized data storage, processing, and retrieval in American life, but they required large spaces and, before the development of transistors, carefully cooled rooms. (International Business Machines)

National Cash Register, Remington Rand, and Underwood—and trailed only Underwood in size.

The demands of the military began reshaping the data-processing industry during World War II. Fed by federal funds, some companies moved beyond the production of tabulators and calculators to make the world's first computers (unlike tabulators, computers have electronic memories that can retain mathematic rules and apply them to new sets of data automatically). IBM, generally more interested in sales than in pioneering new technologies, initially lagged behind Remington Rand and some other companies in developing computers. However, when Thomas Watson, Jr., took over as president from his father in 1952, IBM entered the computer market, and by the mid-1950s it had a line of mainframe computers that competed directly with Remington Rand's UNIVAC. (A mainframe computer is a large, high-capacity computer capable of handling all of an organization's data-processing needs. General Electric became the first private business to own a mainframe computer when it purchased a UNIVAC in 1954.) This first generation of computers was based on vacuum-tube technologies, and the resulting machines were large, bulky, and difficult to cool.

By the 1950s and early 1960s, the first generation of computers was being replaced by a second generation that utilized transistors and diodes rather than vacuum tubes. Smaller, more reliable, and cooler in their operations than their predecessors, these machines represented a major advance in computer technology. Sperry Rand (the Sperry Corporation and Remington Rand merged in 1955) led the industry in making this switch. Characteristically, IBM allowed others to blaze the trail with transistorized computers, only to seize the lead through superior salesmanship and service. "It doesn't do much good to build a better mousetrap," noted Louis Rader of Sperry Rand's UNIVAC division, "if the other guy selling mousetraps has five times as many salesmen."

In 1965, IBM introduced its first third-generation mainframe computer, the "360," in response to moves by several of its competitors, most notably Honeywell. (Using integrated circuits rather than transistors, third-generation computers were faster and less prone to breakdowns than their earlier counterparts.) With gross revenues of nearly $2.5 billion and a net income of $333 million in 1965, IBM commanded 65 percent of the market for computers in the United States. Sperry Rand, its closest rival, controlled only 12 percent of the market. It was said that the computer industry was run by Snow White (IBM) and the Seven Dwarfs (its competitors). In the 1960s and 1970s, IBM successfully withstood antitrust suits mounted against it by the federal government and by other computer companies, and was still clearly America's industry leader as the 1980s opened.

As it grew in importance within the United States, IBM also expanded overseas. In 1949, Richard Watson (Thomas Jr.'s brother) became the head of the newly formed World Trade division. World Trade took charge of all of IBM's foreign operations, controlling production or sales subsidiaries in 130 countries around the globe. With revenues of almost $1.1 billion in 1965, IBM World Trade had become one of America's major multinationals.

As it diversified its product lines and regional coverage, IBM decentralized its management structure. Decentralization occurred within IBM's domestic operations in 1956, when Thomas Watson, Jr., separated the company into five major divisions. This reorganization took place at a three-day conference that Watson convened for more than a hundred IBM managers. "We went in a monolith," Watson later observed, "and we emerged three days later as a modern, reasonably decentralized organization with divisions with profit responsibility and clear lines of authority."

The Booming American Automobile Industry

Just as IBM enjoyed spectacular success as a computer and office-machine business, the American automobile industry typified the prosperity of American manufacturing firms. After 1945 the automobile industry was responsible for one of seven jobs in the American economy, as car manufacturers employed hundreds of thousands of workers directly and, by purchasing supplies and services, even large numbers of persons in such industries as steel, rubber, and petroleum. The automobile manufacturing business was cyclical, with production dropping during periods of recession, but overall production grew dramatically as manufacturers expanded plant capacity to meet the demands of a growing American population. The American love affair with the automobile as a desirable personal and private means of transportation grew ever more torrid as millions of persons moved from central cities to suburban areas and as governments built improved high-speed highways during the postwar years. American manufacturers produced 3 million vehicles in 1946 and then were able to expand capacity dramatically, making just over 11 million cars, trucks, and buses in 1965.

As its importance in the larger business system of the nation increased after 1945, the structure of the automobile industry reflected trends already well established prior to World War II. Industrialist Henry J. Kaiser's attempt to start a new venture to satisfy the enormous postwar demand for passenger cars quickly failed, and older, smaller manufacturers continued to fall by the wayside. When the Packard nameplate disappeared in 1958 and Studebaker quit manufacturing altogether in 1966, only American Motors survived as a combination of the old Hudson and Nash companies to compete with the big three producers: General Motors, Ford, and Chrysler. General Motors continued to lead the industry, emerging from the Great Depression with a 40 percent share of the passenger-car market and building its lead to more than 50 percent in 1955. The American vehicles were typically large, capable of carrying an entire family. They were also profitable, as styling changes added to their dimensions while causing consumers to want to purchase new models. Meanwhile, foreign producers enjoyed only small niches.

The most serious challenge before 1970 came from Germany's Volkswagen. The Volkswagen challenge presaged certain changes in market segments that were on the horizon. Alfred P. Sloan, Jr., had built General Motors into the world's largest industrial corporation by segmenting automobile models according to price. The success of Volkswagen, however temporary, in retrospect represented a segmentation by type of vehicle as well as by price. Although Henry Ford learned that the company might be available for purchase during his visit to Berlin in 1948, he decided against the acquisition because he foresaw complications stemming from Allied occupation policies toward the defeated Nazi empire. Within a few years Volkswagen was part of the "miracle" of German economic recovery, building a small car of uncomplicated design, affectionately dubbed "the beetle" because of its styling. From 1958 to 1960 the German producer mounted a serious challenge in the domestic American market as its car, which underwent incremental improvements but not an annual model change, caught favor. In sharp contrast to the large, heavily chromed vehicles from American firms, the Volkswagen beetle was lightweight, easy to control, and economical to operate. General Motors, Ford, and Chrysler, however, successfully defeated Volkswagen's challenge by introducing smaller models of their own. Ford's success with its Mustang, introduced in the 1965 model year as an inexpensive sports car, was an indication of the changing segmentation of the American automobile market and the potential ability of American manufacturers to satisfy customers' desires.

The large American firms were successful not only at home but also abroad as multinational corporations. In 1950, 10.6 million motor vehicles were produced in the world, of which 8 million were built in American factories. By 1970, the international industry had changed dramatically. While American production totaled 8.2 million vehicles that year, the world's producers made 29.7 million. Much of the world's increase occurred in Britain, Canada, France, and Germany, where General Motors and Ford were significant factors, as well as in Italy; in Japan the American firm's investments were more modest. Henry Ford II carried through his clearly expressed international vision of 1948 as the company successfully continued to expand manufacturing operations abroad, especially in Britain and on the European continent. Within Ford's executive ranks, perceptive executives learned that the surest route to Henry Ford's approval included gaining managerial experience abroad. General Motors, as the largest of the American companies, had become an even greater presence as a multinational firm; in the postwar period it was manufacturing complete vehicles on every continent. Chrysler lagged behind its larger rivals, however. It purchased the French firm Simca in 1958 and British Rootes Motors in 1965. Both subsidiaries were already in financial trouble and unable to compete successfully in European markets, and the parent American firm was not strong enough itself to pose a serious challenge to foreign competitors.

THE MODERN CORPORATE BUSINESS SYSTEM

Conglomerates and multinationals were two variants of big business, and their development continued a trend begun in the mid-nineteenth century: a relatively small handful of big businesses dominated key segments of the U.S. economy, especially manufacturing.

The Scale of Big Business

In 1962, the five largest industrial corporations accounted for over 12 percent of all assets used in manufacturing, the fifty largest possessed over a third of the nation's manufacturing assets, and the top five hundred had over two-thirds. Big businesses advanced in sales and, to a lesser extent, in services as well as manufacturing. Chain stores such as Kroger became very important in food sales, for example. Some companies grew especially large and important. In 1965, three industrial giants—General Motors, Standard

Oil of New Jersey (now Exxon), and Ford—had more gross income than all the farms in the United States. In 1963, the revenues of General Motors were eight times those of New York State and nearly one-fifth those of the federal government.

It was these large diversified firms that dominated the global economy. In 1973, the United States had 89 companies that employed at least 40,000 people apiece. The closest comparison was Great Britain, with only 30 such companies. All of the other nations of Western Europe combined had about the same number as Britain. Nearly all of these big businesses were industrial companies. And the story was the same in the service industries. The strongest in the world, America's banks and insurance companies served much of the globe's financial needs.

The Relative Decline of Small Business

As large firms expanded in the global market and in America's rich domestic market, small business declined in relative importance during the 1950s and 1960s. The number of self-employed business people in America dropped steadily between 1950 and 1972. The total share of employment held by small firms fell only slightly, from 41 percent in 1958 to 40 percent in 1977; but, more tellingly, between 1958 and 1979 the share of business receipts received by small businesses plummeted from 52 percent to only 29 percent of the total for all American firms. As one astute observer noted in 1962, "Small business is not looking particularly healthy these days. . . . Essentially it seems to be hanging on." The decline of small business was particularly pronounced in manufacturing. Single-plant companies (a good proxy for smaller firms) accounted for 39 percent of the nation's industrial output in 1954 but for only 25 percent by 1972.

Beyond manufacturing, the slump in small business was most apparent in farming. A trend toward concentration took place in farming as large farms, "agribusinesses," came to dominate agriculture in the United States. Many family farmers found their economic positions untenable and left farming for other occupations. By 1988, only 2.2 percent of the nation's working population was engaged in agriculture—down from 27 percent in 1920, 14 percent in 1945, and 4.5 percent in 1973. In just one decade, the 1960s, some 900,000 independent farms disappeared, many swallowed up by large corporate farms.

The main problem facing family farmers was the growing need for large amounts of capital. A scientific and technological revolution transformed farming in the postwar years; large tractors and other types of mechanized equipment, hybrid seeds for corn and other crops, and chemical fertilizers all cost money. Large corporate farmers did better than most family farmers in this situation, for they could draw on varied sources of capital to get through hard times. Increasingly, their farms were part of large, vertically integrated agribusiness empires, such as Holly Farms and Cargill, which made profits not from growing food but from processing and marketing it.

BIG BUSINESS AS A SOCIAL INSTITUTION

Big business firms during the postwar decades grew in importance beyond their economic role in American society. These companies offered security and high pay for their workers as well as for their growing numbers of managers. In the 1950s and 1960s, Americans enjoyed the highest standard of living of any people on the globe, one far above those of Japan and Germany, just emerging from the rubble of war. Recessions, compared to the 1930s and what was to come, were short-lived and shallow.

Life in the World of Big Business

In the prosperous postwar decades, managers and even workers were fairly confident of the security of their employment. In the context of economic growth, workers and managers exchanged their security for a loyalty to their firms perhaps unmatched at any other time in American history.

Big companies in turn were loyal to their managers. As modern personnel policies evolved, a typical large American firm provided security and fellowship from the time of initial employment to a person's retirement and beyond. Companies had devised various benefit programs for employees before 1945 that were extended in the postwar prosperity. For instance, in 1950 Du Pont launched a program of classroom instruction on "free enterprise" for its employees. The company titled its employee's magazine *Better Living* and offered job security in exchange for "more work, better work, and more continuous work" from its employees. Corporate Americans enjoyed company-owned recreational facilities, participated in choral groups, attended festive picnics and parties. Employment with a big company often brought with it a sense of security—a sense that the firm, in exchange for years of loyal service, would plan for continual employment even when prosperity temporarily soured. Pension plans supplemented the minimal retirement program provided by the federal social security system after 1945. And perhaps most important of all to the lives of individual employees and their families, as Americans rejected the publicly managed systems of delivering health care that all other industrial nations devised after the war, corporate employment even provided care in times of sickness.

The secure life of corporate employment reached to a limited extent below the ranks of managers into the secretarial and blue-collar industrial work forces. After a round of contentious strikes following the war, labor relations were much more placid than they had been in the 1930s, in part because corporation executives grudgingly learned that improved personnel policies could result in less disruption to the flow of work within a company. Manufacturers also strove to reduce the influence of unions in their plants. Part of Du Pont's motive to improve worker loyalty to the firm was to reduce interest in unionism. The executives were successful; in 1946, 94 percent of Du Pont workers were unionized, a figure that had dropped to 66 percent by 1960. Also, with American manufacturing firms dominant in markets both at home and abroad, big business leaders were able to provide the high wages won by unions to industrial workers, passing along the costs to customers, some of whom were often the workers themselves. Unions in turn were sometimes able to negotiate programs of job and income security for their members.

The Socioeconomic Background of Business Leaders

As in times past, most leaders in big businesses came from the upper-income ranks in the United States. Rags-to-riches stories remained exceptions, not the rule, in American business. Most executives running big businesses came from backgrounds of some privilege. Nearly all were men, and none was from minority groups. Most were well educated. In 1950, three-quarters had attended college. Small business owners differed in their backgrounds from big business executives. Small business people were younger than their counterparts in big businesses, and a higher proportion came from families with nonbusiness backgrounds. Less well educated than big business leaders, small business owners often began as unskilled or semiskilled workers or as clerical employees.

To the extent that they got ahead in business, blacks continued to do so in small firms. In 1969, only 5 percent of the minority-owned businesses in America (of which blacks owned 90 percent) employed more than ten people—compared to 20 percent for white-owned businesses. Most of the black-owned firms remained in services and sales, with relatively few in manufacturing. Although they offered some chance for business advancement, small businesses did not bring economic achievement to blacks commensurate to their numbers in America's population. In 1969, blacks composed 11 percent of America's population but owned just 2 percent of its businesses.

As before World War II, certain other minority groups, especially Asian-Americans, found small business development more rewarding than did blacks. Like Chinese and Japanese immigrants before them, Koreans coming to America looked to small businesses for advancement. Moving into Los Angeles and other cities in the 1960s and 1970s, many set up grocery stores, restaurants, and other service businesses. In part, Koreans formed small businesses to compensate for the lack of job opportunities with larger enterprises. Racism combined with a lack of English language skills and an attachment to Asian customs to prevent their rapid movement into

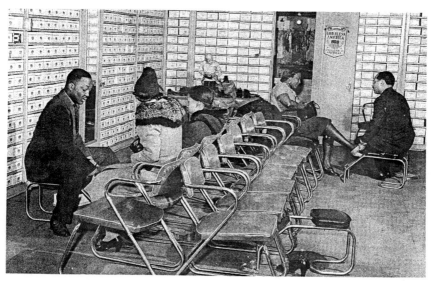

African-American entrepreneurs found that their opportunities were usually limited to serving the needs of black communities and their customers. (Library of Congress)

established large businesses. However, having some wealth and good education allowed them to start small businesses—as did the existence of support groups such as extended families, ethnic clubs, and voluntary organizations. Until the Los Angeles riots of 1992, many Korean firms ventured into black neighborhoods lacking basic business services.

The Organization Man

The term "organization man" best describes the business executives in large corporations during the 1950s and 1960s. Having suffered the disruptions of the Great Depression and World War II, they were most interested in security. These upper-echelon business executives wanted to belong to large business organizations; they sought acceptance as members in their business groups. In 1950, 40 percent of the heads of big businesses in the United States said that their primary road to the top had been their positions as salaried administrators; only 9 percent claimed to have started in business as entrepreneurs. Some 60 percent had been with the same company for at least ten years before becoming the chief executive officer.

Few of these business leaders were innovative risk takers. They were company men who desired success, but not too much success. As one observer of the American business scene noted in 1956, young men entering business would "talk of finding a sort of plateau—a position well enough up to be interesting, but not so far up as to have one's neck outstretched for others to chop at." The 1950s in particular were the years of the man in the gray flannel suit, the business executive who sought to blend into rather than stick out from the crowd. (IBM executives were famous for wearing only blue suits, white shirts, and dark ties.) It was a time of "yes-men," of business leaders who got ahead by agreeing with their superiors rather than by proposing new ideas. In spite of this image, however, large firms sometimes took entrepreneurial risks, such as the decision by Thomas Watson, Jr., to take IBM into computers or Henry Ford's ill-fated venture to gain market share, the Edsel.

Small business owners varied widely from these characteristics. Some were stalwart members of their local communities, operating stable firms. Others were entrepreneurs taking sometimes dramatic risks. Les Wexner, for example, started with a small retail store in women's clothing and eventually built a huge retailing empire around The Limited. For those who succeeded—always a minority of those who owned small businesses—involvement in small business ventures offered possible opportunities for upward social and economic mobility.

Business and the Community

The prosperity of the American economy and the comfortable profits earned by so many corporations were such that executives could build on earlier traditions of social responsibility and play a larger than ever philanthropic role. Big corporations typically formed separate foundations that their officers controlled. Those foundations in turn granted funds to agencies in the local communities where the company had plants, in an attempt to improve the quality of life for all citizens. Sometimes companies worked closely with local officials to develop programs of renewal for the central business district housing the corporate office. Aetna and other large insurance firms, for instance, helped initiate and finance the rebuilding of downtown Hartford, Connecticut, in the 1960s.

One national effort to bring together firms across the spectrum of the American economy was the formation of the National Alliance of Businessmen in 1968. Henry Ford proposed the idea of having business executives work closely with public officials to provide employment for the poorest Americans. Encouraged by President Lyndon Johnson, Ford served as the first Alliance president. The organization focused especially on employment, training, and educational programs among disadvantaged Americans in the hopes of improving opportunities to escape from poverty and build prosperous communities.

THE MODERN COMPANY

By the early 1970s, big businesses in the United States had changed considerably from those of thirty years earlier. Above all, they were more diversified.

They produced and sold a broader range of products for a wider variety of consumer markets both at home and abroad. But big businesses did not squeeze smaller concerns out of the U.S. economy altogether. Although small businesses declined in overall importance to the American economy in the 1950s and 1960s, they remained significant, especially in sales and services. If the opportunities of the postwar world brought changes to the business firm, they also altered the nature of government-business relations in the United States. The growth of a consumer society, based on the outpouring of consumer products from U.S. factories, led the federal government into a much broader range of regulatory activities than ever before.

Selected Readings

Walter Hayes, *Ford: A Life of Henry Ford II* (New York: Grove Weidenfeld, 1990), is an informed, personal account. Douglas Knerr, *Eagle-Picher Industries: Strategies for Survival in the Industrial Market Place, 1840–1980* (Columbus: Ohio State University Press, 1992), explains how one large company transformed after 1945. For a case study on the history of small business, see Mansel Blackford, *Pioneering a Modern Small Business: Wakefield Seafoods and the Alaskan Frontier* (Greenwich, Conn.: JAI Press, 1979). Dorothy Riddle, *Service-Led Growth* (New York: Praeger, 1986), examines the importance of service-industry companies. John L. Shover, *First Majority-Last Minority* (DeKalb: Northern Illinois University Press, 1976), and Jay Staten, *The Embattled Farmer* (Golden, Colo.: Fulcrum, 1987), look at changes occurring in farming.

On the nature of executives in big businesses, see William Whyte, Jr., *The Organization Man* (New York: Simon and Schuster, 1956). Ronald Baily, ed., *Black Business Enterprise: Historical and Contemporary Perspectives* (New York: Basic Books, 1971); Ivan H. Light, *Ethnic Enterprise in America: Business and Welfare Among Chinese, Japanese and Blacks* (Berkeley: University of California Press, 1972), and Scott Cummings, ed., *Self-Help in Urban America: Patterns of Minority Business Enterprise* (Port Washington, N.Y.: Kennikat Press, 1980), are valuable sources on the places of minorities in American business. Finally, Diana Tittle, *Rebuilding Cleveland: The Cleveland Foundation and Its Evolving Urban Strategy* (Columbus: Ohio State University Press, 1992), is a fascinating account of one business organization's involvement in a big city.

IMPORTANT EVENTS, 1946–1972

1946   Congress charters the Council of Economic Advisers in the Employment and Production Act.
General Motors wins a major strike, and union power begins to recede.

1947   The Taft-Hartley Act restricts union activities.

1950   The Celler-Kefauver Act limits horizontal and vertical integration.

1956   Congress funds the Interstate Highway System.

1962   The Trade Expansion Act promotes overseas trade through negotiated tariff reductions.

1964   The Civil Rights Act requires fair employment for minorities and women.

1966   Congress creates the National Highway Traffic Safety Administration.

1970   The Clean Air Act establishes environmental standards.
Congress creates the Occupational Safety and Health Administration.

1972   The Water Pollution Control Act orders a stop to the discharge of industrial pollutants.
Congress creates the Consumer Product Safety Commission.

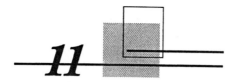

The Political Economy
After World War II

On February 20, 1946, President Harry S Truman signed into law the Employment and Production Act. No other action better symbolized the growth of the government's economic authority resulting from the depression and wartime experiences. The law was a compromise between those Americans who wanted the government to assume responsibility for investment decisions in the economy and those who believed that private interests should determine investment decisions. The measure provided a kind of "economic constitution" of the federal government's responsibilities in managing the overall level of prosperity in the United States; in particular, it chartered the Council of Economic Advisers, a new federal agency, to watch over the U.S. economy. The Council was to inform the president about business conditions, to recommend desirable policies, and to issue an annual report on the nation's economic health. To review the information and recommendations generated by the Council of Economic Advisers, the law set up a Joint Economic Committee in Congress. With the signing of the Employment Act, which received few dissenting votes in the House of Representatives and none in the Senate, ultimate authority for the nation's economic well-being shifted from the private arena of corporate boardrooms to the public arena of legislative and presidential politics.

The experiences of the Great Depression and wartime prosperity had etched themselves deeply on Americans' consciousness, as the passage of the Employment and Production Act clearly demonstrated. Those experiences meant that, after 1945, government exerted more power over business affairs than ever before. Both the depression and World War II had fashioned a stronger federal government that sometimes responded to the wishes of trade unions or others whose interests differed from those of business. The growth of rival sources of power threatened the ability of business executives to act independently, and as the U.S. political economy evolved in the postwar decades, business associations and corporations found it necessary to engage continually in political activities to influence public policies. In general, the political rivals of business were not antagonistic to the values of capitalism. The American public, and often business leaders themselves, still turned to the federal government to guide economic prosperity and to provide a measure of security, and business executives sometimes discovered that their preferences had to give way to the concerns of others.

Three main trends appeared in the American political economy after 1945. Each had antecedents in U.S. history, but each also had a dramatic impact on business after 1945. First, the office of president became deeply involved in guarding the well-being of American capitalism. In the executive branch of the federal government, large, complex bureaucratic agencies mushroomed and sometimes claimed an authority of their own, independent of private corporations and traditional democratic institutions. More and more, the administrative agencies, Congress, and the president relied on advice from professional economists. Second, business began to reduce the power of organized labor. Third, especially after 1960, a reinvigoration of public-interest ideology led to new social and economic regulation of business behavior.

THE FEDERAL GOVERNMENT AND ECONOMIC WELL-BEING

Ever since the rise of big business in the nineteenth century, large-scale, impersonal organizations, which existed independent of the lives of the individuals who constituted them, increasingly characterized American society. The process of bureaucratization occurred not only in manufacturing, financial, and transportation enterprises but also in labor unions, social institutions (such as churches, school systems, and universities), trade associations, and political organizations of various kinds.

The Growth of Federal Bureaucracy

Nowhere was the growth of bureaucracy more apparent, however, than in government. Government—federal, state, and local—grew slowly but steadily throughout the first half of the twentieth century but expanded remarkably during the 1940s and thereafter. Government employment of civilians, including teachers, rose from 9.5 percent of the labor force in 1940 to 16.8 percent in 1986. The federal government alone employed 3.9 percent of the labor force in 1970, up from 2.4 percent in 1940. Clearly, the growth of the public sector reflected the increased activities conducted by governmental agencies.

President Harry S Truman's signing of the Employment Act of 1946 was an important public event, symbolized by the number of souvenir pens he intended to distribute. (Wide World Photos)

The growth of government also meant an expansion of government involvement in the economy. That involvement took a large number of institutional forms, some of which had developed before World War II. In the years after the war, the federal government more than ever assumed responsibilities for the health of the economy to ensure that the end of wartime mobilization would not bring a return of the Great Depression. During the postwar period, the views of professional economists became especially important in shaping fiscal and other policies.

The Employment and Production Act of 1946

The Employment and Production Act of 1946 embodied the desire of America's business and political leaders to prevent the recurrence of the Great Depression. The nation's prosperity due to wartime full employment seemed to confirm Keynes's theory that large public expenditures could create prosperity. Many experts believed that the U.S. industrial economy was "mature," meaning that given the existing inequitable distribution of wealth, there was little reason for business firms to invest in new productive facilities to satisfy already-saturated markets. Encouraged by Keynesian economists, some political and labor leaders agreed that without massive and continual government intervention, the peacetime economy would remain stagnant with an undesirably high level of unemployment.

The Employment Act represented the result of attempts to deal with these concerns. The Senate originally passed a bill with a number of innovations designed to correct the stagnation that had beset the business system during the 1930s. It stated that "all Americans able to work and seeking work have the right to useful remunerative, regular, and full-time employment." To ensure such a sweeping right, the Senate bill proposed a planning mechanism, the National Production and Employment Budget. In this scheme the government would estimate the gross national product necessary to achieve full employment as well as the anticipated volume of investment and spending from the public and private sectors. Any deficiency would first be made up by encouraging private investment and spending and, if that proved insufficient to achieve full employment, by spending federal funds. Such federal spending, it was clear to all concerned, might include public works on the model of the Tennessee Valley Authority, not only for electrical power but also for such broad social goals as health care and housing.

Business leaders sought a greater emphasis on a public-private partnership in postwar economic policy than the Senate's bill provided. They successfully lobbied the House of Representatives to rewrite the legislation. Business leaders had a strong ally during this legislative struggle in the Committee for Economic Development formed during the war years. The Business Council, which advised New Deal officials, had foreseen the need for postwar economic planning. Shortly after the attack on Pearl Harbor, the group's chairman, R. R. Deupree of Procter and Gamble, had voiced his concern: "The challenge which business will face when this war is over cannot be met by a laissez-faire philosophy or by uncontrolled supply and demand. Intelligent planning . . . and courage will be needed to carry us through the reconstruction period." By September 1942, the Commerce Department and the Business Council had cooperated to form the Committee for Economic Development. Its purpose was to combine the talents of professional economists and corporate executives to influence federal policy.

The Committee for Economic Development tried to steer a middle course between older laissez-faire ideas and large-scale state intervention into the economy. The big business leaders and their economists rejected the notion that the American industrial system was mature and therefore stagnant. These executives believed that it was possible to determine the public interest objectively, that there was no necessary conflict between the public interest and the interests of the firms or trade associations for which they worked, and that a cooperative partnership between business and government was desirable and achievable. The Business Council and the Committee for Economic Development thus opposed the full-employment bill because it went too far in removing decisions from the private sector and placing power in the hands of government officials.

If the Business Council and the Committee for Economic Development laid the groundwork, the U.S. Chamber of Commerce was the most directly influential group in lobbying Congress to enact the Employment and Production Act of 1946. Eric A. Johnston, the Chamber's national president during the war, led the Chamber away from its earlier opposition to federal intervention in the nation's economic affairs and pressured Congress to pass a law to the Chamber's liking. Gone was the provision to have public investments to guarantee full employment. Instead, the measure provided for technical expertise in guiding the federal government's promotion of private business initiatives for the expansion of economic activity and thereby of fuller, if not full, employment. The new law contained language intended to safeguard the nation from rampant inflation. It signaled greater acceptance by key business leaders that economic leadership ultimately resided in the policies of the federal government, that business and public officials had to act in concert if the nation was to prosper.

The Rise of Professional Economists in the Federal Government

Although economists had advised the government since the 1920s, their role became much larger after the passage of the Employment and Production Act of 1946. They began to have a significant effect on the conditions in which business executives made decisions in the private sector. Professional economists did not fully come into their own, however, until after John F. Kennedy became president in 1961. By the end of the 1950s, Democratic congressional leaders were voicing complaints about President Dwight D. Eisenhower's willingness to accept recessions in the business cycle and their attendant unemployment. Kennedy agreed with this view and as president sought to reduce the unemployment caused by business downturns, to launch social reform programs aimed at eliminating poverty, and to boost defense expenditures. A rapidly expanding economy, stimulated by the correct federal fiscal policy, would, Kennedy hoped, achieve these goals.

Kennedy found that the tradition of corporatism begun in the early twentieth century served him well in this regard. The president turned for professional advice to Walter Heller, chairman of the Council of Economic Advisers. Following Heller's recommendations, Kennedy proposed reductions in federal taxes to stimulate private capital-goods spending and consumer purchases, while at the same time increasing expenditures for social reform, defense, and a new space program. His aim was to stimulate the economy through deficit spending, anticipating that inflation could be controlled and that eventually an expanded economy would produce greater tax revenues, thereby reducing the federal deficit. The president needed the support of business leaders who could command public attention and congressional backing in order to achieve these goals, but he feared that the nation's business executives would oppose such measures as imprudent. Kennedy's fears proved groundless, however. In fact, the essentials of his proposals agreed with views expressed by the Committee for Economic Development. Late in 1962, Kennedy addressed the Economic Club of New York, and its members received his ideas warmly. The president told Heller that the speech was "straight Keynes and Heller, and they loved it." Later, a National Association of Manufacturers official expressed support for tax reduction "even in the face of a current deficit which can only be partially moderated." Unfortunately, Kennedy's assassination prevented him from enjoying the fruits of his political initiative. After Congress enacted his fiscal program in 1964, the American economy boomed. Soon, however, the costs of the Vietnam War, combined with President Lyndon B. Johnson's reluctance to raise taxes, overheated the economy and inflation rose out of control.

Nonetheless, the success of Kennedy's initiative had the effect of ensuring an influential role for technical economic analysis within the federal government. During the Kennedy-Johnson years, social scientists employed by the federal government were active as never before in providing indicators and guideposts with which the politicians could assess policy. These activities occurred, moreover, in the public sector, quite independent of decisions made in corporate boardrooms. President Johnson began a planning, programming, and budgeting system throughout the executive branch that required agencies to consider the costs and probable economic outcomes of their programs, and their reports were evaluated and programs coordinated by a planning staff. Later, in 1970, President Richard M. Nixon and Congress agreed to change the Bureau of the Budget into an Office of Management and Budget to further evaluate and forecast economic trends and events. Under Nixon, the federal government moved further toward a system of national planning. Nixon created the Domestic Council in an attempt to clarify objectives, explain alternative policies, make policy recommendations, and coordinate and evaluate programs. In 1974, Congress established its own Budget Office to provide the legislators with economic analyses independent of those developed in the executive branch.

GOVERNMENT AND THE FRAMEWORK FOR BUSINESS ACTIVITY

The federal government not only became deeply involved in assuring the economic well-being of the nation in the post-1945 period by seeking general prosperity and growth, but it also engaged in activities deliberately designed to shape the business environment. Economic analyses were one aspect of these activities, as were varying political responses to the specific interests of particular industries or segments of the business community.

Antitrust Policy

Antitrust litigation was another area in which government influenced business decisions in the decades after 1945. Antitrust activity revived during the presidency of Harry S Truman was aborted temporarily by the Korean War from 1950 to 1953, and continued thereafter. Investigations and prosecutions came from both the Antitrust Division of the Department of Justice and the Federal Trade Commission. The effect of this antitrust activity was to limit the ability of big business firms to grow even larger through mergers that fit the traditional patterns of either vertical integration or horizontal combination.

Both the volume of antitrust cases and the size of the government agencies dealing with antitrust issues expanded after World War II. The Antitrust Division of the Department of Justice grew to employ hundreds of attorneys and dozens of economists. Comparable development occurred in the Federal Trade Commission, which formed a separate Bureau of Competition to engage in antitrust activities. This trend in both agencies gave evidence of the growing bureaucratization of antitrust activity as more and more of it was placed in the hands of specialists who engaged in time-consuming court actions involving judicial rulings on arcane points of law.

There were important antitrust policy changes through legislation in the postwar period. Congress provided an important modification of the existing antitrust statutes when it passed the Celler-Kefauver Act of 1950. This measure stated that the government could examine market share as evidence of anticompetitive, monopolistic practice. Earlier, in the Progressive Era, some politicians had unsuccessfully argued that a firm that controlled more than 25 percent of the market in its industry should be declared in violation of the antitrust statutes. Although the Celler-Kefauver amendment did not specify a figure, its passage meant that in the future business executives would have to consider overall market share as a part of their fundamental strategy, lest they run afoul of government litigation. Such considerations, for instance, restrained General Motors from deliberately destroying smaller competitors.

The dynamic of antitrust litigation continued after Truman left office and the Republicans took the reins of the executive branch under Dwight

Eisenhower. Officials in the Eisenhower administration, and after 1960 the Democrats under Kennedy, agreed on the need to limit firm size through antitrust investigations. Democrats and Republicans cooperated to amend the antitrust statutes to allow companies to seek prior approval for proposed mergers. The bipartisan goal was to ensure a substantial measure of price competition among big business firms and to allow small firms to become established and grow.

The antitrust activity of the postwar years, and especially the new rules enacted in the Celler-Kefauver Act, had a powerful influence on big business firms, encouraging them to adopt the conglomerate strategies that became popular by the 1960s. Attorneys specializing in antitrust law after 1950 advised business clients to refrain from merging with other firms in order to improve market positions. They counseled executives to use company assets accumulated in the profitable postwar years to follow a diversification strategy into new lines of production, distribution, or services.

The Military-Industrial Complex

The emergence of the cold war and the need for a continual state of armed preparedness meant that a new situation, labeled "the military-industrial complex" by President Eisenhower, characterized the American political economy during these years. Not only did a large market with only one customer develop in defense but also arrangements were made in which there were sole suppliers for major weapons systems. Traditional practices of competitive bidding by private firms for government contracts simply were not economically feasible in this situation. The technological complexity of aircraft, missiles, ships, and other military goods grew enormously, so much so that private firms lacked the resources to develop them without assurances of their ultimate sales. The Defense Department therefore became a significant source of funds for scientific and engineering research. Between 1955 and 1965, federal spending for science grew from $3.3 billion to $14.8 billion, most of which was defense related. The Defense Department developed close relations with private firms (and, to a lesser extent, universities) for the development of new weapons. Then, typically, when a large firm received a contract for the design and production of a weapon, that firm subcontracted with other companies for assistance. The result was an elaborate network of funding, contracting, and subcontracting that extended across the nation and into a majority of the congressional districts (whose representatives voted the necessary appropriations). Moreover, the defense procurement system was susceptible to abuse. Firms sometimes allied with military officers to produce expensive weapons systems of questionable value, and the extraordinary defense contract profits enjoyed by the unscrupulous became public scandals.

General Dynamics produced military aircraft in its factory in Fort Worth, Texas. As a major supplier of military goods, the company was concerned that it had too much capacity, needed in case of war, to operate efficiently during peacetime. (Lockheed FW Company)

Eisenhower termed these arrangements the military-industrial complex because he was concerned about the "acquisition of unwarranted influence." Eisenhower believed in a "public interest" that transcended the self-interest of the military services and defense contractors who, he feared, were able to arrange decisions that were not always in the nation's best interests. Moreover, there were powerful forces within the business community and the military services to increase funding levels and to maintain cordial relations. In 1958, for instance, the Committee for Economic Development called for larger defense appropriations from which individual members' corporations clearly stood to benefit. Moreover, retired military officers, many of whom still had strong ties with the military, populated defense contractor offices. In 1969, some 2,072 retired colonels, captains, admirals, and generals were employed by defense suppliers.

In the years after Eisenhower's retirement, the issues he had raised caused continuing controversy. President Kennedy appointed Robert S. McNamara of the Ford Motor Company as secretary of defense, and McNamara and his associates used business management principles to try to control the logistics of the military services. Nevertheless, the goods and services of defense dwarfed the sales of even the nation's largest firm, and the problems of dealing with an enterprise of such magnitude remained. In 1965, when American troops began to be sent to Vietnam in large numbers, military expenditures soared even further.

Federal Aid to Business: Highways

From its foundation in 1789, as we have seen, the federal government used its resources to aid business directly in the development of the nation's economy. This developmental activity continued in the middle of the twentieth century. In the nineteenth century, the federal government had helped private entrepreneurs develop railroad facilities, especially when the network approached the trackless barriers of western plains, deserts, and mountains. In the twentieth century, the widespread popularity of automobiles and trucks led the federal government to become heavily involved in the financing of improved roads, once a largely local concern. Eventually, in 1956 the federal government launched an enormous public works project to provide American motorists, and especially American businesses, with express highways.

After World War II, as the popularity of automobiles and trucks continued to grow, motorists and shippers encountered serious problems. Traffic simply did not move freely across the country, and congestion, especially in and around cities, added considerably to the cost of moving goods. The solution seemed to be expressways, divided highways specifically designed for fast travel. City planners liked the concept because they envisioned expressways as devices to shape urban environments in socially desirable ways, and economists concerned about the business cycle saw road construction as a public-works project with the potential for stimulating employment during recessions.

In response, Congress authorized in 1956 the funding of a 41,000-mile National System of Interstate and Defense Highways. The bill created a highway "trust fund" that housed special tax revenues collected from fuel, tires, and other equipment. All motorists would pay for the roads, and all were free to use them, but the main purpose of the construction was to satisfy the requirements of the business firms seeking a more efficient trucking industry. By 1960, some 7,570 miles of expressways were open to traffic, with the remainder under construction or being planned. In short, the federal government had launched a major public-works program in which the public provided capital facilities of use to countless American business firms.

THE NEW REGULATION

As it had from the early 1800s, the federal government continued to shape the political environment within which American businesses operated and

Ralph Nader, pictured here, testified vigorously for consumer and other causes. (The Bettman Archive)

to aid them through developmental economic policies. Along with this aid came federal regulation, and in the decades after 1960, the federal government became involved in a new burst of regulatory activity. Earlier forms of regulation had been political responses to the advent of the new center firms that were reordering business activities in the industrializing economy; the burst of new regulation that occurred after 1960 involved the creation of new government agencies to deal with the broad human, social, and environmental effects of a mature industrial system.

Ralph Nader and the Origins of the New Regulation

On November 29, 1965, an event occurred that more than any other symbolized the appearance of new impulses for the regulation of business behavior: the publication of *Unsafe at Any Speed: The Designed-in Dangers of the American Automobile* by Ralph Nader. The son of Lebanese immigrants, Nader was a brilliant young attorney and free-lance journalist who attacked the nation's largest industrial company, General Motors, for designing and marketing a defective automobile, the Chevrolet Corvair, in which unwitting consumers were maimed and killed. Worst of all, Nader revealed that GM had sold the vehicle knowing that its suspension system was inadequate for certain driving conditions. The company had decided to proceed with the manufacture and sale of the faulty Corvair without regard to public safety, Nader charged, in order to protect its investment.

For Nader, the point of attacking General Motors was not simply to question the motives of its executives but to call attention to a larger issue. "A great problem of contemporary life," he observed, "is how to control the power of economic interests which ignore the harmful effects of their applied science and technology." General Motors and the Corvair's problems were thus symbolic, a point of departure for revival of the idea that the public interest must prevail over the profit motive of powerful corporations. Business executives, as we have seen, sometimes boasted of their social responsibility; Nader demonstrated that their behavior sometimes ran contrary to their rhetoric. The problem was worsened by the ever-growing complexity of the consumer products spewing from modern factories.

The publication of *Unsafe at Any Speed* might not have been a memorable event by itself, but Nader graphically expressed a growing concern among the consuming public. The automobile was not only integral to the American business system but central as well to the lifestyles of the vast majority of Americans. Nader's revelations struck a raw nerve in American culture, because people realized that they could not automatically trust manufacturers to provide reasonably sound products. Nader's concerns got even greater publicity when a congressional committee revealed unsavory behavior on the part of General Motors executives who apparently intended to discredit the author. James P. Roche, the president of GM, apologized to Nader in testimony before the committee.

Two important events followed the revelations of GM's behavior. One was the creation in 1966 of a new regulatory agency, the National Highway Traffic Safety Administration, to govern the design of automobiles sold in the United States. Although Nader was acutely disappointed by the agency's subsequent performance, a new regulatory agency was nevertheless born. Furthermore, riding the crest of his nationwide publicity, Nader established the Center for Study of Responsive Law in 1968 (later, in 1970, he founded the Public Interest Research Group with funds won in a court suit against GM for the firm's invasion of his privacy). Vigorously promoting the use of the law as an agent of social change, "Nader's Raiders," as the press dubbed the men and women associated with Ralph Nader, soon initiated a spate of reports critical of business behavior and the failure of government to regulate that behavior.

Sources of the New Regulation

Before Ralph Nader drew attention to the problems of the Corvair, questions of the public interest had typically arisen from concerns over fairness in apportioning material benefits and entrepreneurial opportunities among business firms, between management and labor, and toward commercial farmers. During the 1960s, the traditional forms of regulation that had begun with the creation of the Interstate Commerce Commission in 1887 continued. However, Nader was able to awaken and mobilize reform impulses arising from an entirely different kind of society, a consumer society concerned about issues relating to material abundance rather than scarcity.

The new regulation that began in the 1960s was in large part a product of the success of the business system. The success of industrialists in organizing the mass production of consumer goods, first so evident in the consumer durables industries in the 1920s and later apparent in the fantastic production achievements of World War II, had created unprecedented material abundance. The confidence of economists, politicians, and business executives in their abilities to foster fiscal policies conducive to permanent plateaus of prosperity contributed to a national mood of complacency. In short, a large segment of the American population came to take for granted not only consumer goods, such as automobiles and electrical appliances, but also amenities, items that increased pleasure. They assumed as their birthright a good life of material plenty, comfort, safety, and security.

Signs of the consumer-amenity society abounded by the 1950s. The executives of industrial firms, as we have seen, increasingly based their strategies on marketing considerations rather than on the more traditional production orientations. Business entrepreneurs developed new technologies to make products more appealing to consumers. Automobile manufacturers promoted automatic transmissions and air conditioning, as well as attractive colors and design details like tail fins, to ease driving and improve passenger comfort. Color film and television replaced black and white images in popular favor, while recorded sound became available in high-fidelity stereo. At the end of the 1950s, historian David Potter described material abundance as a distinguishing characteristic of American civilization, and economist John Kenneth Galbraith, while decrying the continuation of poverty, analyzed what he termed the "affluent society."

The quest for the amenities of life extended far beyond the development of consumer goods and the marketing strategies of large corporations. After 1960, vocal and powerful groups of affluent Americans began to question the side-effects of the headlong drive for material abundance. Some who had moved to the suburbs, for instance, in search of green spaces and fresh air, disliked the decisions of business developers seeking further growth. Environmental pollution became an emotional issue. Other Americans—the conservationists—opposed corporate and governmental development of scenic lands, forests, and rivers. Union leaders and workers expressed the belief that successful corporations should ensure safe and healthful workplaces. Consumer activists like Ralph Nader asserted that marketing strategies must not result in products that unnecessarily endangered human lives. A general concern about the quality of life in the present and the future arose. This concern, in turn, led to political demands for new forms of government regulation to guard the public interest, to protect the quality of life. By the end of the 1960s, many of these groups coalesced into an environmental movement that sought a changed relationship between business and government in which experts guarded the quality of life.

Civil Rights Regulation

Quite apart from the issues arising from the apparent conquest of the age-old problem of economic scarcity came further demands for changes in public policy. The continuation of racial injustice in a nation that officially expressed the ideal of equality produced a powerful civil rights movement in postwar America. The civil rights reformers called upon the nation's institutions to treat all citizens equally. Black leaders demanded fair employment practices in the private as well as the public sector. By the early 1960s, black demands had helped fuel the feminist movement, which maintained that the public interest required equality of treatment between genders as well as between races. Promoters of equal rights for women and blacks sought enhanced government regulation of the employment and personnel policies of business as well as other institutions.

Black Americans had long sought federal help in achieving a greater measure of racial justice in American institutions, including business. As a group they had historically received a disproportionately small share of wealth. One problem was inadequate access to higher-paying and secure jobs. In 1940, as the nation was mobilizing its resources for war, a black union leader, A. Philip Randolph, successfully pressured President Roosevelt to issue an executive order banning racial discrimination in firms receiving defense contracts. As the civil rights movement grew more powerful after World War II, it demanded new federal legislation to bring an end to racial discrimination.

The major result of the civil rights movement, the Civil Rights Act of 1964, contained a provision that had a new regulatory impact on American business. One of the law's provisions outlawed racial and gender discrimination in employment. An Equal Employment Opportunities Commission was established to gather information and emphasize conciliation as a way of ending discriminatory personnel practices. Under the new law, when an individual believed he or she was being treated unfairly by an employer or a union, he or she could institute a court suit to end the practice. The Department of Justice could participate in the suit when it observed "a pattern of practice . . . of general public importance." Under this measure neither employers nor unions would any longer be free to practice racial discrimination in hiring, promotion, or job-security policies. Business, in effect, faced a new round of regulation in its personnel policies.

Environmental Regulation

Many other public-interest demands were met by legislation enacted after 1960. After the laws governing equal rights for citizens came measures

Images such as this one, caused by an oil spill on Alaska's Prince William Sound by the Exxon tanker Valdez *in March 1989, aroused public concern over the despoilation of the environment by business activity. (Alaska Department of Environmental Conservation)*

intended to safeguard recreational and wilderness water and land in perpetuity, as well as laws that regulated the automobile industry. Between 1965 and 1972, a federal policy evolved regarding the protection of the environment. At first the main concern was "ecology," the interrelationships among natural environments and living organisms. By the 1970s, however, public concern had broadened to the point where the human-health issues related to the adverse effects of industrial production predominated.

From the long list of new regulatory measures regarding the environment three actions deserve special notice. In 1967, Congress enacted the Air Quality Act to establish a system by which the federal and state governments could cooperate in efforts to lessen automobile and industrial air pollution. A complex measure that expressed the new concern with environmental quality, it did not seem entirely effective. Congress tried to improve matters with the Clean Air Act of 1970, which required government agencies to establish and businesses to reach clean air standards by 1975. The criteria to be used were based on health considerations, not technological feasibility or economic costs. Then in 1972, again using health criteria, Congress enacted the Federal Water Pollution Control Act to mandate an end to the discharge of industrial pollutants by 1985. In both cases the legislation set clear regulatory goals and a timetable for their achievement. In the meantime, President Nixon consolidated various environmental regulatory functions into the Environmental Protection Agency (EPA), established in 1971, by which means, he said, the government could treat the environment "as a single interrelated system." State governments followed suit, creating environmental agencies to cooperate in solving the problems of air and water pollution at the local level.

Behind all these regulations lay a political commitment to protect the health and welfare of future generations of Americans and a recognition by congressional majorities that the private decisions of business executives did not necessarily conform to that public interest. It had become clear that the criteria of regulation should be scientifically derived by experts not beholden to any particular corporate interest. The legislation, in short, embodied a realization that much more than the factors of production were appropriate considerations in public policy. The regulators assumed that the material abundance of American society was sufficient to justify such health and welfare concerns, and that a "people of plenty" should apply scientific knowledge in maintaining the resources used by all peoples.

Enactment of this new environmental legislation provoked a hailstorm of criticism from business executives and their trade associations. The problem with the new regulations, in their view, lay in the health and welfare criteria that the government wanted to apply to production and marketing decisions. Regulations, business executives complained, must take into account the costs to the firms being regulated (and thereby the costs to society as a whole) and the technological feasibility of achieving clean air and water. Moreover, the complexity of achieving the mandated goals soon mired the EPA and the affected business firms in a morass of bureaucracy that, from the point of view of production- and profit-minded executives, unnecessarily diverted attention from normal entrepreneurial goals. In brief, business complained that the new regulation was impractical.

New Regulation of the Workplace

Closely related to the concerns expressed in the 1960s over the state of the natural environment were matters of health and safety in the workplace. Unrest among workers complaining about health and safety conditions increased during the decade, and, seeing the chance to solidify their support among workers, both Presidents Johnson and Nixon favored legislation intended to improve and safeguard working conditions. In 1970, Congress created the Occupational Safety and Health Administration (OSHA) in the Department of Labor to sponsor research on desirable occupational safety and health standards and to prescribe regulations to achieve them. At the time, in addition to workplace accidents that killed thousands of workers and caused millions of disabling injuries each year, government officials estimated that occupational diseases and illnesses annually killed 100,000 Americans and afflicted 390,000 more.

Business associations were adamant in their opposition to the creation of OSHA and its subsequent regulations. One complaint concerned the costs of meeting the law's requirements. The Chamber of Commerce claimed in 1981 that business already had spent about $48 billion in capital expenses to meet the new requirements, $5 billion in that one year alone. (On the other hand, occupational illnesses were costing the Social Security system and other welfare agencies $3 billion annually during the same period.) Nor were the costs encountered by business the only reason for its opposition. The creation of OSHA enabled workers to complain formally of working conditions to sympathetic federal officials and thereby to gain a greater measure of control over the terms of their employment. Business executives bitterly resisted relinquishing their traditional prerogative of control over working conditions. They complained about federal safety inspectors wasting their time, imposing unreasonable rules, and in general creating confusion and senseless intrusion in factories, workshops, stores, and offices.

New Consumer Regulation

One result of the gradual emergence of an affluent society increasingly concerned with the quality of life was direct federal involvement in the affairs of consumers. As producers of goods, business people, farmers, and workers had learned techniques of organization and political action to protect their interests. Consumers, however, remained amorphous and for the most part unorganized. Yet the right of consumers to have safe products of high quality available at fair prices seemed indisputable, and the political appeal of consumer issues was powerful, as Ralph Nader had demonstrated. Traditionally, Americans had left the safeguarding of consumer interests largely to the collective power of purchasing decisions. In an age when producer interests were well financed and politically powerful, however, the marketplace did not always protect consumers. Moreover, as products became technologically more complex, it was difficult for individual consumers to make rational purchasing decisions.

The new consumer regulation began in 1966 with the formation of the National Highway Traffic Safety Administration. Acting on behalf of its policyholders, the insurance industry aided Nader's cause in order to promote improved safety standards in the design of vehicles. The consumer movement broadened in the 1970s. In 1972, the Supreme Court allowed the Federal Trade Commission wider powers to investigate business practices on behalf of consumers, and Congress created the Consumer Product Safety Commission to set and enforce safety standards for thousands of school, household, and recreational goods. Three years later, Congress passed the Warranty Act of 1975, which required businesses to disclose warranty information to consumers in clear language, to establish meaningful procedures to handle consumer complaints, and to declare the limits of their warranty obligations.

The changes in government regulation of business on behalf of consumers also included the courts. Traditionally, judges had applied the legal doctrine of *caveat emptor*, "let the buyer beware," when consumers complained about the purchase of an inferior product. Consumers could recover from manufacturers of defective products only if they proved negligence. The legal barriers protecting manufacturers crumbled in 1960, however, when the New Jersey Supreme Court ruled that the driver of a new Chrysler automobile whose steering mechanism suddenly failed, demolishing the car and painfully injuring the occupant, did not have to prove that the manufacturer was negligent. In effect, the court ruled that consumers enjoyed an implied warranty from manufacturers. That year there were fewer than 50,000 product-liability cases before American courts, but by 1963 the figure had jumped to 250,000; in 1970 it had climbed to 500,000. After 1960, manufacturers felt that the nation's legal doctrine had become *caveat venditor*, "let the seller beware."

PUBLIC POLICY AND LABOR RELATIONS

Significant political events altered not only government-business relations after 1945 but also relationships between labor unions and business corporations. Legislation passed in the 1930s had granted workers the rights of collective bargaining. The National Labor Relations Act of 1935 combined with worker militancy to produce an industrial union movement that pressed management to make concessions in its traditional prerogatives of wages, hours, and work rules. By producing labor shortages and intense patriotic pressures for full production, World War II furthered the labor movement and made it a factor with which industrial managers had to deal, however grudgingly.

The Right to Manage

American business executives and their trade associations presented a united front on very few issues. New Deal labor policy was one such issue. The impact of the Wagner Act and of the militant upsurge of union sentiment that swept through factories in the 1930s cut across divisions of industry, firm size, and region that otherwise separated business executives. The union movement not only called into question the prevailing distribution of wealth in American society but threatened managerial prerogatives of the governance of firms according to business executives' definitions of self-interest.

The labor movement and its supporters in the federal government represented a pluralist vision of industrial democracy. Workers wanted more than higher wages. They sought a significant voice in determining the rules and pace of work. Especially during the full-employment years of World War II, workers engaged in "wildcat" strikes that interrupted production schedules in order to affect industrial decisions in factories. On occasion, labor leaders even expressed an alternative vision of a socialist industrial system in which democratic processes determined basic managerial decisions, wealth was distributed more equally, and investment decisions were based on social goals rather than profit considerations. Although most national union leaders and government officials during the war cooperated to restrain worker radicalism, government agencies responsible for maintaining full war production sometimes enforced regulations on business that in effect partially removed management's exclusive privilege of operating its plants.

All of these trends affronted management's conception of its role in the industrial system. Most industrial executives thought that they should be responsible for investment decisions, price and cost controls, production schedules, and work rules. When workers accepted employment in a factory, in management's view they agreed to abide by management's decisions, including those dictating the hours of work, the speeds at which machines and assembly lines operated, and the wages paid by the firm.

In the eyes of corporate executives there were thus many problems with the federal government's labor policy as it developed after 1935. Although managers had succeeded in preserving their prerogative to employ whomever they chose by accepting the "maintenance of membership" (union shop) provisions of wartime labor policy, they still saw the unions as far too powerful and intrusive. Events immediately after the war reinforced their view. During 1945 and 1946, a time of reconversion to civilian production, the nation witnessed a record number of strikes involving more workers than ever before. A coal miners' strike threatened the country with cold homes and closed factories, while in the spring of 1946 the railroad workers threatened a general strike of that industry. The government's only recourse to protect the public interest was temporary nationalization of the vital industry. The railroad strike was settled while President Truman was in the process of asking Congress for authorization to draft the workers into the army so that he could order them to their jobs.

The strike during the reconversion period that most threatened corporate executives' right to manage occurred against General Motors. Led by Walter Reuther, the United Auto Workers asked for much more than wage concessions. Faced with the lifting of wartime price controls and the prospect of less than full production, the union sought to protect and augment workers' earnings in case of a recession. Reuther demanded a 30 percent wage increase without compensatory automobile price increases. He demanded the right to inspect the corporation's books to demonstrate that it could pay higher wages from its profits and insisted on a contract that protected union security and improved workers' abilities to control their jobs. Reuther anticipated a victory over the world's largest industrial firm, believing that management would not wish to face a shutdown while its competitors were beginning to satisfy the pent-up demand for consumer goods.

General Motors, however, won the strike, which involved almost 300,000 workers and lasted 113 days. The company resisted sharing corporate financial information with the union and insisted that "wages, hours of employment and other conditions of employment are the only matters which are subject to collective bargaining." Management claimed "sole responsibility" for the firm's affairs, including provisions for disciplining workers who violated their contract with General Motors. The company successfully confined the conflict with the union to strictly economic matters, granting wage increases well below Reuther's original demand and resisting public disclosure of the firm's decisions about prices and wages. After this victory, business executives in general sought to solidify the principle of managerial prerogatives with a general revision of the prevailing labor law, the National Labor Relations Act of 1935.

The Taft-Hartley Act of 1947

The National Association of Manufacturers (NAM), joined by the Business Council, the Chamber of Commerce, and many other trade associations, sparked an effort to revise the National Labor Relations Act of 1935. In so doing, business leaders adopted what they believed was a realistic position. The NAM and its supporting groups recognized that however undesirable unions and collective bargaining might be in principle, they had become deeply entrenched in American industrial society. The best course to follow thus seemed not the union-busting campaigns that had followed World War I but a reshaping of law to restrict union activities to the narrowest possible economic considerations while retarding future union growth.

In preparing the agenda for labor-law reform, the business associations emphasized the importance of the public interest in industrial disputes. The law, they insisted, should place management and labor on an equal footing; in their view, the Wagner Act and wartime government policies had tilted the law in favor of the workers. Industrial relations should take place in an orderly framework in which workers were bound to abide by contracts until they expired. Employers should not have to face jurisdictional disputes in which one union competed with another for workers. Finally, bargaining should never be conducted on an industrywide basis, but only on a plant-by-plant or individual-firm basis unless employers agreed otherwise.

When Congress wrote the Taft-Hartley Act in 1947, it responded to the spirit, if not the specifics, of the business associations' agenda. This lengthy and complex law required union leaders to swear that they were not members of the Communist party, to account for their organizations' finances, and to refrain from making political contributions. The law prohibited the closed shop but allowed the union shop, thereby preserving management's rights to hire whomever it chose. Unions had to provide a sixty-day notice before launching a strike, and the federal government, when it deemed that disputes were adversely affecting the public interest, could order striking workers to return to their jobs for eighty days while bargaining continued. To retard the further growth of unions, the new law allowed states to require the open shop with so-called right-to-work laws. Employers now enjoyed the right to use their resources to try to persuade workers not to participate in unions.

Because Congress had responded favorably to the desires of business to restrict union activity, business leaders generally applauded the Taft-Hartley Act. Union leaders, on the other hand, wanting a system of industrial relations in which workers could participate in shaping corporate policies directly affecting them, sought its repeal. John L. Lewis of the United Mine Workers even called the Taft-Hartley Act "the first ugly, savage thrust of Fascism in America."

Labor Relations After 1947

The passage of the Taft-Hartley Act had important political implications for business and labor alike. No longer did a common antilabor stance unite American business executives and their trade associations. Some large industrial firms withdrew from active participation in the National Association of Manufacturers as the business community split along lines of size, function, and region. For the unions the failure to win broader rights during the reconversion period combined with the effects of the new federal law to produce a situation of stagnation. In general, union membership began a period of long-term decline, falling from a peak of almost 36 percent of the nonagricultural work force in 1945 to slightly more than 25 percent in 1980. As industrial jobs relatively declined in number with changing economic trends, the government's labor policy made it difficult to establish unions in areas where they were not already powerful in 1947.

In the great manufacturing industries that had arisen with the Industrial Revolution, there were, of course, still many serious and bitter disputes between management and labor after 1947. A few firms were intransigent in resisting collective bargaining. But the general pattern of management behavior in dealing with labor was one of aggressive realism. Industrial executives accepted the power of unions but continued to be aggressive about restricting issues to workers' concerns about economic security. And as long as the economy was experiencing long-term growth, management was willing to concede higher wages, which firms could accommodate with automation (replacing workers with machines) and productivity growth or pass along to consumers through higher prices. In 1956, Ford Motors agreed to begin a supplemental unemployment-benefits program to soften the blow for laid-off workers during depressed business cycles, a policy that the unions extended to other firms in contract negotiations. Unions, meanwhile, found that to comply with federal regulations they had to employ specialized experts and improve their systems of disciplining local leaders and rank-and-file members, practices that augmented tendencies toward bureaucratization.

PREPARING FOR THE FUTURE

In the twenty-five years following World War II, the American political economy underwent significant development. Much that was traditional in federal policy toward business remained, but some long-standing attitudes toward regulation took on new forms. Government did little to affect the permanence of big businesses as institutions dominating the production of industrial wealth, even as those institutions themselves were changing with the emergence of multinational and conglomerate forms of organization. Even though big business remained a major feature of the American economic system, other organizations sometimes acted to counteract its power. The union movement, although it never achieved the stature envisioned by some of its founders, remained a significant force into the 1970s. Moreover, the federal government, responding to newly expressed political impulses by enacting the new regulations of the 1960s and 1970s, injected new complexities into the politics of business.

Selected Readings

Historians have only begun to explore the inner workings of the American political economy after 1945. No general treatments of either business history or political history focus on the main themes of their interaction during this period. There are, however, a number of significant if more limited studies.

For information on the relationships between business and federal fiscal policy, two studies stand out: Robert M. Collins, *The Business Response to Keynes, 1929–1964* (New York: Columbia University Press, 1981), and Kim McQuaid, *Big Business and Presidential Power, from FDR to Reagan* (New York: Morrow, 1982). The latter volume focuses on the Business Council, while the former includes much discussion of the Chamber of Commerce and the National Association of Manufacturers. Otis L. Graham, Jr., *Toward a Planned Society: From Roosevelt to Nixon* (New York: Oxford University Press, 1976), is a fascinating introduction to an important subject affecting the political economy.

For a discussion of labor relations and federal policy, see Howell John Harris, *The Right to Manage: Industrial Relations Policies of American Business in the 1940s* (Madison: University of Wisconsin Press, 1982). Mark H. Rose, *Interstate: Express Highway Politics, 1941–1956* (Lawrence: University Press of Kansas, 1979), provides a good analysis of a subject that directly affects everyone. Paul A. C. Koistinen, *The Military-Industrial Complex: A Historical Perspective* (New York: Praeger, 1980), is a collection of important essays. Robert Griffith, "Dwight D. Eisenhower and the Corporate Commonwealth," *American Historical Review* 87 (February 1982): 87–122, is an important addition to the literature of the political economy. On antitrust policy, Richard Hofstader, "What Happened to the Antitrust Movement?" in Earl F. Cheit, ed., *The Business Establishment* (New York: John Wiley & Sons, 1964), remains insightful. And, finally, on the environmental movement, Samuel P. Hays, *Beauty, Health, and Permanence: Environmental Politics in the United States, 1955–1985* (New York: Cambridge University Press, 1987), is encyclopedic.

IMPORTANT EVENTS, 1971–1992

1971   President Richard Nixon abolishes the convertibility of the U.S. dollar into gold.

1973   The United States suffers from an oil embargo, and an energy crisis begins.

1975   Honda begins manufacturing motorcycles in the United States, in preparation for opening an automobile factory.
Microsoft is founded to develop computer software.

1979   The United States experiences a second oil embargo. The federal government rescues the Chrysler Corporation from bankruptcy.

1981   IBM introduces its desktop Personal Computer.

1985   Foreign trade rises to 20 percent of the U.S. GNP. American corporate debt rises to 116 percent of net worth.

1987   Japanese automobile manufacturers capture a 31 percent share of the American market.

1988   Mergers and acquisitions reach a new peak.

1990   Honda's *Accord* becomes the best-selling car model in the United States.

1991   General Motors announces losses of $7 billion.

1992   IBM reports losses of $5 billion.
American businesses "adopt" 40 percent of the nation's elementary schools.

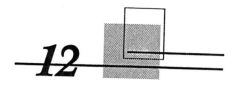

12

Restructuring
American Business

In the autumn of 1961, John D. Ong took a leave from his army duty in Louisiana and came home to Ohio in search of civilian employment. Like so many young men of his generation, Ong was fulfilling an obligatory tour of military duty, now nearing its end. The young officer was a historian turned lawyer, and he was looking for an opportunity to practice his profession as a civilian. Ong had answered an advertisement placed by the legal department of The B. F. Goodrich Company (a diversified rubber manufacturer founded in Akron, Ohio, nearly a century before, in 1870), and the company had brought him to its headquarters for an interview. In his quest for employment, Ong had borrowed a car and traveled around the state for several interviews with law firms. He returned to his army duty, not thinking he would spend his career in business. Then Ong accepted an offer to join the Goodrich legal staff.

At the time John Ong began working in Akron, The B. F. Goodrich Company was the nation's fourth-largest American rubber manufacturer. Best known for its automobile and truck tires, the company made all kinds of rubber goods, from industrial belts to surgeons' gloves. Its chemists and engineers were innovators whose research had led Goodrich into becoming the world's leading producer of polyvinyl chloride, an important source of plastic. The company also made aircraft wheels and brakes, serviced airplanes at major airports, and had supplied America's first astronauts with their space suits. As a multinational firm, Goodrich had rubber and vinyl plants—subsidiary or joint-venture firms—around the world.

Thirty years later John D. Ong served as chairman and chief executive officer of The BFGoodrich Company (the firm had changed its logo in 1974). The company he led was fundamentally different from the one he had joined in 1961. BFGoodrich still appeared on the sidewalls of tires, but the company that manufactured them was owned by Michelin, a French tire manufacturer. Gone were all of the traditional Goodrich rubber manufacturing and distribution facilities. Also gone were thousands of employees; the company had shrunk from about 39,000 workers in 1961 to 13,500 in 1992. Goodrich had transformed into a chemical and aerospace company. While the company remained important as a supplier of vinyl resins for the plastics industry, Ong and his management team were emphasizing investments in specialty chemicals as well as services and products for the aerospace industry, especially for avionics (the application of electronics to flying).

The changes that John Ong witnessed in the decades after he earned degrees at Ohio State and Harvard Universities in history and law were symptomatic of the dramatic transformations that occurred in the American business system after 1971. The public policy framework in which business operated shifted and made international markets less secure for American firms. Market opportunities, investments, and technologies were changing rapidly and on an international basis. Some American firms, like Goodrich, were successful, overall, in adapting to these variations. Others fell by the wayside as an expanding international competition in markets once dominated by American firms swept over them. The BFGoodrich Company survived, and its chief executive eventually succeeded, through a combination of several factors. One was the willingness to sell traditional product lines to other firms able to invest in them. Ong led his firm in shedding the traditional tire business. Another was the realization that large bureaucratic structures in business firms were ineffective in facing competitive challenges. (About 200 persons were employed at the Goodrich corporate headquarters in 1992; the top officers delegated most management responsibilities to executives in the decentralized operating divisions, where the company earned its profits.) A third factor was partly luck—the good luck of being able to sell the tire business in a way that realized substantial capital that Goodrich could invest in lines of business activity that, for it, were more promising.

The route to reforming their corporation was a bumpy one for the Goodrich executives. They made mistakes that lost substantial sums. The firm was strong enough, however, to survive those mistakes and offer a promising future for a new generation of employees and customers. That would not always be the case, however. In the decades after 1970 Americans experienced dramatic changes in economic opportunities—changes that resulted from shifts in investments and competition across the world. These changes, as we shall see in Chapter 13, were also a product of new government policies and new situations in international relations. The restructuring that Ong's BFGoodrich underwent was a response to management's rethinking of profitable strategies. Similar restructurings across the landscape of the American business system dramatically changed the face of American business as the twentieth century entered its last years.

As business strategies shifted and corporate structures took on new shapes, business for Americans after 1970 became more competitive and economic well-being less secure than it had been in the years following World War II. Big business remained a very important part of the American scene, but smaller firms became relatively more important than was the case in the first decades after the war. The shift of employment from manufacturing to service industries, already under way, accelerated by the end of the 1970s. Within the manufacturing sector of the economy, employment opportunities were declining in the face of foreign competition and new technical systems of production that required fewer workers. Big business firms remained important in manufacturing, but smaller firms were increasing their share of manufacturing employment. Within the service sector of the economy, too, small businesses were generating new employment opportunities. In the 1980s, the American economy generated new jobs, but at a rate lower than in the 1970s or 1960s. Employment became less secure. Between 1979 and 1989, the 500 largest industrial firms shed 3.7 million workers.

INTERNATIONAL COMPETITION AND MULTINATIONAL FIRMS

Changes in the structure of multinational industries were important signposts of the world's evolving economic system. In some domestic oligopolies (American industries dominated by a handful of companies), the entry of foreign firms broke down long-standing relationships. Then the domestic oligopolies gave way to worldwide oligopolies. The tire industry was a case in point. Four large firms—Goodyear, Firestone, U.S. Rubber (later Uniroyal), and BFGoodrich—dominated the American market and had extensive facilities abroad, especially in Europe. However, with the growth of world trade and the expansion of motor-vehicle use and tire markets abroad, foreign firms were sometimes more successful than American companies. During his career at Goodrich, John Ong saw his company lose its ability to engage profitably in the tire business in Europe and much of Asia, while rubber manufacturers based in Germany, Britain, Italy, France, and Japan were not only succeeding in their home bases but also penetrating American distribution systems and markets. By 1990 only one large American tire manufacturer—Goodyear—remained, while old American name brands continued under the ownership of foreign-based multinational firms.

The penetration of American industries by foreign firms brought about basic changes in the American business system. One change was the restructuring accomplished by American companies in order to refocus investments. American companies sold divisions in transactions that reshaped ownership patterns in industries and tended to reduce diversification as a business strategy. The refocusing of investments sometimes reduced the size of American companies as they shed factory capacity, product lines, and employees. Another response by American firms was to retreat from foreign markets, where large multinational competitors were stronger. Meanwhile, foreign investments in the United States reshaped the American business landscape with new names from foreign cultures.

The American Automobile Industry and International Competition

Nowhere were these developments more obvious to Americans than in the automobile industry. In 1970, an American oligopoly consisting of General Motors, Ford, and Chrysler dominated the market. Twenty years later the "big three" saw their share of the American market shrink substantially while they competed with manufacturers based in Germany and Japan for design and engineering leadership. As thousands of American automobile workers witnessed the loss of secure employment, political pressures mounted to abandon postwar policies of free trade. Foreign multinational firms established factories in the United States, and the "big three" American companies established new partnerships with them.

Americans drove cars more than ever after 1970, as the historical trend toward private transportation continued unabated despite the distressing oil shocks of 1973 and 1979 and the nation's growing dependence on imported sources of petroleum. (In 1973 and again in 1979, responding to war and bitter political rivalries in the Middle East, the Organization of Petroleum Exporting Countries—OPEC—suddenly withheld oil supplies from world markets, driving prices up to unprecedented levels.) Energy costs played an important role in reshaping the American automobile industry. Energy costs in the United States had traditionally been low, and American automobile companies were not focusing on fuel efficiency. Instead, during the postwar years vehicles grew larger, and the growing sales of larger cars with automatic transmissions and air-conditioning systems effectively increased fuel usage. With the advent of the new regulation of the 1960s and requirements to reduce exhaust emissions (motor vehicles were a major source of air pollution in the United States), manufacturers retrofitted their designs with devices to meet these requirements. Under this procedure, exhaust emissions were, in fact, reduced; but fuel consumption increased. These conditions mattered little to customers, however, as fuel costs remained a very small part of operating costs. American companies seemed to be successfully satisfying tastes in the American car market. But in 1973, and again in 1979, fuel costs suddenly skyrocketed and fuel availability became uncertain. The American car buyer was now conscious of fuel costs as an important factor in weighing purchase decisions.

Multinational automobile firms based in other nations had been eyeing the American automobile market covetously for years. That market, too, was changing in fundamental ways as a result of the prosperity of the postwar years. Except for the short-lived success of Volkswagen in gaining a significant share of the market, foreign firms had fared poorly in their exportation of vehicles to the United States. Volkswagen sales, however, forecast a shift in the market away from product differentiation according to price and toward product differentiation according to vehicle type and performance. In the meantime, either foreign producers lacked the designs suitable for American highways or their ability to invest in the necessary dealers and service networks was insufficient to take advantage of the shifting market. Japanese officials were especially frustrated, for an alliance between government and automobile industry executives there saw growth in automobile exports as vital to that nation's continuing economic revival. The oil shock of 1973 gave them a chance.

High fuel costs in other nations had forced automobile manufacturers to design efficient cars. American customers were now ready to snap up any available fuel-efficient vehicle. Most of those cars were foreign. Sales of Japanese-made vehicles soared as their manufacturers penetrated the American market for the first time. Then the crisis of oil shortages receded and gasoline costs relative to other goods dropped, after which American manufacturers recovered much of the market they had lost.

The American producers' recovery proved only temporary, however, and the American automobile oligopoly began to suffer an ongoing problem. Part of the problem was sheer misfortune, and part of it resulted from management practices. American automobile manufacturers tended to look at returns on their investment as the most important measure of their success, instead of combining that standard with a long-run view of the market and of engineering advances. In short, they were slow to realize that a new type of market segmentation was evolving. The results were damaging. Automobiles designed abroad enjoyed technological advantages, with new designs to meet tough air-pollution standards. Foreign competitors took a contrasting long-run outlook on markets and production. The vehicles themselves represented not only different types of cars but different price ranges as well. Foreign manufacturers were successful in improving product quality both by introducing high standards of quality control on the production line and by motivating production workers.

Bad luck, in combination with poor management practices, wounded the American automobile industry to the point where only a government rescue could save the smallest firm, Chrysler. When the second oil shock hit in 1979, Americans suddenly returned to their earlier desire for fuel-efficient cars. Meanwhile, after carefully studying the American car market, Japanese automobile executives redesigned their products. In 1979, the Japanese producers had large inventories of vehicles on hand, and when American customers snapped them up, they discovered that the Japanese

The flood of foreign compact cars affected the U.S. car industry in recent decades, not only by taking a sizable market share but also by making the American auto firms revise their designs and make smaller cars. This photograph taken in Japan around 1980 shows a cargo of Hondas being loaded for shipment overseas. (Courtesy of American Honda Motors)

cars were typically of high quality in both design and manufacture. This time, the Japanese inroad into the American car market was deep and long lasting.

The Japanese penetration reshaped the American automobile industry in the 1980s. By 1987, 31 percent of the passenger cars sold in the United States were imported. The American manufacturers—allied with their workers, parts suppliers, and dealers—fought to bring an end to free trade. Federal officials negotiated "voluntary" restrictions by the Japanese on their exports of cars to America in 1981. One effect was that costs to American car buyers increased over the next few years by billions of dollars. Another effect was the change in strategy of the Japanese firms and of Ford and Chrysler.

Facing restraints on their vehicle exports to the United States, the Japanese companies responded in three ways. First, because they were able to sell every vehicle offered in the restricted American market, they focused on higher-priced models that earned higher profits, introducing vehicles distinguished by type as well as by price. Second, they worked out multinational alliances with American competitors for the design, production, and distribution of vehicles in the United States. For instance, a joint venture of General Motors and Toyota, the largest Japanese firm, operated a former GM factory in California, assembling vehicles that were sold under different nameplates by Toyota and Chevrolet. Third, the Japanese firms built factories of their own in the United States. Honda was the vanguard. A motorcycle manufacturer, Honda was a relative newcomer to the Japanese automobile industry that needed added factory capacity to satisfy the demand for its *Accord,* a popular model in the United States. Having started out in 1975 with a small motorcycle factory located near Marysville, Ohio, the company soon expanded at the site to assemble automobiles using parts both imported and locally made. By 1990, Honda's factory had become one of the largest in the United States and its *Accord* was the best-selling model in the American market. Other Japanese firms followed Honda's example and established either joint ventures or independent factories in seven states.

The expansion of the Japanese automobile industry led to a situation whereby worldwide factory capacity exceeded market demand for automobiles. Faced with this situation, American firms struggled to compete. Of these firms, Ford Motors was the most successful in the 1980s. Henry Ford II's vision of a multinational company operating in a worldwide market allowed the firm to survive by means of profits earned abroad, even while its domestic American sales sagged in the recession of the early 1980s. When Ford retired as chairman of the company in 1980, he turned it over to Philip Caldwell, who was schooled in the experience of the company's foreign operations. Ford Motors transferred successful manufacturing technologies from its foreign plants while using its profits from multinational operations to invest in new products for the American market, especially the popular *Taurus* model. Ford Motors executives painfully slashed factory capacity to cut costs and learned to involve workers in both the design of vehicles and the control of their quality. Ford Motors also strengthened ties with Mazda, a Japanese company, and arranged a joint venture with Nissan, that nation's second-largest auto firm, in order to offer customers a wider range of models. These multinational measures lowered design costs and improved opportunities to exchange technical advances.

Chrysler, the smallest of the traditional "big three" American auto companies, experienced more checkered results. It lacked the multinational resources upon which Ford had successfully drawn. And its joint-venture arrangements with Mitsubishi, a huge Japanese company that manufactured automobiles among other goods, were less advantageous than those of its competitors. By the end of the 1980s, Chrysler executives had seen their automobile volume slip behind that of Honda, even though its truck sales, especially of "mini-vans," remained strong. In search of more profitable market segements, Chrysler bought the small American Motors and its famous Jeep nameplate in 1987. Then, in 1992, it introduced a newly designed passenger car in hopes of recapturing lost market share.

General Motors also responded less ably than Ford to the new automobile market conditions. Early on, GM had become dominant thanks to the market and product engineering orientation of Alfred P. Sloan, Jr.; but later generations of executives were slow to adapt to the changing nature of vehicle markets. Sloan had created GM's divisions to offer vehicles in different price ranges, but as price distinctions blurred after 1945 and model distinctions became clearer, each of the established GM divisions tried to offer a wide range of model types. One result was clouded product distinction, with one GM division in effect competing with another instead of with rival firms.

Despite the restraints placed on Japanese exports to the United States, General Motors faltered after 1980 and saw its remaining share of the market shrink from 44 percent to 36 percent in 1991. Like Ford and Chrysler, GM designed new models and reduced factory capacity, but it did so more slowly. Advertising messages failed to distract sophisticated customers from the realization that new models did not always fully incorporate the improved technologies used by competitors. Top executives believed that the company would eventually recapture markets lost to those competitors, and they wanted the firm to retain factory capacity to meet the demand; but in the meantime capital costs had to be covered. They launched an entirely new, autonomous division, *Saturn,* to compete directly with imported nameplates, a venture that had succeeded by 1992. In other areas, however, GM was in deep trouble. When the company closed its books on business for 1991, it reported $7 billion in losses. That staggering sum would have been even worse had overseas operations been less profitable.

The GM board of directors intervened on April 6, 1992, with an announcement that stunned the American business world. The board had dismissed the firm's president and its chief financial officer and had removed its chairman, Robert C. Stempel, as head of the board's powerful executive committee. Retired Procter & Gamble chief John G. Smale—an "outside" director, not a member of management—was now in charge of the powerful GM executive committee. In his previous position, Smale had earned a reputation for invigorating a disciplined marketing strategy for Procter & Gamble's diverse consumer products. Although he had no substantial experience as an automobile industry executive, Smale, supported by other outside GM directors, was in effect taking formidable responsibility for the management of the automobile giant. Even before the dramatic intervention by the board of directors, GM had announced the closing of up to 25 North American factories; 80,000 employees expected to see their jobs disappear by 1995. The company's labor costs were not quite double those of Ford Motors in 1992. The company explained that only plants whose workers agreed to more efficient work rules could stay open.

The Merger and Takeover Wave of the 1980s

The American automobile industry represented only part of the story of business restructuring in the period. In the face of new competitive challenges from abroad as well as changing opportunities in both marketing and the harnessing of new communication and computer technologies for profitable ends, American business underwent a substantial merger wave in the 1980s.

Difficulties experienced by conglomerate corporations preceded the most recent merger wave. Conglomerate corporations fell on hard times in the early 1970s. Conglomerates suffered from management failures, as executives exercising financial controls could not effectively lead them without cognizance of market and production conditions. Interest payments on the heavy debts incurred to finance expansion dragged down earnings, and the diversified firms performed better. One symptom was a decline in the number of conglomerate mergers, which, slowed by economic recession, dropped from 715 in 1968 to just 123 in 1975.

The wave of mergers that occurred in the 1980s was enormous, reflecting in part the failure of conglomerate firms' performance. (See Table 12.1.) The merger activity of the 1980s dwarfed that of the 1960s or 1970s and reshaped the map of American business as familiar names fell by the wayside. Some 143 of the 500 largest industrial corporations in the United States—28 percent—were acquired by other companies in the 1980s. Altogether, the total value of business assets changing hands during the decade came to $1.3 trillion.

The purpose of most of the mergers and acquisitions of the 1980s was to refocus a business on its core activities. As business executives came to understand the weaknesses of conglomerates, they sought through takeovers and mergers to build companies that were more specialized in their focus. The goal was apparent when a large company with most of its assets in one field bought another big business in the same industry. Such deals were especially pronounced in the gas pipeline, oil, food, banking, and

Table 12.1   Mergers and Acquisitions in the United States, 1982–1991

Year	Number of transactions	Percentage of change	Value (in $billions)	Percentage of change
1982	1,617	—	57.7	—
1983	1,812	+12.1	48.9	−12.2
1984	2,416	+33.3	121.1	+147.7
1985	2,773	+14.8	141.3	+16.7
1986	3,803	+37.1	200.7	+42.0
1987	3,150	−17.2	171.5	−14.6
1988	3,310	−5.1	232.4	+35.5
1989	3,061	−7.5	244.1	+5.0
1990	3,154	+3.0	164.3	−32.7
1991	2,117	−32.9	98.0	−40.3

SOURCE: *Mergers & Acquisitions*, May/June, 1992, p. 43. Reprinted by permission of Mergers & Acquisitions, Philadelphia.

airline industries. For example, Hercules Inc. sold its Aircraft and Electronics Group to BFGoodrich in 1990 for $176 million, a move that allowed executives in both firms to focus on their core business strategies. After the takeovers, while core businesses were combined, peripheral businesses were often divested. In fact, about 60 percent of the unrelated acquisitions made between 1970 and 1982 had been divested by 1989.

In a second type of takeover, conglomerate firms were acquired for the express purpose of breaking them up. Sometimes corporate raiders, such as Carl Icahn, so-called because they used stock tender offers to purchase companies in hostile (unfriendly) takeovers, bought and sold firms as if they were commodities. (If managers refused to sell to them, the raiders offered stockholders more for their stock than the current price, purchased the company, and put a new management team in place.) The various divisions of the company were then sold off in a "bust-up" to other firms. In other cases, a group of investors, often using borrowed money, bought up the stock of a company to "take it private" (that is, take its stock off of public exchanges) in a leveraged buy-out (LBO). Sometimes the purchasers were former managers of the company who might sell divisions piecemeal. In about 20 percent of the hostile takeovers completed in the mid-1980s, more than half of the assets involved were sold within three years, and in the other 80 percent about a third of the assets were divested. In LBOs, 44 percent of the assets were sold.

An example was the purchase of the cosmetics giant Revlon by the corporate raider Ronald Perelman in 1985 for $2.3 billion. Before the acquisition, Revlon had diversified into fields outside of cosmetics, especially health care. After the takeover, Perelman sold $2.06 billion of Revlon's health care and noncosmetic businesses. About 60 percent of the asset sales were to other companies, but some went to management groups, including groups of managers formerly in charge of some of the Revlon divisions. Perelman revamped Revlon's cosmetics business, tripling its advertising budget, and Revlon's profits rose. He reduced the corporation's headquarters staff but made no reductions in the numbers of blue-collar workers or the amount of capital investments.

Not all of the results were quite so beneficial, however. Some companies struggled in the aftermath of mergers, takeovers, or leveraged buy-outs. The Goodyear Tire and Rubber Company was a case in point. Goodyear had risen to become the world leader in producing tires and other rubber products. Because the tire industry was competitive and profits were low, and because the tire industry prospered or suffered according to the cycles of production in the automobile industry, Goodyear sought to diversify into other manufactured products while maintaining leadership in the tire market. Then, in 1986, a British corporate raider, James Goldsmith, made an unwelcome move to purchase Goodyear stock and take over the company. Goodyear managers resisted Goldsmith successfully, but only by wounding and changing their company. Goodyear sold its aerospace division to raise cash, borrowed $2.6 billion, and purchased 40 percent of its stock in order to drive up the price of the shares and make them unaffordable for Goldsmith. After its victory over the foreign raider, Goodyear continued to sell nontire businesses. Still, its annual interest bill of over $300 million on $3.3 billion of long-term debt reduced earnings and made it more difficult for the company to retain its worldwide leadership in the manufacture and distribution of tires.

Several important factors, both economic and political, abetted the merger wave of the 1980s. Conditions in the stock markets were particularly important. At least until 1985, the prices of many common stocks were low relative to the actual values and earnings potentials of the firms, and this situation encouraged takeovers. Companies or individuals were able to secure the financing required for the purchases; brokerage houses and banks, which earned giant commissions, eagerly arranged the financing. Finally, restraints once imposed by antitrust laws evaporated as key appointees of Ronald Reagan, elected president in 1980, were reluctant to impose traditional threats of lawsuits. At the same time, other restraints imposed by state governments proved ineffective. The Supreme Court struck down state laws that restricted out-of-state companies from buying in-state companies, observing that the laws had the effect of regulating interstate commerce, an exclusive preserve of the federal government.

In the early 1990s, merger activity declined. The combination of a severe recession, which dried up funds, and higher stock prices, which made purchases more costly, slowed the takeover wave. Revelations about unethical practices by some corporate raiders also dampened the movement, and a number of the most notorious went to jail. Then, too, companies devised defenses against unwanted takeovers. The political environment also changed. Although the federal government under President George Bush continued the Reagan policy, doing little to regulate mergers, state governments acted. In decisions involving Indiana and California laws in 1987 and 1990 respectively, the U.S. Supreme Court reversed its earlier stance to allow states to make difficult unfriendly out-of-state purchases of in-state corporations. By 1992, forty states had laws making unwanted takeovers more difficult than in the past.

BIG BUSINESS AND SMALL BUSINESS

The rearrangements of the American business system that mergers, takeovers, and leveraged buy-outs produced had important implications for the ability of American entrepreneurs to respond to shifting markets both at home and abroad. While some of the rearrangements allowed executives in large firms fresh opportunities to focus resources on promising ventures, others burdened managers with heavy obligations that drove prominent firms into bankruptcy. Meanwhile, small companies sometimes prospered, and their success suggested to some observers that the American business system remained dynamic and able to readjust to changing conditions in the international economy.

Small Business and Changing Opportunities

As part of the restructuring of America's business system, small businesses experienced a modest resurgence in the 1970s and 1980s. Between 1976 and 1984, small businesses increased their share of the nation's total employment from 51 percent to 53 percent, and throughout the 1980s they accounted for about 40 percent of America's GNP. Even so, small businesses could not compensate fully for the decline of big businesses and never were in a position to save American society from the hazards of international competition. Small businesses did generate new jobs, probably about half of the total generated during the 1970s and 1980s. On the whole, however, their position varied considerably in the different segments of the nation's business system.

Manufacturing was the most outstanding example of the renewed importance of small business. Small companies increased their share of the nation's total manufacturing output from 33 percent in 1976 to 38 percent ten years later. In addition, they benefited from the growth of a competitive global market, where smaller, more flexible factories often enjoyed advantages in making quick adaptations to changing markets.

The growing importance of small manufacturers was a result of both technological trends and competitive international pressures. The growing availability of computers allowed small manufacturers to undertake jobs that only large firms could handle in earlier times. Computer-aided design (CAD), computer-aided engineering (CAE), and computer-aided manufacturing (CAM) permitted small staffs to enlarge their accomplishments. In industries as diverse as movie making and steel manufacturing, smaller firms began replacing older giant companies. Then, too, the larger companies restructured. Reversing their century-old reliance on vertical integration, more and more big businesses in manufacturing turned instead to small companies to supply components for their finished products. Small companies came increasingly into demand as subcontractors because the larger firms, again responding to the demands of the unstable world market, sought flexibility in their operations. When big businesses reversed vertical integration by relying on small outside suppliers, they also in effect reduced their wage costs, for the typical small manufacturer did not provide industrial workers the incomes enjoyed by employees of large firms. Nonetheless, limits to this type of restructuring appeared in the early 1990s. Small manufacturers lacked the capital needed for fully automated factories and by the early 1990s had fully exploited the CAD, CAE, and CAM technologies.

In foreign sales, the significance of small manufacturers increased after 1970. Of the 243,000 American companies that exported directly through their own sales offices in 1989, 88 percent had fewer than 500 employees, as did half the firms exporting through third parties such as brokers. Altogether, small businesses accounted for about 21 percent of America's manufacturing exports by the early 1990s, considerably more than in earlier years.

In terms of numbers, small businesses dominated the service industries, a growing field in the 1970s and 1980s (although expansion in most service fields slowed during the late 1980s and early 1990s). Big companies, however, became increasingly significant in services as time passed. In 1984, for example, large banks such as Citicorp and Bank of America owned assets twice as large as those of such leading industrial firms as Exxon and General Motors, and the spread of branch banking was ending the independence of local banks. The same revolution in communications and computers that allowed a resurgence of small business in manufacturing threatened small firms in some service fields.

Most of the remaining small firms were in sales, where small firms continued to face strong competition from big companies. Challenged by mail-order houses, department stores, and chain stores in earlier years, independent retailers encountered growing competition from discount stores such as Walmart in the 1970s, 1980s, and 1990s. Suburban shopping malls were another threat to small retailers, who often could not afford their rental fees. The share of total retail sales made by small businesses in the United States dropped from about half to roughly a third in the twenty years after 1958. By the mid-1980s, the nation's largest fifty retailers accounted for a fourth of the nation's retail sales.

The Growth of Franchising

Although the distinction between big businesses and smaller firms had become pronounced in many fields as the twentieth century progressed, some blurring occurred in the form of business franchising. In franchising, a would-be entrepreneur (the franchisee) purchases the right to do business in a certain line of work from a company in that field (the franchiser). In return for this sum, along with yearly payments based on the amount of sales made, the franchisee reaps benefits provided by the parent company. The franchiser usually provides national advertising (including a well-known trademark), advice and guidelines about conducting business (and often training in the business at its national headquarters), and the benefits of mass purchasing discounts. Many Americans came to view franchising as an ideal combination of, or middle ground between, large and small businesses. Franchisees embraced franchising as a way to have the independence and entrepreneurial opportunities that they associated with small business without forsaking what they perceived to be the security of big business. For the franchiser, franchising offered the possibility of rapid business expansion at little cost, since the franchisee supplied most of the capital. And the various annual fees levied on the franchisees promised a prosperous future for any franchiser whose product caught on with the American public.

Franchising evolved over more than a century. Cyrus McCormick used franchised dealers to sell his reapers in the nineteenth century. Building on McCormick's experiences, automobile manufacturers and petroleum companies began selling cars and gasoline through franchised dealers in the opening decades of the twentieth century. Soft-drink makers, led by Coca-Cola, sold their goods through franchised bottlers. And restaurant franchising began in the 1920s with A & W Root Beer and Howard Johnson establishments.

Franchising grew at a phenomenal rate after World War II. By the 1950s and 1960s, it seemed as if everything was being franchised: fast foods (McDonald's, Kentucky Fried Chicken), motels (Holiday Inn was one of many), coin-operated laundries, companies selling household pets, and businesses making security systems. By 1967, sales made by franchised businesses accounted for about 10 percent of America's GNP. Then, in the early 1970s, the franchise boom slowed temporarily, as the economic recession that opened the decade exposed weaknesses in the financing and management of many franchised businesses. During this time it became apparent, above all, that the franchisees were rarely able to obtain independence or even financial stability in the franchise system. The parent company often profited at the expense of the franchisees.

Despite these revelations, the franchise movement recovered momentum during the late 1970s and early 1980s. Americans continued to view franchising as a way to fulfill their dreams of becoming independent entrepreneurs, and franchising spread from lawn care to day care for children. By 1990, 533,000 franchise establishments had sold $716 billion worth of goods and services in America—up from 396,000 outlets selling $120 billion just twenty years earlier. By 1988, 374 American companies also operated 35,000 franchise outlets abroad.

IBM and Changes in American Business

Some small firms did succeed as a result of adaptations to changes in the international economy, and franchising was in part a story of successful innovation; but famous big businesses struggled. No example was more noticeable than IBM. The history of IBM in the tumultuous years after 1970 dramatized some of the rapid changes that swept across the American business landscape.

IBM was a hugely successful multinational corporation that had entered the computer field under the leadership of Thomas L. Watson, Jr., and became dominant by supplying the mainframe computers that did so much to enable large organizations to accumulate, store, process, and retrieve information. The success of IBM symbolized the ability of executives to command huge financial resources both to capture leadership in the information age and to provide secure, well-paid employment to tens of thousands of employees. In the end, however, even IBM had to undergo fundamental reorganization to adapt to changing conditions in the markets it served. It also had to retreat from its long-standing policy of investing in research and development in order to maintain technological leadership.

Because IBM was so successful, government policy affected the company's strategic history. In 1969, as Lyndon Johnson was stepping down as president of the United States, the Department of Justice filed an antitrust suit accusing IBM of monopoly and urging the courts to break it up. The case dragged on for almost thirteen years, and the company's lawyers advised Watson and other IBM executives to change their strategy and restrain market penetration. Because of the antitrust threat IBM did not grow as big as it might have.

In spite of the restraints imposed by the antitrust suit, however, IBM's business did enlarge. IBM had built its computer business by designing, manufacturing, and servicing mainframe computers of high quality that,

McDonald's products were so popular that they were introduced in Moscow before the collapse of communism and the Soviet Union. (Courtesy of Moscow-McDonald's)

while not always at the edge of advances in electronic technologies, performed satisfactorily for their users. By 1980, having combined its computer business with other successful ventures in office equipment (IBM electric typewriters dominated markets worldwide), the company employed 391,000 persons around the globe.

Computer technology was a rapidly developing field, however, and IBM had less success in smaller machines, the so-called mini-computers that were less expensive and met the needs of organizations smaller than large corporations or public agencies. In the 1960s the Digital Equipment Corporation and other firms had profitably entered this line of business, where IBM lagged behind in the market. Meanwhile, by the end of the decade inventors and entrepreneurs were beginning to develop so-called microcomputers, small machines that could sit on an individual's desk and perform less complex information-processing tasks. Steven Jobs and Steven Wozniak had begun Apple Computer in a garage in California in 1976 and built the company into a venture selling a line of desktop microcomputers. Among other tasks, the early line of Apple computers was capable of helping a small business—or an individual in a large organization using a software program, "VisiCalc," developed by two graduate students at the Harvard Business School—to store, process, and analyze financial information on an electronic "spreadsheet." In spite of the success of Apple and other microcomputer manufacturers, however, the machines did not fulfill the promises of the technology; by 1980, at best only 3 percent of corporate employees were using microcomputers regularly, with only a slightly higher usage in small business.

To John R. Opel, IBM's president and chief executive officer (and soon to be chairman) in 1980, a venture into the microcomputer business seemed both a promising business opportunity and a chance to leave a personal imprint on the industry. Such a venture suggested a profitable way of expanding IBM's business without enlarging the firm's share of the mainframe market and encouraging the government to continue its antitrust suit. Opel wanted IBM to maintain its reputation for excellence in marketing and service while it moved to the forefront of technological advances. Microcomputers offered Opel an opportunity to achieve his goals for IBM, so in 1980 he arranged to have a small group of engineers begin planning a microcomputer to be manufactured and sold by the giant company.

Eventually Philip D. Estridge took charge of the project, located in Boca Raton, Florida. Estridge led a small group of engineers and marketing executives whose excitement over designing and producing a new microcomputer on a year's timetable was infectious, a group who enjoyed an autonomy unusual for IBM. The microcomputer group broke with long-standing IBM customs and developed a machine with "open architecture"—that is, one in which the design linking the computer's components (chips, boards, wiring, and the like) was revealed to software developers and parts suppliers at independent companies. Estridge chose the Microsoft Corporation, then a small software company in Bellevue, Washington, to develop the Disk Operating System (DOS) that was the machine's primary software, while other outside vendors wrote application software to make the machine usable for writing and processing information. IBM wanted to encourage outside suppliers and software developers to produce added features in order to enlarge the machine's usefulness and therefore its market. So, instead of patenting large parts of the machine's architecture, IBM chose to protect only the Basic Input Output System (BIOS).

This strategy, and the willingness of the executives in company headquarters to support Estridge's group with infusions of capital without trying to control its progress in detail, proved a stroke of genius. The company also used outside suppliers for key parts, including the microprocessor chip, which it purchased from Intel Corporation. The machine's architecture allowed room for expansion, including the ability to connect to other computers. Introduced in August 1981, just one year from the launching of the project, the Personal Computer (PC), as it came to be called, was an instant success. Buyers paid $2,880 for a desktop machine that used a more powerful microprocessor than the one in rival Apple's machines. The personal computer proved useful in accomplishing work, freeing individuals in business and elsewhere from attachments to mainframe computers and empowering them to shape applications in tailor-made ways for particular tasks. During the few months it was on the market in 1981, the IBM PC earned $43 million in revenues. And by the end of 1984, microcomputer sales had brought $4 billion in revenues to IBM. Its personal computer business alone ranked it as the 74th largest American industrial company that year. In terms of revenue, no other product in American manufacturing history had enjoyed such a spectacular success.

The figures, however, hid the fact that IBM stumbled after its initial success. The company eliminated the microcomputer group's autonomy and organized it as an Entry-Level Systems Division subject to controls from corporate headquarters. An effort to launch a less expensive "home computer," the PCjr., proved unsuccessful. Estridge and other executives insisted on designing new machines based on a more advanced microprocessor. The result, the Personal Computer AT, first introduced in 1984, suffered serious defects that the company was unable swiftly to correct. Meanwhile, Estridge ordered engineers intent on refining existing technologies so as to ensure price leadership in desktop computers to focus their attention on more advanced technologies. Other manufacturers rushed in to fill the gap with "clones," designed to be fully compatible with IBM machines once ways around the patented BIOS had been discovered. The DOS operating system, written by Microsoft and introduced by IBM in 1981, set the industry standard. By 1991, 90 percent of the microcomputers in use were compatible with IBM machines. In the meantime, however,

IBM had lost market share to rival firms. Having long since introduced an advanced line of microcomputers of its own, Apple weathered the recession by cutting prices and saw its market share rise from 8.6 percent in 1990 to 10.7 percent in 1991. In 1984 IBM had 63 percent of the microcomputer market, but it dropped to a 38 percent share in 1987 and to a 15 percent share in 1991.

The trouble that IBM was experiencing in personal computers came to be reflected in the company as a whole by the end of the 1980s. Although the government had dropped its antitrust suit in 1982, by the end of the decade IBM saw the recession erode its sales and profits in mainframe computers. John F. Akers became chief executive officer of the company in 1985, and at about the same time the company began to consider ways of refining a decentralized management structure. The computer business was changing rapidly thanks to quick advances in electronic technologies, and IBM's leaders began to realize that it was difficult for their firm, because of its size, to adapt quickly to those changes. Competitors were sometimes more agile in their use of new technologies to satisfy market needs. In the meantime, advances in microcomputer technology had reduced demand for mainframe computers, long an IBM profit bastion. IBM remained a giant among firms, but even it began to slip in the recession that so damaged the American economy after 1989.

Akers revealed plans for a fundamentally new business strategy and structure in 1991, at a time when the company had lost $2.6 billion. Part of the losses was due to the new strategy. IBM paid employees to leave voluntarily. It planned to trim its payroll to 275,000 employees by the end of 1993. It closed factories as it shed managers. And it developed some 20,000 separate alliances with other companies in different fields related to computers. Most dramatic was the announcement of a joint venture with Apple Computers to develop a new operating system for microcomputers. Finally, IBM created separate subsidiary companies for important lines. The IBM Personal Computer Company, announced in 1992, would operate as a separate unit. In effect, IBM was being transformed into a holding company with thirteen operating companies—nine for specific product lines and four to provide research, marketing, and financial support for the business. The autonomy that had allowed entrepreneurial employees under Estridge's direction in 1981 to change the computing industry had dramatically come full circle. Akers, however, did not survive, as the board of directors, dissatisfied with the firm's perfomance, asked him to resign in 1993.

The Growth of Microsoft

The Microsoft Corporation was a small firm that grew dramatically by developing and distributing computer software. While IBM was reorganizing its businesses and shedding employees, Microsoft was becoming the world's leading provider of software for desktop computers. Microsoft's founder, William H. Gates III, was a genius at devising programs for computers. As a teenager, Gates developed a national reputation as a programmer. He took a leave of absence from high school to accept a $30,000 annual salary from the TRW Corporation to develop computer programs, eventually returning to graduate from high school. He attended Harvard University but, again, at the age of nineteen, dropped out to pursue his dream of participating in the development of the brand-new desktop computer industry. With his friend, Paul Allen, Gates founded the Microsoft Corporation in Bellevue, Washington, in 1975. When Gates learned of IBM's development of the Personal Computer, he worked hard to persuade the giant manufacturer to contract with Microsoft for the development of its operating system (the software any computer requires to integrate its parts) and to provide a platform for "application software" (the programs that enable persons to use the machine to accomplish tasks). In 1980 Gates negotiated a contract between IBM and Microsoft, which had just thirty-two employees, to provide the operating system and a programming language for the new Personal Computer. Microsoft paid $100,000 to another small company, Seattle Computer Products, to adapt for IBM's machine an operating system it was developing. Meanwhile, Gates also worked on software for IBM. The result in 1981 was PC-DOS, an acronym that stood for Personal Computer–Disk Operating System. Each of IBM's customers paid Microsoft a fee to use DOS.

When demand for the IBM Personal Computer far exceeded initial expectations in 1981, the concurrent sales of PC-DOS began to enrich Gates and Microsoft. Gates and Microsoft worked closely with IBM's engineers to improve the operating system and to adapt it to evolving technological advances in the desktop computer industry. When competitors began selling "clones," Microsoft provided the operating system, then called MS-DOS for Microsoft–Disk Operating System. Microsoft's operating systems for both IBM and its competitors were nearly identical, and the application software was interchangeable regardless of who manufactured the machine. Microsoft shared knowledge of its operating system with other companies that developed application software, for Gates understood that computer sales would expand rapidly as more and more useful software became available for customers.

Gates was not content to draw the line at operating systems, however. He reinvested the substantial profits earned from DOS to compete in applications software markets. As the company grew rapidly after 1981, Gates was careful to keep Microsoft decentralized, with small groups of programmers and marketing experts assigned responsibility for competing in particular computer markets. By 1992, Gates' strategy had made Microsoft the largest software vendor in the world. The company had offices in 25 nations, employed almost 12,000 persons, and enjoyed sales of $2.76 billion. Gates had become one of the nation's wealthiest citizens.

REFORMING THE MANAGEMENT OF BUSINESS

As the stories of IBM and Microsoft indicate, the management of business changed along with the restructuring of the business system. The most important trend was a renewed emphasis on decentralized responsibility within large corporations. Big firms like the BFGoodrich Company, when they underwent a restructuring, also developed management practices that shrewdly combined production, marketing, and financial responsibilities in the operating units. The purpose was to allow the company to adapt quickly to changing conditions in markets affected by international forces.

Consequences of Mergers

The mergers of the 1980s had important consequences in addition to reducing diversification among big businesses. The takeover wave combined with the growth in international competition to spark a slimming down of management. Many American businesses had more levels of management than their foreign competitors. By the early 1970s, General Motors had twenty major layers of management; Toyota, by contrast, had nine. These layers of management made it difficult for American firms to respond quickly to rapidly changing global situations. As U.S. companies were acquired, broken up, and sold, layers of management were peeled away in an attempt to cut costs and regain competitiveness. Over time, this process— along with divestitures and the return to a focus on companys' core capabilities—offered to make U.S. businesses more competitive globally.

The merger binge, however, also tended to reinforce a major problem in the ranks of big business: shortsightedness. Faced with the possibility of an unwanted merger, managers often found it difficult to plan for the future. They tended to emphasize the importance of short-term results, quarterly profits, instead of long-term results, such as the international competitiveness of their firms. American business leaders were more shortsighted than their counterparts in Japan and Western Europe. Executives spent valuable time and funds trying to avoid unwanted takeovers instead of using resources to bolster their market positions in the global economy.

Short-Term Strategies

The merger wave, however, was not solely responsible for the shortsighted approach of American business leaders. More and more business leaders received college educations in finance that emphasized short-term solutions to business problems on a case-by-case approach. Reward systems that had little to do with the long-term health of their companies reinforced business leaders' myopic approach to their firms' concerns. And investors proved increasingly unwilling to wait for long-term profits. More and more stockholders were institutional investors (with investments in employee pension plans for instance), not individual investors. Judging by the performance of their stock portfolios on an annual basis, the managers of pension plans and other institutions took little interest in the long-term health of the companies in which they invested: after all, it was easier to sell the stock of a company in trouble than to try to work with its managers to solve its problems.

America's legal system encouraged business executives to stress quarterly results. The law prohibited commercial banks from owning stock in industrial companies to which they loaned funds. This policy lessened any interest that bank executives might have had in working with their counterparts in industry to try to ensure the long-term profitability of American business. (In Germany and Japan, by contrast, banks owned large shares of industrial firms and bankers worked very closely with industrialists in bad times as well as good.) Similarly, laws prevented institutional investors from owning more than 10 percent of the stock of any company in which they invested, thereby decreasing close, long-term investor interest in the companies. (Congress had passed these laws in the wake of the Great Depression of the 1930s in an attempt to solve perceived financial problems that had contributed to the hard times.)

The short-term approach to business resulting from the takeovers and other factors hindered commercial research and development activities in America. Particularly bothersome in this respect was the growth of corporate debt. Corporate raiders taking over companies and firms acquiring other companies usually did so with borrowed money. Likewise, companies mounting defenses against takeovers—by, for example, purchasing their own stock to keep it out of the hands of raiders—incurred deep debts. As a proportion of the net worth of American corporations, corporate debt rose from 86 percent in 1971 to 116 percent by 1985. To pay the interest on this mounting debt, business leaders often starved research and development, falling behind foreign competitors. As research and development expenditures lagged, so too did economic growth.

THE BUSINESS EXECUTIVE

As we have seen, substantial changes occurred in American business during the last decades of the twentieth century. The nature of business leadership changed too, if somewhat less substantially. With the growth of opportunities in small business came more opportunities for Americans traditionally excluded from the upper echelons of big business. Even in the corporate offices of large businesses, opportunities for women and members of minority groups expanded after 1970. Most executives had the benefits of a college education, while growing numbers had earned graduate degrees, especially the Master of Business Administration (MBA). Moreover, with the rise of financial controls in large corporations came the rise to leadership of executives with backgrounds in corporate finance. In 1979, 33 of the leaders of the 100 largest firms had a background in finance, up from 14 in 1949.

Women in Business Management

In 1992, only one woman was a chief executive officer running one of the 1,000 largest publicly held companies in the United States—Linda Wachner, the head of Warnaco, a cosmetics firm. Indeed, women remain underrepresented in the ranks of top management. In 1991, women composed 46 percent of the nation's labor force but made up only 1 percent of the senior management of large businesses.

More progress has occurred at entry-level and middle-management ranks. In the early 1970s, women typically made up about 5 percent of the MBA classes at most institutions; but a decade later, as the MBA was fast becoming the degree needed for advancing up the ranks of management, women composed a third or more of such classes. By 1991, women made up 41 percent of the entry-level and middle-level management in large firms, up from just 27 percent ten years before, and they could be found in manufacturing, not just in sales and services. In addition, more women held line positions that placed them in charge of the operations of their firms, rather than simply advisory staff positions.

Nonetheless, what observers have called a "glass ceiling" kept all but a few women from advancing to top executive posts. Women often found their careers stalled at middle levels. A 1992 report by *Business Week* showed that 70 percent of women managers in large firms believed that a male-dominated corporate culture remained a very significant barrier to their rise within the ranks. In the same year, a broad-ranging study prepared by the U.S. Department of Labor found that recruitment practices, advancement policies, and a general lack of commitment to moving women into senior management hindered their ascent.

Charlotte Beers was one of very few women who did reach the top in a large American firm. In the summer of 1992 she became chairperson and chief executive officer of Ogilvy & Mather Worldwide, the nation's fourth-largest advertising agency. At Baylor University, Beers had majored in mathematics and sciences. She began her advertising career as a brand-manager for Uncle Ben's, where she launched the firm's long-grain and wild rice lines. In 1971 she moved to J. Walter Thompson, one of America's leading advertising and marketing companies, where she quickly gained a reputation for very careful handling of clients. Beers was one of the first female executives at Thompson to be assigned to the Sears, Roebuck account. She impressed Sears' executives when she nonchalantly disassembled one of the firm's power drills while explaining a new marketing plan. Despite her mechanical aptitude, Beers explained her business success as having resulted from her "laughter and energy and wit." "Women are

After Sylvia Rhone graduated from the Wharton School, she found that a career in banking was less to her liking than working in the music industry. Eventually Rhone became co-president and Chief Executive Officer of East West Records America. (Anthony Barboza)

comfortable with those things." Later, Beers went on to Tatham RSCG, a midsized Chicago advertising agency, and then to Oglivy & Mather.

Few women were as successful in big businesses as Beers. Rebuffed in large companies, women frequently left them to start their own smaller firms. As one woman business writer explained in 1992, "What we have is not a glass ceiling, but a rubber roof. And the more women that hit it, the more that are bouncing out of the organization and off on their own." Women started businesses at twice the rate of men in the late 1970s and early 1980s. Although the gap lessened in later years, they were still forming small businesses at a faster rate than men in the early 1990s. And they did so over a broader range of industries than before: by 1992, women owned nearly a third of all companies in the United States. Even so, companies owned by women generated less than 10 percent of the sales made by American businesses.

Minorities in Business

Opportunities for African-Americans and other minorities in the upper ranks of corporate management have been even more limited than for women. Most blacks and other minorities have never enjoyed the opportunity even to try to succeed in white-owned businesses. In 1990, for instance, blacks composed just 5 percent of the managerial force of companies with 100 or more employees. Hispanics made up under 3 percent, and Asians less than 2 percent. Some companies—most notably, Merck, Xerox, McDonald's, and Kentucky Fried Chicken—have moved minorities, especially blacks, into management positions. At Xerox, in 1990, 14 percent of the managers at the vice president level were minorities, up from 3 percent a decade before; and at Kentucky Fried Chicken a third of the 161 middle-management positions were held by minorities. But these companies were exceptions, not the rule. Like women, minorities complained that too often a "glass ceiling" has obstructed their advance. Hindering their rise in management ranks, they pointed out, were such factors as an absence of performance feedback, a lack of guidance, exclusion from corporate social life, and stereotyping.

For some minorities, small business has seemed to offer an avenue to economic success; but the degree of opportunity varies greatly by ethnic group. Asians have led Latinos, who, in turn, have led blacks in their rate of small business formation (all three groups have trailed far behind whites). A comprehensive study by the U.S. Small Business Administration in 1988 suggested that, among the many factors responsible for the low rate of small business formation by blacks, two stand out: the inability of most black business owners to find markets beyond the black community and the lack of mentoring by successful business people. There are simply too few African-Americans who have succeeded in small firms whose sales extend beyond the black community to serve as informal instructors for small business aspirants.

BUSINESS AND SOCIETY

Prodded by the federal government, and by the desires of business executives to win social acceptance for themselves and their companies, U.S. corporate leaders have espoused the doctrine of the "social responsibility" of business. By this doctrine they have meant that their companies would act responsibly toward the American public on such matters as truth in advertising, the hiring of women and minorities, and cleaning up the environment. Like their predecessors in the 1920s, business leaders of the 1970s, 1980s, and 1990s have asserted that their companies exist to serve society, not simply to make a profit. Although they have accomplished less than they claimed, corporate involvement has helped local communities adjust to the changes wrought by international competition.

The Social Responsibility of Business

An area that attracted particular attention from business leaders in the late 1980s and early 1990s was education. As they perceived that a decline in America's educational system was affecting the international competitiveness of their firms, business executives became reformers. At one extreme were entrepreneurs who sought to dismantle the nation's public school system via school choice; in effect, they hoped to place public, private, and parochial schools on an "equal" footing in the competition for student "customers." At the other extreme were business leaders who wanted to preserve and bolster public schools by altering them to ensure fulfillment of the needs of every American to learn the skills needed to face work pressures in the global market.

From the mid-1980s into the 1990s, those business executives seeking to alter public schools moved through several overlapping stages of involvement. Most popular were "adopt-a-school" programs whereby companies provided goods and services, including guest speakers, employee tutors, small grants, and computers. By 1992, 40 percent of the nation's elementary schools had been "adopted." In a second type of endeavor, business leaders worked with schools to change particular academic programs, often utilizing a "school-within-a-school" approach. For instance, American Express sponsored academies in finance, travel, and public services in high schools. By the early 1990s, 140,000 academic-corporate partnerships of various sorts had been established in 30,000 elementary and secondary schools, about half the schools in the nation. In a third and still-broader type of involvement, businesses worked together to try to improve education within school districts. The Cincinnati Business Committee's Task Force on Schools and Chicago's Leadership for Quality were examples of this approach. Business leaders designed these interventions to bring such management principles as delegating responsibility and decentralizing authority to bear on school administrators and teachers. Finally, business leaders and organizations worked to reform educational policies at the state level.

Loss of Confidence in the Business System

Americans have generally lost confidence in the ability of their business system to compete effectively with international rivals and thereby provide steadily rising income levels. Several events and trends prompted this lack of confidence. In the mid- and late 1980s, for instance, scandals that besmirched the reputations of several of the nation's leading brokerage houses attracted much public attention. Investigations by the Securities and Exchange Commission revealed that prominent members of brokerage firms had used knowledge gained from their work in arranging mergers and had personally speculated in the stocks of the companies involved in the mergers. Called insider-trading, this practice blatantly violated federal statutes and traditional ethical norms. Michael Milken's downfall in 1990 was the most dramatic example. Convicted on six counts of manipulating securities markets, evading net capital rules, and cheating the government of taxes, Milken was forced to pay back the $600 million he had acquired from his financial transactions and was sentenced to years in prison. As a result, the brokerage firm for which Milken worked and the one that had pioneered in financing takeovers, Drexel Burnham Lambert, soon went bankrupt.

The takeover wave helped end the sense of confidence that Americans had had in their nation's economy during the 1950s and 1960s. Instability replaced stability as both managers and workers found themselves laid off when firms pared down their work forces. Industrial workers, in particular, felt betrayed. The "guarantee" of ever-higher wages and better benefits, in return for greater productivity and no strikes, fell apart in the 1970s and 1980s under the pressure of foreign competition. At the same time, business had succeeded in weakening labor unions (the Reagan administration was itself a union buster), thus further diminishing the protection of workers' interests. Meanwhile, employment patterns changed. In 1969, *Fortune* 500 companies employed roughly 21 percent of America's nonfarm work force and had annual sales equal to 46 percent of the nation's GNP; but twenty years later they employed only about 11 percent of the nonfarm workers and had sales equal to just 42 percent of GNP. Clearly, the large companies were becoming more efficient: they were producing only slightly less of the nation's growing GNP with far fewer workers. It was this drop in employment that worried Americans most: the big businesses had employed 16 million workers in 1979, but a decade later this figure had plummeted to 12 million.

Laid off by the largest industrial corporations, the fired workers had to seek new jobs, often at lower wages in new locations. Even those who kept their positions suffered as real wages fell. Between 1973 and 1990, real hourly wages for nonsupervisory workers (about two-thirds of the nation's work force) dropped 12 percent. And as real wages for nonsupervisory workers declined, disparities in income and wealth increased. From 1977 to 1989, the American economy grew at a rate that would have raised everybody's real income by about 10 percent, if the gains had been evenly distributed. Instead, the top 1 percent of the nation's families—in 1989, the 1 million families with an income of at least $165,000 per year—saw their average incomes soar 80 percent, while the incomes of most other Americans stagnated or declined. By 1989, the richest 1 percent of the families owned 37 percent of the net worth of all American families, up from 31 percent in 1983.

THE AMERICAN BUSINESS FIRM AT THE CLOSE OF THE CENTURY

The stagnant or declining standard of living that so many Americans experienced in the last decade of the twentieth century was an indication that the American business system was still struggling to adapt to changing international economic conditions. Some firms, such as The BFGoodrich Company, appeared to have prospects for long-term health; others, like its rival in the traditional tire business, Goodyear, seemed able to survive with savvy leadership and marketing acumen. On the other hand, investors at the end of 1992 had lost confidence in IBM's ability to return to high levels of profit, and the value of its stock and bonds plummeted to levels below the prices paid in 1982. Meanwhile, small business publicists proudly pointed out that their sector was adding employment opportunities. Yet doubts among Americans remained. Small business and service industry wages were usually well below the standard once expected by American industrial workers. For some citizens, the political economy seemed to offer solutions, hearkening back to traditions of governmental support for business firms through the developmental policies that were so much a part of the historical fabric of American public policy.

Suggested Readings

Michael Dertous, Richard Lester, and Robert Solow, *Made in America: Regaining the Productive Edge* (Cambridge, Mass.: MIT Press, 1989); Michael Jacobs, *Short-Term America: The Causes and Cures of Our Business Myopia* (Boston: Harvard Business School Press, 1991); and Lester Thurow, *Head to Head: The Coming Economic Battle Among Japan, Europe, and America* (New York: William Murrow, 1992), offer provocative looks at American business in the global economy. Max Holland, *When the Machine Stopped: A Cautionary Tale from Industrial America* (Boston: Harvard Business School Press, 1989), is a superb case study of the history of a leading company in the American machine-tool industry. On the significance of the takeover wave of the 1980s, see Andrei Shleifer and Robert Vishny, "The Takeover Wave of the 1980s," *Science* 249 (August 1990) 245–249; and C. K. Prahalad and Gary Hamel, "The Core Competence of the Corporation," *Harvard Business Review* 68 (May/June 1990): 79–91. Pietro S. Nivola, "The New Protectionism: U.S. Trade Policy in Historical Perspective," *Political Science Quarterly* 101, no. 4 (1986): 577–600, provides a good overview of U.S. trade policy.

Much has recently been written about the significance of small business in the modern American economy. Among the most valuable works on this topic are William Brock and David Evans, *The Economics of Small Business* (New York: Holmes & Meier, 1986); Zoltan Acs and David Audretsch, *Innovation in Small Firms* (Cambridge, Mass: MIT Press, 1990); and John Case, *From the Ground Up: The Resurgence of American Entrepreneurship* (New York: Simon & Schuster, 1992). Thomas S. Dicke, *Franchising in America: The Development of a Business Method, 1840–1980* (Chapel Hill: University of North Carolina Press, 1992), explores the important phenomenon of franchising.

Scattered sources examine the place of women and minorities in modern American business. "Pipelines of Progress: A Status Report on the Glass Ceiling," published by the U.S. Department of Labor in August 1992, is a useful place to start in examining some of the problems that women face in reaching the top ranks of management. Joanne Wilkens, *Her Own Business: Success Secrets of Entrepreneurial Women* (New York: McGraw-Hill, 1987), profiles women who succeeded as business owners in the 1970s and 1980s. The 1988 report of the U.S. Small Business Administration, Office of Advocacy, presents a valuable survey of small business involvement by women and minorities. Finally, on minorities in recent American business, see Glegg Watson, *Black Life in Corporate America* (Garden City, N.Y.: Doubleday, 1982); Edward Irons and Gilbert Moore, *Black Managers: The Case of the Banking Industry* (New York: Praeger, 1985); and Ivan Light and Edna Bonachich, *Immigrant Entrepreneurs: Koreans in Los Angeles, 1965–1982* (Berkeley: University of California Press, 1988).

1971 President Richard Nixon abolishes the convertibility of the U.S. dollar into gold.
The Federal Election Campaign Act allows corporations to form political action committees, which in turn are permitted to engage directly in election campaigns.

1972 The Business Roundtable forms to influence the new regulation of the 1960s.

1973 The United States suffers from an oil embargo, and an energy crisis begins.
President Nixon begins removing banking regulations in order to increase competition among banks.

1975 Congress charges the Federal Reserve System with adjusting the money supply to control the economy.

1978 The Airline Deregulation Act begins deregulation of an important industry.

1979 The United States experiences a second oil embargo.
The federal government rescues the Chrysler Corporation from bankruptcy.

1981 Japanese automobile manufacturers agree to restrain exports to the United States.
Large tax incentives are initiated in the hopes of stimulating private investment.

1989 The United States and Canada sign a free-trade agreement; German reunification begins.

1991 The Soviet Union collapses.

1992 The United States, Canada, and Mexico sign the North American Free Trade Agreement, while twelve European nations create the European Community.

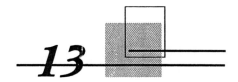

Challenges to American Business at Home and Abroad

On Monday morning, December 14, 1992, Bill Clinton, president-elect of the United States, took a seat in an auditorium in Little Rock, Arkansas, his native state. Clinton was leading a national conference on the condition of the economy intended to clarify the choices facing his new administration. Clinton had won the presidency a month before, observers agreed, because a majority of American voters were uneasy with the course of the economy. Unemployment rates were high, recovery from recession was anemic, the requirements of funding huge government deficits were dragging down private investment opportunities, and many citizens worried that they, their children, and their grandchildren were ill-equipped to face the ongoing challenges of international competition. Clinton had promised voters that upon his election as president he would focus "like a laser beam" on their country's economic problems—on both unemployment and the long-term issues of government deficits and international competition.

The economic conference, unprecedented in the nation's history, was one result of Clinton's pledge. A wide spectrum of Americans came to Little Rock. Prominent economists who had long advised the Democratic party spoke, as did political scientists and leaders engaged with the social problems that had arisen from economic ailments. The leaders of important trade unions, as well as executives from large corporations, participated in the deliberations. Robert Cizik, chairman of Cooper Industries and president of the National Association of Manufacturers, and John D. Ong, chairman of The BFGoodrich Company and head of the Business Roundtable (a lobbying organization of big business executives formed in 1972), both told reporters after the deliberations that they were cautiously optimistic about the new administration's willingness to develop policy initiatives helpful to

Robert Reich, soon to be named Secretary of Labor, and President-elect Bill Clinton and Vice-President-elect Al Gore helped focus Americans' attention on the solution of economic problems at Little Rock, Arkansas in December 1992. (Wide World Photos)

the American business system. "I have never voted for a Democrat in my life, but I must say I've been impressed," Ong said after the conference ended. He added that Clinton "has an obvious command of the issues, but we don't know what his program will be."

Whatever the details of the president's program, Clinton generally respects the tradition begun in 1789 of federal support for developmental economic policies. Among Clinton's closest friends over the previous twenty-five years is Robert Reich, a prominent lecturer and author whom Clinton called to Little Rock to take charge of the economic part of the transition to his presidency. Reich came with Ira Magaziner, an old college friend turned business consultant with whom Reich had written *Minding America's Business* in 1982, a book that unfavorably compared American business performance with economic performance in Germany and Japan. Reich and Magaziner had called for "industrial policy," an invigorated alliance among public agencies, private firms, and trade associations intended to change the course of business investment and performance in the face of the new realities of international competition. As Reich's thinking evolved over the ensuing decade, he began to advocate extensive public investment in worker education and training as a way of allowing American society to participate fully in the material plenty of the new international economy that had emerged after 1970. Clinton appointed Reich as secretary of labor in support of those ideas.

Robert Reich, his friend Bill Clinton, and co-author Ira Magaziner were active participants in a national debate that arose in the 1970s with regard to government-business relations and economic policy. Since the experience of the Great Depression of the 1930s, American policy makers and their economic advisers had focused on fiscal and monetary policy on demand. (And at least since Adam Smith's time, economists had looked upon economic activity as a balance between the demand for goods and services and their supply.) As global economic conditions changed after 1970, however, and as some American firms started to suffer in the competitive environment, politicians and their advisers began reconsidering ways of using government to stimulate the supply of goods and services—a system that in the 1980s came to be known as "supply side economics." President Jimmy Carter, who served from 1977 to 1981, and his advisers began thinking of fresh ways for government to aid sectors of the American economy that were suffering from international competition. In particular, the Democratic approach specified an important role for public decision making in helping business firms develop strategies to compete internationally. In contrast, President Ronald Reagan, who served from 1981 to 1989, promoted massive tax reductions intended to boost the supply of goods and services in which government's role was more passive, leaving strategic business decisions in private hands. These differing approaches led to a national debate in the 1980s over "industrial policy," a debate in which Robert Reich was a leading participant.

However, as Americans sought to use their government to help adjust to the international competition, much more was involved than the issues of investment summarized by the phrase "industrial policy." The federal government began to "deregulate" important industries in the 1970s. As prominent corporations and entire industries stumbled in the newly competitive business environment, government sometimes intervened to rescue them. And American leaders worked out a new international arrangement for free trade in North America in the hopes of revitalizing economic activity on a long-term basis.

AN UNSTABLE INTERNATIONAL
BUSINESS ENVIRONMENT

As the international business environment transformed after 1970, American companies adjusted. But the instability of this business environment sparked controversy over the political economy. The situations with which Clinton, Reich, and Ong, as well as other business executives across the nation, had to deal were unfamiliar territory for Americans. International currents outside of direct American control were dramatically affecting relationships between government and the economy, and the appropriate policy responses were unclear.

Shocks to the Postwar International Economic Order: Currency, Trade, and Oil

When the Bretton Woods Agreement ended in 1971, the global market became a less predictable arena in which to do business. After 1965 the nation was straining to fight a war in Vietnam without demanding substantial economic sacrifices at home, and inflationary pressures mounted. Foreigners were exchanging billions of dollars for gold, causing a "gold drain" away from the United States. The fixed exchange rates of the Bretton Woods Agreement and the convertibility of the dollar into gold could not withstand the pressure. Faced with this situation and a severe domestic recession, President Richard Nixon ended the convertibility of the U.S. dollar by foreigners to gold in August 1971. Convertibility had been the bedrock on which the Bretton Woods Agreement was based, with respect to fixed currency exchange rates among nations. From 1971 on, exchange rates were "free-floating," with currencies worth what market forces decreed.

Even as the Bretton Woods Agreement was collapsing, the GATT began to erode. As economic uncertainty increased after 1971, pressures mounted to restrain the movement toward free trade. By the 1980s, free trade among nations remained the official goal of the nations belonging to the GATT, but the reality was that various types of official and unofficial trade barriers began to be raised in response to popular pressures to protect domestic markets that had traditionally led to prosperity for American firms and their workers. "Voluntary" export restrictions were most noticeable in the automobile industry after 1981, as Japanese manufacturers successfully took markets from producers headquartered in Detroit. By the early 1990s, about a quarter of exports to America were subject to nontariff restrictions.

Inflation and "oil shocks" also hurt American businesses in their competition with foreign firms. In 1973 and 1979, oil-producing nations, through the cartel known as OPEC, sharply increased the price of crude oil to other countries. In 1973, in response to the Arab-Israeli War, they hiked prices fourfold. A similar action occurred in 1979. The oil shocks, in turn, stimulated inflation, augmenting business uncertainties. By the early 1980s, despite a recession, inflation had climbed to well over 15 percent a year in the United States. Japanese and German business leaders adjusted relatively smoothly to these changes by boosting the productivity of their factories while their governments successfully dampened inflationary forces. But

American business executives experienced more difficulty in their efforts to accommodate the inflation. One dramatic result: America's global share of manufactured goods exports fell from 15 percent to only 11 percent in the 1970s. As American firms were less able to compete internationally, the nation suffered trade deficits. The United States last earned a trade surplus (of $6 billion) in 1982. Trade deficits peaked at $144 billion in 1987.

The New World Order

Adding to the confusion arising from economic factors were dramatic changes in the world's political arrangements at the end of the 1980s. With those changes, American business and political leaders had to alter their thinking about economic arrangements. The cold war, which had appeared in the aftermath of World War II, shaped political and economic decisions for more than four decades. It ended suddenly with the reunification of Germany beginning in 1989 and the collapse of the Soviet Union in 1991.

The end of the cold war meant that the political map of Europe had to be redrawn, with new nations appearing in what was once the Soviet Union and with Eastern European nations long dominated by Soviet power now free to pursue their separate destinies. The political changes brought new risks to the international economy as western nations, including the United States, sought to extend credits and to encourage capitalist reformation of former socialist economies. Economic collapse threatened to accompany these political changes, especially in Russia. And European, Japanese, and American leaders faced the prospect of massive loan defaults disturbing capital markets across the globe.

For Americans, the end of the cold war brought dramatic changes in business activity. As always, political arrangements shaped business opportunities. Government expenditures for the cold war dropped considerably, and firms and regions whose prosperity had been closely tied to military expenditures suffered dearly. Worst off was southern California, whose economy had boomed after 1940 with the expansion of aircraft and other defense-related industries. There companies laid off production workers, engineers, and managers, driving the regional economy into depression. If the end of the cold war brought wrenching and painful change to what Eisenhower had labeled the "military-industrial complex," however, it also created new opportunities. Multinational firms based in the United States and elsewhere were now cautiously looking at Eastern European nations as new investment opportunities. At the end of 1992, for instance, Procter & Gamble announced an agreement to produce detergents in Russia. Already the firm's worldwide sales had reached $30 billion, half of its total sales, and P & G executives hoped the Russian venture would lead to further multinational expansion.

DOMESTIC POLITICS AND ECONOMIC UNCERTAINTY

The abandonment of the Bretton Woods monetary system indicated the magnitude of public policy's role in creating the uncertain conditions characterizing American business after 1970. The inflation that hurt the American economy in the 1970s seemed to lead to a new set of economic conditions, dubbed "stagflation," wherein inflation continued in the absence of robust economic growth. (Previous experience had suggested that economic stagnation reduced prices.) A sharp recession from 1981 to 1983, the worst downturn since the 1930s, wrenched severe inflation from the American economy. A boom in the middle years of the 1980s brought about important shifts in business opportunities. The boom was followed, in turn, by another bust, and the recession that began in 1989 was worse even than the severe one that had wracked the economy at the beginning of the decade.

Banks, Money, and Economic Theory

Issues arising from monetary and banking practices were one result of America's experience with inflation in the 1970s. The once-vehement conflict over the metallic base for the nation's coinage had ended, and now, especially with the emergence of stagflation, the issue involved new ideas about the relationship between the supply of money and the nation's economic health.

Within the long span of history, the widespread worries about inflation were relatively new. As the nation became more affluent, economists' concerns about scarcity began to recede and to be replaced by concerns about inflation. Historically, inflation had accompanied wars, and prices had dropped in postwar recessions; but after World War II, prices did not go down. In fact, the long-run trend of the U.S. economy in the twentieth century was toward inflation. Because inflation affected business investment decisions and the costs of labor and materials, it evolved as an area of lively political dispute and vitally affected federal policy.

During the 1960s, an economic theory known as *monetarism* emerged as a powerful idea. Associated with Milton Friedman, an economics professor at the University of Chicago, the monetarists challenged the federal government to follow a new course regarding inflation. Having observed that inflation and the supply of money were historically closely related, Friedman urged the government to monitor and control the money supply in order to control inflation. In his view, since the banking industry provided money to business firms and consumers, the Federal Reserve Board, which governed the banks, had to become the principal agency in the fight against inflation.

Congress responded in 1975. A joint resolution charged the Federal Reserve System with watching and controlling the money supply in order

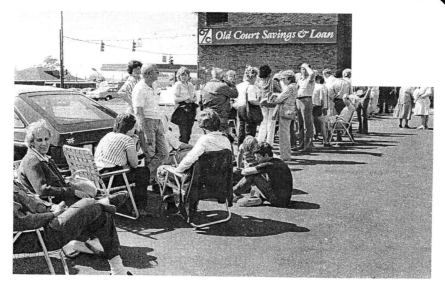

When Congress intervened in the failure of savings and loan banks to allow deposit insurance to protect the public, scenes such as this one of panicked customers were prevented from spreading across the United States. Before the advent of federal deposit insurance in 1933, customers lined up in front of failing banks in hopes of withdrawing their funds before doors closed permanently. (Wide World Photos)

to produce "maximum employment, stable prices, and moderate long-term interest rates." The Federal Reserve Board began reporting regularly on its policies of monetary growth. But the problems of stagflation continued into the 1980s. Keeping tight reins on the supply of money had the effect of raising interest rates, slowing business investment and consumer spending, and threatening depression levels of unemployment. Nevertheless, monetary policy had become another significant area wherein public action set the boundaries within which business executives arrived at investment, employment, and production decisions.

Rescuing Corporations

The use of federal resources to rescue ailing corporations was a departure in government-business relations that represented a new approach to the uncertainties of the new international business conditions. As economic growth faltered and stagflation set in after 1970, some major corporations fell into deep trouble. One response to such failure was to invoke bankruptcy laws and allow private investors, under court supervision, to reorganize the firm's assets. Another response was to use federal resources to refinance the failing firm. Indeed, government leaders followed this latter course when the failed firms were among the largest in the American business system, even though the policy flew in the face of traditional rhetoric regarding competition, risk taking, and free enterprise.

This new approach to business failure began with the bankruptcy of the Penn Central Railroad in 1970, the largest such failure in American history. The government made large investments in the nation's northeastern railroads in order to ensure continuing service to the region. To save the Lockheed Corporation, America's largest defense contractor, the Nixon administration arranged another rescue. But the most spectacular rescue of all began in 1979, during the administration of President Jimmy Carter, when the nation's tenth-largest industrial firm, Chrysler, which had been losing money in its automobile business, informed the nation that without additional credit it would fail.

The federal government agreed to guarantee $1.5 billion of credit to rescue the ailing Chrysler corporation. The arrangement included substantial wage concessions from the members of the United Auto Workers in exchange for placing a union representative on Chrysler's board of directors. The subsequent performance of the firm was monitored by a special Loan Guarantee Review Board headed by the secretary of the treasury. Government officials were willing to make such a large commitment in the hopes of saving the firm and maintaining employment. Finally, after several years of operating on the brink of default, Chrysler was able to reestablish itself, earn profits, and repay its loans in 1984.

Nor was the federal rescue of ailing corporations confined to industrial firms. The recession of the early 1980s produced insolvency in some important banks as well. The New Deal banking reforms had included federal depositor's insurance. When insolvency loomed, the usual government policy was to arrange a merger of the insolvent bank with a solvent bank as a less costly way of protecting deposits. However, in the case of the insolvency of the Continental Illinois National Bank and Trust in the summer of 1984, officials of the Reagan administration decided to provide government guaranteed loans to Continental Illinois, forcing management changes as a condition; Continental Illinois's liabilities were simply too large to force a merger with a healthy bank.

DEREGULATION

A movement to break with the tradition of federal regulation gained momentum in the 1970s as government officials grappled to check inflation. Beginning with the push for railroad regulation in the nineteenth century, some business firms and trade associations actively sought government assistance in reducing the potential destructiveness of competition and in adjudicating differences arising from firm size or regional location. To a considerable extent the movement for the regulation of business had been sparked by businesses themselves. The movement for deregulation, however, stemmed largely from the technical and theoretical concerns of the Council of Economic Advisers, expressed in their required annual report. When deregulation appeared, its results added competitive uncertainties to business conditions.

By the 1970s, social scientists were voicing discontent with existing regulatory practices. Basically, economists observed that regulatory agencies had institutionalized a "command-and-control" view of business activity in which expert bureaucrats determined the public interest and issued rules to control the behavior of corporations. Meanwhile, political scientists argued that regulatory agencies experienced a life cycle in which they may have begun as watchdogs of the public interest but soon were "captured" by the industries they sought to govern. Empirical observation of the regulation of transportation industries—and, later, of energy, communications, and financial industries—seemed to indicate that regulation failed to realize the public interest and instead resulted in a bureaucratic tangle that entwined private corporate interests, legislators, and the regulatory agencies in self-serving ways. To both the economists and the political scientists some system of decentralized decision making seemed desirable. They believed that government responsibility should be limited to establishing appropriate frameworks within which business executives, observing market opportunities, could make decisions on how best to serve the public most efficiently and at the lowest cost.

The views of the social scientists were intellectually, but not politically, powerful. However, when they were combined with policy needs as defined by elected officials, including the president and influential congressional leaders, a potent movement for deregulation developed. At first, deregulation emerged as a body of ideas that seemed appropriate for certain ailing industries. President Richard Nixon and his successor, Gerald Ford, echoed the complaints of business that federal regulation imposed higher costs and therefore unwarranted burdens on consumers. Both presidents thus sometimes resisted imposing new regulations on business. By the end of the 1970s, the control of inflation had become the first priority in the nation's economic policy. Seeking to slow inflation substantially without providing intolerably high levels of unemployment, President Carter turned to deregulation as a policy that would decrease business costs, restore the pressures of price competition on some firms, and thereby cut into the inflationary spiral.

Deregulating Transportation Industries

Transportation industries were the first to experience the full force of deregulation in the 1970s. The Airline Deregulation Act of 1978 led the way, soon followed in 1980 by the Rail Act and the Motor Carrier Act. Sometimes opposed by the business firms most directly affected, since such firms generally preferred the security that regulation offered, each of the laws tried to restore price competition and thereby lower costs to consumers. They allowed regulated industries more flexibility to adapt to changing market conditions and technologies, thus producing in the long run more efficient transportation services within the American economy.

The federal government, through the Civil Aeronautics Board (CAB), had regulated the airline industry since the 1930s. The CAB controlled both the fares that carriers could charge and the routes the airlines could fly. The original purpose of those restraints on competition was to encourage investors to develop the airline industry. By the 1970s, however, that objective no longer seemed valid. Instead, regulation appeared to provide an environment of safe capital investments, little managerial initiative, high wages for airline employees, and, of course, high costs for travelers. The growth of successful, low-cost intrastate carriers in California and Texas, operating outside of CAB rules, gave evidence that the American airline industry was inefficient and costly.

The reform of the airline industry began in 1976, when the CAB started to ease restrictions on routes and fares. Under the leadership of Alfred Kahn, an economics professor appointed chairman of the Civil Aeronautics Board in 1977, deregulation moved forward steadily. The airline companies, fearful that losses in route monopolies would endanger profits, and the airline unions, believing that deregulation would result in enormous pressures to reduce wages, resisted. Under Kahn's leadership, however, the CAB allowed more and more fare discounting and granted carriers entry into new markets. When the results of increased competition appeared to be better service at lower costs, while the airline companies continued to enjoy profits thanks to higher passenger traffic, Congress was won over. The Airline Deregulation Act of 1978 called for the dissolution of the CAB over a six-year period, with free entry of airline companies into routes of their choosing at fares determined by competition. The first major victory of deregulation had been won. Subsequently, competition forced rapid change in the airline industry's business structure. By 1988, six firms controlled 90 percent of U.S. domestic air travel, and fares were rising.

After deregulating the airlines, Congress turned to trucks and railroads in 1980. Economists had complained that the regulation of the trucking industry since 1935 by the Interstate Commerce Commission had resulted in gross inefficiencies. The ICC had allowed the truckers to establish regional rate bureaus to fix prices, and the commission's regulations sometimes necessitated circuitous routing or required carriers to drive empty trucks on return trips. Regulations also prevented new firms from entering the business. Not only did prices to shippers seem to be high as a result, but regulations were costing the nation valuable fuel resources. In 1980,

Congress responded to those arguments, presented by the Council of Economic Advisers and representatives of President Carter, by making it easier to enter the trucking business and allowing competitive forces to determine rates. After deregulation, some large trucking firms went bankrupt, while others, applying capital resources and managerial skills, captured the less-than-full-truckload business. The larger trucking firms increased their share of the industry's business under deregulation, and thousands of independently owned operators entered the field.

Similarly, the Rail Act of 1980 allowed rail executives much greater flexibility in charting the course of their firms. The railroads could now make separate contracts with individual shippers. They were allowed to adapt more fully to new technologies by loading containers or trailers on flatcars. Congress instructed the ICC to show more leniency in allowing mergers between rail firms, especially mergers that would improve operating efficiency, and between railroads, barge lines, and trucking companies. After passage of the new law, some of the largest railroads began to combine in an effort to provide more traffic sources that could now move over longer routes. Once, fears that the industry would be dominated by a few huge firms had prevented mergers, but now that trucking was providing a competing mode of transportation, those fears seemed unimportant.

Deregulating Banking

The deregulation movement of the 1970s also profoundly affected the banking industry. Some economic experts and politicians became concerned in the 1970s about the rate at which capital was accumulating to meet the nation's business needs. In 1970, President Nixon expressed his worry over the low rate of "national savings" and their effective utilization, and he appointed a special presidential commission to recommend new policies. In 1973, this commission called for more competition in the banking industry in order to improve the efficiency by which savings were accumulated and capital transferred to borrowers. Then, as the inflation rate worsened during the decade, economists voiced concerns that banks were no longer able to attract savings under existing rules.

Before the 1970s, Congress had enacted legislation to encourage stability in the banking industry while at the same time preventing monopolies from forming. Some regulations of the 1930s, which had been a response to problems associated with the banks and the depression, were lifted. In the 1970s, with the advent of extraordinarily high inflation and new electronic technologies applicable to financial firms, pressures for change mounted. As securities firms began offering accounts paying savers high rates of interest, huge sums of capital flowed to them out of banks, thrifts, and insurance companies, all of which were hurt in their ability to make loans for new homes, factories, and machinery.

The Depository Institutions Deregulation and Monetary Control Act of 1980 reversed the earlier policy. With the new law, the federal government created a framework in which the three types of institutions could compete with one another for deposits and loans. Thrift institutions (savings and loan banks) could write loans on more than real estate mortgages, and both they and the banks could raise interest rates paid to depositors. Banks began entering the securities business by offering brokerage services. Banking service charges for small depositors grew substantially under deregulation as banks tried to attract depositors with larger savings. The banking industry began a wave of mergers as larger institutions sought to do business with depositors as well as borrowers on a national basis.

Deregulation combined with economic circumstances to bring about unexpected and unwanted changes in the nation's savings and loan industry. Laws passed in 1980 and 1982 allowed the thrift institutions, which had traditionally made long-term loans to homeowners, to enter new fields. Seeking higher returns on their loans than could be obtained in the residential housing field, the savings and loan banks made real estate development and construction loans, which carried a high degree of risk. Inexperienced in these fields, and sometimes engaging in fraudulent activities, savings and loan executives often found themselves overextended. The failure of federal agencies to monitor the activities of the thrift institutions made the problem worse. Cutbacks in regulatory staffs meant that no one was watching what the officers of the savings and loan institutions were doing. As a result, by 1989 some 500 of the nation's 3,000 savings and loan banks were insolvent, and Americans faced a bill in excess of $500 billion to protect depositors. That year Congress passed the Financial Institutions Reform, Recovery and Enforcement Act to bail out the failed thrift banks and, in effect, to reregulate the industry.

Deregulating Communications

The deregulation of communications industries began in the 1980s, again under the belief that competition would ultimately result in greater efficiencies and lower costs for the consumer. In 1980, the Federal Communications Commission allowed the nation's largest firm, the American Telephone and Telegraph Company, to begin selling (as opposed to leasing) communications equipment to its customers. In 1981, the same agency began removing restraints on the operation of commercial radio stations, while Congress extended the life of television broadcast licenses from three to five years and reduced government surveillance of the broadcasters.

An antitrust agreement with AT&T in 1982, while technically not a deregulation, conformed to its general spirit. The antitrust tradition involved a commitment to price competition among firms, exactly the situation deregulation was intended to obtain. The nation's largest firm in terms of assets, AT&T provided 70 million customers with high-quality telephone service at low rates. It employed 1 million people, had 3.2 million shareholders, and borrowed more money than any institution but the federal government. Because of an antitrust suit begun in 1974, this giant had to divest itself of its local operating companies, an undertaking of staggering complexity.

The case against AT&T arose initially because of government accusations of anticompetitive practices, not from an upswell of public outrage. Earlier, the Justice Department had obtained an agreement that prevented AT&T from entering the computer industry, even though its Bell Laboratories had provided major technological innovations that made modern computers possible. This earlier agreement had protected firms in the computer industry, including IBM, from the enormous resources at AT&T's command, resources that the communications firm might have used to dominate the computer industry. After AT&T agreed to divest itself of its local companies, however, the government allowed it to enter the computer business. In 1984, the smaller but still sizable AT&T began marketing computers in competition with IBM and other firms.

THE EMERGING GLOBAL ECONOMY

After decades of tension, the cold war ended in 1991 with the collapse of the Soviet Union and its power in Eastern Europe and Asia. This dramatic international political watershed offered prospects for peace. Yet in unexpected ways the end of the cold war added to Americans' uncertainties regarding their business system. Federal spending for armaments had for generations provided prosperity for defense contractors and their employees, spending that now was likely to fall. Especially hard hit was California, a state whose population began growing rapidly with the mobilization effort of World War II and continued to expand thereafter during the cold war. The world economy had changed rapidly and not always to the advantage of American business after the downfall of the Bretton Woods system. Now the world's political arrangements underwent momentous changes as well.

Regional Trading Blocks

Even before the cold war ended, the commitments to free trade that American leaders had promoted after 1945 were easing. The United States was far from alone in erecting trade restrictions. Five years of negotiations about GATT, known as the Uruguay round, stalled in 1992 without achieving further tariff reductions. In place of the relatively free worldwide trade of the 1950s and 1960s, global trading blocs were emerging after 1970, with trade between the blocs facing restrictions. With no one economy dominant in the world, government leaders in different capitals were trying to advance the well-being of their citizens by replacing free trade with managed trade. Three trading blocs were of greatest importance: North America, Europe, and Japan-Asia.

Following World War II, American policy had encouraged the international economic integration of European economies as a way of strengthening the region during the cold war. European leaders began to dream of integration, first in coal and iron production and later in other fields, as a way of ensuring that no Western European nation would ever again have the capability of waging industrialized combat against its neighbors. With the revival by the 1960s of the West German economy as a powerful entity and a generally high level of prosperity across the continent, leaders began to consider more and more ways of effecting economic union, even with a view toward political integration. The European Community (EC) of twelve nations was the result. Members of the EC planned the full integration of their markets by the end of 1992, creating thereby the world's largest single unified market of some 380 million people.

The formation of the EC was a dramatic event in the course of European history. The member nations allowed the free movement of goods, people, and capital across national boundaries. Indeed, the EC offered a glittering market for American goods. Once an American product adhered to the rules and regulations of one EC member, it could be sold to all. Some American companies were quick to take advantage of this new environment. One was Campbell Biscuits Europe, a subsidiary of Campbell Soups. Beginning in 1990, the company sought to distribute products efficiently to the entire twelve-nation market. It reorganized its European corporate structure, centralizing marketing and standardizing packaging—objectives it could not accomplish when the European market had been divided among autonomous nations.

For American firms, however, these opportunities were not always easy to realize. A major purpose underlying the formation of the EC was to protect European nations from foreign competition, whether from America, Japan, or elsewhere; and many American business leaders viewed the EC as "Fortress Europe." Despite assurances to the contrary, there were disturbing signs that the EC would restrict imports from America. One early dispute involved financial services. Under the principle of reciprocity, the EC could keep American banks out of Europe or stop the expansion of those already there. If European banks did not have access to all of the United States—and, like American banks themselves, they in fact did not because of continuing restrictions on branch banking—then American banks could be denied access to all of Europe. Another controversy involved manufacturing. The EC proposed limiting Japanese auto makers to 16 percent of the European market (including cars made in Japanese-owned factories in the United States).

Meanwhile, the American government set about developing a trading bloc for North America. The North American Free Trade Agreement (NAFTA) began to take shape in 1989, when the United States and Canada signed a Comprehensive Free Trade Agreement and began lowering trade barriers, a process to be completed in 1998. Almost immediately economic benefits appeared to flow as a result of the agreement. Merchandise shipments between the United States and Canada rose 35 percent between 1987 and 1991, and each nation gained about 2 million jobs as a result. Then, in 1992, both countries expanded their trade agreement to include Mexico. As trade restrictions eased over time, the three nations—with a total population of about 360 million in the early 1990s—began to form a large unified market for goods and services. By 1992, Mexico was already America's third-largest market, after Canada and Japan.

The creation of NAFTA did not occur without adding to uncertainty in the economies involved. American banks and insurance companies, long frozen out of Mexico, looked forward to benefiting from the arrangement. American manufacturing was relocating into Mexico well before NAFTA to take advantage of the lower wage scales south of the border, a trend that NAFTA appeared to accelerate. And American industrial workers saw NAFTA as a political action that threatened to corrode their job security and standard of living even further.

Reacting to the formation of NAFTA and the EC, Japan stepped up its backing for the creation of an Asian trading bloc in the early 1990s. First proposed by Australia, this bloc, called the Asian Pacific Economic Cooperation, would be composed of Japan, Australia, and the nations making up the Association of Southeast Asian Nations (ASEAN)—Thailand, Singapore, Malaysia, Indonesia, Brunei, and the Philippines. Great uncertainties surrounded the possible formation of this trading bloc. In the early 1990s, Japan, while boosting its support for the group, proved unwilling to provide wholehearted backing. Then, too, some of the ASEAN nations had closer economic ties to the United States than to one another—for instance, two of the "four tigers" of Asia, Singapore and Malaysia—and did not want to endanger those connections.

Policy Debates

The formation of NAFTA and the recognition that other nations had abandoned free trade in favor of managed trade also involved a recognition that the United States should reconsider its traditions of government-business relations. The distress that the American business system experienced after 1970 was partly a result of government policy changes, beginning with Nixon's decision to end the Bretton Woods agreement. Issues thus arose about changing the direction of public policy in order to foster economic growth and international competitiveness; in the ensuing discussion, business corporations and business associations played an active role.

Traditional fears about the power of large corporations undermining American democracy and individualism receded somewhat inasmuch as large corporations themselves were apparent victims of policy and economic forces beyond their direct control. In the past, laws had forbidden corporations from participating directly in political campaigns. The Federal Election Campaign Act of 1971 changed that ban and allowed corporations to form political action committees (so-called PACs) with the authority to raise money from employees and stockholders and contribute up to $5,000 directly to political campaigns. After this change, the number of PACs exploded as corporations and trade associations attempted to influence public policy to their advantage.

The associations of corporations and of executives that had formed earlier, such as the Committee for Economic Development, continued their activities, promoting policies that business leaders favored. A significant new association, the Business Roundtable, appeared in 1972 as a direct response to the new regulation of the 1960s. Trade associations and individual corporations had at times bitterly fought enactment of new regulatory laws, claiming they placed undue burdens on firms already struggling to overcome the pressures of inflation and of the virulent competition that was emerging in the world economy. The Business Roundtable took a different approach: meeting quietly, it practiced practical politics. Its usual strategy was to accept the goals of the new regulation but to argue that realism demanded substantial modifications of policy. Using a small lobbying force consisting of the top executives of the largest industrial firms, the Roundtable became especially effective in the late 1970s. Roundtable lobbying prevented the establishment of a consumer protection agency that reformers wanted as a further expansion of regulation. Members of the Roundtable also helped influence fiscal policy during the Carter administration, although they were unsuccessful in restraining budget deficits under Presidents Reagan and Bush.

The Business Roundtable helped Congress amend the air and water pollution laws in 1977. Significant amendments accepted the complaints of industrialists concerning the economic and technological feasibility of achieving regulatory goals. Congress also changed or extended the deadlines it had imposed earlier for achieving significant reductions in air and water pollution. After 1977, regulators tried to account for the views of industrialists as well as environmentalists and to weigh the costs as well as the benefits of specific regulatory policies. In the 1980s, the measurement of regulatory costs and benefits by economic analysis became the standard policy of the Reagan administration. Later, President George Bush, asserting that the regulations placed undue burdens on firms in international competition, assigned Vice President Dan Quayle the task of removing them altogether. Meanwhile, in 1992, Congress responded to consumer complaints of high prices by passing (over Bush's veto) a bill regulating the cable television industry.

THE UNCERTAIN FUTURE

These actions were controversial, but nothing was more contentious than the larger debate concerning the appropriate role of government in helping business adjust to competition so that American prosperity would return to the high growth rates it had sustained before 1970. In the 1980s, Americans engaged in a debate over the best means of devising policies to facilitate the United States' ability to supply goods and services under the new conditions of the international economy. Harking back to the tradition of government support for business begun in the first meeting of the Congress in 1789, some economists and experienced public administrators began arguing for more than managed trade through voluntary export restrictions and other devices. Usually affiliated with the Democratic party, these advocates of "industrial policy" suggested processes whereby American public officials and business leaders would collaborate in developing carefully considered long-range approaches toward business. Their critics, usually affiliated with the Republican party, decried the notion of an American industrial policy as unwarranted interference in the private affairs of business. With Republicans in control of the presidency in the 1980s, federal policy toward business rested on the idea of lowering taxes to foster private decisions for capital investment.

The industrial policy debate revealed that Americans held no consensus on public policy measures designed to bring greater prosperity to the nation and security for individuals and their families. By the last decade of the twentieth century, much had changed since American power had peaked in 1945. A widespread popular unease about the economic future had replaced the confidence of the generation that had successfully mobilized the nation during World War II and had joined together during the cold war to resist communism. The business system itself had changed significantly after 1970, and even the largest corporations were not immune to worldwide political and economic trends. The most successful large ventures appeared to be ones whose executives had learned to combine financial, market, and production outlooks in a decentralized corporate structure, while small firms promised to offer desirable flexibility in adapting quickly to the world's changing circumstances.

In the 1990s, another generation of Americans faces the uncertainties of historical change. Businessmen, businesswomen, workers, consumers, government officials—indeed, all Americans—face new challenges as the twentieth century comes to a close. The nation and its business system have entered a still-unnamed "postindustrial" era, and fundamental changes are

Americans joined Europeans, as well as Africans, Latin Americans, and Asians, in trying to enlarge opportunities for trade on a worldwide basis in the 1990s. (Marie LaFrance)

occurring everywhere Americans look. Most employment opportunities are now found in service, not manufacturing, industries. Manufacturing industries, in turn, remain important to the overall health of the economy, but the production of goods in many cases requires a less intensive use of labor. (Robots, for instance, are replacing humans in repetitive factory jobs in key industries.)

Just as changes wrought by the Industrial Revolution were unclear to the entrepreneurs who initiated it, the government officials who encouraged it, and the business managers who consolidated it, so too are the changes in the business system and the larger society being wrought by postindustrial conditions not yet fully clear. What is clear, however, is that Americans still have faith in their business system and still venerate the successful entrepreneur, whether he or she gains that success in new, venturesome small firms or in large-scale corporations. As they try to reach ever-higher levels of material abundance for themselves and their children, Americans will demonstrate again and again that they have not forsaken their tradition of valuing the individual, the entrepreneur, and the profit motive.

Selected Readings

On the industrial policy debate, Otis L. Graham, *Losing Time: The Industrial Policy Debate* (Cambridge, Mass.: Harvard University Press, 1992), is seminal. Other key works in that debate include Ira Magaziner and Robert Reich, *Minding America's Business: The Decline and Rise of the American Economy* (New York: Harcourt Brace

Jovanovich, 1982); Reich, *The Next American Frontier* (New York: Times Books, 1983); and Reich, *The Work of Nations: Preparing Ourselves for 21st-Century Capitalism* (New York: Alfred A. Knopf, 1991).

Peter Temin and Louis Galambos, *The Fall of the Bell System* (New York: Cambridge University Press, 1987), is a model study of recent history that explains the importance of ideology for understanding deregulation. Robert Reich and John Donahue, *New Deals: The Chrysler Revival and the American System* (New York: Times Books, 1985), is also revealing. Finally, Pietro S. Nivola, "The New Protectionism: U.S. Trade Policy in Historical Perspective," *Political Science Quarterly* 101, no. 4 (1986): 577–600, provides a good overview of U.S. trade policy.

Index